GROWING UP
ASIAN
AMERICAN

GROWING UP
ASIAN
AMERICAN

An Anthology

Edited and with an Introduction by
MARIA HONG

Afterword by
STEPHEN H. SUMIDA

WILLIAM MORROW AND COMPANY, INC.
New York

Library of Congress Cataloging-in-Publication Data

Growing up Asian American : an anthology / edited and with an
   introduction by Maria Hong : afterword by Stephen H. Sumida.
        p.   cm.
   Includes bibliographical references.
   ISBN 0-688-11266-8
   1. American literature—Asian American authors.   2. Asian American
families—Literary collections.   3. Asian Americans—Literary
collections.   4. American literature—20th century.   I. Hong,
Maria.
PS508.A8G76   1993
810.8'0895—dc20   93-14033
                                                                     CIP

Printed in the United States of America

First Edition

1 2 3 4 5 6 7 8 9 10

To my brothers, Will and Ed,
and to Stefan
with love

Contents

7

Contents

Contents

ACKNOWLEDGMENTS

I am very grateful to the following people for generously giving me their suggestions regarding this book: Randolph Arguelles, Maureen Aung-Thwin, Vijay Balakrishnan, Carol Bruchac, Joseph Bruchac, Jeffery Paul Chan, Julie Chang, Rafael Chang, Fay Chiang, Curtis Chin, Peggy Choi, Lawrence Chua, Cathy Song Davenport, Sid Hajari, Lane Hirabayashi, Wendy Ho, Marlon Hom, Florence Hongo, Garrett Hongo, Evelyn Hu-Dehart, Zia Jaffrey, Kavery Kaul, Akemi Kikumura, David D. Kim, Elaine Kim, Robert Ku, Marie G. Lee, Marjorie Lee, Phillip Lee, Lamgen Leon, Russell Leong, Amy Ling, Mary Lui, Wing Tek Lum, Wesley Macawili, Fay Chew Matsuda, Sucheta Mazumdar, Ameena Meer, Janice Mirikitani, Fernando Chang Moy, Jim Okutsu, Oscar Peñaranda, Wei-Chi Poon, Corin Ramos, Gerard Raymond, Anjani Shah, Tony Suh, Stephen Sumida, Judy Susman, Sam Tagatac, Renee Tajima, Jack Tchen, Monique Truong, Lily Tsong, Sauling Wong, Loli Wu, Jeff Yang, Grace Yun, and Judy Yung.

I am indebted to Mei-Lin Liu of the Chinatown History Museum library in New York, the New York Public Library (especially the interlibrary loan department), and the Brooklyn Public Library for use of their precious books and journals. Without these unique resources many works would have been inaccessible.

I would also like to thank Ronald Takaki, whose book *Strangers from a Different Shore: A History of Asian Americans,* I consulted for historical background, and Stan Mark of the Asian American

Legal Defense and Education Fund, who updated me on the Japanese American redress situation.

Special thanks to Bill Adler and Julie Rosner of Bill Adler Books for confidence and patience throughout the process of putting together this anthology, and to my editor, Will Schwalbe, and his assistant, Zach Schisgal, for their unfaltering enthusiasm and savvy editorial advice.

I am especially grateful to Suelain Moy for giving my introduction her expert eye, and to Jean Jung for kindly alerting me to this project. For overall support and inspiration, I would like to thank my mother, Anna Hong, and my early teachers, particularly Eleanor Josset. And finally, my deepest gratitude to Stefan Smagula, Karen Shen, Pamela Renner, and Taehee Kim, for love, friendship, and believing.

INTRODUCTION

Named heir to family history,
I did not ask for unspoken details,
though I yearned for names, dates and roads.
I did not question his account,
though now I wonder, was it stove, lamp or match?
Instead, as any child would do,
I sat and marvelled as he spun wondrous tales
of small children, nascent moons
and journeys set foot in the night.
            —*from "Ohio" by Curtis Chin*

Each of us remembers stories from childhood and adolescence. As we grow older the meanings of these stories change. Once mysterious adult behavior becomes more understandable, while our own seemingly innocent actions may be viewed with more complexity. Our knowledge of other stories—both the comforting and the disturbing—can transform the way we look at our own experiences.

The essays, excerpts, and short stories in this anthology are all previously published works about growing up in the United States. And they have all been written by authors identified as Asian American.

These selections illuminate universal themes and events common to all coming-of-age literature: parent-child relationships, rebellion, feelings of being uniquely misunderstood, first love, sexual discovery, bewilderment, and vulnerability in the face of the adult world.

As works of a particular American racial and ethnic group, these stories and essays raise questions of identity, assimilation, cultural history, and heritage. How these issues are explored varies tremendously within the collection, according to each author's individual voice and situation.

The collection reflects the diversity of its authors' backgrounds. Many of the writings are by Chinese and Japanese

Americans, but there are also works by writers of Filipino, Korean, Indian, and bi- and multiracial descent. While most of the selections are by second- and third-generation authors, there are stories by first-generation writers who immigrated to the States as children and by fifth-generation authors whose ancestors built American institutions like the transcontinental railroad during the nineteenth century.

Temporal and geographic location also contribute to the diversity of perspectives. Chronologically, the collection begins with Sui Sin Far's short story, "Pat and Pan," from the late nineteenth century, and ends with contemporary writers R. A. Sasaki and Indira Ganesan. Many authors were raised in long-established Asian American communities in California and Hawaii. A few, like Tooru J. Kanazawa, draw on their experiences growing up in multicultural communities such as Juneau, Alaska, in the 1910s. Others recall early experiences of ethnic isolation, like Lydia Minatoya, who was raised in upstate New York during the 1950s.

Although several writers have roots in urban centers like New York City, Los Angeles, and San Fransisco's Bay Area, the focus of each work shifts dramatically depending on whether the author grew up in a community of his/her ethnic group. For example, the Chinatown setting of Jade Snow Wong's *Fifth Chinese Daughter* is very different from the mostly African American neighborhood of Gus Lee's *China Boy*; yet both stories take place in San Francisco.

And not surprisingly, the social and economic status of the authors' families influenced how they grew up. As Louise Leung Larson recounts in *Sweet Bamboo,* the effects of prejudice can be mitigated by the benefits of affluence. On the other hand, the forces of racism combined with poverty can make childhood an arduous experience, as was the case for Mary Paik Lee, growing up during the 1910s in rural California.

It may seem superficial to gather together writers from such diverse backgrounds and to label them all as just Asian American. However, the kinship among their stories is manifested not only by the recurrence of certain themes, but also by the sense of recognition many Asian American readers will experience when reading them.

This bond of recognition is especially significant within the context of race and ethnicity. As a racial minority, Asian Americans traditionally have been excluded from representation in mainstream American media. During our 160-year history, most portrayals of Asian Americans have perpetuated insidious stereotypes including the Eurocentric perception of Asian Americans as foreign, exotic, and non-American. There have been few images that reflect the complexity of Asian American experiences.

As a Korean American growing up in a mostly Jewish American suburb of New York City during the 1970s and 1980s, I was unaware of the flourishing Asian American cultural movement taking place in Manhattan, less than fifty miles away. During this time, seminal organizations like New York's Basement Workshop were inspiring artists and activists to create plays, visual art, poetry, fiction, and music.

Later, in college and while working at New York's Chinatown History Museum, I learned about this cultural movement and other ongoing creative efforts. Reading poems and stories from Asian America and working in a community of Asian American historians, artists, and writers, I felt both comforted and empowered. The affirmation of my perceptions of racism made me feel strangely at ease. The literal and literary presence of other Asian Americans enabled me to explore my concerns in a validating way.

Over the last two decades the number of published writings by Asian Americans has grown tremendously. Yet much of the literature remains inaccessible to a broad audience. While the novels of best-selling author Amy Tan are readily found in most libraries and bookstores, other works require persistence and luck to find. Many journals and books have gone out of print, leaving few copies behind outside of individual collections. I hope this collection will make some of these stories widely available, especially to young people growing up today.

I have tried to make this anthology as inclusive as possible. However, certain themes and groups remain under- and unrepresented. Within the body of Asian American literature, there are many stories about growing up in Asia and coming to America. However, prose pieces about coming of age in America are relatively scarce. This is particularly true of Filipino American literature, which, despite its long history, consists mostly of poetry, stories of adulthood, and stories that take place in the Philippines.

Immigrant groups must often be in America for at least two generations before producing and publishing literature about growing up here. The Southeast Asian American literatures are in their early stages and very little has been written relating to childhood. Similar circumstances account for the absence of gay and lesbian writings, which often focus on coming out as adults and on life after adolescence. As more stories are written and published, this collection will be expanded and revised.

In order to preserve the unique voices of the different authors, the stories are presented as they originally appeared, or as later revised by their authors. For this reason, certain matters of style (and romanization of some words) are not consistent throughout the collection. No glossary is provided because many of the writers strongly believe that words from Asian languages should not need to be explained. The sense of most words, however, is indicated by context.

I have divided this anthology into three sections, which roughly correspond to the progression from child to young adult. Rather than using age as a strict guideline, I have situated the stories according to the types of experience they portray.

The first section, called "First Memories," is devoted to stories of childhood. Parents and stepparents figure prominently in many of these works, as in Toshio Mori's "Through Anger and Love." Teachers and early school experiences are also important in some stories, like Marie Hara's "Fourth Grade Ukus (1952)." Nostalgia and a child's forthright observation characterize many of these selections.

The second section, "The Beginnings of Identity," is composed of stories of early adolescence. Steps toward independence and initiation into teenage life mark these works. The protagonists often have the ability to perceive the hypocrisy and idiosyncrasy of the adult world. They challenge authority accordingly, as in Garrett Hongo's personal essay "Kubota" and the excerpt from Cynthia Kadohata's *The Floating World*. Several stories depict first sexual experiences.

In the final section, "Growing Up," the narrators are either teenagers, or adults looking back on their early lives. Some stories, like Kartar Dhillon's "The Parrot's Beak," span growing up from childhood through adulthood. Others, like Mavis Hara's "Carnival Queen," take place during the time just before young adulthood.

The beginning of the second section contains autobiographical accounts of growing up during the internment of Japanese Americans during World War II. These stories have been grouped together and placed at the beginning of the identity section because of the internment's significance within Asian American history.

As the most horrifying example of widespread hostility toward Asian Americans, the internment represents an abrupt end of innocence, a transition from childhood to adolescent doubt and rage. A historical account of the internment precedes the memoir excerpts. In addition to these stories about the internment, the internment's effect on later generations emerges in some of the other selections.

The purpose of this anthology is not to define rigidly what it means to grow up Asian American, but rather to enable individual readers to determine for themselves what we share and where we diverge by reading a collection of works on this subject. Each author offers a different perspective on what growing up and being Asian American means. And as I mentioned, many voices have yet to be represented.

One thing that emerges upon reading this anthology is the presence of a strong narrative tradition within Asian American literature. Above all else, these are beautifully written stories, rendered with eloquence, passion, and precision. I hope that they will be enjoyed as such and will inspire others to write their stories.

—*Maria Hong,*
Brooklyn, NY, 1993

FIRST
MEMORIES

"PAT AND PAN"

Sui Sin Far
(a.k.a. Edith Eaton) (1867–1915)

During the late nineteenth and early twentieth centuries, Americans of Asian descent faced prejudice from individuals as well as widely institutionalized, systematic forms of racism. American legislation reflected the prevalence of an extremely hostile attitude toward Asians and Asian Americans. The Chinese Exclusion Acts of 1880 and 1882 severely restricted immigration from China compared with immigration from European nations. Similarly, the California Alien Land Act of 1913 prohibited Asian American farmers from owning land.

Given this context, Edith Eaton's embracing of her Chinese heritage, as expressed in her writings, suggests a uniquely courageous and formidable spirit. Writing under the pseudonym Sui Sin Far ("Water Lily" in Cantonese), Ms. Eaton wrote fiction, autobiography, and articles about the Chinese communities in America and her personal experience. The daughter of an English man and a Chinese woman, she grew up in the United States and Canada.

Although she did not achieve the literary popularity of her sister, Winnifred, who wrote under a Japanese pen name, Onoto Watanna, Ms. Eaton was published widely in mainstream magazines and newspapers. She was also recognized by the Chinese American community for her pioneering work. "Pat and Pan" was published in her only book, a prose collection entitled Mrs. Spring Fragrance (A. C. McClurg, 1912). Her work has been republished in several anthologies and discussed in scholarly books

such as Between Worlds: Women Writers of Chinese Ancestry
by Amy Ling.

I

THEY LAY THERE, IN THE ENTRANCE TO THE JOSS HOUSE, SOUND
asleep in each other's arms. Her tiny face was hidden upon his
bosom and his white, upturned chin rested upon her black,
rosetted head.

It was that white chin which caused the passing Mission
woman to pause and look again at the little pair. Yes, it was a
white boy and a little Chinese girl; he, about five, she, not more
than three years old.

"Whose is that boy?" asked the Mission woman of the peripa-
tetic vendor of Chinese fruits and sweetmeats.

"That boy! Oh, him is boy of Lum Yook that make the China
gold ring and bracelet."

"But he is white."

"Yes, him white; but all same, China boy. His mother, she
not have any white fiend, and the wife of Lum Yook give her
lice and tea, so when she go to the land of spilit, she give her
boy to the wife of Lum Yook. Lady, you want buy lichi?"

While Anna Harrison was extracting a dime from her purse
the black, rosetted head slowly turned and a tiny fist began
rubbing itself into a tiny face.

"Well, chickabiddy, have you had a nice nap?"

"Tjo ho! tjo ho!"

The black eyes gazed solemnly and disdainfully at the
stranger.

"She tell you to be good," chuckled the old man.

"Oh, you quaint little thing!"

The quaint little thing, hearing herself thus apostrophized,
turned herself around upon the bosom of the still sleeping boy
and, reaching her arms up to his neck, buried her face again
under his chin. This, of course, awakened him. He sat up and
stared bewilderedly at the Mission woman.

"What is the boy's name?" she asked, noting his gray eyes
and rosy skin.

His reply, though audible, was wholly unintelligible to the American woman.

"He talk only Chinese talk," said the old man.

Anna Harrison was amazed. A white boy in America talking only Chinese talk! She placed her bag of lichis beside him and was amused to see the little girl instantly lean over her companion and possess herself of it. The boy made no attempt to take it from her, and the little thing opened the bag and cautiously peeped in. What she saw evoked a chirrup of delight. Quickly she brought forth one of the browny-red fruit nuts, crushed and pulled off its soft shell. But to the surprise of the Mission woman, instead of putting it into her own mouth, she thrust the sweetish, dried pulp into that of her companion. She repeated this operation several times, then cocking her little head on one side, asked:

"Ho 'm ho? Is it good or bad?"

"Ho! ho!" answered the boy, removing several pits from his mouth and shaking his head to signify that he had had enough. Whereupon the little girl tasted herself of the fruit.

"Pat! Pan! Pat! Pan!" called a woman's voice, and a sleek-headed, kindly-faced matron in dark blue pantalettes and tunic, wearing double hooped gold earrings, appeared around the corner. Hearing her voice, the boy jumped up with a merry laugh and ran out into the street. The little girl more seriously and slowly followed him.

"Him mother!" informed the lichi man.

II

WHEN ANNA HARRISON, SOME MONTHS LATER, OPENED HER school for white and Chinese children in Chinatown, she determined that Pat, the adopted son of Lum Yook, the Chinese jeweller, should learn to speak his mother tongue. For a white boy to grow up as a Chinese was unthinkable. The second time she saw him, it was some kind of a Chinese holiday, and he was in great glee over a row of red Chinese candles and punk which he was burning on the curb of the street, in company with a number of Chinese urchins. Pat's candle was giving a brighter and bigger flame than any of the others, and he was jumping up and down with his legs doubled under him from the knees like an india-rubber ball, while Pan, from the doorstep of her father's store, applauded him in vociferous, infantile Chinese.

Miss Harrison laid her hand upon the boy's shoulder and spoke to him. It had not been very difficult for her to pick up a few Chinese phrases. Would he not like to come to her school and see some pretty pictures? Pat shook his ruddy curls and looked at Pan. Would Pan come too? Yes, Pan would. Pan's memory was good, and so were lichis and shredded cocoanut candy.

Of course Pan was too young to go to school—a mere baby; but if Pat could not be got without Pan, why then Pan must come too. Lum Yook and his wife, upon being interviewed, were quite willing to have Pat learn English. The foster-father could speak a little of the language himself; but as he used it only when in business or when speaking to Americans, Pat had not benefited thereby. However, he was more eager than otherwise to have Pat learn "the speech of his ancestors," and promised that he would encourage the little ones to practise "American" together when at home.

So Pat and Pan went to the Mission school, and for the first time in their lives suffered themselves to be divided, for Pat had to sit with the boys and tiny Pan had a little red chair near Miss Harrison, beside which were placed a number of baby toys. Pan was not supposed to learn, only to play.

But Pan did learn. In a year's time, although her talk was more broken and babyish, she had a better English vocabulary than had Pat. Moreover, she could sing hymns and recite verses in a high, shrill voice; whereas Pat, though he tried hard enough, poor little fellow, was unable to memorize even a sentence. Naturally, Pat did not like school as well as did Pan, and it was only Miss Harrison's persistent ambition for him that kept him there.

One day, when Pan was five and Pat was seven, the little girl, for the first time, came to school alone.

"Where is Pat?" asked the teacher.

"Pat, he is sick today," replied Pan.

"Sick!" echoed Miss Harrison. "Well, that is too bad. Poor Pat! What is the matter with him?"

"A big dog bite him."

24

That afternoon, the teacher, on her way to see the bitten Pat, beheld him up an alley busily engaged in keeping five tops spinning at one time, while several American boys stood around, loudly admiring the Chinese feat.

The next morning Pat received five strokes from a cane which Miss Harrison kept within her desk and used only on special occasions. These strokes made Pat's right hand tingle smartly; but he received them with smiling grace.

Miss Harrison then turned to five-year-old Pan, who had watched the caning with tearful interest.

"Pan!" said the teacher, "you have been just as naughty as Pat, and you must be punished too."

"I not stay away flom school!" protested Pan.

"No,"—severely—"you did not stay away from school; but you told me a dog had bitten Pat, and that was not true. Little girls must not say what is not true. Teacher does not like to slap Pan's hands, but she must do it, so that Pan will remember that she must not say what is not true. Come here!"

Pan, hiding her face in her sleeve, sobbingly arose.

The teacher leaned forward and, pulling down the uplifted arm, took the small hand in her own and slapped it. She was about to do this a second time when Pat bounded from his seat, pushed Pan aside, and shaking his little fist in the teacher's face, dared her in a voice hoarse with passion:

"You hurt my Pan again! You hurt my Pan again!"

They were not always lovers—those two. It was aggravating to Pat, when the teacher, finding he did not know his verse, would turn to Pan and say:

"Well, Pan, let us hear you."

And Pan, who was the youngest child in school and unusually small for her years, would pharisaically clasp her tiny fingers and repeat word for word the verse desired to be heard.

"I hate you, Pan!" muttered Pat on one such occasion.

Happily Pan did not hear him. She was serenely singing:

"Yesu love me, t'is I know,
For the Bible tell me so."

But though a little seraph in the matter of singing hymns and repeating verses, Pan, for a small Chinese girl, was very mischievous. Indeed, she was the originator of most of the mischief which Pat carried out with such spirit. Nevertheless, when Pat got into trouble, Pan, though sympathetic, always had a lecture for him. "Too bad, too bad! Why not you be good like me?" admonished she one day when he was suffering "consequences."

Pat looked down upon her with wrathful eyes.

"Why," he asked, "is bad people always so good?"

III

THE CHILD OF THE WHITE WOMAN, WHO HAD BEEN GIVEN A BABE into the arms of the wife of Lum Yook, was regarded as their own by the Chinese jeweller and his wife, and they bestowed upon him equal love and care with the little daughter who came two years after him. If Mrs. Lum Yook showed any favoritism whatever, it was to Pat. He was the first she had cradled to her bosom; the first to gladden her heart with baby smiles and wiles; the first to call her Ah Ma; the first to love her. On his eighth birthday, she said to her husband: "The son of the white woman is the son of the white woman, and there are many tongues wagging because he lives under our roof. My heart is as heavy as the blackest heavens."

"Peace, my woman," answered the easygoing man. "Why should we trouble before trouble comes?"

When trouble did come it was met calmly and bravely. To the comfortably off American and wife who were to have the boy and "raise him as an American boy should be raised," they yielded him without protest. But deep in their hearts was the sense of injustice and outraged love. If it had not been for their pity for the unfortunate white girl, their care and affection for her helpless offspring, there would have been no white boy for others to "raise."

And Pat and Pan? "I will not leave my Pan! I will not leave my Pan!" shouted Pat.

"But you must!" sadly urged Lum Yook. "You are a white boy and Pan is Chinese."

"I am Chinese too! I am Chinese too!" cried Pat.

"He Chinese! He Chinese!" pleaded Pan. Her little nose was swollen with crying; her little eyes red-rimmed.

But Pat was driven away.

Pat, his schoolbooks under his arm, was walking down the hill, whistling cheerily. His roving glance down a side street was suddenly arrested.

"Gee!" he exclaimed. "If that isn't Pan! Pan, oh, Pan!" he shouted.

Pan turned. There was a shrill cry of delight, and Pan was clinging to Pat, crying: "Nice Pat! Good Pat!"

Then she pushed him away from her and scanned him from head to foot.

"Nice coat! Nice boot! How many dollars?" she queried.

Pat laughed good-humoredly. "I don't know," he answered. "Mother bought them."

"Mother!" echoed Pan. She puckered her brows for a moment.

"You are grown big, Pat," was her next remark.

"And you have grown little, Pan," retorted Pat. It was a year since they had seen one another and Pan was much smaller than any of his girl schoolfellows.

"Do you like to go to the big school?" asked Pan, noticing the books.

"I don't like it very much. But, say, Pan, I learn lots of things that you don't know anything about."

Pan eyed him wistfully. Finally she said: "O Pat! A-Toy, she die."

"A-Toy! Who is A-Toy?"

"The meow, Pat; the big gray meow! Pat, you have forgot to remember."

Pat looked across Pan's head and far away.

"Chinatown is very nice now," assured Pan. "Hum Lock has two trays of brass beetles in his store and Ah Ma has many flowers!"

"I would like to see the brass beetles," said Pat.

"And father's new glass case?"

"Yes."

"And Ah Ma's flowers?"

"Yes."

"Then come, Pat."

"I can't, Pan!"

"Oh!"

Again Pat was walking home from school, this time in company with some boys. Suddenly a glad little voice sounded in his ear. It was Pan's.

"Ah, Pat!" cried she joyfully. "I find you! I find you!"

"Hear the China kid!" laughed one of the boys.

Then Pat turned upon Pan. "Get away from me," he shouted. "Get away from me!"

And Pan did get away from him—just as fast as her little legs could carry her. But when she reached the foot of the hill, she looked up and shook her little head sorrowfully. "Poor Pat!" said she. "He Chinese no more; he Chinese no more!"

"From Gee Sook to Beatty"
from *Sweet Bamboo: Saga of a Chinese American Family*
Louise Leung Larson (1905–1988)

Sweet Bamboo *is Louise "Mamie" Leung Larson's autobiographical account of her Chinese American family's life in Los Angeles during the first decades of the twentieth century. The story begins with her parents' lives in China and ends with her coming of age as an independent adult in America. Sweet Bamboo (Gum Jook) is the Tom Leung family village in Guangdong China.*

As the daughter of a successful herbalist, Tom Leung, Ms. Larson grew up in an unusually privileged environment. The following excerpt illustrates her young life at 1619 Pico Street in a wealthy residential section of Los Angeles.

Ms. Larson was born in 1905 in Los Angeles. After graduating from the University of Southern California in 1926, she became one of the first Asian American journalists. From the 1920s through the 1940s, she wrote for major newspapers, including The Los Angeles Record, Chicago Daily News, *and* Los Angeles Daily News. *During her lifetime she received many awards for her work from women's, Asian American, and government organizations, including the Pioneer Woman's Award of the Chinese Historical Society of Southern California (1978), a commendation from the Los Angeles mayor's office (1984), and an award for her role as a pioneering journalist from the Asian American Journalists Association (1988).*

Readers of this piece need to know that E Bok Foo is Tom Leung's older cousin. E Bok Foo established the herb company in which Mr. Leung trained as a young man. The two men were partners in the Foo and Wing Herb Company for many years prior to the beginning of this excerpt.

EVEN THOUGH WE RESENTED RACIAL SLURS, WE WERE NOT WITH-out prejudice against other minorities. We felt superior to blacks, or *hak gways* (black ghosts) as we called them. My best friend at Tenth Street School was a black girl, though very light colored, but when a family friend asked me why I chose a *hak gway* for my chum, I was embarrassed. After this, to my regret, I tried to distance myself from my friend. We also spoke disparagingly of *Jew gways* (Jew ghosts) and *union gways* or *goong gways* (union ghosts or laborers). As *sahm yup* Cantonese, we looked down on *say yup* Cantonese, who spoke a different dialect and whom we thought were lower class. When we became college students, we felt superior to the "market bunch," young men who worked in the produce market. We did not live in Chinatown, so we considered those who did, not quite as elite as we. But we called all Orientals, including ourselves, *wong gways* (yellow ghosts). Papa couldn't vote, not being a citizen, but he was always sympathetic to Republicans. At presidential elections, we always supported the Republican candidate. The Democratic Party, in our opinion, was the party of poor people or *goong gways*, so we sided with the Republicans. However, we were more or less apolitical. It wasn't until after I had graduated from college and was working that I cast my first vote—as a Democrat. Mama had no interest in what went on in the American political scene, but she was an avid reader of Chinese newspapers. Perhaps one reason we grew up with this snobbish attitude was because we had a cook, a maid, and a nurse, and we noticed that most people didn't. We were proud that our father was the most successful herbalist in Los Angeles, and that he was highly respected by the Chinese community. Yet our parents did not foster these opinions. Perhaps it was our life style. Much later, we were to learn what it meant to be poor.

The move to "1619," where Papa set up business under the name of T. Leung Herb Co., and the breakup of the partnership with E Bok Foo, were causes for rancor. In fact, E Bok Foo was very angry. When Papa first broached the subject of moving to a bigger house, there were angry discussions. E Bok Foo spent much time in his offices in Oakland and Boston. When he returned to Los Angeles, he wanted to move into "1619." He wanted control of the herb business there. Papa was willing to share fifty-fifty, but E Bok Foo insisted he should have half interest in the house also. He ordered Papa to get out of the herb business and leave the city. One night, the argument got so heated that E Bok Foo threw a flower pot at Papa, who left the room. E Bok Foo probably reasoned that he had invited Papa to come to this country in the first place and had taught him the herb business. He moved into "1619," and Mama gave him her room. He worked and ate at Olive street and came to "1619" to sleep. Papa and Mama kept their bedroom door shut, and E Bok Foo stayed in his room. The second floor "parlor" was unused. This uncomfortable situation went on for two or three months, when E Bok Foo finally went back to "903," but the family squabble was never settled, and E Bok Foo and Papa were no longer partners, but competitors.

Gee Sook, our cook who had been with us so long at Olive street, came with us to "1619." He continued to live in Chinatown, arriving early each morning on the "P" streetcar. We children had by this time given up eating *jook* (rice gruel) for breakfast. Sometimes we had cornflakes, but more often than not we would go to school without breakfast. Our parents began eating oatmeal for breakfast, which Mama cooked. At Olive Street, Gee Sook had made sandwiches for Lillie and me for our school lunch, but he cut the bread so thick that we were ashamed to eat in front of the other children and began making our own lunches. In the early afternoon, Gee Sook took his straw basket, boarded the "P" car, and went to Chinatown to shop for our evening meal, just as he had done at Olive street. He used the wood stove, winter or summer. He sat at the top of the basement steps and ate. He never felt quite at home in the new house. Papa insisted that the white tile kitchen floor be mopped daily and that the stoves and counters be kept clean. After a year or two, he told Papa he was going back to China, that he was getting old and wanted to die there. He had saved enough money from his small earnings to buy a ticket home to Canton. His departure was a blow to our parents. They wanted to continue eating Chinese meals as they had since they'd left

China, and they tried in vain to find a replacement for Gee Sook. Finally they gave up this quest and hired a *hak gway* cook named Beatty from an employment agency. She turned out to be a Southern cook of gourmet quality. Since I didn't like Chinese food, I was ecstatic.

The first breakfast Beatty cooked still stands out in my memory. It was served, fittingly, in the breakfast room, an airy, light room that opened onto the back garden. The chilled melon was cut with scalloped edges, the eggs were scrambled just right, and I had never tasted such fluffy, delicious biscuits. Even Mama ate a whole biscuit. Beatty had certain specialties, such as oxtail soup and fried sand-dabs, which were Papa's favorite. Mama, whose taste for American food was lukewarm, genuinely liked not only Beatty's biscuits, but her spoonbread. She jealously guarded her recipes, and long after she had left, we tried in vain to duplicate her spoonbread. The Johnson sisters found her strawberry shortcake especially mouth-watering. They tried to wheedle and bribe the recipe from Beatty, who shut herself into the pantry when she stirred up the batter. I gorged on the meals, gaining weight. But our parents still yearned for their Chinese food. On Beatty's day off, Mama tried her hand at cooking. She had watched Gee Sook and had picked up some rudiments of Chinese cooking—things she had never learned during her pampered girlhood. Eventually she became a good cook and knew how to make Papa's favorite dishes. She taught Lillie too, and later, Holly; they both became excellent cooks—American and Chinese style—but in the kitchen I was known as *lun jun* or clumsy and slow.

The garden at the back of the new house was laid out in formal style, according to Papa's plan. There was a fountain in the middle and a summerhouse in the back. Gravel paths divided the planting plots. Two plots in front were planted in grass. Papa ordered all the trees, flowers, and shrubs from his old friend and teacher Paul Howard of the Howard and Smith Nursery, which was on its way to becoming one of the most successful nurseries in Los Angeles. The nursery also did the soil preparation and planting at the cost of $3.50 per day per man. At that time, the plantings were practically given away. We have a bill dated March 31, 1914 for $140.33 which covered all the original landscaping—labor included. Among the plantings listed are bay and rubber trees, bamboo, 18 varieties of shrubs, 100 dusty millers, phlox, ficus, 24 petunias, 50 calla lillies, jasmine, magnolia, a dozen hanging baskets, and roses (including two climbing Cecil Brunners.) I remember the latter well because they bloomed so profusely, almost covering the summer house with tiny pink roses. The garden was enclosed by a decorative, white fence, high enough to insure complete privacy, not only from neighbors, but also from the utility part of our yard where the woodshed and clothesline were. Since the plants were mature, not seedlings, the garden soon was a pleasure to enjoy. Papa installed lights for nighttime enjoyment.

Monroe's lively document about the family (written about 1940) describes Papa's love of his garden:

Every morning before going to his office, he would smoke his water pipe in the back porch (which overlooked the garden) and look at his plants, especially the ones lining the porch rails and stone steps. This is one *definite habit* I will always remember he did. On rainy days he'd merely stand by the screen door of the breakfast room and peer out. He did this before and immediately after his breakfast which was at about 10 a.m. When he came home at night he would do the same. One night he noticed a pair of cat's eyes in the dark and seemed very interested. He described them as being like *two lanterns.* Whenever there was a full moon he used to keep the garden lights closed and admire the moonlight. He admired the moonlight just like I do now. Dad kept up an endless vigil against scraps of paper and leaves on the ground and always made us pick them up. My dad was *always neat.*

Mama also smoked a water pipe, but not outdoors. When she woke in the morning, she would take her first smoke in the bathroom, sitting on the stool by the toilet. After she came downstairs, she smoked two or three times a day—always sitting in the chair by the kitchen stove. For a while, it was my job to clean these water pipes, a smelly job that I intensely disliked. Mama also smoked cigarettes. She had started smoking them when she was a young girl, but she told Myra Lee, "I don't want my girls to smoke." We never did. Papa never

smoked cigarettes; he smoked cigars and a pipe. He was particular about what he smoked and patronized an exclusive place
called John's Pipe Shop in downtown Los Angeles. Their delivery wagon made frequent trips to our home; it was in the form
of a large pipe drawn by a pony. Papa always bought the best
in tobacco, imported mixtures, and a brand called Long Cut
Tobacco which he and Mama used in their water pipes. He kept
the tobacco in a jar with a lettuce leaf over it to keep it fresh
and moist. His favorite pipe was made in Ireland. When we
were very young, Lillie and I loved the fancy paper rings that
came around the cigars, and later, we vied for the wooden cigar
boxes in which to keep our treasures. The cigar smell clung to
them no matter how long we kept them.

Monroe was correct in stating that Papa was neat. Papa had
Mabel type up these instructions for the maid:

> All the floors must be swept with a broom once a week;
> the first floor on Friday, the second floor on Saturday, and
> the third floor on Tuesday.
> Scrub the bathrooms on the first and third floors twice a
> week.
> Scrub bathroom on second floor every day.
> Sweep the steps twice a week, and dust them every day.
> In the kitchen clean the stoves, icebox, woodwork, etc.,
> every Thursday.
> Use the hose on the front and back porches on Tuesday
> and Saturday. Sweep them every day.
> If the rooms are not very dirty, they need not be swept,
> but only dusted and mopped, except the children's rooms,
> which must be swept every day.
> Sweep the roof garden once a week.

Since the maid also had to do the huge daily washings and
look after the young children, she had her hands full. However,
I doubt that the instructions were followed to the letter because
the maids seemed to have plenty of time to take us to the parks
or to the movies in the afternoons.

Originally, the front porch extended the width of the house;
but Papa soon decided that his office was too cramped and
small, so he had about a third of the porch glassed in, doubling

his office space and still leaving plenty of porch. He was always making improvements. After Gee Sook left, there was no need for the woodshed so that was torn down. (There was no need for the wood stove either, but it was built into the kitchen and too difficult to remove.) A structure was built at the back of the utility section of the yard. For a short time it was used as a playhouse but soon became living quarters for students. One was C. C. Lee, a silent young man, who gave us Chinese lessons. There were steps leading from this structure to the flat roof where the clotheslines were placed. This made even more work for the maid, who had to bring the wet laundry up the steep basement stairs, outdoors to the yard, and then up the steps to the clotheslines. Lillie and I learned how difficult this was when we did the laundry, though our task was much easier. By that time, we had a wringer-type washing machine which was on the back porch; we had to carry the clothes basket up only one flight of stairs, but we complained bitterly.

Sometimes Papa would have his morning smoke on the sec-ond-floor balcony, which extended the width of the house; the sitting room and Mama's bedroom opened onto this balcony. Chinese ceramic pots planted with flowers in season were dis-played on the wide shelf atop the balcony railing. On warm evenings the whole family would sit out there. The view here— of traffic on Pico Street—was less than desirable. For some reason, we seldom made use of the roof garden, where there was the most privacy and quiet and a comfortable lawn swing. Here again, Papa had potted plants. In the fall, the chrysanthe-mums were a riot of color. The petals were used in a fish dish that Papa liked. The Fourth of July was one time when we would gather on the roof garden, to watch the fireworks display from Exposition Park.

"FRONTIER HOME"
from SUSHI AND SOURDOUGH
Tooru J. Kanazawa (1906–   )

Sushi and Sourdough *tells the story of Japanese Americans living in the territory of Alaska from the late 1890s through the early 1920s. During this period—Alaska's gold rush—Issei, first-generation Japanese Americans and Nisei, second-generation Japanese Americans, joined the multiethnic ranks of fortune-seekers throughout the area, often departing from points in Washington and Northern California. Other Japanese American men traveled north to work in Alaskan salmon canneries, where many Chinese and Filipino Americans also labored. On the heels of these migrations, families and single men settled in Alaskan towns, some of them forming early, small Japanese American communities.*

Sushi and Sourdough is a novel based on Tooru Kanazawa's experiences growing up in the frontier gold-mining town of Juneau. In the following excerpt the protagonist, Joe "Thor" Toranosuke Fuse, explores the unspoiled wilderness of that region.

Mr. Kanazawa was born in Spokane, Washington, in 1906 and moved with his family to Douglas, Alaska, in 1912. Two years later the family moved to Juneau, where his father worked as a barber. Mr. Kanazawa graduated from the University of Washington, Seattle, with a B.A. in journalism in 1931, and later wrote for publications including The Christian Science Monitor, Common Ground, *and several Japanese American newspapers such as the* Japanese American Courier, New York Nichibei, *and* Rafu Shimpo. *In 1943, he volunteered for the 100–442nd Regimental Combat Team, a regiment composed of Nisei from Hawaii and the internment camps, which fought in Italy and*

France. The famous 442nd became one of the most decorated units in American history. Mr. Kanazawa was awarded a Bronze Star for meritorious service, and served as a radio operator assigned to rifle companies and as a citations writer. From 1952–1987, he worked as vice president of the New York Travel Service. He lives in New York City.

THOR DISCOVERED IN THE STREETS OF THE TOWN AND IN THE wilderness of the mountains and creeks almost inexhaustible opportunities to develop his initiative and resourcefulness. Although he was neither avaricious nor needy, if some of his numerous activities brought him income he considered it sugar on his buttered bread. Mama could not afford cake except on birthdays. She was saving what she could for the family's future.

Much of the money he earned went to buy sweets. He did not correlate sugar with his frequent toothaches and reluctant visits to the dentist. Mama scolded but to no end.

On most Saturday mornings Thor turned scavenger. It took Mama several weeks to realize that it was impractical to lay out freshly laundered clothing for him on Saturdays. At least her son had sense enough to wear his clodhoppers on his forays. He would tuck a gunnysack under his arm and disappear beneath the piers.

The sandy beach of this underworld was slimy and the acrid air smelled of sewage. He learned to avoid the sudden flushing of toilets but could not evade the constant drops of water that fell from the street planks. Overhead he heard the *clip, clop, clip, clop* of hooves and the rumble of steel-tired wagon wheels. The log pilings, eroded by tide and marine life into elongated hourglass shapes, were encrusted with knife-edged barnacles and tiny mussel shells. In the dim light emanating from the edge of the pier, he searched for soda-water bottles and an occasional reed-encased demijohn bottle that was worth a quarter.

He emerged on the street with a sack full of bottles, smelling of hemp, stale beer, seaweed, and slimy clay. Dampness had climbed the ironed legs of his denim pants, water had darkened his blue cambric shirt, and his shoes were soaked and caked with brine.

One Saturday Mama met him emerging from the nether-world. "Komaru ne!" she said, her voice betraying all the meanings of the word: embarrassment, perplexity, annoyance. "What will the neighbors think! Not of you!" she emphasized. "Of me! Me!"

She threw up her hands in defeat as he bore his clinking burden to Dolly Gray's bottling works, where he dumped the bottles into a large wooden tank of water. He scraped off the labels and emptied the sand out of the bottles. He watched in fascination as Dolly placed the bottles over the whirling brushes of a machine that thoroughly cleansed the insides.

The bottles were filled with fruit syrup and carbonated water, capped, and labeled. Dolly rewarded Thor with two cents a bottle and a soda. His favorite flavor was strawberry. Instead of removing the cap he would drive a nail through it and so prolong his enjoyment.

At the bowling alley across the street—he was always on call—he attained a speed setting up pins on ten black dots that earned him a nickel a game. The charge was twenty-five cents a line, with the winner paying ten cents and the loser fifteen. Thor usually received a tip from the bowlers, who skidded the money down the maple alleys. He dreaded the big Swedes who used brute force rather than finesse just to see the pins fly.

One night at the pool hall up the street, Thor and Gus were watching Ken when the butt of Ken's cue hit Gus in the eye. Ken apologized, though Gus was wrong, standing too close, and gave him a silver dollar.

"What an easy way to make a buck," Thor said.

"You know, that hurt. I saw stars."

Thor examined the eye. "Yeah, it's going to get black."

"Your brother's a sport. C'mon, let's go have a soda."

The two boys, one of Swedish forebears, the other of Japanese, were the closest of friends and almost inseparable. Gus was about the same height, with flaxen hair, blue eyes, and a round face. Gus had a habit of ducking his head when he made a mischievous remark, as if he were trying to hide his expression. He had a flexible and loose scalp so he was able to wiggle his ears. This ability was Thor's despair because no matter how much he tried, he could not duplicate what he considered a remarkable feat.

Gus had round shoulders, partly the consequence of a fall he had taken up on the mountainside. He had fallen from the lip of a frozen waterfall, and escaped serious injury only because he landed on a steep, icy slope, sliding rather than falling flat. Thor had been shaken by his friend's close call, but was relieved to find him in good spirits when he visited him in the hospital.

Thor also had misadventures. One Saturday at the pier he was helping George the Greek lower provisions to a boat by means of a rope. The weight of a sack of potatoes pulled his hand forward before he could even think of letting go. His first and middle fingers were caught between the edge of the pier and the running rope that burned off the flesh.

The doctor applied salve to his wounds; he never forgot the smell of the yellow ointment, the stained gauze and adhesive tape which became soiled and had to be changed. He watched with awe as nature healed the raw flesh and covered it with skin. He bore the scars for years.

In July George commissioned Thor to pick some blueberries at ten cents a pound. He expected Thor to fill a five-pound, Swift lard pail, but he returned with a water pail more than half full. George wanted to pay him with an equivalent value of fruit, but Thor wanted cash. He had risen before the sun, raided his favorite patches on the Silver Bow Basin road where the berries grew as big as nickels. Now he thought of the time and labor spent and his resentment grew.

Angrily he stalked the stand, strongly tempted to push over some of the displays in revenge. Fear restrained him. His home was just across the street.

"I won't buy anything from you for my mother," he threatened. When George offered him half of what he had earned, Thor slapped the coins out of the extended hand. As he started to run away George grabbed him. He struggled furiously as the strong arms carried him toward the cash register. Three silver dollars were placed in his hand and his fingers were closed over the money. He stood wiping the tears from his eyes. He returned one dollar. "You owe me only two dollars," he said.

George threw up his hands and raised his eyes to the twilight sky. "All this commotion for what. I was only teasing."

"You were not," Thor retorted hotly. "You're a mean man."

Mama wondered why he went blocks out of his way to buy

green groceries when all he had to do was walk across the street. He refused to tell her what was wrong. This was between him and that bugger. It was weeks before George could mollify him. After that Mama would wonder why Thor brought home more fruit and vegetables than her money would normally buy.

Weddings were of more than romantic interest to the boys. At the reception, usually held in the dining room of a hotel, the boys would gather in the street outside and wait for the ushers or friends of the groom to come out. Invariably they would toss silver dollars and two-and-a-half-dollar gold pieces out into the street, and the boys would scramble for their share.

At one of the wedding receptions, Thor snatched a gold piece from under the hand of Ettore Lucano, a newcomer who tended to bully the younger boys. Ettore had a complexion that always looked flushed, with a white scar across his left jawbone.

"Gimme," Ettore said. "That's mine."

Thor backed away. "Is not. I got it first." He added, "Slow-poke."

That was a mistake. Ettore reddened to the roots of his bad-ger-colored hair. He stalked Thor and suddenly grabbed for him. Thor took to his heels, closely pursued by the older boy. Thor sought refuge in his home, slamming the door on Ettore's panting breath.

As Thor stood gasping for breath in the kitchen, his sister Helen reported to him, "Ettore says the money is his."

"Tell him it's mine and I'm going to keep it."

Helen returned. "He says he is going to come in after you."

"I dare him to."

"He's much larger than you," Helen observed.

"I don't care."

Helen carried the message. "He says he will split with you."

Thor was tempted but said, "I beat him to it. He's a slow-poke."

"He's going to get real mad."

"See if I care,"

"You want me to say slowpoke?"

"Sure."

Ettore entered the kitchen, casting uneasy glances over his shoulder.

"Now, you going to give me that money?"

"No!"

As they glared at each other, Thor glimpsed his father coming down the hall from the barbershop. On impulse Thor hit Ettore in the mouth as hard as he could. As Ettore staggered back, Papa entered the room.

"What is going on here?" he asked.

"Nothing," Thor said.

Ettore slipped away through the kitchen door. Helen reported that he was real mad. He was walking back and forth like a lion in a cage. He was red in the face and talking to himself. Sometimes he would hit his hand with his fist. Oh, he was real mad!

As the saying goes, Thor thought discretion was the better part of valor.

The next day he was playing casino with Gus on the front porch. From time to time he would stand up and glance up and down the street. He was apprehensive and couldn't keep his mind on the cards. Gus sensed what was bothering Thor but kept silent. Thor had done what none of them dared to do, but now he had to take the consequences. Ettore appeared but Thor remained on his knees, dealing the cards without a break. Ettore nudged him in the back with his knee.

"What you mean, hitting me?"

"You had no business coming into the house."

"I ought to sock you one."

Thor played a card, but remained silent. He was on edge, aware of the menace that kept muttering threats over his head.

"One of these days," Ettore said, and left.

Gus took a deep breath. "I'll be a son of a gun," he said. It was a favorite expression of his. "Man, you really must have socked him."

Thor disclaimed any hint of prowess. He would rather run than fight. He was never forced to do either. Although Juneau was a frontier town, its residents were relatively quiet and peaceful. His encounter with Ettore was a rare exception.

Thor never saw knives used as weapons. If two boys were to fight it was fair and square, with bare fists. Knives were used to whittle, make whistles out of an elderberry twig, cut bait, but mostly for mumbletypeg. In one version the small blade was kept extended straight out, with the large blade at right angles. In another version the game was played with only the small blade extended straight out. The loser had to pull a peg out of the ground with his teeth.

With regional variations and modifications the childhood games of Main Street, U.S.A., were borne to the territorial appendage of Alaska. Thor disdained the games his sisters played: jackstraws, jump rope, hopscotch, and beanbags. The only interest Thor had was in trying to juggle three or four beanbags at a time.

Thor's childhood games ran the gamut of kick the can, pom pom pullaway, and Annie, Annie over. In kick the can, Thor griped that the smaller boys always seemed to be "it." More to his liking was pom pom pullaway. The one who was "it" stood in the center of the street while the rest lined up on the edge of the sidewalk.

"Pom, pom, pullaway, if you don't come I'll pull you away."

The boys tried to run across the street without being tagged. Those tagged joined the one who was "it" until all the boys were caught. The space for crossing was limited by outside boundaries. The game ended when the last boy was tagged. The first one tagged became "it" for the next game. This was a game he never saw played when he went Outside.

In "Annie, Annie over, dachshund free" (or that was the way it sounded to Thor), in which girls also joined, those on one side of a house would throw the ball over the roof while those on the other side would try to catch the ball before it hit the ground.

In a mining town of fewer than four thousand residents, many of them bachelors, there were not enough children to have organized sports. The boys occasionally played pick-up baseball on the sand flats along Willoughby Avenue until the incoming tide was washing around their shoes. One Saturday when the rising tide was lapping at Thor's heels, the ball was hit over his head and plopped into the sea. He stood a moment in indecision, took off his shoes and stockings, waded knee-deep to the ball, and retrieved it while the batter circled the bases for a home run. There was no ground-rule double.

Except for a game of catch, he hung up his glove for many years. He disliked making a fool of himself and the traumatic experience of being the last one picked to a side.

Perhaps the most important influence in his life at this time was Toby Thompson, the son of the town foundryman who cast parts for the machinery in the stamp mills and mines. Every village and town has a genius who grows up with a hammer in one hand and a monkeywrench in the other. He could fix his mother's wringer or sewing machine, adjust his father's boat engine, learn to drive and repair the first automobile, and make his own crystal radio set from raw material.

One day Thor labored industriously on a model car he felt would beat all the others in town. It ran well on the planked streets, but when he tried it out on a gravel road, the rear axle assembly collapsed under him. His vexation was so great he was tempted to leave his creation on the spot.

Toby came upon him wiping tears that left smears on his cheeks. He squatted on his haunches and examined the two-by-fours Thor had spiked together to hold the axles.

"You was thinkin' wishful," Toby said. "You need long bolts and nuts to hold those two-by-fours together. You got a bit and auger? You bore holes all the way through; thick bolts will hold those boards together. The blacksmith should have some long enough."

Toby looked at Thor. "I could do it for you but then it wouldn't be yours."

"I'll feel like a fool dragging that thing through the streets."

"Let them laugh. If they don't like it they can lump it." It was Toby's favorite expression. "Never quit. See it through."

"Like shooting a shotgun. Or carrying that stove up to our treehouse."

"Sure. That's what I mean."

Thor nodded. He watched the older boy walk away. He's someone special, he thought. He's not mean like Cecil Rhodes, the son of Old Man Rhodes who had named his son after the British Empire builder. The town egotist would jeer, "That's for me to know and for you to find out."

Toby would say, "When your time comes will be soon enough."

Toby had taken Thor, Gus, and George Oja up to Silver Bow Basin and spent an entire afternoon teaching them how to shoot his shotgun. He had labored over several weekends helping them build a treehouse. Like most playthings it fell into neglect as the boys moved on to other things, but it had been a game more important than most.

Thor watched winter approach on the mountain tops. The days were usually raw and threatening. He went to bed with rain pattering on the window pane. In the morning, as clouds climbed the sky, the bald heads of the three mountains were crowned with snow. Each day the snowline crept further down into the timber belt. He rescued his ice skates from the corner of a closet and industriously sharpened and oiled them each night by lamplight.

Then one evening large, fat snowflakes floated down and peered through the windows. Winter had come. Restless days were spent testing the ice on Evergreen Pond. After one heavy rainstorm, an Arctic front moved in and the pond was a huge sheet of glass.

On this Saturday morning Thor emptied the last of the condensed milk from a can—mystified Mama was certain she had had enough for Papa's morning coffee—and with can and a branch shaped like a hockey stick hied himself to the pond. His skates cut the first strokes on the deserted and virgin surface of the ice. He never forgot the intoxication of that first stride, the cold bite of the air on his cheeks, of unused muscles quivering in their sheaths of thigh, calf, and ankle. He loved to play shinny and because of his skill on skates was a match for the older boys.

Reality brought him back to earth. One enchanted moonlit night as he was guiding a can up the ice, a high school student picked up his can and threw it far into the woods. The act was so unexpected that Thor stood dumbfounded. The anger came later, but what could he do about it? He reasoned that the skittering noise of the can had annoyed the student's girlfriend.

Thor literally grew up on skates in winter. After school and on weekends, Evergreen Pond, moonlit or starlit, was the home of his soul.

A big thrill was to be allowed to ride on a bobsled with the older boys. Toby Thompson saw to that. He had taken a two-by-twelve plank and attached small wooden sleds with steel runners at front and back, with a steering wheel assembly to guide the front sled.

At the top of frozen Gold Street the boys, alternating sides, would give the bobsled a running start, swing on in unison, and race downward, gaining momentum every second. Hugging the boy in front of him Thor lifted his legs as high as he could for fear they might be snapped off by the hurtling ground underneath.

On either side the sidewalks with their wooden railings posed the constant threat of death or mutilation should the human juggernaut hurtle off course. The ride was especially thrilling at night, as there were only the dim street-corner lights, the shadows of the houses, and the white gleam of the snow to guide Toby. The younger boys had the honor of pulling the heavy bobsled up the hill.

When northern lights shuttled across the loom of the sky Thor was aware of some force beyond his ken. One night as he skated on Auk Lake in the starlight, the northern lights hung like celestial curtains above the stage of Mendenhall Glacier, parting and then drawing together as if at some ghostly standing ovation. He felt that he was seeing the colors of the spheres. He was transported beyond himself as though in religious ecstasy. His trance held him captive, although mechanically he went home in Toby's truck with his noisy peers and lay sleepless in his bed.

Another treat was the class sleigh ride in winter, with hay softening the wooden floor of the sled and blankets to keep warm. The night chosen for the outing came clear and cold. Starshine etched its spell among the trees that lined Glacier Highway, the crusty blanket of snow, the sleeping giants of mountains. After the tittering and snickering subsided the class sang Christmas carols, and what was more appropriate than "Jingle Bells"? There was nothing, he thought, to equal the smoothness of steel runners on ice, like a magic carpet flying through the air. He listened to the muffled plop of the horse's hooves, the rustle of the runners, the wind whispering in his ears. The sleigh ride went into a treasury of little hours gathered to exalt his heart.

An abiding influence in Thor's growth and development was his inheritance, the wilderness, in which Juneau was set like an anachronism. At one with nature and its living creatures among his beloved mountains and waters, he lived from day to day unfettered by the concerns that warped and deformed his elders.

Mat envied Thor and tried through meditation to reach his son's state of grace. Thor watched curiously as Papa sat Turkish fashion on the floor, his back straight as Mama's broomstick, his hands resting on his lap, his eyes closed. Twenty minutes every morning before breakfast. Sometimes he would hold his hands in prayer position and vibrate them as if he were calling on invisible powers. Practical Mama wished Papa would use his meditation to stop his drinking.

Mat tried to bring nature into the home in the form of *bonkei*, a miniature tray landscape. George the Greek brought him a flat cherry crate. Mat had Thor gather white sand, pebbles, and the short moss that grew on Gold Creek's boulders, and the longer moss found on forest floors. Using wooden match sticks and a piece of windowpane glass for a lake, he created a creditable *bonkei*. Displayed in the barbershop window, it drew favorable comment. In his fashion Mat brought one of the arts of Japan to this outpost of civilization.

Thor's first efforts at expressing himself were to copy what he saw, such as the labels on the ends of orange crates that depicted the blossoms, leaves, and fruit. He drew by rote, just as he memorized his lessons. The symbolism of Papa's landscape, unsophisticated as it was, escaped him.

As he grew, his inclination was more toward the visual than the aural. To him the earth was a palette of color that appealed more to his senses than the sound of music. Of all his joys the greatest was to find remnants of the rainbow reborn in field and wood, on mountain and in the sea.

He admired the courage of the crocuses, as strong in their instincts as the salmon running upriver, reaching for the pale sun through imprisoning snow. He feasted his eyes on the rash yellow flowerlets of pussywillows nurtured in nooks of Silver Bow Basin, a vast bowl concentrating solar heat. He loved to run his fingers over the silvery down of the catkins, a sensual pleasure. He would bring shoots of the first pussywillows to school and for art class he would draw brownish-green shoots and—such sacrilege—paste catkins on the drawing to imitate nature.

On the road to Thane he sought the shy gold of the first

yellow violets near rivulets, knowing almost to the day when they would greet him, winking their tiny purple lashes. Pink carillons of blueberry flowers swung on crimson branches along Glacier Highway, while the salmonberry flowers were pink stars on bright brown shoots.

In the Mendenhall meadows of the delta dairy lands, buttercups, clover, and marigolds wove designs richer than Persian rugs. Wild roses were a treasure infrequently found, their fragrance more subtle than all the perfumes of Grasse. Acres of pink lupine shot spikes into the summer sky and lavender iris grew in the marshes. Alaskan cotton, Michaelmas daisies, and goldenrod decorated earth's autumn canvas.

The Alaskan spring came in various guises: cold driving rains, cloudless skies, or dangerous white cloaks of snow. All winter long Thor walked the treacherous streets with guarded tension in his calves, but when spring came the feeling was different. As the last ice melted on the planked streets beneath the young sun, the soles of his feet, through leather, through wood, held communion with earth. Never mind the calendar, this was his vernal equinox.

One morning he left his sleeping family and went out on the deserted Sunday street. He looked at the refuse of winter and had a thought. He walked up Front Street, turned left on First Street, and passed Seward. He looked up Main Street toward City Hall. Yes, he was right.

The town firemen had brought out their truck, unreeled their hose and started down Main Street, washing it from sidewalk to sidewalk. The stream of water cleansed the wooden planks of gravel, sand, salt and coal ashes—all the grime of winter, until the wet wood surfaces sparkled in the sunlight. He retreated before the spray that made small rainbows in the air.

He kept pace with the firemen, sometimes ahead, sometimes behind, as they moved from hydrant to hydrant down Front Street. When he mocked them they directed the water at his flying feet and he would race away simulating terror. Once he dodged the wrong way and was bowled over. A fireman in his rubber boots ran over, swung him high in the air and said, "That didn't hurt, young man, did it?"

He wiped the tears from his eyes and laughed. "I was scared." At City Dock the firemen completed their chore, rolled up their hose and returned to the firehouse. He watched them leave with regret.

Thor held the firemen in deep respect. Every Fourth of July program listed a firemen's hose contest. Two teams of firemen dressed in slicker hats with chin straps, oilskin coats, and rubber hip boots lined up ahead of two hydrants. Leading from each hydrant lay three lengths of hose, like a white snake ready to be coupled together.

At a given signal, two men coupled the hose and nozzle together while another attached the hose to the hydrant and turned on the water. As the men finished coupling the hose they ran to help anchor their leader, who directed his stream of water at the leader of the other team.

At five to ten yards the force of the water could bowl a man over or stagger a team of four as each side struggled to score a direct hit on the other. The team that drove the other behind a designated line won the contest.

On an unseasonably warm day Thor walked up the gravel road that ran beside Gold Creek into Silver Bow Basin. High overhead where the eagles soar, on the shoulders of Mount Juneau, acres of snow trembled on their uneasy beds. Underneath, water from melting ice leaped from the lip of each ravine and poured a thousand feet into the canyon, living columns as graceful as any in Ionia. Through the spring, sitting in his classroom, Thor had heard the roar of avalanches and longed to dash outside to watch the spectacle.

The roar of a minor avalanche from a neighboring ravine made Thor jump. The reverberations should have alerted him. He looked across the creek and up the rocky slope created by previous avalanches. He stared straight up at the snow mass that was bulging over the mountain's shoulder.

He disobeyed the premonition that told him to flee. He was spellbound, as though the white mass was a predatory animal ready to pounce on him. Even as he watched, the overhang of snow a thousand feet above his head started to move. It was like slow motion. So engrossed was he, like a cameraman shooting oblivious to a danger threatening him, that he only started to run when it was almost too late.

The roar as tons of white hit the slope across Gold Creek several hundred feet away shattered the air. Snow and ice, clawing up gravel and boulders, raced downward toward the creek. He glanced back once and forever remembered the fearful grandeur of the oncoming tide, a wave crested with clouds of snow that glowed like glory in the sunlight.

Another fleeting glimpse from the corner of his eye and he felt he was out of danger. The snow dust devils escorting the main mass of snow could hardly harm him.

Just then the concussion hit him as if he had fallen from the roof of his home. A live force tumbled and rolled him over until he fetched up against a snowbank. Bruised and uncomprehending, he watched as the flying snow dissipated, leaving an awesome mass blocking the highway.

He lay in a state of shock. It did not occur to him that his body could have been entombed without anyone knowing until the trucks and snowplows came to clear the road. He got up and started walking toward town. Soon he was running with a fixed look in his eyes, down Gold Street and then Front Street to his home.

At the kitchen table he sat unseeing, unrecognizing, as though in a trance. Mama hovered over him with small questions and his siblings stared at him as though he were a stranger. The trembling left his limbs and a deep lassitude possessed him. He lay down for a nap. By evening he was enjoying his dinner. Not to alarm his mother, he kept his adventure a secret. Between mouthfuls he considered the invisible force that had almost killed him. So, an explosion is accompanied by concussion.

This homing instinct possessed him on at least two other brushes with nature—and possible death. With Gus and George he was fishing a pool in Gold Creek up in the basin. This was no quiescent water but more like a whirlpool formed as the spring-swollen stream poured into a large pool, made a complete circle, and dashed out on the other side.

A piece of the decaying stump to which he was clinging with one hand while he cast with the other gave way, and he was plunged into the white water. Unable to swim, he held his breath and thrashed the numbing cold, trying to keep afloat. Gus and George were too petrified to even move.

Thor circled the whirlpool once and on his second round the force of the circling water cast him ashore near the outlet. He clawed his way out of the tugging waters and lay several moments gasping to regain his breath.

The chill penetrated his body and drove him to his feet. Without a word to his friends he started walking toward town. Soon he was running past the melting mass of the avalanche that had almost sent him into oblivion. In his eyes was the same fixed, unnatural stare. His wet pants rubbed the skin between his thighs. Warmth had returned to his body by the time he reached home and changed into dry clothing. He did not analyze his actions. He had run to keep warm; he had sought the refuge of his home. To Mama he explained that he had fallen into Gold Creek.

A third accident occurred one spring dusk on the steepest part of Gold Street near St. Ann's Hospital. Instead of cycling down the steep wooden sidewalk, he chose the unpaved street. When he tried to brake his momentum he realized his rear tire could not get traction on the gravel and large stones.

Frightened and desperate, his arms like steel rods and his hands clamped like vises around the handlebars, he bounced crazily from stone to stone, steering as straight as he could toward where the wood planking started on Gold Street. He was short of safety when the front wheel hit a large stone. He was catapulted from the bicycle, slammed against the ground with stunning force, and almost knocked senseless. He lay prone for moments regaining his wits.

In the corner playground some girls were swinging and singing in the Alaskan dusk. They couldn't care less if I'd been killed, he thought, bitterly though unjustly. They could not see him where he lay. Painfully he picked himself up and limped home because his handlebars had been twisted askew. No fixed stare in his eyes this time. He hurt too much in every bone of his body.

Mama happened to be standing on the porch. In the dusk she did not see that gravel had scraped one cheek raw. She was looking for the other children to call them in for dinner. She could not know that he had bitten the inside of his lower lip. A lump formed there that his tongue toyed with over many years.

"THROUGH ANGER AND LOVE"

Toshio Mori (1910–1980)

*"*T*hrough Anger and Love" was written in 1950, but not
published until 1979 in Toshio Mori's second collection of short
stories,* The Chauvinist and Other Stories. *Like much of his
fiction, "Through Anger and Love" depicts scenes from a
community of first-and second-generation Japanese American
gardeners, shopkeepers, nursery owners, and their children in the
San Francisco Bay Area of the 1930s.*

Mr. Mori's first book, Yokohama, California, *was published
in 1949. He was a prolific writer, and his many stories appeared in
publications such as* Pacific Citizen, Hokubei Mainichi,
Common Ground, New Directions in Prose and Poetry,
Writer's Forum, Amerasia Journal, *and* Iconograph.

*Mr. Mori was born in Oakland, California. While interned at
the Central Utah Relocation Center in Topaz, Mr. Mori started
and wrote for the publications* All Aboard *and* Trek. *His novel,*
Woman from Hiroshima, *was published in 1979 by Isthmus
Press. His work has been republished in numerous anthologies and
textbooks, including* The Best American Short Stories of 1943.

FROM A PARKED AUTOMOBILE HARUO STUCK HIS HEAD OUT A LITTLE
and peered across the street. Yes, he was still standing by the
entrance talking to several men. His old man was talking and
laughing as if nothing had happened yesterday. Had he forgotten already? No, his old man couldn't forget that easily. Haruo

cautiously drew back and sat on the fender. Five minutes to seven by the City Hall clock. Promptly at seven, he knew, the flower market was going to open. What should he buy? What flowers were most popular, and most profitable? Suddenly he heard footsteps approaching the car. Instantly he was on his feet, and without looking back scurried around the corner. Safely past the corner he increased his pace. At a hundred yards he began to puff with exertion and slackened a bit. Just ahead he spied an alley and ran for it. Puffing and coughing he rested his nine-year-old body, his eyes trained on the sidewalk. Two minutes passed and nobody came after him. Slowly he came out and looked down the street and sighed with relief.

The market was open by now. Well, let the others go in first. He would walk around the block and take his time. Unhurriedly he stopped and looked at the store windows. Every now and then he looked up and down the street. Watching his chance he would slip in the market and make his purchase. He must look out for his old man. Then he must act natural when buying from the wholesalers so they would think that he was buying for his old man. Several minutes ago he was unsure of himself. He couldn't believe that he would be able to go through with it. Now he was sure of himself. He knew what flowers to get and where to get it from. His father bought a lot of things from Matsumoto and Toscana. Matsumoto was a grower of carnations and Toscana raised roses. They knew him well. It would be easy. If only his old man would not appear at the wrong time.

Nearing the market once more Haruo slowed down. His eyes darted from the market entrance to the adjoining wholesale stores. Cautiously he stepped behind the row of parked cars watching for his father. He was not in sight. Should he take a chance now or wait awhile? He watched a number of people coming in and out of the market. Flower business must have been good yesterday. Almost all the florists were present. Should he hurry and buy before the flowers were all gone? Several more florists came out with armfuls of flowers. Haruo became desperate. He hurriedly crossed the street to a spot near the entrance. Growing bolder he peered through the window, watching all sides, and then he saw his father.

His father was in the rear of the market purchasing cyclamen and mixed plants. He looked very much absorbed in the plants. Should he slip in now? Haruo could see Matsumoto, whose table was near the entrance. At least he could get the carnations. Wait a minute. He became suspicious, cautious. Was his old man purposely in the rear so he would fall in a trap? Maybe his old man had seen him a few minutes ago and asked Matsumoto to look out for him. That would be terrible. Then he would have to go back home crawling on his knees. Undoubtedly his father would further humiliate him and kick him out of the house. Maybe Matsumoto did not know. He looked keenly at the carnation grower's face, watching for a tell-tale sign that he was looking out for his old man. No, he did not know. Matsumoto's face was calm and relaxed. His eyes did not shift about. Then he looked in the rear of the market watching for his old man. He was not around. He was gone. Eagerly he walked in heading straight for Matsumoto's table.

Haruo's face fell. Matsumoto's table was bare. Where did his flowers go? Did he sell out? He hesitated in his tracks. Matsumoto's eyes brightened.

"Hello, Haruo!" he cried. "How are you? My, you've grown. And how is your mother?"

"Fine," Haruo said hurriedly. He looked over the table. "Did you sell out? Have you any carnations left?"

"Do you want carnations?" Matsumoto asked. "Let's see. How many do you want?"

"Ten bunches," Haruo said eagerly.

The man looked under the table and started unwrapping a big bundle. "All right, Haruo," he said. "I'll give you ten. Mixed colors?"

"Yes, but give me lots of red."

Matsumoto laughed heartily and his belly shook. "You're a smart boy, Haruo. You know what sells."

Haruo looked about. Matsumoto laughed and talked too loud. He must get away. "Will you please wrap it up?"

"Are you going to take it with you now or is your father coming to pick it up?" he asked.

"I want it now," Haruo said quickly.

Matsumoto hummed a tune and took his time wrapping. Finally he handed over the package. "All right, Haruo."

"How much is it?" Haruo asked.

"Dollar and a half. I'm charging you only fifteen cents a bunch."

"Pay you next time," Haruo said.

"Sure. That's all right," Matsumoto cried, waving his hand.

Haruo fairly ran to Toscana's table. He must hurry. His father might return any minute. His eyes brightened at the sight of Toscana's good roses piled high on his table.

"Hello, boy," called the Italian. "Do you want to buy nice roses? I'll give you a bargain today."

Haruo picked up a bunch to see if the outer petals of the roses were bruised, and then satisfied examined the bases of the stems for the telltale mark of old flowers. Toscana chuckled and picked up several bunches for Haruo to examine.

"All fresh flowers, my boy. No kidding," he said. "You want to buy for your papa?"

"How much?" Haruo asked hurriedly.

Toscana counted off six bunches. "Two dollars to you. A real bargain."

"I'll take it." He said quickly.

Haruo looked about while he waited for the man to finish wrapping. He must get away. Any minute now his old man would be coming back. Which entrance should he take, the front or the rear? Eagerly he accepted the package from Toscana.

"All right, boy," the nurseryman said, nodding and smiling.

With both arms loaded with packages Haruo walked off excitedly. He must hurry. He must catch a bus and ride back to his district and start selling his flowers. He quickened his little strides in the direction of the rear entrance. Suddenly from the front entrance came a familiar cry. "Haruo! Come back! Haruo!"

Terror-stricken he broke for the rear door. Gripping his bundles tight to his sides he ran past several tables unheeding the cries. Reaching the sidewalk he cut sharply to his right and then across the street. He must not be caught. It would be the end of him. He must get away. Running swiftly around the corner he headed for Seventh. He must shake his father off his trail. Should he go up or down Seventh? He must go up to reach the bus line, but suppose his old man was waiting for him at the next block? No, that wouldn't do. Should he run straight for First and wait around the pier, and later retrace his steps? That would be loss of time. No, he must go down Seventh and walk back to Twelfth. Then he remembered the jitney running on Seventh and his eyes brightened. His father would never think of the jitney.

To make sure his old man was not following, Haruo ran a couple of blocks more and headed for Sixth. At the corner of Sixth he sat puffing on the gutter looking in all directions, expecting the appearance of his father. Anxiously he looked to see if the flowers were bruised and the stems broken. They looked all right, and his anxiety turned to relief. He must sell them before noon while in good condition. In the afternoon they would start wilting without water.

Five minutes went by and his father did not appear. Cautiously he walked back to Seventh and waited for the jitney. Time after time he hid among the buildings whenever a figure appeared on the street. When the jitney came he boarded quickly and asked for a transfer. He slid low in his seat so he would not be noticed from the street. Several times the driver stopped the car for passengers. Haruo held his breath at every stop, expecting his father to jump aboard. At Clay the jitney turned left and passed Eighth, Ninth, and Tenth. He noticed the tall buildings coming into view. Three more blocks and he must get off and catch his bus. Maybe he should get off a block away and make sure his old man wasn't waiting at the spot. Scrambling to his feet he asked the driver to stop at the next corner.

No sight of his old man. He walked eagerly to the corner of Thirteenth and Clay for his bus. He wished the bus would hurry. Several minutes of waiting brought restlessness and uneasiness. Was the bus never coming? Then he caught sight of it in the distance. At last!

Safely on the bus and bound for his district Haruo leaned back with relief. His father would never find him now. With his feet on the front seat Haruo braced himself. His shoes did not reach the floor. Every now and then he looked into the packages to see if the flowers were all right. A dollar and a half to Matsumoto and two dollars to Toscana. He must pay them next time. He must sell pretty nearly all his flowers to make a good profit. He had ten bunches of carnations and six bunches of roses. That would mean twenty dozen carnations and twelve dozen roses.

He must sell cheaper than his old man. How much should he charge? Twenty-five cents a dozen for carnations and thirty-five cents a dozen for roses would be a bargain. Anybody would buy at that price. First, he would go to the shops in the district that knew him. Mazzini, the Browns, Nick, Hamilton Hardware, Rosloff Service Station, Riley, Joe, and the rest. They were friends of his old man. They would be glad to see him.

Haruo took out his pencil and pad and figured. The car moved and vibrated. Several times the flowers started to slip off the seat. Twenty dozens at twenty-five cents a dozen would be five dollars. Twelve dozen roses at thirty-five would amount to four dollars. Nine dollars for the day! That would be swell. He would give his uncle fifty cents a day for room and board.

The bus stopped and lurched. Haruo looked out of the window. Pretty soon he must get off. He put his pencil and pad in his pocket. He had better start selling right away. He must make good today. If he failed and had to go back begging for forgiveness his old man would laugh at him and give him a stick. No, he couldn't fail. When a boy has run away from home for good he should not think of going home. Even if it killed him he shouldn't. He should move on and take the consequences.

Gripping the packages tightly he waited for his block. Familiar buildings came into view. The Woolworth, Safeway, Gibson Drug, Palace Theater, Texaco Station, and Bank of America. His eyes brightened and he eagerly went forward to be let off. He could see Rosloff gingerly wiping a customer's windowshield. He could see that the Browns were doing a good business. He smiled. His hometown.

Haruo got off at the next corner. For a moment he stood bewildered and hesitating. What was his plan? Where should he go first? Again the dread of uncertainty and the fear of his future shook his nerve. Did he do right by leaving home? Was he at fault and not Father? How did the quarrel begin? His cheeks burned at the thought of it. Last night his father slapped him in the face in front of his brothers and sisters and called him a fool. His brothers laughed and his sisters looked with astonishment. They saw him crying, and the hard shaking he got in addition. What did he do? He had done nothing. What was it? He didn't know. The quarrel began a long time ago. He must be bad, or his old man mistaken? Was it his quick temper or his father's? He leaned against the telephone pole wondering what to do. Suppose the folks did not want to buy flowers today? Suppose he couldn't sell enough to pay back Matsumoto and Toscana? He would be in a fix. He couldn't live at his uncle's any length of time without paying room and board. Then he heard Rosloff's familiar voice calling, "Hello there, sonny! Come over here!"

Haruo eagerly ran across the street, his packages dangling. "How are you, Haruo?" asked the service station man. "What you got there?"

"Flowers," Haruo said eagerly. "Carnations and roses. Would you like to buy some, Mr. Rosloff?"

He laid the packages on the ground and quickly unwrapped one of them. He held a bunch of carnations in each hand. "They're nice and fresh, and a bargain. Twenty-five cents a dozen."

The man laughed. "Come inside of the station," he said. "You don't want the sun on your flowers."

Inside his cool office Rossloff picked up red and white carnation bunches. "These are swell flowers."

Haruo nodded his head. He was busy unwrapping the other bundle. "I have some nice roses too. They're thirty-five a dozen."

"Are these your dad's or your own?" the man asked.

"They're my flowers. I'm selling them," Haruo replied.

"Your dad was here five minutes ago," Rosloff said.

Haruo looked quickly at his friend. He could not tell what the man meant by it. He kept still, busying himself with the flowers.

"I'll take a dozen of pink roses and a dozen each of red and white carnations," the man said. "I'm going to take them home and surprise my wife."

"Gee, thanks!" Haruo's eyes danced as he cut the strings of the bunches and started counting.

The man took a seat and examined a headlight globe. "You cut school today, Haruo?" he asked casually.

Haruo did not look up. He kept counting the flowers slowly. "Yes, I was busy this morning."

"You should be busy in school," Rosloff quietly said. "Let your father sell flowers and worry about money."

"I can't."

"Why?" The man carefully laid the globe on the shelf.

Haruo handed over the carnations and the roses to Rosloff. Hurriedly he wrapped his remaining flowers. "I can't tell you, Mr. Rosloff."

"Did you have a fight with your dad?"

Haruo nodded his head.

"Pshaw! That's all right, son. Forget it," Rosloff said. "Sometimes you've got to taste vinegar, and sometimes honey. That's the way it goes, Haruo, whether you're young or old."

He stood shifting his weight from one foot to the other.

"Oh, I forgot, Haruo. How much do you want?"

"Eighty-five cents," Haruo said.

The man opened the register and counted the money.

"Mr. Rosloff, please don't tell my father I was here," Haruo begged. "I've run away from home."

"I won't squeal on you," the man said. "You can depend on me."

Outside Haruo stepped along gingerly, his coins jingling in the pants pocket. Eighty-five cents to the good. A swell start. With luck he might make nine dollars. He hummed a tune. He'll show his father. This was his world. Why had he been afraid several minutes ago? He knew flowers. He liked flowers, Where did his fear come from? He laughed and wondered where to try next. Up ahead the Browns' two shops bustled with activity. Miss Brown's stationery shop always had customers. She was nice to everybody. He would go in there next. Maybe her father who ran a cigar-stand next door would also buy flowers.

Haruo walked in and found a lot of customers at the counters. Almost instantly he was the center of attraction. He smiled gratefully to Miss Brown who ordered him to open the packages. People cluttered about him. A lady wanted a dozen mixed carnations. One old gentleman bought two dozen roses. A young girl took a dozen carnations for her mother. Miss Brown purchased two dozen roses, and finally escorted him to her father's place. "Dad, why don't you buy some beautiful roses for mother?" she said. "He has some of the nicest colors."

Her father looked up from his work and examined the roses. He bought two dozens. Haruo walked away, his head high in the air. He chuckled and hummed. Flushed with confidence he went in Mazzini's, Hamilton Hardware, Riley's and Joe's Garage right after another. When he came out of Joe's his packages were light. Four bunches of carnations and three bunches of roses left. His two pockets were bulging with small coins. How much had he made? He laughed. He must count the money. This was fun. Tomorrow he would take another portion of the town and keep rotating his route. He could go on forever. He smiled happily.

Haruo ran across the street to the park and sat under the shade of a tree. First, he tackled one pocketful of money and then the other. Three dollars and forty cents plus three dollars and sixty cents equals seven dollars. Seven dollars! He must have sold many dozens. Yes, sixteen dozen carnations and nine dozen roses. He could easily make nine dollars. He looked across the street at the bank clock. It was almost noon. His stomach felt empty. Nick's Cafe stood invitingly at the corner. Should he go in now and eat? He looked at the remaining carnations and roses. They were in pretty good condition. Yes, he could go in Nick's and eat and sell his flowers at the same time. He dumped his money in his pockets and picked up the flowers.

His hands bumped against the bulging pockets as he walked, and his thoughts returned to his triumph. Nine dollars gross profit minus three dollars and fifty cents cost equals five dollars and fifty cents net profit. He could do it. It meant freedom and pride. He could do as he pleased. On the way to Nick's he stopped short in front of a maroon Ford DeLuxe. It looked familiar. There was no one in it and he looked closely at the license plate. Quickly his eyes darted about the stores expecting to see his old man. His easy, springy stride of a moment ago became short hesitant steps. Somewhere in town his father was making his rounds. Where could he be? Suppose his father caught him by surprise? A look of terror crossed his face. He must get rid of his flowers right away and slip away from the district. Every few yards Haruo looked across the street and behind him expecting his father to jump out of hiding. Hurriedly he looked in Nick's. His father wasn't there. He felt hungry, he swallowed his saliva. He could go for three hamburger sandwiches, a pie, and a glass of milk. Cautiously Haruo stood at the corner and peered inside Nick's to make sure his father wasn't among the customers. Satisfied he crossed the street for Nick's.

At the doorway Haruo hesitated. Was he taking a chance? Suppose his father should come in while he was eating and grab a hold of him? His father would surely explode and soundly spank him in front of Nick and everybody. No, he mustn't take such a risk. First, he would go around the block and see if his father was in any of the stores. Then he would hurry back, order just a hamburger, and move on.

All around the block Haruo looked in every shop. He was sure that his father wasn't nearby. He broke into a run. Perhaps he could eat a piece of pie if he hurried. That would be swell. A banana cream or pineapple. He mustn't forget to ask Nick about the flowers. Maybe some of his customers would also make purchases.

Breathlessly he ran in the cafe and carefully laid his packages in the corner. First he saw Nick, who broadly grinned at him. "Hello, young man!" he cried. "How are you?" Then he noticed his father sitting and facing him, his small gimlet eyes studying him with a sly smile. For a second Haruo stood open-mouthed and then backed away quickly to the corner to pick up the packages and run outside.

"Haruo!" cried his father, smiling and holding up his hand. "Haruo, come back here."

Haruo hesitated. His father was still sitting leisurely. He could get away easily. He could run out, hide, and never allow his father to touch him. There was danger in remaining. Still he hesitated.

"Come here, Haruo. How are you doing?" his father said. "Business good today?"

Haruo slowly approached his father. "I made seven dollars already," he said.

"Good! You're doing fine," his father said. "Sit down here, Haruo, and let's have lunch together."

"What'll you have, young man?" Nick asked.

Haruo sat down, looking cautiously at his father. "I want a hamburger and a banana cream pie," he said.

Nick went away to fill the order. His father looked in the corner.

"You still have some flowers to sell?" he asked.

Haruo nodded. "I have four bunches of carnations and three bunches of roses left."

"You sell them easily," his father said cheerfully. "Over seven dollars for the day. Not bad. I know you could earn it every day. You're pretty smart."

Nick came back with the order.

"Let's eat, Haruo," his father said. "I like Nick's hamburgers best. They're always good. How about you, Haruo?"

Haruo nodded his head while his mouth bit into the sandwich.

"I don't worry about you, Haruo," said his father. "No, sir. You can go out in the world today, and I know you can make a living. But your mama. She's worried about you. She wants you to come home. You don't want to worry her, Haruo."

Haruo sat silently munching his hamburger. He glanced at his father, who smiled back. Nick whistled and watched the hamburgers sizzle in the pans. A noon whistle went off at the factory several blocks away. Presently people cluttered in Nick's. All around him Haruo listened to the talk of business and of labor. He listened importantly to their talk and watched his banana cream disappear.

"Anything else, young man?" Nick asked him.

Haruo smiled and shook his head. His father got up and paid the bill.

"Come home when you're through selling the flowers. Mama will be expecting you," his father said. "I have to go home now and watch the store. You take your time, Haruo."

His father went away. Haruo sat sipping his milk and listened to the men talking of inflation, civil liberties, and sports. When he was finally through with his lunch Nick came over and bought a dozen carnations. "Goodbye, young man," were the departing words of Nick.

Outside Haruo walked up and down the main street carrying his packages without attempting to sell a bunch. The sun shone brightly. This was a swell day. A swell day to go to the ball park and see the Oaks and the Seals tangle. No, it was a greater day than that. He could leap, sing, and run all the way home. This was something he had never before experienced. This was a great thrill. Then he remembered his greatest disappointment, bitterness, and loneliness of last night as a prelude to joy. His warm laughing face became solemn. Suddenly tears filled his eyes. He wiped his tears with his sleeves and wondered if the people were noticing him in such a condition.

"AND THE SOUL
SHALL DANCE"

Wakako Yamauchi (1924–   )

"*A*nd the Soul Shall Dance" *was first published in* Rafu
Shimpo *in 1966 and has been reprinted in several anthologies as both
fiction and drama. As a play, it won the American Theatre Critics
Regional Award for Outstanding Play in 1977 and was broadcast on
television by PBS and others. This classic short story evokes scenes
from childhood in rural southern California, where many Japanese
Americans farmed during the 1930s.*

*Ms. Yamauchi was born in Westmorland, California, a desert
township near Mexico, and she grew up in Imperial Valley,
California, where her father leased land and farmed during the Great
Depression. In 1942, she and her family were incarcerated in the
Poston internment camp in Arizona.*

*Both her fiction and her drawings have been published frequently
in* Rafu Shimpo *since the 1950s. Her plays and short stories have
also appeared in* Amerasia Journal, Southwest, The Christian
Science Monitor, Bamboo Ridge: The Hawaii Writers'
Quarterly, *and numerous collections.*

*She lives in Gardena, California, where she now concentrates on
playwriting. A recipient of many awards, including grants from the
Rockefeller Foundation, she has had her plays produced by a broad
range of companies such as East West Players, the Yale Repertory
Theatre, Pan Asian Repertory Theatre, and the New York Public
Theater.*

IT'S ALL RIGHT TO TALK ABOUT IT NOW. MOST OF THE PRINCIPALS are dead, except, of course, me and my younger brother, and possibly Kiyoko Oka, who might be near forty-five now, because, yes, I'm sure of it, she was fourteen then. I was nine, and my brother about four, so he hardly counts at all. Kiyoko's mother is dead, my father is dead, my mother is dead, and her father could not have lasted all these years with his tremendous appetite for alcohol and pickled chilies—those little yellow ones, so hot they could make your mouth hurt; he'd eat them like peanuts and tears would surge from his bulging thyroid eyes in great waves and stream down the dark coarse terrain of his face.

My father farmed then in the desert basin resolutely named Imperial Valley, in the township called Westmorland; twenty acres of tomatoes, ten of summer squash, or vice versa, and the Okas lived maybe a mile, mile and a half, across an alkaline road, a stretch of greasewood, tumbleweed and white sand, to the south of us. We didn't hobnob much with them, because you see, they were a childless couple and we were a family: father, mother, daughter, and son, and we went to the Buddhist church on Sundays where my mother taught Japanese, and the Okas kept pretty much to themselves. I don't mean they were unfriendly; Mr. Oka would sometimes walk over (he rarely drove) on rainy days, all dripping wet, short and squat under a soggy newspaper, pretending to need a plow-blade or a file, and he would spend the afternoon in our kitchen drinking sake and eating chilies with my father. As he got progressively drunker, his large mouth would draw down and with the stream of tears, he looked like a kindly weeping bullfrog.

Not only were they childless, impractical in an area where large families were looked upon as labor potentials, but there was a certain strangeness about them. I became aware of it the summer our bathhouse burned down, and my father didn't get right down to building another, and a Japanese without a bathhouse . . . well, Mr. Oka offered us the use of his. So every night that summer we drove to the Okas for our bath, and we came in frequent contact with Mrs. Oka, and this is where I found the strangeness.

Mrs. Oka was small and spare. Her clothes hung on her like loose skin and when she walked, the skirt about her legs gave her a sort of webbed look. She was pretty in spite of the boniness and the dull calico and the barren look; I know now she couldn't have been over thirty. Her eyes were large and a little vacant, although once I saw them fill with tears; the time I insisted we take the old Victrola over and we played our Japanese records for her. Some of the songs were sad, and I imagined the nostalgia she felt, but my mother said the tears were probably from yawning or from the smoke of her cigarettes. I thought my mother resented her for not being more hospitable; indeed, never a cup of tea appeared before us, and between them the conversation of women was totally absent: the rise and fall of gentle voices, the arched eyebrows, the croon of polite surprise. But more than this, Mrs. Oka was *different*.

Obviously she was shy, but some nights she disappeared altogether. She would see us drive into her yard and then lurch from sight. She was gone all evening. Where could she have hidden in that two-roomed house—where in that silent desert? Some nights she would wait out our visit with enormous forbearance, quietly pushing wisps of stray hair behind her ears and waving gnats away from her great moist eyes, and some nights she moved about with nervous agitation, her khaki canvas shoes slapping loudly as she walked. And sometimes there appeared to be welts and bruises on her usually smooth brown face, and she would sit solemnly, hands on lap, eyes large and intent on us. My mother hurried us home then: "Hurry, Masako, no need to wash well; hurry."

You see, being so poky, I was always last to bathe. I think the Okas bathed after we left because my mother often reminded me to keep the water clean. The routine was to lather outside the tub (there were buckets and pans and a small wooden stool), rinse off the soil and soap, and then soak in the tub of hot hot water and contemplate. Rivulets of perspiration would run down the scalp.

When my mother pushed me like this, I dispensed with ritual, rushed a bar of soap around me and splashed about a pan of water. So hastily toweled, my wet skin trapped the clothes to me, impeding my already clumsy progress. Outside, my mother would be murmuring her many apologies and my father, I knew, would be carrying my brother, whose feet were already sandy. We would hurry home.

I thought Mrs. Oka might be insane and I asked my mother

about it, but she shook her head and smiled with her mouth drawn down and said that Mrs. Oka loved her sake. This was unusual, yes, but there were other unusual women we knew. Mrs. Nagai was bought by her husband from a geisha house; Mrs. Tani was a militant Christian Scientist; Mrs. Abe, the midwife, was occult. My mother's statement explained much: sometimes Mrs. Oka was drunk and sometimes not. Her taste for liquor and cigarettes was a step into the realm of men; unusual for a Japanese wife, but at that time, in that place, and to me, Mrs. Oka loved her sake in the way my father loved his, in the way of Mr. Oka, the way I loved my candy. That her psychology may have demanded this anesthetic, that she lived with something unendurable, did not occur to me. Nor did I perceive the violence of emotions that the purple welts indicated—or the masochism that permitted her to display these wounds to us.

In spite of her masculine habits, Mrs. Oka was never less than a woman. She was no lady in the area of social amenities; but the feminine in her was innate and never left her. Even in her disgrace, she was a small broken sparrow, slightly floppy, too slowly enunciating her few words, too carefully rolling her Bull Durham, cocking her small head and moistening the ocher tissue. Her aberration was a protest of the life assigned her; it was obstinate, but unobserved, alas, unheeded. "Strange" was the only concession we granted her.

Toward the end of summer, my mother said we couldn't continue bathing at the Okas'; when winter set in we'd all catch our death from the commuting and she'd always felt dreadful about our imposition on Mrs. Oka. So my father took the corrugated tin sheets he'd found on the highway and had been saving for some other use and built up our bathhouse again. Mr. Oka came to help.

While they raised the quivering tin walls, Mr. Oka began to talk. His voice was sharp and clear above the low thunder of the metal sheets.

He told my father he had been married in Japan previously to the present Mrs. Oka's older sister. He had a child by the marriage, Kiyoko, a girl. He had left the two to come to America intending to send for them soon, but shortly after his departure, his wife passed away from an obscure stomach ailment. At the time, the present Mrs. Oka was young and had foolishly become involved with a man of poor reputation. The family was anxious to part the lovers and conveniently arranged a marriage by proxy and sent him his dead wife's sister. Well that was all right, after all, they were kin, and it would be good for the child when she came to join them. But things didn't work out that way; year after year he postponed calling for his daughter, couldn't get the price of the fare together, and the wife—ahhh, the wife. Mr. Oka's groan was lost in the rumble of his hammering.

He cleared his throat. The girl was now fourteen, he said, and begged to come to America to be with her own real family. Those relatives had forgotten the favor he'd done in accepting a slightly used bride, and now tormented his daughter for being forsaken. True, he'd not sent much money, but if they knew, if they only knew how it was here.

"Well," he sighed, "who could be blamed? It's only right she be with me anyway."

"That's right," my father said.

"Well, I sold the horse and some other things and managed to buy a third-class ticket on the Taiyo-Maru. Kiyoko will get here the first week of September." Mr. Oka glanced toward my father, but my father was peering into a bag of nails. "I'd be much obliged to you if your wife and little girl," he rolled his eyes toward me, "would take kindly to her. She'll be lonely."

Kiyoko-san came in September. I was surprised to see so very nearly a woman; short, robust, buxom: the female counterpart of her father; thyroid eyes and protruding teeth, straight black hair banded impudently into two bristly shucks, Cuban heels and white socks. Mr. Oka brought her proudly to us.

"Little Masako here," for the first time to my recollection, he touched me; he put his rough fat hand on the top of my head, "is very smart in school. She will help with your school work, Kiyoko," he said.

I had so looked forward to Kiyoko-san's arrival. She would be my soul mate; in my mind I had conjured a girl of my own proportions: thin and tall, but with the refinement and beauty I didn't yet possess that would surely someday come to the fore.

My disappointment was keen and apparent. Kiyoko-san stepped forward shyly, then retreated with a short bow and small giggle, her fingers pressed to her mouth.

My mother took her away. They talked for a long time— about Japan, about enrollment in American school, the clothes Kiyoko-san would need, and where to look for the best values. As I watched then, it occurred to me that I had been deceived: this was not a child, this was a woman. The smile pressed behind her fingers, the way of her nod, so brief, like my mother when father scolded her: the face was inscrutable, but some-thing—maybe spirit—shrank visibly, like a piece of silk in wa-ter. I was disappointed; Kiyoko-san's soul was barricaded in her unenchanting appearance and the smile she fenced behind her fingers.

She started school from third grade, one below me, and as it turned out, she quickly passed me by. There wasn't much I could help her with except to drill her on pronunciation—the "L" and "R" sounds. Every morning walking to our rural school: land, leg, library, loan, lot; every afternoon returning home: ran, rabbit, rim, rinse, roll. That was the extent of our communication; friendly but uninteresting.

One particularly cold November night—the wind outside was icy; I was sitting on my bed, my brother's and mine, oiling the cracks in my chapped hands by lamplight—someone rapped urgently at our door. It was Kiyoko-san; she was hysterical, she wore no wrap, her teeth were chattering, and except for the thin straw zori, her feet were bare. My mother led her to the kitchen, started a pot of tea, and gestured to my brother and me to retire. I lay very still but because of my brother's restless tossing and my father's snoring, was unable to hear much. I was aware, though, that drunken and savage brawling had brought Kiyoko-san to us. Presently they came to the bedroom. I feigned sleep. My mother gave Kiyoko-san a gown and pushed me over to make room for her. My mother spoke firmly: "Tomorrow you will return to them; you must not leave them again. They are your people." I could almost feel Kiyoko-san's short nod.

All night long I lay cramped and still, afraid to intrude into her hulking back. Two or three times her icy feet jabbed into mine and quickly retreated. In the morning I found my mother's

70

gown neatly folded on the spare pillow. Kiyoko-san's place in bed was cold.

She never came to weep at our house again but I know she cried: her eyes were often swollen and red. She stopped much of her giggling and routinely pressed her fingers to her mouth. Our daily pronunciation drill petered off from lack of interest. She walked silently with her shoulders hunched, grasping her books with both arms, and when I spoke to her in my halting Japanese, she absently corrected my prepositions.

Spring comes early in the Valley; in February the skies are clear though the air is still cold. By March, winds are vigorous and warm and wild flowers dot the desert floor, cockleburs are green and not yet tenacious, the sand is crusty underfoot, everywhere there is the smell of things growing and the first tomatoes are showing green and bald.

As the weather changed, Kiyoko-san became noticeably more cheerful. Mr. Oka, who hated so to drive, could often be seen steering his dusty old Ford over the road that passes our house, and Kiyoko-san sitting in front would sometimes wave gaily to us. Mrs. Oka was never with them. I thought of these trips as the westernizing of Kiyoko-san: with a permanent wave, her straight black hair became tangles of tiny frantic curls; between her textbooks she carried copies of *Modern Screen* and *Photoplay*; her clothes were gay with print and piping, and she bought a pair of brown suede shoes with alligator trim. I can see her now picking her way gingerly over the deceptive white peaks of alkaline crust.

At first my mother watched their coming and going with vicarious pleasure. "Probably off to a picture show; the stores are all closed at this hour," she might say. Later her eyes would get distant and she would muse, "They've left her home again; Mrs. Oka is alone again, the poor woman."

Now when Kiyoko-san passed by or came in with me on her way home, my mother would ask about Mrs. Oka—how is she, how does she occupy herself these rainy days, or these windy or warm or cool days. Often the answers were polite: "Thank you, we are fine," but sometimes Kiyoko-san's upper lip would pull over her teeth, and her voice would become very soft and she would say. "Drink, always drinking and fighting."

At those times my mother would invariably say, "Endure, soon you will be marrying and going away."

Once a young truck driver delivered crates at the Oka farm and he dropped back to our place to tell my father that Mrs. Oka had lurched behind his truck while he was backing up, and very nearly let him kill her. Only the daughter pulling her away saved her, he said. Thoroughly unnerved, he stopped by to rest himself and talk about it. Never, never, he said in wide-eyed wonder, had he seen a drunken Japanese woman. My father nodded gravely, "Yes, it's unusual," he said and drummed his knee with his fingers.

Evenings were longer now, and when my mother's migraines drove me from the house in unbearable self-pity, I would take walks in the desert. One night with the warm wind against me, the dune primrose and yellow poppies closed and fluttering, the greasewood swaying in languid orbit, I lay on the white sand beneath a shrub and tried to disappear.

A voice sweet and clear cut through the half-dark of the evening:

> Red lips press against a glass
> Drink the purple wine
>   And the soul shall dance

Mrs. Oka appeared to be gathering flowers. Bending, plucking, standing, searching, she added to a small bouquet she clasped. She held them away; looked at them slyly, lids lowered, demure, then in a sudden and sinuous movement, she broke into a stately dance. She stopped, gathered more flowers, and breathed deeply into them. Tossing her head, she laughed— softly, beautifully, from her dark throat. The picture of her imagined grandeur was lost to me, but the delusion that transformed the bouquet of tattered petals and sandy leaves, and the aloneness of a desert twilight into a fantasy that brought such joy and abandon made me stir with discomfort. The sound broke Mrs. Oka's dance. Her eyes grew large and her neck tense—like a cat on the prowl. She spied me in the bushes. A peculiar chill ran through me. Then abruptly and with childlike delight, she scattered the flowers around her and walked away singing:

Falling, falling, petals on a wind . . .

That was the last time I saw Mrs. Oka. She died before the spring harvest. It was pneumonia. I didn't attend the funeral, but my mother said it was sad. Mrs. Oka looked peaceful, and the minister expressed the irony of the long separation of Mother and Child and the short-lived reunion; hardly a year together, she said. We went to help Kiyoko-san address and stamp those black-bordered acknowledgments.

When harvest was over, Mr. Oka and Kiyoko-san moved out of the Valley. We never heard from them or saw them again and I suppose in a large city, Mr. Oka found some sort of work, perhaps a janitor or a dishwasher and Kiyoko-san grew up and found someone to marry.

"Fourth Grade Ukus (1952)"
Marie Hara (1943–   )

"*F*ourth Grade Ukus (1952)" humorously portrays early *experiences in a Hawaiian non-English Standard elementary school. Prior to becoming an American state in 1959, the territory of Hawaii operated two kinds of public schools. English Standard schools accepted mostly Caucasian students and a few non-European Americans who passed the language tests. Other students, mainly of Asian and Native Hawaiian descent, attended the non-English Standard schools, which were considered less appealing and less academically rigorous.*

Marie Hara was born in and grew up in Hawaii. Her stories have been published in Bamboo Ridge: The Hawaii Writers' Quarterly, Chaminade Literary Review, Honolulu Magazine, *and several anthologies. She co-directed the first Talk Story Conference for writers in 1978, and has worked for the Hawaii Literary Arts Council to promote the literature of Hawaii. "Fourth Grade Ukus (1952)" is part of her forthcoming novel,* Lei. *In addition to writing fiction, Ms. Hara is a teacher, journalist, and publicist. She lives in Honolulu.*

"DA BOLOCANO," I REPEATED POLITELY AT THE CONE-SHAPED mountain where a spiral of smoke signaled into the crayon-shaded air. She must have drawn it.

The woman tester was young and Japanese and smiley. I relaxed, thought for sure I wouldn't have to act "put on" with her. But she kept after me to say the printed words on the picture cards she, unsmiling, held before my eyes.

She shook her head. "Again."

"Da bolocano," I repeated loudly. Maybe, like O-jiji, she couldn't hear. "We wen' go see da bolocano," I explained confidentially to her. And what a big flat puka it was, I thought, ready to tell her the picture made a mistake.

"It's the vol-cano," she enunciated clearly, forcing me to watch her mouth move aggressively. She continued with downcast eyes, " 'We went to see the vol-cano.' You can go and wait outside, okay?"

Outside I wondered why—if she had seen it—she drew it all wrong.

Mama shrugged it off as we trudged home.

"Neva mind. Get too many stuck shet ladies ova dere. People no need act, Lei. You wait. You gon' get one good education, not like me."

That was how I ended up at Kaahumanu School, which was non-English Standard, but sported massive flower beds of glowing red and yellow canna lilies arranged in neat rows, which were weeded and watered daily by the students. Teachers at Kaahumanu were large in size, often Hawaiian or Portuguese with only an occasional wiry Chinese or Japanese. There was a surprise haole teacher who came in to teach art and hug kids. Many teachers wore bright hibiscus blooms stuck into their "pugs" of upswept hair. They didn't hold back on any emotions as they swept through the main yard like part of a tide of orderliness, lining up their wriggly classes. They cuffed the bad and patted the heads of the obedient as they counted us. They were magnetic forces with commanding voices, backbones at full attention and bright flowers perched like flags on the tops of their heads. When we stood in formation, the first ritual of the morning, rumors of all kinds went through our lines. I learned that on special holidays the cafeteria might even serve laulaus and poi, which we would help to prepare. Now that was worth waiting for.

I was in a dreamy mood when I first ran into Mrs. Vincente, who was to be my teacher. As a human being she was an impressive creation since her bulk was unsettling and her head quite small. As she waddle-walked toward me, I made a fatal error. I mistook her for an illustration in a library book I had grown fond of in Kohala. She was a dead ringer for the character I thought I was seeing right before my nose. And why not? The first day of school was the beginning of a new chapter in my life. Everything so far had been surprising.

Therefore, I squealed out loud in pleasure, "Oh, Mrs. Piggy-Winkle!" at the sight of the pink-fleshed mountain topped by a salad-plate-sized, orange hibiscus. Did I truly think she would be equally delighted to see me? Mrs. Vincente, as I learned later, would never forget me. At the moment of our meeting, she grabbed me by the back of my neck and shook me fiercely until I blubbered.

Teachers came running; students formed a mob around us, and the school principal, Mrs. Kealoha-Henry, saved me.

As I stood sobbing and shivering from the wild shaking, Mrs. Vincente lectured me on good manners. I shook my head, no-no, when she asked in an emotional voice, "Do you understand?" It took all of Mrs. Kealoha-Henry's counsel to keep Mrs. Vincente away from me.

Grabbing the opportunity, I ran all the way back home where, after she came home from work, Mama found me hiding out in the laundry shed. I didn't return to school for several days after that. But my mother's continual nagging, bribery and just plain boredom finally wore me down. I vowed not to talk at school, in the name of personal safety. And I would forget imagination.

Hanging high on the wall against the painted white wood, positioned to face the person entering up the broad steps through the columned entrance was a large portrait of Queen Kaahumanu, our school's namesake. I studied her fully fleshed face, the insignia of rank in the background and her guarded expression. In return her eyes reviewed me, a small girl who wasn't sure what to do next.

As I stalled and paced the corridor, the morning bell rang and all the other children disappeared. Alone in my patch of indecision, I balanced on one bare foot and then the other while I studied the ancient lady's clear-eyed regard.

When Mrs. Kealoha-Henry found me, she laughed in surprise.

"So you did come back. And now you have met the Queen. Do you know her story? No? I thought so."

The principal, a plump woman who wore old-fashioned glasses, which dangled from a neckpiece onto the front of her shirtwaist, told me then and there about Queen Kaahumanu, the Kuhina Nui. I learned that she was a favorite child and a favorite wife, that her hair was called ehu, meaning that it was reddish unlike that of other Hawaiians of her time, and that she was hapa—of mixed blood, probably from Spanish ancestors. Mrs. Kealoha-Henry suspected the Conquistadors, whose helmets the Hawaiian alii had copied in feathers, had been the first Europeans to Hawaii. I heard the kindly stranger saying that I, too, must be hapa. She suggested a visit to the school library where I would be welcome to read more about the Queen and what she did with the tremendous power she held at the end of her life. Mrs. Kealoha-Henry put her hands on my shoulders and turned me in the direction of the steps that led to the second floor. She would take care of the absences.

Although I hoped that the principal had not confused me with someone else who was Hawaiian by blood, I was very pleased with the thrilling story. Her comments became the bond between the Queen and me. I felt lucky that I went to a school where a hapa was the boss, in fact, commanded tribute. After all, I did have the reddish hair—or some of it—and if I was hapa as she said, then that was the reason for my being different from the others. I felt clearer whenever I looked at Queen Kaahumanu's portrait from then on. Every day the Queen's round face gave me a signal that I was okay; a small thing, but necessary for someone so hungry for signs.

Still, no matter how hard I squinted, the hair depicted in the painting showed no sign of being red. Never mind, I told myself, she was right there, up high, and she looked at me affectionately, if I kept up the squint. Whenever I needed to, I found my way back to the hallway to stand in the breeze and acknowledge the power of our kinship.

"Pssssssssst . . ."

I felt a nudge from one side and a soft pinch from the other.

Just before the first morning bell rang, the whispers traveled around. We were aware that our teacher was moving down the line to study each one of us. Our voices were high, and our faces as busy as the noisy birds in the banyan outside. Always chattering, always in tune with our buddies, always watching, we knew how to move together without getting caught. We studied how to do it.

"Joseph. Make quick. We gotta line up; no talk. Standup-straight. Sing loud or she gon' make us guys sing one mo' time."

"She checking the guys' clothes first, if clean or what. Bumbye she gon' look our finganail and den check our hair behind the eah, l'dat."

The clanging bell brought us to silent attention.

Joseph looked completely blank. Unconcerned, he, being new, had no understanding of the importance of our morning ritual. He didn't even pretend to mouth the words of Mrs. Vincente's favorite greeting, "Good Morning, Dear Tea-cha, Goooood Mor-ning to You."

Before I could answer importantly, "Cuz got ukus, some guys, you stupid doo-doo head," and think, "But not us guys," our teacher was standing right in front of us. Mrs. Vincente looked grim. Her gold-rimmed eyeglasses gave off glints in the pools of sunlight, evidence of real daylight outside, which invaded our dark, wood-paneled classroom.

She was the one who taught us to sing "Old Plantation Nani Ole" (Oooll . . . Plan-tay-shun . . . Na-ni . . . Ohlay) and "Ma-sa's (never her way, Massa's) in the Cold, Cold Ground," her favorite mournful melodies. She had turned to making us sing in order to drill us on our English skills, so lacking were we in motivation.

Frequently Mrs. Vincente spoke sharply to us about the inappropriate silences of our group. She complained that too often we spoke out of turn but "rarely contributed to the discussion." She must have believed that we didn't absorb anything that she lectured about repeatedly. She often confided aloud that she was "disappointed in" us or we had "disappointed Teacher" or she was "sorry to have to disappoint" us, "however," we had done something wrong again.

She was a puzzle.

The Oriental kids—for that was our label—in the room knew

better than to open their mouths just to lose face, and the part-Hawaiian kids knew they would get lickings one way or another if they talked, so we all firmly agreed that silence was golden.

Never would an adult female loom up as large to me as Mrs. Vincente did then. I could see her face only when I sat at a safe distance with a desk for protection. If she approached—in all her girth she was most graceful moving across her neatly waxed floor—her hands took my complete attention. When they were ready to direct us, I felt the way I did when Mama showed me what the red light at the crosswalk was for. When Teacher stood very near me, I couldn't see her tiny eyes, because the soft underpart of her delicate chin transfixed me so that I could not understand the words she mouthed.

Once I overheard her passionate argument with another teacher who wanted to introduce the hula in our P. E. exercises. Mrs. V.'s reasoning escaped me, but I knew she was against it. I stayed hidden in the ti leaves under her window just to hear the rush of her escaping emotions as she grew angrier.

Mrs. Vincente's face was often averted from the horrors she saw represented in the existence of our whole class. We were not by any means brought up well, didn't know our p's and q's and refused moreover to speak properly or respectfully as soon as her back was turned.

Our concentrated looks centered on her totally. We followed her every move, a fact which unnerved her briefly each morning as evidenced by her perspiration, followed by a swabbing of her face with a lace-trimmed hankie.

She shook her head at Francene Fuchigami, whose mother made her wear around her neck an amulet in a yellowed cotton pouch, which also contained a foul incense and herbs. The blessed omamori guaranteed the absence of both slippery vermin and casual friends. Francene and I competed for Mrs. V.'s favor, no matter how much we accepted her obvious but peculiar interest in the boys only. She favored them shamelessly, but bullied them at every opportunity.

We would bring Mrs. Vincente anthuriums, tangerines and sticky notes, "Dear Mrs. V., Your so nice. And your so pretty, too," with high hopes. Maybe she would like me then, ran the thread of wishful thinking. Winning her favor took all of my attention. I had to stay neat and clean and pretend to be a good girl, somebody who could "make nice-nice" and "talk high maka-mak." To win Mrs. Vincente over, I saw that I would have to be able to speak properly, a complicated undertaking demanding control of all my body parts, including my eyes and hands, which wandered away when my mouth opened up. Therefore, in a compromise with my desire to shine, I decided to keep absolutely quiet, stand up with the stupid row and ignore the one I wanted to impress.

Mrs. Vincente was one of us, she claimed, because she herself had grown up in our "very neighborhood." Her school, too, she once let out, had been non-English Standard. We were surprised to hear her say that her family was related to the Kahanus, who owned the corner grocery store. We knew them, the ones who used to have money. She spoke, dressed and carried herself in a manner that was unlike any of the women I observed at home, but she fit right in with our other teachers who, like her, had gone to Normal School and shared her authoritative ways.

Difficult as she was, we could understand her preoccupation. Getting rid of ukus was a tedious job connected with beratings from your mother and lickings from your father. We always knew who carried ukus and were swift to leave that child alone. News traveled fast. All the same we could each remember what it felt like to be the "odd man out," which was the name of one of our favorite games.

To have ukus, to tell your close friends not to tell the others, and to have them keep the secret: that was the test of friendship. Like the garbage men who worked under the uku pau system, which meant that no gang or worker was finished until everybody on that truck helped the final guy unload his very last bag and everybody could quit, uku season wasn't over until every kid got rid of every last clinging egg.

At Christmas time Mrs. Vincente would wrap up a useful comb for each and every one of us. At the end of the year we would race each other to be the first of the crowd lined up at her massive desk.

We would each shyly request her autograph with the suggested correct phrases, "Please, Mrs. Vincente," and "Thank you, Teacha," so she must have been what we had grown to expect a teacher to be.

Because of Mrs. Vincente I wanted to become a teacher, wield power and know how to get my way. I wanted to be the one who would point out a minute, luminous silver egg sac stuck on a coarse black hair; shake it vigorously with arm held out far away from body, and declare victoriously, "Infestation . . . of . . . pediculosis!"

She would then turn to address the entire class. "This child must go directly to the nurse's office." She would speak firmly but in a softer tone to the kid. "Do not return until you can bring me the white clearance certificate signed by both of your parents."

Completely silent during class, I practiced those words at home while I played school. I turned to the class. I gave the warning to the kid. Mrs. Vincente was not to be taken lightly.

The day Joseph learned about ukus, I figured out teachers.

Facing him, Mrs. Vincente demanded to know the new boy's name from his own mouth.

"Joseph Kaleialoha Lee."

"Say ma'am."

"Hah?"

"You must say Joseph Kaleialoha Lee, ma'am."

"Joseph-Kaleialoha-Lee-ma'am."

"Hold out your hands, please."

Evidently he had not "paid attention," the biggest error of our collective class, one which we were to hear about incessantly. He had not watched her routine, which included a search for our hidden dirt. He held his hands palms up. I shuddered.

Mrs. Vincente studied Joseph with what we called the "stink eye," but he still didn't catch on. She must have considered his behavior insubordinate, because he did not seem retarded or neglected as he was wearing his new long, khaki pants and a freshly starched aloha shirt.

She reached into the big pocket of her apron and took out a fat wooden ruler. Our silence was audible. She stepped up a little nearer to Joseph, almost blocking out all the air and light around us so that her sharp features and steely voice cut through to reach our wobbly attention.

"What grade are you in now, young man?"

Joseph was silent as if in deep thought. Why wouldn't he say the answer? I nudged him quickly on his side with the hand nearest his body.

"Fot grade," he blurted in a small, panicky wheeze.

She turned on us all, enraged at our murmurs of anticipation. We knew for sure he would get it now.

Some girl giggled hysterically in a shrill whinny. "Heeng-heengheeng . . ." Probably Japanese.

"Quiet."

Business-like, she returned to Joseph with her full attention, peering into his ear. "Say th, th, th. Speak slowly." He heard the warning in her voice.

"Tha, tha, tha." Joseph rippled droplets of sweat.

"Th, th, th . . . everyone, say it all together: the tree!"

We practiced loudly with Joseph leading the chorus, relieved now to be part of the mass of voices.

"Say the tree, not da chree."

"The tree, not da chree."

"Fourth grade, not fot grade."

"Foth grade, not fot grade."

With a rapid searching movement which most of us missed, Mrs. Vincente swung around to face Darcy Ah Sing, whose hand was still stuck in her curly brown hair, scratching vigorously. Mrs. V. stared blackly into Darcy's tight curls with unshakable attention. In a matter of seconds, with an upward swoop of her palm, Teacha found the lice at the nape of the exposed neck and pronounced her memorable conclusion, ending with "by both of your parents," indicting Darcy's whole family into the crime.

"March yourself into the office, young lady." Mrs. Vincente wrung a hankie between her pudgy hands with tight motions. Head hanging, Darcy moved out wordlessly to the school nurse's station for the next inspection. We knew that she would be "shame" for a long time and stared at our bare feet in hopeless sympathy.

When we were allowed to sit at our desks (after practicing the "sks" sound for "desks": "sssk'sss, ssk,sss, dehss-kuss, dehss-kuss, dehss-kuss, not dessess, dessess, dessess") we were hooked into finishing our tasks of busywork and wearing our masks of obedience, totally subdued.

Then she read to us, as she explained that she would be "wont to do when the occasion arose," while we sat at our desks with our hands folded quietly as she had trained us. She enunciated each word clearly for our benefit, reminding us that by the time we graduated we would be speaking "proper English," and forgot the uku check for the day. Her words stuck like little pearly grains into the folds of my brain.

"The child . . . the school . . . the tree . . ." I could not hear the meaning of her words and scratched my head idly, but in secret. I yearned to master her knowledge, but dared not make myself the target of her next assault. I was not getting any smarter, but itchier by the minute and more eager to break free into the oasis of recess.

When the loud buzzer finally shattered the purring motor of her voice, we knew better than to whoop and scatter. We gathered our things formally and waited silently to be dismissed. If we "made noise" we would have to sit inside in agony, paying attention to the whole, endless, meaningless story, which sounded like all the ones before and wasted our precious time. Even Joseph caught on.

Once outside two teams of the bigger boys pulled at a heavy knotted rope from opposite ends. Joseph's bare toes dug into the dust right in back of Junior Boy, the tug-of-war captain. Clearly he wouldn't need any more of my prompting if Junior Boy had let him in. Beads of wetness sparkled off their bodies as the tight chain of grunting boys held fast under the bright sun.

Noisy clumps of kids skipped rope and kicked up the ground, twisting bodies and shining faces, all together in motion. Racing around the giant banyan, for no good reason, I scream-giggled, "Wheeeeeha-ha-hah!" Like a wild cat I roared up the trunk of the tree . . . just to see if I could.

While the girls played jacks, and the boys walked their stilts, we moved around groups trading milk bottle covers and marbles. We wondered aloud to each other. We spread the word.

"Ho, whatchoo tink?"

"Must be da teacha wen' catch ukus befo."

"Not . . ."

"*Not* not!"

"Yeah?"

"Ay, yeah. O how else she can spock 'em l'dat fast?"

That made me laugh, the thought of Mrs. V. picking through her careful topknot. She would have to moosh away the hibiscus to get in a finger. I mimed her by scratching through the hair I let hang down in front of my face. When I swept it back professionally with the palm of my hand, I threw in a cross-eyed, crazy look. Joseph pretended to "spock ukus" in my hair as he took on Mrs. V.'s exaggerated, ladylike manner to hold on to one of my ears like a handle and peer in to the endless puka.

"Ho, man," he proclaimed, "get so planny inside."

The recess bell rang, ending our sweet freedom. We pranced back to the classroom in a noisy herd. Teacha gave us the Look. We grew cautious. We would spend the next hour silently tracking Mrs. Vincente's poised head, while Joseph and I smiled knowingly at each other.

Eyes gleaming, Mrs. Vincente never disappointed any of us because she always stuck right on her lessons and never let up at all. She stayed mean as ever, right on top of the class. As for us, fourth grade ukus could appreciate the effort . . . so much not letting go.

"TOUSSAINT"
from *CHINA BOY*
Gus Lee (1946–   )

C hina Boy *is author Gus Lee's first novel. It tells the story of Kai Ting, the youngest child and only son of a Shanghainese American family living in San Francisco during the 1950s. Kai faces a common childhood challenge, learning to defend himself against neighborhood bullies, who taunt him with the nickname "China Boy." His trials are compounded by several factors including the death of his mother, the presence of an abusive stepmother (Edna), and being one of the few Asian Americans in a poor, primarily African American neighborhood.*

Gus Lee was born in San Francisco. He attended West Point where he studied under General H. Norman Schwarzkopf. He graduated with a law degree from the University of California at Davis and has served as deputy district attorney in Sacramento and as director of legal education for the State Bar of California. He is also the author of the novel Honor and Duty. *He lives in Burlingame, California.*

A RAIL-THIN NINE-YEAR-OLD NAMED TOUSSAINT LARUE LOOKED on during these beatings and only hit me once. I therefore assumed that he occupied some lower social niche than mine. Like a snail's.

He took no pleasure in the China Boy rituals. He instead talked to me. I suspected that he had devised a new method of pain infliction.

"Toussaint," he said, offering his hand. "Ya'lls supposed ta shake it." He grinned when I put my hand out with the same enthusiasm with which I would pet Mr. Carter's bulldog. Toussaint, like Evil, had a big gap between his front teeth.

Toussaint would become my guide to American boyhood.

My primary bond to him was for the things he did not do. He did not pound or trap me. He never cut me down. Or laughed with knives in his eyes. Then he opened his heart by explaining things to me, giving me his learning, and taking me into his home.

"China. Don be cryin no mo'. Don work on dis here block, no sir, Cap'n! Give 'er up. When ya'll cry, hol' it insida yo'self. Shif' yo' feet an air-out, go park-side. Preten ya'll gone fishin. Don run, now. Ain't cool."

"Fish in park?" I asked.

"Cheez! Ya'll don colly nothin! Ferget da fish, China. Dry yo' tears."

He told me about the theory of fights. That kids did it because it was how you became a man later on.

"Momma tole me," he said, "in ole days, no Negro man kin hit or fight. We belongs to da whites, like hosses.

"Man fight 'notha man, be damagin white man goods. So he get whipped. An I mean *whipped*." He shook his head and rubbed the top of it, easing the pain of the thought.

"Now, ain't no mo' dat," he said, smiling. "We kin fights, like men." He was speaking very seriously. Fighting was a measure of citizenship. Of civilization. I didn't think so.

"China, stan up."

"Why?" I whined.

"Putchur fists up. Make a fist! Right. Bof han's.

"Dis one—," he said, holding my left. "It fo' guardin yo' face. Dis here one—dat's fo' poundin da fool who call ya out. Here come a punch, and ya'll block it. China—you listenin ta me?"

"No fight, no reason!" I said hotly.

"No reason!?" he yelled. "You can fight wif no *reason*? Boy! What-chu *talkin* about?"

Uh-oh, I thought. Toussaint's hands were on his hips.

"Evera kid on dis here block like ta knock you upside da head and make you *bleed* and ya'll got no *reason*? China. Ain't no dude in da Handle got mo' cause fo' fightin *evera* day den *you!*"

"Too many boy fight," I said, drawing back from his heat.

"Uh-*uh!* No sir, Cap'n! Big-time nossir! Lissen. Some kids, dey fight *hard.* But ain't *never* gonna be no gangin up on one kid. *Dat* ain't cool." He shook his head. "Kid stan on his feet. No one else feet. Ain't *nobody* gonna stan inaway a dat. An youse best colly dat."

"Hittin' long," I tried.

"Say what?" he said.

"Long. Not light!"

"Wrong? Ya'll sayin fightin's *wrong?*"

"Light," I said.

"Howzat?"

"Bad yuing chi," I explained.

"Say *what?*"

"Bad, uh, karma!" I said, finding the East Indian word often used by my sisters.

"Well, China, ya'll thinks awful funny. Don have nothin ta do wif no *caramels.* No matta Big Willie take yo' candies. Ain't *candies.* It not bein *chicken.* Not bein yella. Ya'll don havta like it. Sakes, China, no one like ta Fist City. Well, maybe Big Willie, he like it. But like it or don like it, no matter none. Ya'll jus *do* it."

He invited me to play in his house. Many of the games involved capturing cockroaches. "Ya'll ready?" he would ask, and I would nod, nervously. Toos would kick the wall next to the sink, and roaches would slither out of the dust and the cracked plaster. Toos would use his plastic cup, smacking it quickly onto the floor, smiling as he watched the captured roach's antennae struggle to escape, its hard body clicking angrily against the plastic.

He made his closest buddies tolerate me. His mother took me to the church of Reverend Jones on Sundays until Edna changed my religion. The simple presence of his company, and that of his pals, saved me from innumerable trashings and gave me time to breathe.

I had never had a friend before, and I cared for him as few lads have for another. My heart fills now when I think of him. That will never change.

Toussaint was, next to me, the skinniest kid on the block. He ran no faster than I since he lacked the sincerity of my efforts, but he was as tough as a slum rat and had the guts of Carmen Basilio. Basilio, the big-headed middleweight who fought while his blood ran down his bruised face like cascading crimson rain in a summer monsoon. Basilio, whose busted face was on the front page of every pinned-up sports section in every barbershop in the city. Kids respected bravery above all else. It was what allowed you to put your pants on in the morning.

My courage was so low that putting on my big-boy underpants was a task. Toussaint was deemed crazy to buddy with me. But he was my friend because I needed one. He got nothing for himself, in the hard world of our peers' respect, for his generosity.

Outside of a table service, we had few possessions and less cash, but Toos's home made ours look like a gilded palace of Babylon. The LaRue family lived in a windowless converted storage room in a shambling tenement on Masonic, next door to Brook's Mortuary. The stone steps to the main door were chipped, crumbling, and dangerous for old people and toddlers. The entryway was a garbage dump for rotted food, and the stairways reeked of old and pungent uric acid.

A sad, small alcoholic named Sippy Suds lived next door to Toussaint. Suds's apartment produced the worst smell in the Panhandle, a rancid sour waft of vomit and urine so strong in the closed space of the hallway that it made you crazy with the badness of it. He used to mess on himself. Suds was one of several people in the 'hood whose speech evaded understanding. I thought it was related to my eyes. Whenever I concentrated and tried to fight through his thick, inebriated Mississippi babble, my eyes watered from the pungent toxins in the air. Suds had everything no one wanted, down to flies that liked his clothes and odors that would cause others to change jobs.

Many of the kids on the block despised Suds, taking his pitiful coins by incessant begging.

"C'mon, Suds, gimme nickel. Yeah! Gimme dollah!"

Toussaint respected him.

"Leave da man be," he said to a whole battalion of yammering kids. "Ain't cool, takin poor man's coins. C'mon! Back off!"

he shouted, pushing them back. "'Sides. Man yoosta be a fighta," he said.

Heck, I thought. *Everyone* around here is a fighter.

I had seen dead rats before in our house, looking pitiful and scary in the traps, their little feet tucked up in death, thick round tails looking like remnants of ancient lizards. But I had never seen families of them alive. They were on Toussaint's stairs, sluggish, bunched up, and squeaky, and the first time I saw them I stopped and cried. Toussaint looked at me, nodding his head. The rats were pushy and one ran over my foot, small, heavy, sharp-clawed, and warm.

"Won hurtcha none," he said, taking my arm as I began to faint.

An elderly and toothless woman lived in a shamble of newspapers and produce cartons on top of the stairs in the hall. Toussaint called her Missus Hall. She wore old shawls, discarded and unmatched men's shoes, and staggered on broken hips with wriggling loose shoelaces, aided by a short stick wrested from a fruit crate. She would sit on the neighborhood stoops, her crackled fingers pulling splinters from each other, her aged and wrinkled face scrunched with the effort of finding the torment in her hands. During these efforts, her fleshy nose could touch her lips. She was missing clumps of hair, eyelashes, eyebrows. Missus Hall did not look like someone who had been very pretty in her youth. But her durability, her will to survive, were attractive, and I liked her very much.

My mother had been beautiful. And she had died.

Missus Hall would relieve herself on old newspapers in the alleyways on Central Avenue. She never spoke to anyone but would nod at Toussaint, who brought her shares of their meager food. The LaRue and the Ting families did not look even a little bit alike, but we had the same caloric intake, while enjoying strong differences on the meaning of Christian charity.

Mrs. LaRue offered to feed me as well, and I was inclined to eat anything that wasn't going to run away from me. This easily included plain, unbuttered grits, which resembled *tze*, rice gruel. But Toussaint's friends never took food from his mother. Her son was too thin.

One Halloween night, after I had been friends with the

LaRues for more than five years, Missus Hall smiled at me. I remember that when she showed her teeth I thought she was angry. It took a moment to realize that she was greeting me with a smile, and I beamed back at her, offering her witches' teeth candy, the world full of light.

I asked Mrs. LaRue why Missus Hall never spoke.

"I honestly don't know, Kai," she said. "I figure somethin almighty drastic happened in her life, and it probly happened twice. Once early, and once late. She's not gonna do nothin fancy with her life. She's jes getting ready for the next blow."

The LaRue home had no furniture, only milk cartons and fruit crates that his momma got from the Reliance Market.

Toussaint had no toys and never asked to play with those belonging to others. He had no father. His mother was wonderful and caring and had convinced Toos that toys and living fathers were not necessary in this mysterious physical world. She carried the whole load, all the way. Toussaint had the gift of love, and they shared everything they had. I was testament to that fact. His smile, shining from a high-cheekboned, high-foreheaded, almost skull-like face, was beatific and had the force of the Prophet. I thought he was the handsomest boy in the world.

As a streetfighter, Toussaint was unusual. He cared nothing for style, which was becoming an extremely big deal to the others.

"Toos," said Jerome Washington. "Ya'll fights like a ole' lady. Ya'll fights like Missus Hall." He giggled. "Ain't dat right, Toos?" Jerome was not looking for a fight. He just enjoyed stirring feces with his tongue.

"Dat probly be true, Jerome," said Toussaint, slowly. He was smiling, frustrating Jerome in some mysterious way. Jerome cursed and moved on.

"See, China? Jerome don mess wif me. He wanna hurt mah feelins, an I jes talk blahdee-blah trash back at 'em. 'China Bashers.' Dat's a lota *crap*. Misser Pueblo, in Cutty's Garage. He tole me: fight fo' da fight. Don pay no mind ta no lookers. Style, dat fo' *girls*.

"Fists. Be fo' da boy dookin Fist City wif ya."

Toos threw unending series of berserk punches, ignoring incoming rounds as if they were raindrops on a pleasant spring day. He would punch until the fight was over—until Toussaint collapsed or the other kid stopped. I didn't know how he could do that.

When he fought, the smile beat feet, and he became all business. He did not have to do this often. It usually occurred when a Haight kid crossed the border of Fell Street and strutted north up Masonic, looking to break some bones.

Toos's home was on the cross-'hoods thoroughfare. It was Indian Country; trouble came calling with the rising sun.

Toos was skinny and occasionally got picked. He would stand up straight, like an older boy, and roll his shoulders back, like a grown man. He would measure the challenge, giving the Handle crosser a chance to move on. Sometimes his quiet, unfearing gaze was as articulate as my mother's face. When parley failed, he met aggression with his own fury. He was never called out twice by the same youth.

The Haight, six blocks south, was boogeymanland. Boys carried knives, men had zip guns, and women looked more dangerous than twenty San Juan streetfighters with switchblades. Some of the Haight boys wore old-skinned Big Ben coveralls and carried barber shaving razors in the cup of the hand, hiding the flash of steel inside their arm-swaying struts. They could punch a guy and move on. It took a moment to realize that the face had been opened, blood everywhere, the searing pain following long moments after the incision.

"Ya'll stay outa dere," said Toussaint, pointing with a long and skinny thumb at our rival 'hood. "Be boogeymen, big-time."

Until I learned English, I understood it as The Hate.

The Panhandle lay between our 'hoods like no-man's-land, a DMZ that operated without U.N. intervention. Panhandle boys entered the park with great care and only in daylight. It was a jungle of thick eucalyptus, corpses, tangled azalea, and memories of aimless nocturnal screams. Men gathered there at night to smoke and drink and discuss this new land of California. When they disagreed, people died.

The Haight was largely populated by trekkers from Alabama and Louisiana. Mrs. LaRue said their heartaches came from not having a minister. Reverend M. Stamina Jones had followed the LaRues, the Joneses, the Scotts, and the Williamses—the

Panhandle families—from Georgia. Others in the neighborhood hailed from Mississippi, Maryland, and Tennessee. I thought they were names of streets.

"No ministers in the Haight, just knife fighters," she said. "They'se lost. Toussaint LaRue and Kai Ting, you listen to Momma! Don't be goin into the Haight, no how and no way. Now. *That* be gospel."

Toussaint taught me about music. He tried to translate the words of the chorus in the church of Reverend Jones, but I always suspected that he lacked certainty in his explanations. But he knew that the chorus moved me, and would rub the hair on my head whenever I found myself weeping in time with its singing. I did not have to be an Imperial Scholar to know that crying in this temple house was accepted; the congregation's choral majesty was salted with tears and accented by open weeping. Sobs often served as confirmation of the truth of Reverend Jones's ministry. A dry-eyed assembly meant that his delivery was off the mark.

Toos also introduced me to Mr. Carter, who owned Evil the bulldog. Mr. Carter was a shipyard worker at Hunters Point who lived across the street from us, with the LaRue home around the corner. He had a platoon of exwives, no prospects of any more, two radios and a record player, and everyone on the block liked him while hating his dog.

Evil was moody. Somedays he raised his black-and-white head to you on a loose leash, anxious for a pat, his eyes half-closed, his teeth looking sadly overused and brownishly old.

Other days he growled, the fangs angry and huge and brightly wet. He would run around like a broken top with his jaws open, all the kids screaming as they scattered. Evil never caught me; I was the flight expert. He would clamp his maws around a kid's leg and throw his neck back and forth and Mr. Carter would blow that whistle in Evil's ear until he let go. He would then use a fat clothes-hanger dowel to beat the starch out of the dog, and I was the only one who felt sorry for him.

"Oughta jes give dat dog *away*," said Toos.

I shook my head. "Give doggie mo' food," I said. "He too much hungry."

"China, you'se a very funny boy," he said. "Now. Don let

94

no dog smell yo' fear. He smell dat, he get feared hisself and eat yo' pants in a *big* hurry."

The men who had been in the army would sit on the wide stairs of Mr. Carter's place and sing. "What the Best-Dressed Man in Harlem Is Wearing Tonight," "The Blues in the Night," and I could close my eyes and sway to their unearthly beautiful voices. They also sang songs they called Jodies. I knew them; my father used to chant them while he chopped vegetables in the kitchen when our mother was still alive.

"Yo' momma was dere when ya lef'"
"YO' RIGHT!"
"Jody was dere when ya lef'"
"YO' RIGHT!"
"Sound off—"
"ONE-TWO!"
"Sound off—"
"THREE-FO'!"
"Bring it on down—"
"ONE-TWO-THREE-FO'!"
"ONE-TWO-THREE-FO'!"

"Jody got somethin dat you ain't got"
"I'S BIN SO LONG AH ALMOS' FO'GOT"
"Yo' baby's as lonely as lonely can be"
"WIF ONLY JODY FO' COM-PANY"
"Ain't it great ta have a pal"
"TA HELP KEEP UP HER MO-RALE"
"Sound off. . . ."
"Yo' not gonna get out till da enda da war"
"IN NINET'IN HUNDRA' AN' SEVENTY-FOUR. . . ."

Adults and kids gathered on Mr. Carter's stoop to sing and clap hands, or to gently swing to "Harlem Nocturne" and the high throaty jazz of Billie Holiday's "Strange Fruit," "The Way You Look Tonight," and "God Bless the Child." Toos told me that the words to that song meant that if God did not love you, you were soon dead, because little came to short people without God's grace.

"Good news is, China," said Toos, "dat God love all chillun."

"Me, too?" I asked.

"Dat *gotta* be true," he said. "God get dibs on all da little chillun he kin find. And," he said, elbowing me, "you'se little."

We would keep time and tap with one foot while keeping the other ready to exit stage left if Evil felt the urge. The muse didn't come cheap in the Panhandle.

"Mista Carter," said Toussaint's mom. "That's not right, namin a dog Evil. You can come up with a better name'n that, I know you can. Callin somethin a name sometime make it so."

"Charlotte, you think it be a big favor to all de chillun on dis block be comin up ta dis here dog an callin 'em *Spot*? or *Fido*?

"See. His firs' name, it was Winston. The name offered no warnin. Folks like ta pet 'em. Den he start ta eat kids? He gots too much crust. I call 'em what he is: Evil." He whacked his pants leg with the dowel.

Kids learned to make their own music, without radios. I thought this was because of Evil, since the price of listening to radios could be a pint of dog-drawn blood. But I was wrong. Kids, even poor and unhappy ones, love to sing, warbling the purity of expression, the unsullied and miraculous poetry of a child's honesty. Happy kids sing better. Toos sat on his crumbling steps with Titus McGovern and Alvin Sharpes—boys who had pledged their lives to him—to sing the "Papa Ditty," and other rapadiddle tunes from the not-so-distant South.

> *Well, I don know but I been tole,*
> *Papa gonna buy me a pile a coal.*
> *If dat coal don burn fo' me,*
> *Papa gonna take me to da sea.*
> *If dat sea don make me wet,*
> *Papa gonna sink us deeper in debt.*
> *If dat debt don eat our food,*
> *Papa gonna thank da good Saint Jude.*

And so on.

Each kid would sing a two-line stanza, making it up as he went. I always shook my head, lowering it as I blushed when it was my turn.

"Dang!" cried Alvin Sharpes. "Lookit China's face. It all red! How you do dat, China?" It was easy. I couldn't rhyme.

"Missa LaRue," I asked, struggling to align the *L*'s and the *R*'s. "Kin rearn me 'Papa Ditty'?"

"The 'Papa Ditty'? I don't think I know that, Kai. Can you sing a little of it for me?"

I tried. She laughed and hugged me.

"Oh, sweetnin, that's 'The Mockinbird's Song.' Listen to me," she said, bending over, her smoothly angular and pretty face bright with life, looking at me with a great smile, singing in a deep mystic voice that scratched the itches in my heart.

> *Well, I'll tell you what I've learned:*
> *Papa's gonna buy me a mockinbird.*
> *If that mockinbird don't sing,*
> *Papa's gonna buy me a diamond ring.*
> *If that diamond ring don't shine,*
> *Papa's gonna buy me a bottle of wine.*
> *If that bottle of wine don't pour,*
> *Papa's gonna take us to the shore. . . .*

"My momma rike shore, rike ocean," I said.

"Well, Kai, that big blue sea, it's somethin, all right."

Toussaint told me that Big Willie Mack, the glandular error in the guise of a twelve-year-old, had been the first to punch me on my inaugural day on the street. Big Willie was the toughest dude on the block, a bad combination of vicious clothes-taking bully and mean, gutsy fighter.

Toussaint had hit me on the arm that day with that second, harmless blow, to make sure that Willie didn't wind up and do it again.

"China, ya'lls gotta fight. Pretty soon, he be takin yo' clothes."

"No. Crows too small. Him long size," I said.

"China. He don't take 'em ta wear. He take 'em to *take 'em.* You'se gotta punch it out wif him, China."

"Ohnry make worse, mo' hit."

"Den *you* hit back mo'. Dat how it is. It hard be livin, be a

stan-up-boy on dis here block, ya'll don fight. Don havta *win*,
jes *fight*. Make it so's da other boy think fightin you's too much
work! Make it easy on *bof* of us."

"Kin *you* whup Big Wirry?" I asked.

"Nah, don think so. But he know I fights 'em, won give in.
He wan *my* shoes, he gonna havta give me some *blood*."

We both looked at Toos's shoes. I didn't think Toos had to
worry about anyone taking them unless Evil went crazy or a
starving rat was driven to extreme means.

I tried to explain yuing chi, the responsibility of the future,
God's ever-watchful scorecard, to Toussaint, but the concept
exceeded my vocabulary. I had understood the idea so easily
when it was conveyed by the dark, shimmering, expressive eyes
of my mother. I was so anxious to explain that fighting was
wrong, and would cause later pain, but winning this inarticulate
debate was as difficult as prevailing in its subject matter.

I thought desperately about fighting but could not figure it
out. I would be noticed, cut down, called horrific names, shoul-
der-bumped or shoved into the soft tar of the old streets of the
Handle. A kid would challenge me and fear would rise inside
my stomach like fog on the Bay and swamp me. My lights
would get punched out and I would bawl like a newborn.

Flight always overcame Fight.

The very best I could do was control my tears, to a point. It
was my only victory over the weakness of my body, the paucity
of my combat power, the horror of fighting.

"China, I need yo' help someday too," said Toos.

I looked at him, confused.

"Say dude from da Haight strut here wif a razor, break mah
bones and bleed me. Hustle to yo' door, ya'll lemme in. Right?"

I thought of Edna. Edna wouldn't let *me* in.

"Hmm," I said.

Toussaint was a preacher of the handshake. He already knew
at this tender age that people got by because they gave each
other the biggest gift in the book: time. His momma provided
it for him whenever he wanted it. They had a handshake on it,
and it gave him the strength of angels.

"You'all lookin at me kinda strange, Kai. Whatcha thinkin?"
said his momma, as Toos went out the door.

"Toos ask fo' wata. You *give* wata."

She studied me for a bit, passing me a sad little cup of water, as well. I drank. "Say that again?" she said. So I did.

"Kai. I love my son. Now look here. *Everybody* love their kids. Yo' daddy and his wife, they surely love you, too. Jus' everabody don't know *how*.

"If the Good Lord took my boy from me I would curl up and die; I truly would," she said very solemnly. "He sent me Toussaint LaRue so's I could *love* him, give him my life, my heart." She smiled. "I have the Lord Jesus and I have Toussaint, and they'se my joys.

"Kai. You 'member this, chile. Someday you'all gonna have yo' own little Kai, a little Janie Ting. When yo' child want yo' time, you *give* it. That's our—our *callin*. I *love* my boy, but sometime he want ta play the cockroach game and I'm jes sick of it? Oh, Lord, *really sick of it*." She looked down at the old floor, clicking her tongue. "Or, he tell me the mos' *borin*, stop-your-mind stuff *ever*? My little man, Toussaint, he tell the longest and mos' unfunniest jokes in the world! But I *listen*, and I laugh fo' his joy, and I play him roaches, cuz I'm his momma, and he's my son. It's my God-given duty."

She dried her hands on a rag, and exhaled, looking away from me. "Toussaint's daddy got killed in truck acciden' in Benning," she said softly. "He was an officer. He went inta the army a private, and came back a cap'n, two bright silver railroad tracks on his collar. Lord, what a man he was! Well. The war, it was over, and he made it back from overseas, a pure hero, and he gave me Toussaint, and then we lost him. . . ." Her voice faded.

"He was a good man, Little Kai, and I miss him *evera day*." Her voice was choked. She stopped to blow her nose, shaking her head, hot tears coursing down her cheeks. "God wanted him bad, and took him." She looked toward the door. "Oh, Lord. What a price You exact. . . .

"John LaRue made a promise to me. I think his son done made one to you. Promises be powerful things. I take care of my son's wants. Then he give water to other men when they need it. And we'll have another John LaRue in the world. You want some more water?"

That was yuing chi, karma! And she let Missus Hall and the rats live on the stairs, and roaches in the wall. Mrs. LaRue was Chinese! She just didn't *look* it.

Could you give water to children who asked for it *and* beat the stuffing out of them if a fight was offered? I frowned with the difficulty of the riddle. She was offering me more water.

I took the plastic cup from Mrs. LaRue again, looking at the liquid within it as I drew it to my mouth. The plastic was old and scarred, with a history probably longer than mine. Innumerable scratches and half-cracks made it look tired, as if the serving of its masters and the catching of roaches had some-how cost too much. The water inside the cup sloshed, like the surf in the ocean, and for a transcendent moment all the scale and sense of proportion in the world dissolved, and I could see my mother placing her feet in the roaring waters of the cup. She was communicating with Na-Gung, an ocean away, and with me, from another world. My eardrums tickled, making me shudder, with her reaching for me. The cup was against my lip, and I stared inside it, cross-eyed. I could not drink this water.

"Tank you. Momma," I said. "I keep wata?"

"You want ta take it on home?" she asked.

"No. Want keep here, on sink. Same wata," I said. "Special. Uh, big-time, special."

"You can take it, chile."

"No," I said, shaking my head. "Mo' betta here." I heard Toos come in. Mrs. LaRue took the cup and placed it on the sink.

"China. Ya'll wanna be mah fren'?" asked Toos. Mrs. LaRue smiled and moved away from my field of vision. Maybe three feet.

"Chure, yep," I said. I sensed something weighing in the balance, an unasked question, a favor awaiting fulfillment.

"Den shake on it," he said, extending his hand. Again? I wondered. He took my hand and molded it into his. His was so hard, so rough.

"Squeeze, squeeze hard, China," he said, "like milk'd come out if ya squoze hard. You'se gotta know how." I gripped, and he smiled.

"Now. We'se frens, fo' sure," he said.

"An you can ask him yo' question, honey," said Momma.

"China," said Toos.

"Toos?" I said.

"China. Tell me 'bout yo' daddy."

I frowned. "Tell what?" I asked.

"Anythin, China. Jes *talk* 'bout him."

I began breathing heavily, not knowing what to say.

"I think yo' daddy was in the war, right?" said Mrs. LaRue. I nodded. "He in China army, for war," I said. "He fry airprane wif guns, bomb. He—" I made motions with my hands—"fall in pallashoot. Shoot gun. Save my ma-ma." I was licking my lips. "He very smart. Read books. Pray catch wif me. . . ."

There was a long silence.

"Thanks, chile," said Momma. "Listen. You share yo' daddy with Toussaint, hear? Dat's what frens do."

Toussaint was all smiles, and I halfway grinned at him, trying to hide my teeth so the Teeth God would not want them.

It was now another day, and my friend, my friend of the handshake, my friend of the water, was staring at me. I jumped a little when I realized he had been staring at me.

"China, ya'll knows how ta laff?" asked Toos. We had been playing marbles. I was pretty good at marbles, for the short shots. I was also becoming something of a demon in penny-pitching, and card-tossing. Parlor games, not at the level of the Bigs of street-thumping and ball-playing, but something, after all. It was all in the wrist.

"Chure, yep," I said, worried by his question.

He opened his eyes wide and showed his teeth. He giggled. It was high, and silly, and warm.

"So les hear yo' laff!" he giggled.

I started to explain to him about the Teeth God, realizing that I could neither describe it nor prove its existence. I didn't even know if it was a boy or a girl. This was, like karma, a matter of faith. I suddenly wondered what all this god-fearing was worth. Mother had respected every god known, and they had taken her.

I opened my mouth and tried to make a laughing sound. It must've been ridiculous, because Toos bent over and guffawed, slapping his knees and putting his head between his knees while making a wonderful sound of a strange animal. My ears perked as I heard what I could later favorably compare to a spasm-ridden rum-crazed jackass. Now I was hearing something that reminded me of the distant laughter of my father. I giggled with him, still holding back.

Even through the laughter came the whistle of my stepmother. She never called when I needed her.

I could not discuss my street whippings at home. Stepmother Edna pretended that no problem existed, washing out the blood from my clothes with astounding tolerance. I began to believe that she took pleasure in my fear. I felt that my shame was mine, and somehow my father's and even my mother's, and did not see it as transferable.

Janie was involved in a struggle for survival with Edna. It was a war between two de facto mother figures. One by blood and death, one by marriage and expectation, neither by choice.

As the lastborn kid of four, I did not understand Janie's tenacious resistance to Edna's supreme power. Kids in the lower birth order, like me, seldom resisted parental authority as did the firstborn, the vanguards. Jennifer Sung-ah and Megan Wai-la were in Berkeley; Janie was now the functional older sibling.

Edna was a grown-up and could slap you silly and dance fandangos on your face. But she hadn't touched Jane for months. If Edna had left me alone like that I would have written poetry for her.

"Kai. I'm doing this for both of us. She is *not* our mom."

"I know dat," I said. I just didn't know what it meant. Janie's eyes were bright in anger.

"Edna told me not to read this to you," she said, pulling a stained and torn book from her aging schoolbag. "It's called *Hansel and Gretel*. It's about a stepmother who gets the father to get rid of the kids. Edna threw it out, and I dug it out of the garbage." Janie looked very intense, very determined.

We sat on the front stairs of our house. I pretended to look at the book, but was watching for Big Willie and the Bashers.

"You China Boy sister?" asked Reginald Tufts.

"His name is Kai," said Janie. "Can you say that? Kai."

"Kai," said Reginald. My mouth was, again, as open as the Red Sea was for Moses. Hearing a boy say my first name was astonishing, and I squinted with the pressure of it, waiting to see what else in the world might change next.

"I'm going to read a book. Want to listen?" she asked.

"A book? Yeah!" he cried, and I glared at him, not wanting to share Janie with a Basher, or a friend of a Basher. Even if he had said my name.

Janie opened the book, which was missing its cover.

"Once upon a time," she began, "there was a poor woodcutter who lived at the edge of a large forest with his wife and two children. The boy was named Hansel, and the girl was named Gretel. Many years before, his wife had died, and he had remarried. They had always been poor. . . ."

Toos and Alvin Sharpes arrived and sat on the stairs to listen to the story and stare at the storyteller. Janie smiled at them and received their smiles in return. I grinned.

The stepmother in this story gave the two children a last meal and left them in the woods to be taken by wolves. She had done this to allow the father and stepmother to live without the burden of the kids, whose voracious appetites were consuming too much of the limited food. It was a credible tale.

I later asked Toos what he would do if his momma left and another mother moved in.

"My momma, she no go nowhere wif out me. Dere ain't no other momma," he said.

"But she go bye-bye anyway," I said.

"Den I goes wif her."

"If she jus, *gone*?"

"I fin her," he said.

"Can fin her, den . . . ?"

"Keep lookin," he said.

"Where rook?" I asked.

"Dunno, China. Lord. *All* over." He looked at me. "Ya'll miss yo' momma, doncha. Yeah." Then he looked up, squinting. "I 'member her. She yoosta tote da um-brella when dere was no rain. Ya'll was a big saprise, comin outa dat 'partment. Didn know you'se in dere."

I looked down at the stairs.

"Ya'll don like yo' stepmomma?"

I shook my head, fearing that somehow, even around the corner of buildings and the rise of streets, she knew I was admitting it, and that this knowledge would hurt me.

"She be a white lady," he said, and I nodded. "Wif yella hair," he added. "Don think she like *us*," he concluded.

"What I do, Toos?" I asked.

"She yo momma, now. Dang, China. I get it; dat's hard."
He studied it for a bit. "I'd as' da Lord."

"I did dat," I said.

To my father, the combat between the females was Women's
War, the incomprehensible tensions between disenfranchised
females. In Shanghai, there was an unquestionable hierarchy,
an immutable order of rank. It did not call for the involvement
of men, and he had no experience to make himself Ward
Cleaver, who in any event was a fantasy designed to sell Mapo.
He could not find an intellectual guide to the current problem
and knew that he did not wish to reestablish the old order. I
found guidance in comic books.

I loved Superman and Mighty Mouse. I had lost my funnies
in the revolutionary storm. Alvin Sharpes had a deep and endless
collection and I began to draw from his castaways. I read them,
two inches from my face, again and again. I began to imagine
myself as a fighter. Who did good for others and beat the crap
out of bad guys. Good karma. I projected myself into the cartoon sequences. I was unconquerable. Here I come, to save the
day. . . . It means that Mighty Mouse is on his way. . . .

After my stunning victories over evil incarnate, I received the
appreciative accolades of my family, laurels from a grateful
nation, a citation from the President of the United States, free
milk at our doorstep, and a new copy of *The Tales of Lu Hsun*.

After a pounding on the street, I would take out my comics
and pore over them with shaking hands and a teary face, trying
desperately to incorporate their messages into my body. But
the correspondence-school method of streetfighting proved un-
successful.

Then I tried reason. Be pal? I would offer. Pow! I don wan
twubble wit you. Wham! Here, candy? Snatch!

Forget reason. I returned to comics and running.

Then Edna rediscovered the comic books, and they were
gone.

I wondered if I was going crazy. I would awaken at night,
crying from a dream in which I was fleeing my stepmother.
Edna would enter my room and slap me in an effort to stop the

weeping, which had awakened her. By the time I figured out that the dream had merged with reality, she was gone and I would squint at the closed door, trying to separate images of light and dark.

Despite the fact that I now had Toussaint and his mother in the periphery of my life, I tried to run away again.

Knowing that silence was imperative to successful flight, I took my time. It was not difficult to sneak down the staircase, my footfalls absorbed by the carpet that had through long wear become part of the risers. The front door made a sound like a cherry bomb when opened by the remote handle. I had seen Father lubricate it. I put oil in the hinges and gave the task five minutes, and the door opened with all the sound that a mouse makes when it sniffs cheese.

Golden Gate Avenue was utterly dark and surprisingly cold, the lone streetlamp at the corner of Central Avenue offering few clues and no warmth. But the street was mine, surrendered only for blinding moments as cars with overbright headlights passed.

The first time a car approached I ran from it, thinking it was an agent of Edna in hot pursuit. I could run very fast on a cold night on an empty sidewalk, my lungs bellowing as I humped arms high and hard to let my legs pump, my head vibrating synchronously with the effort as I fled my fears.

I roamed McAllister, leaning against the cold steel doors of Cutty's Garage, peering into the barred windows of the Reliance Market, missing the winos who kept guard at the Double Olive Bar, trying to recapture the now departed aromas of sizzling french fries in the General Lew Wallace Eatery. I wondered if Rupert and Dozer, the fratricidal siblings, argued after they closed the Eatery and went home to the large apartment building on Grove. Without the aromas of food, McAllister smelled sour and old. I played imaginary checkers on the linoleum grid of the barbershop floor. I projected the more complex figures of Chinese chess, *shiang chi*, onto the black-and-white squares, but could not remember all the moves for both players.

I strolled to Broderick Street, over the pavement where I had once raced when I had a home in which to hide. I looked through the iron-grate fence of Fremont Elementary, retracing beatings by Big Willie and the Bashers. I surveyed the kickball-field benches, the lunch tables, where food had been taken and little bodies stomped. I looked at that spot of the yard, knowing a truth lay in it. I looked away.

Cats chased shadowy rats on the street where Big Willie had stood on my chest. Dogs rousted garbage cans. One growled at me and I froze, waiting ten or fifteen minutes like a man who has stepped on a pressure-release-trigger landmine, until the dog had taken his pleasure with the waste. With light feet, his mangy tail down, he padded away from me and I breathed again. ,

This was my street, McAllister. Now, in the solace of the night, with its bullies and angry words and fists absent, I liked it. I wanted to sleep by day and to walk McAllister to the east at night. It felt safe, the biting cold welcome and fitting. For an instant, I did not want to go any farther, my feet immobilized by the vast, dark unknowns that surrounded the 'hood. I wondered if *wupo*, witches, awaited me in side alleys, or if *dufei*, bandits, were hoping to snatch the only son of the Ting clan tonight.

Ah, I thought. The *wupo* is *inside* the house, not here.

Feeling mildly suicidal, I crossed McAllister to Fulton, which was bold for any kid north of the park. I headed south, keeping to the shadows, crossing Grove, Hayes, and Fell, the final boundary between sanity and simple stupidity. I watched the night traffic on Fell, a big, wide thoroughfare. Where were these people going? Could I go too?

Now I was in the tall eucalyptus trees of the Panhandle itself, the glare of the streetlights swallowed in the darkness of gnarled, interwoven trees. I was in the demilitarized zone, the place of mysterious human sounds, secret passions, and dark bleeding. This was not a child's place.

I crept through the brush as only a boy with bad night vision can. Slowly, patiently, silently, over a detritus of cans, wrappers, boxes, papers. If I made a noise, I stopped. I crawled past a man and a woman, whispering to each other with an intensity beyond comprehension. I shimmied up to a group of talkers sitting around a burning trash can. The fire crackled and cloaked my advance.

I listened to the men in the park. "Boogeymen" from the Haight, with deep, gravelly, bitter voices, raspy with old rumbling hungers. The humor was strained. Some of the speakers were drunk and flared at each other like the trash fire finding fuel to combust in gunfirelike consumption.

What would they do if they found me? I wondered. Nothing, I decided. They didn't care about little boys. There was little talk about sports and fighting. Someone mentioned Joe Louis, and I heard DiMaggio's name.

They were mostly concerned with women, and their meanness and beauty. The mystery of women. These men blamed women for all their woes. Always taking things, wanting more, refusing love, yelling, complaining, comparing. I nodded my head, watching the shadowed figures gesturing, belching in hunger, nodding heads, tippling bottles.

One man held their attention as he spoke of the great Southern Pacific trains that ran from the China Basin docks to Mexico with empty freight cars, no railroad police, and a free meal at the train stops for veterans. I was the son of a veteran. Did that count? I didn't have a mother. Did that matter?

China Basin. It was somewhere in San Francisco, and it sounded like China Boy, like me. It was *my* train. I could go to Mexico. No Edna. No Willie and no Bashers. I would be leaving Janie. Could I do that?

In my mind I heard the wail of the engine calling, its thunderous power promising fast, determined movement, high-pumping wheels chugging tirelessly, taking me away even while I slept in its cars.

I watched the firefly sparks of the trash fire flicker into the night sky, looking like the stack flames of a southbound freight, disappearing into the swallowing blackness. For years I would deride myself, assailing my manhood, for not taking the China Basin train. The decision had been in my hands, but I lacked the ability to seize an early opportunity to die a boy's lonesome death on a distant track.

When I reached Masonic and Golden Gate, I was drawn to Toussaint's apartment building. I climbed the outside stairs with great stealth, thinking of Mrs. LaRue, wanting a glass of water, happy with the mere thought that she was on the other side of the door, resting. Truly there, actually alive, to be seen and heard again. I touched a leg. A big leg. I knew that I was dead from fright and would be beaten afterward for clumsiness.

It was Sippy Suds, his horrendous odors mysteriously absent in the cool of the night. He stirred slightly and began to snore softly. He looked huge lying down, folded inside his faded, moth-eaten, navy pea jacket. In his bent, inebriated, staggering postures on the street, I had thought him as short as Missus Hall. He was actually a tall man. His hands were pinned between his drawn-up knees. They were huge, the fingers bent and black with the dirt of past labor. His wrists were bony but very thick. Hands that gave precious coins to greedy children.

His face looked as if it had been hit often by hard objects or by an angry stepmother. It was square and hard, different colors shading it. Bruising colors. His nose was very flat at the bridge, the bottom of the nose turned to the side, as if an anvil had been dropped on it from an angle. The closed, trusting eyes were surrounded by scars and small mounds of built-up skin. The rough pebbles of scar tissue interrupted the deep lines that laughter had once carved into his temples.

He was a fighta, Toussaint had said.

I sat next to him, looking at him, edging closer, absorbing his kindly silent companionship, feeling safety, defeating loneliness with every moment in his company. I held my breath.

Then we breathed together, and I matched his cycle, my small puff of air emerging with his thicker cloud, both of us slowly exhaling our fatigues with bright, streetlit, vaporous breath into the foggy night. My lungs filled with soulful strength.

I wanted him to awaken and to tell me about his fights. I wanted to hear that he had won, somehow, somewhere, in his past. Together, I thought, the two of us could do anything. I sat until my bottom ached from the hardness of the stairs, and I began shivering, my thin body capsized in cold.

Bye-bye Suds, I whispered, smiling as he stirred again. I returned with small steps to the house of my stepmother, ready for neither the beginning of sleep nor the start of day.

"TRANSFORMATION"
from *TALKING TO HIGH MONKS IN THE SNOW: AN ASIAN AMERICAN ODYSSEY*

Lydia Minatoya (1950–   )

Lydia Minatoya's memoir intertwines memories of childhood, *graduate-school study in psychology, her career as a university professor, and her travels in Asia. Like "Fourth Grade Ukus (1952)" (by Marie Hara, see pages 75–85), the following excerpt recalls elementary school experiences and teachers. However, it is told from the point of view of ethnic isolation in upstate New York during the late 1950s. This chapter foreshadows the author's transformative moments of self-discovery which characterize her later journeys.*

Ms. Minatoya was born in Albany, New York. After receiving her Ph.D. from the University of Maryland in 1981, she began an assistant professorship in the field of counseling psychology. From 1983 to 1985, she taught and traveled throughout Asia.

She received the 1991 PEN/Jerard Fund Award and a grant from the Seattle Arts Commission for Talking to High Monks in the Snow, *which is her first book. She lives in Seattle, where she is a community college counselor and faculty member.*

PERHAPS IT BEGINS WITH MY NAMING. DURING HER PREGNANCY, my mother was reading Dr. Spock. "Children need to belong," he cautioned. "An unusual name can make them the subject of ridicule." My father frowned when he heard this. He stole a worried glance at my sister. Burdened by her Japanese name, Misa played unsuspectingly on the kitchen floor.

The Japanese know full well the dangers of conspicuousness. "The nail that sticks out gets pounded down," cautions an old maxim. In America, Relocation was all the proof they needed.

And so it was, with great earnestness, my parents searched for a conventional name. They wanted me to have the full true promise of America.

"I will ask my colleague Froilan," said my father. "He is the smartest man I know."

"And he has poetic soul," said my mother, who cared about such things.

In due course, Father consulted Froilan. He gave Froilan his conditions for suitability.

"First, if possible, the full name should be alliterative," said my father. "Like Misa Minatoya." He closed his eyes and sang my sister's name. "Second, if not an alliteration, at least the name should have assonantal rhyme."

"Like Misa Minatoya?" said Froilan with a teasing grin.

"Exactly," my father intoned. He gave an emphatic nod. "Finally, most importantly, the name must be readily recognizable as conventional." He peered at Froilan with hope. "Do you have any suggestions or ideas?"

Froilan, whose own American child was named Ricardito, thought a while.

"We already have selected the name for a boy," offered my Father. "Eugene."

"Eugene?" wondered Froilan. "But it meets none of your conditions!"

"Eugene is a special case," said my father, "after Eugene, Oregon, and Eugene O'Neill. The beauty of the Pacific Northwest, the power of a great writer."

"I see," said Froilan, who did not but who realized that this naming business would be more complex than he had anticipated. "How about Maria?"

"Too common," said my father. "We want a *conventional* name, not a common one."

"Hmmm," said Froilan, wondering what the distinction was. He thought some more and then brightened. "Lydia!" he declared. He rhymed the name with media. "Lydia for *la bonita infanta!*"

And so I received my uncommon conventional name. It really

did not provide the camouflage my parents had anticipated. I remained unalterably alien. For Dr. Spock had been addressing *American* families, and in those days, everyone knew all real American families were white.

Call it denial, but many Japanese Americans never quite understood that the promise of America was not truly meant for them. They lived in horse stalls at the Santa Anita racetrack and said the Pledge of Allegiance daily. They rode to Relocation Camps under armed guard, labeled with numbered tags, and sang "The Star-Spangled Banner." They lived in deserts or swamps, ludicrously imprisoned—where would they run if they ever escaped—and formed garden clubs, and yearbook staffs, and citizen town meetings. They even elected beauty queens.

My mother practiced her okoto and was featured in a recital. She taught classes in fashion design and her students mounted a show. Into exile she had carried an okoto and a sewing machine. They were her past and her future. She believed in Art and Technology.

My mother's camp was the third most populous city in the entire state of Wyoming. Across the barren lands, behind barbed wire, bloomed these little oases of democracy. The older generation bore the humiliation with pride. "*Kodomo no tame ni,*" they said. For the sake of the children. They thought that if their dignity was great, then their children would be spared. Call it valor. Call it bathos. Perhaps it was closer to slapstick: a sweet and bitter lunacy.

Call it adaptive behavior. Coming from a land swept by savage typhoons, ravaged by earthquakes and volcanoes, the Japanese have evolved a view of the world: a cooperative, stoic, almost magical way of thinking. Get along, work hard, and never quite see the things that can bring you pain. Against the tyranny of nature, of feudal lords, of wartime hysteria, the charm works equally well.

And so my parents gave me an American name and hoped that I could pass. They nourished me with the American dream: Opportunity, Will, Transformation.

When I was four and my sister was eight, Misa regularly used me as a comic foil. She would bring her playmates home from school and query me as I sat amidst the milk bottles on the front steps.

"What do you want to be when you grow up?" she would say. She would nudge her audience into attentiveness.

"A mother kitty cat!" I would enthuse. Our cat had just delivered her first litter of kittens and I was enchanted by the rasping tongue and soft mewings of motherhood.

"And what makes you think you can become a cat?" Misa would prompt, gesturing to her howling friends—wait for this; it gets better yet.

"This is America," I stoutly would declare. "I can grow up to be anything that I want!"

My faith was unshakable. I believed. Opportunity. Will. Transformation.

When we lived in Albany, I always was the teachers' pet. "So tiny, so precocious, so prettily dressed!" They thought I was a living doll and this was fine with me.

My father knew that the effusive praise would die. He had been through this with my sister. After five years of being a perfect darling, Misa had reached the age where students were tracked by ability. Then, the anger started. Misa had tested into the advanced track. It was impossible, the community declared. Misa was forbidden entry into advanced classes as long as there were white children being placed below her. In her defense, before an angry rabble, my father made a presentation to the Board of Education.

But I was too young to know of this. I knew only that my teachers praised and petted me. They took me to other classes as an example. "Watch now, as Lydia demonstrates attentive behavior," they would croon as I was led to an empty desk at the head of the class. I had a routine. I would sit carefully, spreading my petticoated skirt neatly beneath me. I would pull my chair close to the desk, crossing my swinging legs at my snowy white anklets. I would fold my hands carefully on the desk before me and stare pensively at the blackboard.

This routine won me few friends. The sixth-grade boys threw rocks at me. They danced around me in a tight circle, pulling at the corners of their eyes. "Ching Chong Chinaman," they chanted. But teachers loved me. When I was in first grade, a third-grade teacher went weeping to the principal. She begged to have me skipped. She was leaving to get married and wanted her turn with the dolly.

When we moved, the greatest shock was the knowledge that I had lost my charm. From the first, my teacher failed to notice me. But to me, it did not matter. I was in love. I watched her moods, her needs, her small vanities. I was determined to ingratiate.

Miss Hempstead was a shimmering vision with a small up-turned nose and eyes that were kewpie-doll blue. Slender as a sylph, she tripped around the classroom, all saucy in her high-heeled shoes. Whenever I looked at Miss Hempstead, I pitied the Albany teachers whom, formerly, I had adored. Poor old Miss Rosenberg. With a shiver of distaste, I recalled her loose fleshy arms, her mottled hands, the scent of lavender as she crushed me to her heavy breasts.

Miss Hempstead had a pet of her own. Her name was Linda Sherlock. I watched Linda closely and plotted Miss Hempstead's courtship. The key was the piano. Miss Hempstead played the piano. She fancied herself a musical star. She sang songs from Broadway revues and shaped her students' reactions. "Getting to know you," she would sing. We would smile at her in a staged manner and position ourselves obediently at her feet.

Miss Hempstead was famous for her ability to soothe. Each day at rest time, she played the piano and sang soporific songs. Linda Sherlock was the only child who succumbed. Routinely, Linda's head would bend and nod until she crumpled gracefully onto her folded arms. A tousled strand of blond hair would fall across her forehead. Miss Hempstead would end her song, would gently lower the keyboard cover. She would turn toward the restive eyes of the class. "Isn't she sweetness itself!" Miss Hempstead would declare. It made me want to vomit.

I was growing weary. My studiousness, my attentiveness, my fastidious grooming and pert poise: all were failing me. I changed my tactics. I became a problem. Miss Hempstead sent me home with nasty notes in sealed envelopes: Lydia is a slow child, a noisy child, her presence is disruptive. My mother looked at me with surprise, "*Nani desu ka*? Are you having problems with your teacher?" But I was tenacious. I pushed harder and harder, firmly caught in the obsessive need of the scorned.

One day I snapped. As Miss Hempstead began to sing her wretched lullabies, my head dropped to the desk with a powerful CRACK! It lolled there, briefly, then rolled toward the edge with a momentum that sent my entire body catapulting to the floor. Miss Hempstead's spine stretched slightly, like a cat that senses danger. Otherwise, she paid no heed. The linoleum floor was smooth and cool. It emitted a faint pleasant odor: a mixture of chalk dust and wax.

I began to snore heavily. The class sat electrified. There would be no drowsing today. The music went on and on. Finally, one boy could not stand it. "Miss Hempstead," he probed plaintively, "Lydia has fallen asleep on the floor!" Miss Hempstead did not turn. Her playing grew slightly strident but she did not falter.

I lay on the floor through rest time. I lay on the floor through math drill. I lay on the floor while my classmates scraped around me, pushing their sturdy little wooden desks into the configuration for reading circle. It was not until penmanship practice that I finally stretched and stirred. I rose like Sleeping Beauty and slipped back to my seat. I smiled enigmatically. A spell had been broken. I never again had a crush on a teacher.

from CEBU
Peter Bacho (1950–   )

Peter Bacho's debut novel chronicles the life of Ben Lucero, a young Filipino American priest struggling with issues of identity, religion, and morality. The book is set both in Ben's hometown of Seattle and the Philippine city of Cebu, which he visits for the first time for his mother's funeral. The following passage depicts a scene from Ben's childhood in the States.

Mr. Bacho was born in Seattle and grew up in the city's Central District, then a mostly Filipino and African American neighborhood. His fiction has been published in Seattle Review, Amerasia Journal, Zyzzyva, and other journals and anthologies. Also a journalist and attorney, he has written for The Christian Science Monitor and The Oregonian. For many years he taught law and Philippine history at the University of Washington. He now lives in San Francisco, where he teaches creative writing and literature.

IT WAS PART OF THE LEGEND BROUGHT BACK BY AMERICAN TROOPS after they conquered the Philippines in 1902—Filipinos and dogs, dogs and Filipinos. The relationship shocked the soldiers who, in the defense of canines, slaughtered Filipinos like the dogs the natives ate.

Growing up in the States, Ben had heard the story often enough in different schools in different army towns. For a while, he tried to ignore it. Their family, he always explained, had a dog. Eating her was the last thing on their minds. He felt that his explanation should have settled the matter, burying forever, in the mind of the listener, the evil rumor that Filipinos ate their pets.

It was seldom enough, and Ben, when faced with the invincible ignorance of a classmate, just turned and walked away. He heeded the counsel of Remedios, who abhorred fighting.

In the fifth grade, Ben finally changed his approach.

"Hey, Benny," a tall redheaded boy taunted. "I hear Filipinos eat dogs."

"Look," young Ben explained calmly. "We got a pet dog and we ain't never gonna eat her."

"Just a matter of time, dog eater," the tall redhead said, his smirk saying more than his words.

Ben glanced at his tormentor once, then turned away before reversing direction and pivoting back hard. His clenched backhand—the left, his strongest—was aimed straight at the redhead's smile, which didn't even have time to disappear.

Two seconds later, Ben's target was out cold—two teeth to the minus—and Ben was out of school, suspended for fighting.

At home that evening, Remedios both scolded and soothed her son by saying that he shouldn't fight and that their pet wouldn't be eaten. At the house that night was Uncle Chris, who tried hard not to laugh.

Chris was a character, one of his parents' lifer soldier friends. As Remedios talked, he grinned evilly, eyeing Harriet, the family mutt named after Ozzie's prim woman. Chris and Remedios went back a long time, to childhood in Cebu and war in the hills.

After an hour or so, Remedios was through with her lecture, and Chris politely waited until she had finished.

"Good with beer," he said gruffly, pointing to the innocent animal. Harriet, otherwise the most courageous of canines, immediately left the room.

Basically, Chris was a good guy, as kind and gentle as any Filipino uncle, except when he drank. And that night, he had drunk too much. Ben's mother and father were seated with him around the kitchen table; his father was imbibing while his mother, as usual, was not.

"Psst," Remedios hissed loudly.

That sound, which young Ben's American ears once heard as some sort of imperfect whistle, was really quite perfect and versatile. Ben eventually came to learn Filipinos used it in a variety of ways—to summon, warn, or, in this case, scold—accompanied by an array of eye, eyebrow, mouth, and head movements. That evening, however, old drunk Chris was beyond warning and even reprobation.

"Oh, come on, Reming," Chris said. "The boy's eleven. It's OK. He should know how Filipinos really are. We survive, Benny, here or there, it don't much matter. The kids got it good here in the States—we all do—but back home, you know, it's hard."

Remedios, struck by the simple truth of Chris's statement, was silent for a moment, allowing him to continue.

"There are times," Chris paused, red-eyed, and turned toward Ben, who stood behind his mother, "when if it walks it's cooked. Even Harriet."

"Psst," Remedios hissed again, while furiously raising and lowering her eyebrows. Ben knew it meant he should leave the room, but he ignored the signs, wanting to hear the end of this gruesome tale. Among family, Remedios would simply have told Ben to leave, but Chris's presence changed the equation, by bringing into play her profound sense of *delicadeza*, a trait that seeks avenues of grace, however narrow, in ungraceful situations.

Remedios was reduced to a mad, futile fit of pssting and twitching, and Ben ignored her. He knew that later there'd be the devil to pay—usually in the form of a strap across the back of his legs—but that was later.

Uncle Chris, when drunk, was entertaining and, since his mother's order was implied rather than explicit, Ben could plead cultural ignorance, which Remedios would accept because she didn't want to beat him anyway.

"But Mom," he had said in an earlier successful defense, "I'm American."

So he was, and so he stayed at the table, his mother pssting and twitching like a snake in a frying pan as Uncle Chris continued his morbid Philippine tale.

It began with a question. "Remedios, do you remember the time when Clara's patrol brought back two freshly dead Japs and . . ."

Remedios, knowing the end of the story, was horrified. Chris was on the verge of going much too far. She looked desperately around for help but found none; Albert had passed out, his head slumped on the table.

"Go to your room, Ben!" Remedios said in loud and precise English, her sense of *delicadeza* gone.

Slowly, Ben turned toward his room. A direct order in English—no pleading ignorance on this one.

Chris was so full of booze, he didn't even notice him leave.

"Benny," he heard Chris bellow. "You pound the meat long enough, use enough vinegar, it's good as dog. No, better."

In those days, Ben was a quiet kid and a bit small, until he caught his growth at fourteen. Worse, he was unusually shy. His father knew he had little chance of surviving life in army towns unless something was done.

One Friday evening, as Albert was sitting in his usual place—two feet in front of the small black-and-white television in the living room—he turned to Ben.

"Benny," he announced, "you gonna be like Sugar Ray." The weekly fights were on and Sugar Ray was, of course, the great Ray Robinson. Even when pressed, Sugar Ray never seemed to panic, never even sweat, for that matter.

Opposites attract. The principle was never truer than in Albert Lucero's adulation for Ray Robinson, the epitome of style, boxing and otherwise. Whenever he fought and the bout was televised, Albert was there, staring hard at the tiny black vision before him.

On that evening, Sugar Ray was pumping straight and hard left jabs into the face of some artless bruiser. He would then dance lightly around the ring, avoiding his foe's enraged rushes, suffering only the gusts of air as punches sailed harmlessly past their target. What was amazing on this and other Friday evenings was that Sugar's hair never seemed to get mussed. Pompadoured, processed, and slick, there was never a wayward strand. It was always like Sugar Ray, after disposing of his faceless opponents, had more important things to do, like maybe post-fight cocktails with Lena Horne.

"Look at that," Albert cackled to Ben, who, despite his exposure to scores of matches, was still unaware of the nuances. "Sugar don't never get his hair mussed."

"Me neither," Ben said solemnly. He was eight years old and wore a crewcut.

"Ah, Benny," Albert said patiently, "it's different. You don' understand.

"You can be like that," Albert added quickly. He was leading up to something and Ben was puzzled.

He looked at his father. "You mean, not get my hair mussed?"

"That," he said, "and more." Albert paused, then added quickly, "You know Uncle Sergio?" Sergio Arena was another of Albert's lifer pals. In the Philippines, he had been an amateur boxing champ.

Ben nodded.

"He's gonna teach you, Benny," Albert declared. "And you gonna need it, believe me, skinny and soft as you are. Maybe you be like Sugar Ray?"

"You mean like wearing my hair that way?" Ben asked. He didn't like his crewcut, and the thought of a change in style, even to artificially processed, colored hair, appealed to him.

"No," Albert said, "something better."

Ben's boxing career started shortly thereafter, and it carried through to just before he left for the seminary. In every army town, or wherever the family moved, Albert made sure his son had a good boxing coach, first Sergio, then a host of others.

Ben didn't like it much, particularly at first, but like anything else, he adapted. He was a thin, almost frail boy, and his features dictated his style. Sergio turned him around, fighting him left-handed, teaching him to lead with his right and move continuously away from orthodox, or right-handed, left-leading fighters.

It's a boxing axiom: against orthodox boxers, who are the majority, southpaws are poison. They're awkward, hard to hit, cowardly things, moving constantly away from orthodoxy's thunder—a dangerous and cocked right hand held in close.

In all of his years, Ben was rarely struck with a solid right, and that was fine with him. Fighting became, above all else, a game, and his greatest pleasure came not from belting a foe—he wasn't very mean and didn't have much power anyway—but from making him miss, miss, and miss again.

Away from the gym, his skill as a boxer paid dividends. The black and Mexican kids, despite Ben's inoffensive mien, usually left him alone, allowing him the rare teenage freedom to pick friends and activities. He would spend hours in the library—Remedios insisted—and hang with the boys, even the very bad colored ones. But because he was a boxer and, more important, his mother's son, he would step away before the action got hot or the cops came. Not a word would be said by his friends in protest.

Sitting in the car, Ben recalled that he absorbed Chris's story but kept it secret. As a kid, he had known some Japanese Americans in the various army towns. He also had known other Filipinos. He couldn't help but notice a difference between the two. As a whole, the Filipinos were rowdy and, depending on the city and its demography, usually consorted with blacks or Mexicans to wreak different types and degrees of juvenile havoc.

The Japanese, however, were different. They gave no one any trouble. They couldn't, laden as they were with books, rulers, and, Ben assumed, a full list of parental do's and don'ts.

The young Japanese tended to avoid Filipinos. Ben wondered if it was because they knew, or their parents knew, that Filipinos ate them. He couldn't tell, and, as he grew older, its importance disappeared.

"THE MONKEYMAN"
Zia Jaffrey (1959–   )

Zia Jaffrey's modernist short story, "The Monkeyman," evokes
the emotions and situations of childhood, rather than specific
instances or characters. Although no age is specified, the story
belongs to the realm of early memories as a tale of vulnerability,
excitement, and terror.

Ms. Jaffrey was born in New York City and spent time in New
Delhi, India. She attended Barnard College, where she majored in
English, and Columbia University's Graduate Writing Division for
fiction. She has published articles and book reviews in The Nation,
The Village Voice, and Elle magazine, where she was a
contributing editor. "The Monkeyman," written when she was
twenty-one, was published in Polygraph. She is the author of the
forthcoming book, tentatively titled Travels in the Mughul
Empire. She lives in New York City.

ONETWOTHREEONETWOTHREE

In they run.

"Can we see the monkeyman, can we?"

The children sit with the yellow frocks with the white trim
and the small white bow, legs folded in the grass, elbows in
their knees, palms in their cheeks, like a row of tea-colored glass
dolls, with the sun, west, insulating like a tea-cosy.

The monkeyman faces his audience. He crouches below them

in the driveway, inside the looming black iron gates which clatter when the lock is dropped. He assembles his props: a newspaper fragment, yellowish and soft; a gray cup; a black plastic comb; a brown saucer, a ragged yellow carnation.

The two monkeys pace at the ends of their cords, crossing each other's paths, unaware of their colliding shadows. The monkeyman restricts their movements with his right hand, in which he holds two wooden bars, attached to the cords which fasten around the waists of the monkeys. The bars are now put under his right foot, and with his left hand he reveals a small hourglass drum; he shakes it forward and back, forward and back to create the background beat to his story:

OnetwothreeOnetwothree

With his right hand he places a soiled navy handkerchief on the cement, and leads the female, dressed in a tight parched smokeblue frock, and the naked male, to the "blanket." He prods them in the sides with a crooked stick, to lie down. They lie down, their pink hinds up in the air, facing each other with wide open blinking eyes. The children clap. The monkeyman explains, tossing the drum forward and back, voice straining and loud over the beat:

"This is Mr. and Mrs. Mehta. They are at home. It is morning and they are sleeping."

The eyes flutter, open, wide, blinking.

"It is now time to get up."

The monkeyman prods Mr. Mehta in the neck. Mr. Mehta will not get up.

"Get up, Mr. Mehta," he prods a little harder in the neck. The eyes blink. But Mr. Mehta will not rise. He will not rise. He will not rise.

The drum beat stops. A large hand pushes Mr. Mehta. The eyelids blink. But Mr. Mehta will not rise.

"Arré!"

The monkeyman takes the stick and beats Mr. Mehta harder and harder over the head.

"Come quick! The monkeyman is beating Mr. Mehta! Come quick, O Abba, come!"

The monkeyman stops at the children's cries. He pets Mr. Mehta on the head and wipes his hand loosely on his dhoti.

"Get up, Mr. Mehta!"

Mr. Mehta rises. He moves away from the blanket and lifts the comb which lies before the monkeyman's foot. The drum beat continues.

OnetwothreeOnetwothree

Mr. Mehta returns to the blanket with the comb and rouses Mrs. Mehta. She sits up, and Mr. Mehta begins to comb her head, updown, updown, updown, Mr. Mehta looks around, the eyes blinking. The children clap. Mr. Mehta drops the comb on the cement. He begins to pull the head of Mrs. Mehta, pulling the ear, dragging her weight with the blanket, now by the tail, around the monkeyman, behind the monkeyman, back the other way, around the driveway, back the other way, Mrs. Mehta and the blanket, dragging the props in the wake of the blue blanket with Mrs. Mehta, O, the clattering cup, and the carnation! The monkeyman's eyes are wide and blinking. The drum is abandoned. Hands are groping for an edge of anything. One wooden bar is crossed over from one foot to the other.

"Abba! Come! Please come! Mr. Mehta is beating his wife, O Abba, come!"

Now, the monkeyman, releasing the bar from underfoot, grabs Mr. Mehta by the neck and throws him into the burlap bag, tying it with the handkerchief. He collects his things: a foot presses down on the burlap; the handkerchief is untied; a head pops out, a hand pushes it in; and in go the comb, the cup, the saucer, the newspaper, the carnation with a broken stem. In his haste, the bundle of quietness over a shoulder, a female dragged and blinking back, the gate left open.

THE BEGINNINGS OF
IDENTITY

Tragic Transition:
The Internment of Japanese
Americans (1942–1945)

T he following two selections (from *Farewell to Manzanar* and *In Search of Hiroshi*) are stories about growing up during the Second World War and the internment of Japanese Americans. I have chosen to put these two stories at the beginning of the section on adolescence to signify an end of innocence, which the internment represented. The placement of these two pieces here also puts later selections in the context of this full-scale violation. The following historical summary is given as background to the excerpts.

In the aftermath of the Japanese bombing of Pearl Harbor on December 7, 1941, wartime hysteria and decades of prejudice against people of Asian descent created one of the great horrors of American history—the mass relocation and imprisonment of Japanese Americans in internment camps. From 1942 through 1945, more than 120,000 Japanese Americans, American citizens and Japanese nationals alike, were uprooted from their lives on the West Coast and Hawaii and incarcerated in detention camps.

Despite reports by the FBI, the War Department, and the President's own investigative team that Japanese Americans posed no military threat, xenophobic military and political leaders pushed for the internment of first-, second-, and third-generation Japanese Americans, declaring that they constituted an internal threat to national security as possible spies and saboteurs. Racist anti-Japanese sentiment was fueled by mainstream press editorials and articles in publications such as *Time, The Los Angeles Times*, and *The Washington Post*, and bolstered the position of relocation movement leaders such as Lieutenant General John L. DeWitt, head of the Western Defense Command.

On February 19, 1942, President Franklin Delano Roosevelt signed Executive Order 9066. Order 9066 directed the Secretary of War to prescribe military areas from which persons could be excluded at the discretion of the U.S. military. Although the order directly violated the constitutional rights of Japanese-American citizens, who comprised two-thirds of the interned population, it gave full authority to remove them from their homes and place them first in assembly centers and then in internment camps.

Most internees (119,000) were taken from the states of California, Washington, and Oregon. Due to their vital importance to Hawaii's labor pool (as over one third of the population) and because of Hawaii's multiethnic history, a much smaller number of Japanese Americans were interned from the Hawaiian Islands (1,444).

Instructed to bring only what they could carry, internees were given little notice—a week or less—to get ready for the evacuation, and many lost their homes and livelihoods in the process. Families were forced to register by number and were taken to assembly centers, which were often stockyards, fairgrounds, and racetracks ordinarily used to house animals. Later, they were taken by train to one of ten camp locations: Topaz in Utah, Poston and Gila River in Arizona, Amache in Colorado, Jerome and Rohwer in Arkansas, Minidoka in Idaho, Manzanar and Tule Lake in California, and Heart Mountain in Wyoming. Most of these sites were in desolate desert areas.

As Jeanne Wakatsuki Houston recounts in *Farewell to Manzanar*, conditions in the guarded, barbed wire–enclosed camps were bleak. Only the bare necessities were provided for and there was little or no privacy.

Some families were split up among different camps. Prior to the internment, Japanese Americans were subjected to raids on their homes by government officials looking for evidence of treason. Many men, especially community leaders, were taken in for questioning only because they were of Japanese descent. Following the interrogations, some men were deported to all-male relocation camps and interned separately from their families.

In September of 1942, the Selective Service had classified all men of Japanese descent as IV-C, or enemy aliens. However, on February 1, 1943, President Roosevelt wrote a letter to Secretary of War Henry L. Stimson stating that all U.S. citizens regardless of their ancestry would be allowed to fight in the armed forces. In spite of his earlier evacuation order, President Roosevelt thereby made many male Nisei (second-generation Japanese Americans) eligible for the draft. These orders often forced young men to choose between fighting for a country that was imprisoning their families or being sentenced and jailed separately for draft resistance.

Some Nisei defied the relocation orders because they believed they were unconstitutional. Acting independently, Minoru Yasui of Portland, Fred Korematsu in California, and Gordon Hirabayashi in Washington were among those who refused to obey the evacuation orders and the curfew orders that preceded the internment. All three men were arrested, convicted, and sent to prison. At the time, their cases were heard in the Supreme Court, which upheld their criminal convictions, stating that the government's policies were based on "military necessity." It wasn't until the 1980s that their cases were appealed and overturned by courts that found that the U.S. government had suppressed evidence indicating that Japanese Americans posed no security threat and therefore no "military necessity" for their removal existed.

During the 1970s and 1980s, many Asian American and civil-rights groups campaigned for redress for interned Japanese Americans. These efforts resulted in the signing into law of the Civil Liberties Act of 1988 on August 10, 1988. The act provided for an official apology for the government's internment of Japanese Americans, individual compensation of $20,000 to each of the estimated sixty thousand internment survivors, as well as a fund for a public educational program to prevent the recurrence of such injustice. The act is significant in its recognition that the U.S. government had committed an egregious violation of rights against its own people.

Even after the internment had ended, Japanese Americans felt the devastating effects of this injustice for many years. After being released from the concentration camps, some returned to their hometowns only to find their homes and businesses destroyed and struggled to rebuild their lives. The sense of being singled out as untrusted members of American society also haunted younger Nisei, who passed this on to later generations.

In addition to the following passages, which illustrate life during this period, many Sansei and Yonsei (third- and fourth-generation Japanese Americans) have written about how their parents' and grandparents' internment memories affected their lives.

from *FAREWELL TO MANZANAR*

Jeanne Wakatsuki Houston
(1934–   )
and James D. Houston
(1933–   )

F arewell to Manzanar *is Jeanne Wakatsuki Houston's autobiographical account of her childhood experiences before, during, and just after her family's internment in the Manzanar concentration camp in Owens Valley, California. The following passage recounts the evacuation and her life in the camp.*

Ms. Houston was born in Inglewood, California. She attended San Jose State College, where she received her B.A. in journalism and sociology. Her second book, Don't Cry, It's Only Thunder, *was published in 1984. Her nonfiction has been published in several anthologies including* Common Ground: A Thematic Reader. *She has received many awards for her writing including the Humanitas Prize in 1976 and the Christopher Award for her screenplay of* Farewell to Manzanar. *She wrote the book and screenplay of* Farewell to Manzanar *with her husband, writer James D. Houston. Mr. Houston has written many books, including* Californians: Searching for the Golden State, *which won the Before Columbus Foundation American Book Award.*

SHIKATA GA NAI

IN DECEMBER OF 1941 PAPA'S DISAPPEARANCE DIDN'T BOTHER ME nearly so much as the world I soon found myself in.

He had been a jack-of-all-trades. When I was born he was farming near Inglewood. Later, when he started fishing, we moved to Ocean Park, near Santa Monica, and until they picked him up, that's where we lived, in a big frame house with a brick fireplace, a block back from the beach. We were the only Japanese family in the neighborhood. Papa liked it that way. He didn't want to be labeled or grouped by anyone. But with him gone and no way of knowing what to expect, my mother moved all of us down to Terminal Island. Woody already lived there, and one of my older sisters had married a Terminal Island boy. Mama's first concern now was to keep the family together; and once the war began, she felt safer there than isolated racially in Ocean Park. But for me, at age seven, the island was a country as foreign as India or Arabia would have been. It was the first time I had lived among other Japanese, or gone to school with them, and I was terrified all the time.

This was partly Papa's fault. One of his threats to keep us younger kids in line was "I'm going to sell you to the Chinaman." When I had entered kindergarten two years earlier, I was the only Oriental in the class. They sat me next to a Caucasian girl who happened to have very slanted eyes. I looked at her and began to scream, certain Papa had sold me out at last. My fear of her ran so deep I could not speak of it, even to Mama, couldn't explain why I was screaming. For two weeks I had nightmares about this girl, until the teachers finally moved me to the other side of the room. And it was still with me, this fear of Oriental faces, when we moved to Terminal Island.

In those days it was a company town, a ghetto owned and controlled by the canneries. The men went after fish, and whenever the boats came back—day or night—the women would be called to process the catch while it was fresh. One in the afternoon or four in the morning, it made no difference. My mother had to go to work right after we moved there. I can still hear the whistle—two toots for French's, three for Van Camp's—and she and Chizu would be out of bed in the middle of the night, heading for the cannery.

The house we lived in was nothing more than a shack, a barracks with single-plank walls and rough wooden floors, like the cheapest kind of migrant workers' housing. The people around us were hardworking, boisterous, a little proud of their nickname, *yo-go-re*, which meant literally *uncouth one*, or roughneck, or dead-end kid. They not only spoke Japanese exclusively, they spoke a dialect peculiar to Kyushu, where their families had come from in Japan, a rough, fisherman's language, full of oaths and insults. Instead of saying *ba-ka-ta-re*, a common insult meaning *stupid*, Terminal Islanders would say *ba-ka-ya-ro*, a coarser and exclusively masculine use of the word, which implies gross stupidity. They would swagger and pick on outsiders and persecute anyone who didn't speak as they did. That was what made my own time there so hateful. I had never spoken anything but English, and the other kids in the second grade despised me for it. They were tough and mean, like ghetto kids anywhere. Each day after school I dreaded their ambush. My brother Kiyo, three years older, would wait for me at the door, where we would decide whether to run straight home together, or split up, or try a new and unexpected route.

None of these kids ever actually attacked. It was the threat that frightened us, their fearful looks, and the noises they would make, like miniature Samurai, in a language we couldn't understand.

At the time it seemed we had been living under this reign of fear for years. In fact, we lived there about two months. Late in February the navy decided to clear Terminal Island completely. Even though most of us were American-born, it was dangerous having that many Orientals so close to the Long Beach Naval Station, on the opposite end of the island. We had known something like this was coming. But, like Papa's arrest, not much could be done ahead of time. There were four of us kids still young enough to be living with Mama, plus Granny, her mother, sixty-five then, speaking no English, and nearly blind. Mama didn't know where else she could get work, and we had nowhere else to move *to*. On February 25 the choice was made for us. We were given forty-eight hours to clear out.

The secondhand dealers had been prowling around for weeks, like wolves, offering humiliating prices for goods and furniture they knew many of us would have to sell sooner or later. Mama had left all but her most valuable possessions in Ocean Park, simply because she had nowhere to put them. She had brought along her pottery, her silver, heirlooms like the kimonos Granny had brought from Japan, tea sets, lacquered tables, and one fine old set of china, blue and white porcelain, almost translucent. On the day we were leaving, Woody's car was so crammed with boxes and luggage and kids we had just run out of room. Mama had to sell this china.

One of the dealers offered her fifteen dollars for it. She said it was a full setting for twelve and worth at least two hundred. He said fifteen was his top price. Mama started to quiver. Her eyes blazed up at him. She had been packing all night and trying to calm down Granny, who didn't understand why we were moving again and what all the rush was about. Mama's nerves were shot, and now navy jeeps were patrolling the streets. She didn't say another word. She just glared at this man, all the rage and frustration channeled at him through her eyes.

He watched her for a moment and said he was sure he couldn't pay more than seventeen fifty for that china. She reached into the red velvet case, took out a dinner plate and hurled it at the floor right in front of his feet.

The man leaped back shouting, "Hey! Hey, don't do that! Those are valuable dishes!"

Mama took out another dinner plate and hurled it at the floor, then another and another, never moving, never opening her mouth, just quivering and glaring at the retreating dealer, with tears streaming down her cheeks. He finally turned and scuttled out the door, heading for the next house. When he was gone she stood there smashing cups and bowls and platters until the whole set lay in scattered blue and white fragments across the wooden floor.

The American Friends Service helped us find a small house in Boyle Heights, another minority ghetto, in downtown Los Angeles, now inhabited briefly by a few hundred Terminal Island refugees. Executive Order 9066 had been signed by President Roosevelt, giving the War Department authority to define military areas in the western states and to exclude from them anyone who might threaten the war effort. There was a lot of talk about internment, or moving inland, or something like that in store for all Japanese Americans. I remember my brothers sitting around the table talking very intently about what we were going to do, how we would keep the family together. They had seen how quickly Papa was removed, and they knew now that he would not be back for quite a while. Just before leaving Terminal Island Mama had received her first letter, from Bismarck, North Dakota. He had been imprisoned at Fort Lincoln, in an all-male camp for enemy aliens.

Papa had been the patriarch. He had always decided everything in the family. With him gone, my brothers, like councillors in the absence of a chief, worried about what should be done. The ironic thing is, there wasn't much left to decide. These were mainly days of quiet, desperate waiting for what seemed at the time to be inevitable. There is a phrase the Japanese use in such situations, when something difficult must be endured. You would hear the older heads, the Issei, telling others very quietly, "*Shikata ga nai*" (It cannot be helped). "*Shikata ga nai*" (It must be done).

Mama and Woody went to work packing celery for a Japanese produce dealer. Kiyo and my sister May and I enrolled in the local school, and what sticks in my memory from those few weeks is the teacher—not her looks, her remoteness. In Ocean Park my teacher had been a kind, grandmotherly woman who used to sail with us in Papa's boat from time to time and who wept the day we had to leave. In Boyle Heights the teacher felt cold and distant. I was confused by all the moving and was having trouble with the classwork, but she would never help me out. She would have nothing to do with me.

This was the first time I had felt outright hostility from a Caucasian. Looking back, it is easy enough to explain. Public attitudes toward the Japanese in California were shifting rapidly. In the first few months of the Pacific war, America was on the run. Tolerance had turned to distrust and irrational fear. The hundred-year-old tradition of anti-Orientalism on the West Coast soon resurfaced, more vicious than ever. Its result became clear about a month later, when we were told to make our third and final move.

The name Manzanar meant nothing to us when we left Boyle Heights. We didn't know where it was or what it was. We went because the government ordered us to. And, in the case of my older brothers and sisters, we went with a certain amount of relief. They had all heard stories of Japanese homes being attacked, of beatings in the streets of California towns. They were as frightened of the Caucasians as Caucasians were of us. Moving, under what appeared to be government protection, to an area less directly threatened by the war seemed not such a bad idea at all. For some it actually sounded like a fine adventure.

Our pickup point was a Buddhist church in Los Angeles. It was very early, and misty, when we got there with our luggage. Mama had bought heavy coats for all of us. She grew up in eastern Washington and knew that anywhere inland in early April would be cold. I was proud of my new coat, and I remember sitting on a duffel bag trying to be friendly with the Greyhound driver. I smiled at him. He didn't smile back. He was befriending no one. Someone tied a numbered tag to my collar and to the duffel bag (each family was given a number, and that became our official designation until the camps were closed), someone else passed out box lunches for the trip, and we climbed aboard.

I had never been outside Los Angeles County, never traveled more than ten miles from the coast, had never even ridden on a bus. I was full of excitement, the way any kid would be, and wanted to look out the window. But for the first few hours the shades were drawn. Around me other people played cards, read magazines, dozed, waiting. I settled back, waiting too, and finally fell asleep. The bus felt very secure to me. Almost half its passengers were immediate relatives. Mama and my older brothers had succeeded in keeping most of us together, on the same bus, headed for the same camp. I didn't realize until much later what a job that was. The strategy had been, first, to have everyone living in the same district when the evacuation began, and then to get all of us included under the same family number, even though names had been changed by marriage. Many families weren't as lucky as ours and suffered months of anguish while trying to arrange transfers from one camp to another.

We rode all day. By the time we reached our destination, the shades were up. It was late afternoon. The first thing I saw was a yellow swirl across a blurred, reddish setting sun. The bus was being pelted by what sounded like splattering rain. It wasn't rain. This was my first look at something I would soon know very well, a billowing flurry of dust and sand churned up by the wind through Owens Valley.

We drove past a barbed-wire fence, through a gate, and into an open space where trunks and sacks and packages had been dumped from the baggage trucks that drove out ahead of us. I could see a few tents set up, the first rows of black barracks, and beyond them, blurred by sand, rows of barracks that seemed to spread for miles across this plain. People were sitting on cartons or milling around, with their backs to the wind, waiting to see which friends or relatives might be on this bus. As we approached, they turned or stood up, and some moved toward us expectantly. But inside the bus no one stirred. No one waved or spoke. They just stared out the windows, ominously silent. I didn't understand this. Hadn't we finally arrived, our whole family intact? I opened a window, leaned out, and yelled happily. "Hey! This whole bus is full of Wakatsukis!"

Outside, the greeters smiled. Inside there was an explosion of laughter, hysterical, tension-breaking laughter that left my brothers choking and whacking each other across the shoulders.

We had pulled up just in time for dinner. The mess halls weren't completed yet. An outdoor chow line snaked around a half-finished building that broke a good part of the wind. They issued us army mess kits, the round metal kind that fold over, and plopped in scoops of canned Vienna sausage, canned string beans, steamed rice that had been cooked too long, and on top of the rice a serving of canned apricots. The Caucasian servers were thinking that the fruit poured over rice would make a good dessert. Among the Japanese, of course, rice is never eaten with sweet foods, only with salty or savory foods. Few of us could eat such a mixture. But at this point no one dared protest. It would have been impolite. I was horrified when I saw the apricot syrup seeping through my little mound of rice. I opened my mouth to complain. My mother jabbed me in the back to keep quiet. We moved on through the line and joined the others squatting in the lee of half-raised walls, dabbing courteously at what was, for almost everyone there, an inedible concoction.

After dinner we were taken to Block 16, a cluster of fifteen barracks that had just been finished a day or so earlier—although finished was hardly the word for it. The shacks were built of one thickness of pine planking covered with tarpaper. They sat on concrete footings, with about two feet of open space between the floorboards and the ground. Gaps showed between the planks, and as the weeks passed and the green wood dried out, the gaps widened. Knotholes gaped in the uncovered floor.

Each barracks was divided into six units, sixteen by twenty feet, about the size of a living room, with one bare bulb hanging from the ceiling and an oil stove for heat. We were assigned two of these for the twelve people in our family group; and our official family "number" was enlarged by three digits—16 plus the number of this barracks. We were issued steel army cots, two brown army blankets each, and some mattress covers, which my brothers stuffed with straw.

The first task was to divide up what space we had for sleeping. Bill and Woody contributed a blanket each and partitioned off the first room: one side for Bill and Tomi, one side for Woody and Chizu and their baby girl. Woody also got the stove, for heating formulas.

The people who had it hardest during the first few months were young couples like these, many of whom had married just before the evacuation began, in order not to be separated and sent to different camps. Our two rooms were crowded, but at least it was all in the family. My oldest sister and her husband were shoved into one of those sixteen-by-twenty-foot compartments with six people they had never seen before—two other couples, one recently married like themselves, the other with two teenage boys. Partitioning off a room like that wasn't easy. It was bitter cold when we arrived, and the wind did not abate. All they had to use for room dividers were those army blankets, two of which were barely enough to keep one person warm. They argued over whose blanket should be sacrificed and later argued about noise at night—the parents wanted their boys asleep by 9:00 P.M.—and they continued arguing over matters like that for six months, until my sister and her husband left to harvest sugar beets in Idaho. It was grueling work up there, and wages were pitiful, but when the call came through camp for workers to alleviate the wartime labor shortage, it sounded better than their life at Manzanar. They knew they'd have, if nothing else, a room, perhaps a cabin of their own.

That first night in Block 16, the rest of us squeezed into the second room—Granny, Lillian, age fourteen, Ray, thirteen, May, eleven, Kiyo, ten, Mama, and me. I didn't mind this at all at the time. Being youngest meant I got to sleep with Mama. And before we went to bed I had a great time jumping up and down on the mattress. The boys had stuffed so much straw into hers, we had to flatten it some so we wouldn't slide off. I slept with her every night after that until Papa came back.

A DIFFERENT KIND OF SAND

WE WOKE EARLY, SHIVERING AND COATED WITH DUST THAT HAD blown up through the knotholes and in through the slits around the doorway. During the night Mama had unpacked all our clothes and heaped them on our beds for warmth. Now our cubicle looked as if a great laundry bag had exploded and then been sprayed with fine dust. A skin of sand covered the floor. I looked over Mama's shoulder at Kiyo, on top of his fat mattress, buried under jeans and overcoats and sweaters. His eyebrows were gray, and he was starting to giggle. He was looking at me, at my gray eyebrows and coated hair, and pretty soon we were both giggling. I looked at Mama's face to see if she thought Kiyo was funny. She lay very still next to me on our mattress, her eyes scanning everything—bare rafters, walls, dusty kids— scanning slowly, and I think the mask of her face would have cracked had not Woody's voice just then come at us through the wall. He was rapping on the planks as if testing to see if they were hollow.

"Hey!" he yelled. "You guys fall into the same flour barrel as us?"

"No," Kiyo yelled back. "Ours is full of Japs."

All of us laughed at this.

"Well, tell 'em it's time to get up," Woody said "If we're gonna live in this place, we better get to work."

He gave us ten minutes to dress, then he came in carrying a broom, a hammer, and a sack full of tin canlids he had scrounged somewhere. Woody would be our leader for a while now, short, stocky, grinning behind his mustache. He had just turned twenty-four. In later years he would tour the country with Mr. Moto, the Japanese tag-team wrestler, as his sinister assistant Suki—karate chops through the ropes from outside the ring, a chunky leg reaching from under his kimono to trip up Mr.

Moto's foe. In the ring Woody's smile looked sly and crafty; he hammed it up. Offstage it was whimsical, as if some joke were bursting to be told.

"Hey, brother Ray, Kiyo," he said. "You see these tin can lids?"

"Yeah, yeah," the boys said drowsily, as if going back to sleep. They were both young versions of Woody.

"You see all them knotholes in the floor and in the walls?"

They looked around. You could see about a dozen.

Woody said, "You get those covered up before breakfast time. Any more sand comes in here through one of them knotholes, you have to eat it off the floor with ketchup."

"What about sand that comes in through the cracks?" Kiyo said.

Woody stood up very straight, which in itself was funny, since he was only about five-foot-six.

"Don't worry about the cracks," he said. "Different kind of sand comes in through the cracks."

He put his hands on his hips and gave Kiyo a sternly comic look, squinting at him through one eye the way Papa would when he was asserting his authority. Woody mimicked Papa's voice: "And I can tell the difference. So be careful."

The boys laughed and went to work nailing down lids. May started sweeping out the sand. I was helping Mama fold the clothes we'd used for cover, when Woody came over and put his arm around her shoulder. He was short; she was even shorter, under five feet.

He said softly, "You okay, Mama?"

She didn't look at him, she just kept folding clothes and said, "Can we get the cracks covered too, Woody?"

Outside the sky was clear, but icy gusts of wind were buffeting our barracks every few minutes, sending fresh dust puffs up through the floorboards. May's broom could barely keep up with it, and our oil heater could scarcely hold its own against the drafts.

"We'll get this whole place as tight as a barrel, Mama. I already met a guy who told me where they pile all the scrap lumber."

"Scrap?"

"That's all they got. I mean, they're still building the camp, you know. Sixteen blocks left to go. After that, they say maybe we'll get some stuff to fix the insides a little bit."

Her eyes blazed then, her voice quietly furious. "Woody, we can't live like this. Animals live like this."

It was hard to get Woody down. He'd keep smiling when everybody else was ready to explode. Grief flickered in his eyes. He blinked it away and hugged her tighter. "We'll make it better, Mama. You watch."

We could hear voices in other cubicles now. Beyond the wall Woody's baby girl started to cry.

"I have to go over to the kitchen," he said, "see if those guys got a pot for heating bottles. That oil stove takes too long—something wrong with the fuel line. I'll find out what they're giving us for breakfast."

"Probably hotcakes with soy sauce," Kiyo said, on his hands and knees between the bunks.

"No." Woody grinned, heading out the door. "Rice. With Log Cabin Syrup and melted butter."

A COMMON MASTER PLAN

I DON'T REMEMBER WHAT WE ATE THAT FIRST MORNING. I KNOW we stood for half an hour in cutting wind waiting to get our food. Then we took it back to the cubicle and ate huddled around the stove. Inside, it was warmer than when we left, because Woody was already making good his promise to Mama, tacking up some ends of lath he'd found, stuffing rolled paper around the door frame.

Trouble was, he had almost nothing to work with. Beyond this temporary weather stripping, there was little else he could do. Months went by, in fact, before our "home" changed much at all from what it was the day we moved in—bare floors, blanket partitions, one bulb in each compartment dangling from a roof beam, and open ceilings overhead so that mischievous boys like Ray and Kiyo could climb up into the rafters and peek into anyone's life.

The simple truth is the camp was no more ready for us when we got there than we were ready for it. We had only the dimmest ideas of what to expect. Most of the families, like us, had moved out from southern California with as much luggage as each person could carry. Some old men left Los Angeles wearing Hawaiian shirts and Panama hats and stepped off the bus at an altitude of 4000 feet, with nothing available but sagebrush and tarpaper to stop the April winds pouring down off the back side of the Sierras.

The War Department was in charge of all the camps at this point. They began to issue military surplus from the First World War—olive-drab knit caps, earmuffs, peacoats, canvas leggings. Later on, sewing machines were shipped in, and one barracks was turned into a clothing factory. An old seamstress took a peacoat of mine, tore the lining out, opened and flattened the sleeves, added a collar, put arm holes in and handed me back a beautiful cape. By fall dozens of seamstresses were working full-time transforming thousands of these old army clothes into capes, slacks and stylish coats. But until that factory got going and packages from friends outside began to fill out our wardrobes, warmth was more important than style. I couldn't help laughing at Mama walking around in army earmuffs and a pair of wide-cuffed, khaki-colored wool trousers several sizes too big for her. Japanese are generally smaller than Caucasians, and almost all these clothes were oversize. They flopped, they dangled, they hung.

It seems comical, looking back; we were a band of Charlie Chaplins marooned in the California desert. But at the time, it was pure chaos. That's the only way to describe it. The evacuation had been so hurriedly planned, the camps so hastily thrown together, nothing was completed when we got there, and almost nothing worked.

I was sick continually, with stomach cramps and diarrhea. At first it was from the shots they gave us for typhoid, in very heavy doses and in assembly-line fashion: swab, jab, swab, *Move along now*, swab, jab, swab, *Keep it moving*. That knocked all of us younger kids down at once, with fevers and vomiting. Later, it was the food that made us sick, young and old alike. The kitchens were too small and badly ventilated. Food would spoil from being left out too long. That summer, when the heat got fierce, it would spoil faster. The refrigeration kept breaking down. The cooks, in many cases, had never cooked before. Each block had to provide its own volunteers. Some were lucky and had a professional or two in their midst. But the first chef in our block had been a gardener all his life and suddenly found himself preparing three meals a day for 250 people.

"The Manzanar runs" became a condition of life, and you only hoped that when you rushed to the latrine, one would be in working order.

That first morning, on our way to the chow line, Mama and I tried to use the women's latrine in our block. The smell of it spoiled what little appetite we had. Outside, men were working in an open trench, up to their knees in muck—a common sight in the months to come. Inside, the floor was covered with excrement, and all twelve bowls were erupting like a row of tiny volcanoes.

Mama stopped a kimono-wrapped woman stepping past us with her sleeve pushed up against her nose and asked, "What do you do?"

"Try Block Twelve," the woman said, grimacing. "They have just finished repairing the pipes."

It was about two city blocks away. We followed her over there and found a line of women waiting in the wind outside the latrine. We had no choice but to join the line and wait with them.

Inside it was like all the other latrines. Each block was built to the same design, just as each of the ten camps, from California to Arkansas, was built to a common master plan. It was an open room, over a concrete slab. The sink was a long metal trough against one wall, with a row of spigots for hot and cold water. Down the center of the room twelve toilet bowls were arranged in six pairs, back to back, with no partitions. My mother was a very modest person, and this was going to be agony for her, sitting down in public, among strangers.

One old woman had already solved the problem for herself by dragging in a large cardboard carton. She set it up around one of the bowls, like a three-sided screen. OXYDOL was printed in large black letters down the front. I remember this well, because that was the soap we were issued for laundry; later on, the smell of it would permeate these rooms. The upended carton was about four feet high. The old woman behind it wasn't much taller. When she stood, only her head showed over the top.

She was about Granny's age. With great effort she was trying to fold the sides of the screen together. Mama happened to be at the head of the line now. As she approached the vacant bowl, she and the old woman bowed to each other from the waist. Mama then moved to help her with the carton, and the old woman said very graciously, in Japanese, "Would you like to use it?"

Happily, gratefully, Mama bowed again and said, "*Arigato*" (Thank you). "*Arigato gozaimas*" (Thank you very much). "I will return it to your barracks."

"Oh, no. It is not necessary. I will be glad to wait."

The old woman unfolded one side of the cardboard, while Mama opened the other; then she bowed again and scurried out the door.

Those big cartons were a common sight in the spring of 1942. Eventually sturdier partitions appeared, one or two at a time. The first were built of scrap lumber. Word would get around that Block such and such had partitions now, and Mama and my older sisters would walk halfway across the camp to use them. Even after every latrine in camp was screened, this quest for privacy continued. Many would wait until late at night. Ironically, because of this, midnight was often the most crowded time of all.

Like so many of the women there, Mama never did get used to the latrines. It was a humiliation she just learned to endure: *shikata ga nai*, this cannot be helped. She would quickly subordinate her own desires to those of the family or the community, because she knew cooperation was the only way to survive. At the same time she placed a high premium on personal privacy, respected it in others and insisted upon it for herself. Almost everyone at Manzanar had inherited this pair of traits from the generations before them who had learned to live in a small, crowded country like Japan. Because of the first they were able to take a desolate stretch of wasteland and gradually make it livable. But the entire situation there, especially in the beginning—the packed sleeping quarters, the communal mess halls, the open toilets—all this was an open insult to that other, private self, a slap in the face you were powerless to challenge.

from *In Search of Hiroshi*

Gene Oishi (1933–)

I*n the last chapter of* In Search of Hiroshi, *Gene Oishi describes the inspirational character of Hiroshi as "the whole child . . . he was neither American nor Japanese, but simply me." He began searching for Hiroshi when he started writing about his childhood, which was marked by his internment in the Gila River and Poston detention camps. The following passage describes his life in the camps and the complex issues of loyalty that the internees grappled with while imprisoned.*

Mr. Oishi was born in Guadalupe, California. For most of the years preceding World War II, his father was a prosperous farmer in California's Santa Maria Valley. He attended the University of California at Berkeley, and later began his career as a journalist at the Los Angeles Bureau of the Associated Press in 1963. For many years he wrote and reported for the Baltimore Sun, *as Washington correspondent and bureau chief in Bonn, Germany. His personal essays have been published in* The New York Times Magazine *and* The Los Angeles Times' West Magazine. *In 1981, he delivered a briefing paper to the Commission on the Wartime Relocation and Internment of Civilians. He lives in Baltimore, Maryland, where he works as a public relations specialist for the Maryland State Teachers Association.*

DURING THE FIRST YEAR OF OUR INTERNMENT, THE BURNING ISSUE in the camps was the question of loyalty, whether the Japanese were loyal to Japan or to the United States. Our family, like many others, was split by the issue. My two brothers, Yoshiro and Goro, were pro-American. Simply stated, they wanted America to win the war. My oldest brother Nimashi and my brother-in-law Nobuo were *kibei*—U.S.-born Japanese who were educated in Japan. They joined the Seinen-kai, or young men's association, which was viewed by authorities, and many *nisei,* too, as a bunch of pro-Japanese agitators. When Nimashi or Nobuo made what sounded like an anti-American comment about the war or the loyalty issue, Yoshiro, the most hot-tempered of my brothers, would retort angrily. He would be restrained by Mama from saying more and would go stomping out mumbling under his breath. After a while, Nimashi moved to another block where he lived with friends so we didn't see him anymore. Nobuo, however, continued to live in the next compartment and the relationship between him and Yoshiro was tense.

One morning on the way to school one of my friends pointed to the top of a nearby butte. There unfurled and waving in the wind was the Hinomaru, the flag of Japan. We laughed. We wanted to believe that it was put there as a prank, but we were all uneasy. The thought passed through my mind that Nimashi might have had a hand in it. Shortly after that, Mrs. Smith, our fourth-grade teacher, called me and a girl—I will call her June—to her desk. Mrs. Smith was a tall, slender woman in her late twenties. She often wore dark glasses, something Japanese rarely did, and was always applying lipstick and powdering her face at her desk. She often looked sad, as if she were trying to overcome a personal sorrow. At times, when the children were busy at their places doing an assignment, she would sit at her desk with her head in her hands, as if asking herself, "What in the world am I doing in a place like this?" She seemed a little cold, as if she didn't like us Japanese children very much, which made me wonder, too, why she had come to Gila to teach. She might have been married to one of the administrators who lived in a special white people's compound behind the administration building. That would explain how she knew about Nimashi. Mrs. Smith said to June, "June, I'm so sorry about your father." June nodded her head and might have said something like, "Oh, that's all right, Mrs. Smith." I thought her father had died.

Then Mrs. Smith turned to me and said, "I'm so sorry about your brother." I stood dumbfounded. I had not the slightest idea what she was talking about. "Isn't your brother's name Nimashi?" Mrs. Smith asked. I nodded. "You know, don't you?" she said. "He was arrested last night."

Nobuo was arrested too, and I learned about it only by listening to family conversations, mainly between Hiroko and Mama. Hiroko had another baby shortly after we arrived at Gila and at the time her husband was taken away she was already pregnant with a third. She was normally a cheerful woman who laughed easily, but after Nobuo was arrested her shoulders sagged and she looked tired and worn out. She was the way Mama had been in Guadalupe after the FBI came and took Papa away.

I was aware in a general way of the political controversy raging in the camp. But I didn't talk about it. None of the children did even though we all knew that our older brothers and sisters were arguing about the war, the internment, and what the government had done to us. While still in Guadalupe, I asked my sister Hoshiko, "You want Japan to win or you want America to win?" I don't remember her answer; she probably didn't give me one. I didn't ask such questions in camp because the loyalty question was splitting our family and I was afraid of it. After Nimashi and Nobuo were taken away I was even more wary of the subject.

During our first year at Gila, the government began allowing people to leave the camps for jobs on the outside if they pledged loyalty to the United States. Yoshiro was the first in our family to leave. He went to Detroit where he worked in a factory. About once a month, he sent us a box full of candy bars, which seemed to me like some fabulous treasure chest from the Arabian Nights. He didn't have many friends in Detroit and he was lonely. There were race riots there at the time and once a white mob stopped a bus he was riding and dragged a black passenger out. One of the mob saw my brother and said, "Hey, there's a jap. Let's get him." But the others ran off saying, "Naw, we're after niggers tonight." Shortly after that, Yoshiro volunteered for the Army and was sent to Camp Shelby, Mississippi, where an all-*nisei* combat unit was being trained.

Goro, a pre-med student at Stanford, went to St. Louis, where he worked as a laboratory technician at a hospital. The hospital was run by a religious order of brothers and he got along very well there, but he was drafted after a few months and like Yoshiro sent to Camp Shelby.

After their arrest, Nimashi and Nobuo were sent to a special detention camp in Moab, Utah, and later to another in Leupp, Arizona. Later, Nobuo was allowed to rejoin his family but they were transferred to the Poston, Arizona, camp. None of the so-called "troublemakers" were allowed to return to the camp from which they were removed. Nimashi came to Gila for a brief visit to marry a girl he knew from Guadalupe. After that, he and his bride were sent to the camp at Manzanar, California.

For me, the loyalty question was like a disease that had infected the family and was eating away at it. It had started with Papa being arrested in the middle of the night. Then, in camp, Nimashi and Nobuo were taken away. Yoshiro and Goro went into the Army. Hiroko and her two children left to join Nobuo at Poston. Hoshiko graduated high school and when she was accepted and offered a scholarship by Carlton College in Minnesota, she left too. The family was being scattered and perhaps destroyed and the loyalty issue was somehow at the bottom of it, but I never stopped to sort out precisely why and how. I didn't want to think about it.

Many years after the war, when I began reading about the internment, I was distressed to see how divisive the loyalty question was to the Japanese community. From the point of view of the government, the issue was settled by summarily putting all of us in detention camps. Government officials acknowledged that most Japanese were probably loyal Americans, but they argued that because of Japanese inscrutability there was no reliable way to weed out the disloyal from the loyal. Most assumed as a matter of faith that there were Japanese, both aliens and American citizens, who, given the opportunity, would commit acts of sabotage and espionage, and when there was no evidence of their doing so, it was taken as an ominous sign. Men like Earl Warren, then Attorney General of California, and Walter Lippmann argued that the absence of overt, hostile acts indicated that the Japanese living in the United States were highly disciplined. They were holding back until a Japanese invasion when they could strike with maximum effect.

Because of the immediate arrest of men such as my father, the Japanese community was left leaderless after the outbreak of the war. The leadership devolved by default on the Japanese American Citizens League, which was made up mainly of college-educated, second-generation *nisei*. The league leaders initially opposed proposals for "evacuating" everyone of Japanese ancestry from the West Coast. Caught up in the hysteria of the time, one *nisei* leader, eager to demonstrate Japanese American loyalty, went so far as to propose the creation of a Japanese-American "suicide battalion" to fight in the Pacific. After its initial protests, however, the Japanese American Citizens League accepted the conclusion that "the evacuation" of all Japanese, U.S. citizens and aliens alike, from the West Coast was "a military necessity" and cooperated with the program. It even discouraged legal challenges, arguing that cooperating with "the evacuation" was a way for Japanese Americans to demonstrate their loyalty and to contribute to the war effort. After the Japanese were interned, the league petitioned the government to allow Japanese Americans to volunteer and serve in the armed forces. The league also wanted Americans of Japanese ancestry to be subject to the draft just like everybody else. (After the outbreak of the war, Japanese Americans were no longer drafted and were not allowed to volunteer for the armed forces.)

Such ultra-patriotism, particularly in a concentration-camp setting, was strongly resented by many, even by some who were fundamentally pro-American. There was also strong suspicion that some league leaders were secretly working with camp authorities and informing on groups and individuals espousing what appeared to be anti-American views. Some of them were set upon and beaten. Ultimately, however, Washington agreed to the creation of all-Japanese American combat units to fight in Europe and reopened the Selective Service System to Japanese Americans.

The War Relocation Authority had previously begun a program for releasing at least a portion of the camp population. Japanese were still banned from the West Coast, but they could be settled in the East. One reason for the program was a *habeas corpus* case brought by Mitsye Endo, one of the internees, challenging the constitutionality of the detention. Government attorneys were worried about losing this case and wanted to set up a procedure for "sifting" loyal Japanese Americans from the disloyal so that they would be in a position to demonstrate to the courts that there was a system of due process in place. When the War Department changed its policy on the question of military service the release program was intensified. As a preliminary step, all persons seventeen years and older in the camps were required to fill out a questionnaire. Those who formulated the questions were appallingly insensitive to the extraordinary situation in which the Japanese found themselves. U.S. laws did not allow Japanese immigrants, or any Asian immigrants, to become American citizens. In 1922, the Supreme Court had ruled that naturalization privileges were limited by law to "free white persons and to aliens of African nativity and to persons of African descent." First generation immigrants, *issei,* therefore, could not become American citizens and in spite of that they were asked in the camps to renounce their loyalty to Japan. In effect, to declare themselves stateless persons.

Aside from the loyalty question, most *issei* did not want to leave the camps for the big cities of the East. Even after decades in America most of them spoke little English and had never lived outside of rural or urban Japanese ghettos on the West Coast. The idea of being cast out to fend for themselves in a strange city full of what were probably hostile white people was understandably frightening to them.

As for their children, they were U.S. citizens by birth, but their citizenship, as it turned out, was less important than their race. Now, while placed in camps against their will and in violation of their rights as citizens, they were asked if they were willing "to serve in the Armed Forces of the United States on combat duty wherever ordered." The authorities, moreover, could not resist asking Japanese Americans to "forswear any form of allegiance or obedience to the Japanese emperor, to any other foreign government, power or organization." This was comparable to asking Joe DiMaggio, the son of an Italian immigrant, to forswear allegiance to Mussolini. But even the best intentioned white men of that time had difficulty thinking of people of the yellow race as Americans. That is difficult for many people to do even today.

The questionnaire for *issei* was changed so that they were asked only to abide by the laws of the United States and not interfere with U.S. war efforts. When the *issei* were further assured that there would not be another forced resettlement while the war continued, more than ninety percent of them answered "yes" to the loyalty questions. As for *nisei*, a "yes" answer made them subject to the draft and they had more reason than their alien parents to be resentful about how they were being treated. Nevertheless, more than three quarters of them did pledge their allegiance to the United States. Many of them volunteered for the Army or were drafted and were assigned to the all-*nisei* 442nd Regimental Combat Team. Fighting in Europe, the 442nd and the 100th Battalion—another all-*nisei* unit made up mainly of men from Hawaii—were among the most decorated and bloodied units of the war. Thousands of other Japanese Americans, including many *kibei,* served in the Pacific theater as interpreters and translators and were credited with having given U.S. military intelligence an important advantage over the enemy.

I have compassion today for those *nisei* who answered "no" to the two critical loyalty questions. They were branded as "no-no boys" and viewed as traitors by some of the more zealous pro-American *nisei*. Some, mainly Japanese-educated *kibei,* were openly pro-Japan, but others answered "no" because they could not overcome their sense of betrayal and their resentment over how they were being treated by their government. One embittered World War I veteran renounced his U.S. citizenship, saying he wanted to become "a jap a hundred percent." Others wanted to give conditional answers, such as, "Yes, if my rights as a citizen are restored," or "No, not unless the government recognizes my right to live anywhere in the United States," but the government would only accept unconditional pledges of allegiance and loyalty. A third group answered "no" out of a sense of duty to their parents. At Gila there was a family from Guadalupe with six sons, three of them of draft age. At Guadalupe they had lived isolated on a farm far in the country. The family was different from ours, more old-fashioned and "countryish." The parents were fiercely loyal Japanese, not because they were any more patriotic than my parents, but because all their basic relationships were more intense. Even by Japanese standards they were an extremely close-knit family. I could not imagine any of them taking a course of action that would have separated them from their parents or from each other. All of them answered "no" to the loyalty questions. Many years after the war, I visited the family at their farm in California, but we did not talk about Gila. I was doing research on Japanese in the United States and I would have liked to have asked them why they answered "no." But I could not get myself to intrude on their privacy, and besides I already knew the reasons. They answered "no" because they could not repudiate their parents, who were loyal Japanese. Whatever fate was in store for them, they would endure it together as a family. From Gila, the family was sent to a camp at Tule Lake, California, which was designated as the camp for "disloyals." At some camps "loyal" *nisei,* many of them preparing to be inducted into the Army, taunted the departing "disloyals" saying such things as, "Go on, you dirty japs. We'll kill you the next time we see you."

My brother Nimashi, like my brother-in-law, ended up answering "yes" to the loyalty questions. When I asked him years later why, he said, "Because I didn't want to go to Tule Lake." At the time, many people thought that those who were sent to Tule Lake would be deported to Japan after the war. Some were.

Many *nisei,* especially the super patriots, assumed at the time that all or most *kibei* were anti-American and pro-Japan. It was not as simple as that. Nimashi, who in many ways was a typical *kibei,* saw much that was attractive about America and the American way of life. But his English was not fluent and he spoke with a heavy accent. The *nisei* could dream of one day being accepted as Americans, but the *kibei* saw themselves as permanent outsiders. Nimashi's hero was not John Wayne or James Stewart, it was George Raft, the quintessential anti-hero who operated outside the pale of society. It was infinitely more difficult for a *kibei* to say yes to America and no to Japan, when in his heart he knew that America did not want him and probably never would.

In 1982, while working on a magazine article about the Japanese in the United States, I interviewed a researcher on the staff

of the U.S. Commission on Wartime Relocation and Internment of Civilians, which was created by Congress to reexamine
the forced relocation of Japanese and Aleuts during World War
II. In the course of our talk, I mentioned that my brother Nimashi was arrested at Gila for joining what authorities thought
was a pro-Japanese organization and sent to a special detention
camp in Utah. Whereupon, the researcher took out a slim,
official-looking volume from the shelf, and asked, "What was
your brother's name? Nimashi? Let's see. . . . Here's an entry
. . . Oishi, Nimashi, granted leave to visit family. . . ." I didn't
hear much more than that; I was stunned. My brother's name
was being read out of government records that had been kept
in the 1940s at a World War II detention camp. When I didn't
show any interest, the researcher changed the subject and began
talking about other matters. I thought I was getting sick and
tried to find an excuse for breaking off the interview and leaving
when, suddenly, I began to cry. The researcher, a kindly sympathetic woman, did not seem at all alarmed. "That's all right,"
she said. "It happens all the time." She walked to the door and
closed it, returned to her desk and continued chatting until I
was able to regain control of myself. Such a thing had never
happened to me before, and I was embarrassed about my mo-
mentary breakdown. But it was also good to know, even forty
years later, that I was emotionally affected by the arrest of my
brother and the tension that surrounded it. I began to see that
the most important aspect of my research was not the knowledge and understanding I gained about the internment, but my
emotional reaction to it. I could finally shed those tears that I
could not shed as a child.

Soon after we arrived at Gila, our family began to petition the
government to "parole" Papa, who was being held in an Army
camp in Missoula, Montana. Every member of the family wrote
a personal letter and I was also asked to write one, which I did
without enthusiasm. My family was very upset with me.
"Don't you want Papa back with us?" they asked. "Sure, I do,"
I said. But I was lying. My father, in my eyes, had been a huge
and powerful presence. The whole family, perhaps even the
whole world, trembled before him. Yet, when the war started,

he was plucked out of our house by two FBI agents like a feather. I did not want to see him again.

My father was finally "paroled" around the middle of the second year of our internment and he was allowed to join us at Gila. He was much changed, more quiet and less temperamental. He was sixty years old and for the first time he struck me as an old man. He occupied his time playing *go*, a Japanese board game, and practicing *joruri*. From time to time some ladies in our block would come to our compartment and my father would sing for them some tragic story of noble sacrifice. While he chanted the ladies would take out their handkerchiefs and dab their eyes.

By the time my father joined us at Gila, the political controversy had died down. Most of the young activists were gone— to the Army, to jobs on the outside, and, in the case of the "troublemakers," to other detention camps. That was no doubt the reason the authorities allowed my father and other former community leaders to rejoin their families. It was mainly children and old folks who remained in the camps and life settled to a quiet existence. There were Kabuki performances, *go* tournaments, and art exhibits, mainly of ironwood sculptures. The children played baseball and football and explored the desert.

I had expected the desert to be hot and dry so I wondered when we first got to Gila why there were oil heaters in every compartment. With the onset of winter, the reason for them became clear. At night, it got freezing cold and in the morning everything was covered with frost. It did not rain often, but when it did, it rained as I had never seen it rain before. Storm clouds rolled in quickly with thunder and lightning that left a sooty smell in the air. Then the rain would come pouring down. It did not start with a few sprinkles and grow slowly as it did in Guadalupe, but fell immediately in torrents. Once I was caught in the middle of a firebreak when it started to rain and suddenly I was knee-deep in water. The field looked like a churning lake. Wading home I stepped into a trench and found myself up to my chest in water. I finally made it back to our compartment drenched but feeling rather proud of myself.

The desert was like that, a little scary but challenging. It made you feel you accomplished something when you learned to get around in it. Once we got used to our surroundings, my friends and I went exploring. We flushed brightly colored desert birds out of the brush, caught horned toads, swam in the irrigation canal, and climbed the buttes. Some of the older boys went into the desert in the early evening to hunt rattlesnakes for fun. Sometimes one of them would come back holding the head of a diamondback that was wrapped around his arm. You could hear the buzzing sound made by the rattles from one end of the block to the other.

It was my brother Goro who first took me out into the desert. We often climbed one of the buttes in the evening to watch the sunset. Goro was twenty-two, twelve years older than I, but we had some wonderful talks. Goro was quiet and the most bookish of my brothers and sisters. He was shy with adults, but he loved to talk and play games with children. In one game we played, I pretended I was playing "I Dream of Jeannie with the Light Brown Hair" on a violin and Goro would clutch his heart and pretend he was in ecstasy, saying, "Oh, oh, I can't stand it." But he could be serious, too. Once, while sitting on top of the butte, he explained to me why the people in China were not upside down and his explanation helped me understand gravity as I never had before. He would also try out some of his social theories on me. Christianity, he once told me, was really not a religion in America; it was more of a social sort of thing. When I repeated this theory as best I could to Yoshiro, he laughed and said, "That Goro, he's sure a crazy guy."

We lived close to the edge of camp and the block directly behind us was empty. In one of the barracks were piles of books, mainly used textbooks donated by various groups on the outside. My friends and I would climb through a window of the locked barrack to browse. Most of the books were Dick and Jane type readers and were of little interest. But I did find one volume called *The Golden Treasury of Verse*. I took the book back to the compartment and showed it to Goro, who was delighted with my prize. We read many of the poems together. Goro particularly liked "Annabel Lee" by Edgar Allan Poe, which he recited with great feeling. Then I would recite it and Goro would clutch his heart just as he did when I pretended to play a violin. We also read "The Village Blacksmith" by Henry Wadsworth Longfellow and "O Captain! My Captain!" by Walt Whitman. The three poems remained my favorites and I read them over and over again after Goro left. They sounded like faraway voices calling me.

In college I majored in literature and read a lot of poetry, but I never again developed a relationship with a poem as I did in Gila with my brother and that stolen book. When I read those poems today, it is clear that what appealed to me was the sense of loss they conveyed: a lost love, a lost father, a lost way of life. The poem I understood least well, but which thrilled me the most was Whitman's. It spoke of "My Captain" who is also "My father," a conquering hero, who, having completed a fearful mission, lies on the deck of his ship, "fallen cold and dead." I mourned this fallen man secretly and it seemed to give me some comfort. I wondered uneasily whether the good feeling this poem gave me meant I wanted my own father dead.

The school was housed in barracks in the middle of the camp and had a faculty that was about equally divided between whites and Japanese. The principal at the elementary school was Mr. Strickland, a tall, gaunt man with thinning brown hair and an eagle nose. One day he came into our fifth-grade class to lead us in singing and before he left he taught us this song:

> I ain't got no use for women,
> A true one is seldom to be found,
> They'll use a man for his money,
> When he's flat they'll turn him down.
>
> They're all alike at the bottom,
> Selfish and grasping for all,
> They'll stay by a man while he's winning,
> And laugh at his face at his fall.

Mr. Strickland came into our class a couple of more times to lead us in singing, and each time we also sang "I ain't got no use for women." The girls, of course, didn't like it, and even the boys thought it was a strange song to sing in school, but Mr. Strickland sang it with gusto and waved his long arms like a symphonic conductor as he led the class in singing it. I don't know whether there was a Mrs. Strickland, but in later years when I thought about Gila and Mr. Strickland I imagined that he was a man whose heart had been broken by a woman and who had gone to Gila to escape from his sorrows, just as some men join the French Foreign Legion to hide from their past.

Mr. Strickland, despite his apparent disdain for women, was a kind and outgoing man who seemed to have a genuine liking for us. Around the second year at Gila a school mess hall was opened where we children had lunch. The food there was better than what we got at our block mess hall and we were given second helpings, which we ate like stolen bread, for nobody in any of the other mess halls got second helpings. Once a week there was even ice cream, made with cream, sugar, and dry ice, that Mr. Strickland somehow provided. I assumed that the school mess hall was Mr. Strickland's doing, too, for he made it a point to eat with us, unlike the other white teachers who went to their quarters for lunch.

My school days in Gila were happy ones, but there was one bitter moment. The physical education teacher, a young *nisei* man, had organized us into a Cub Scout troop and he was going to take us to a boys' camp at Prescott, which was in a wooded area to the north of us. We looked forward to the trip for days, but it was canceled because the people in Prescott did not want Japanese there. We had nearly forgotten why we were at Gila in the first place. We had begun to think that we were like everybody else, playing football, having track meets, joining the Cub Scouts. With the cancellation of the Prescott trip we were confronted again with the reality of our internment. We grumbled among ourselves about it, saying things like, "*Hakujin* people are dumb," and "*Hakujin* people really hate us."

Long after the war, I learned that among the white people in the camps were anthropologists who were sent to study the Japanese so that the government would have better insight into the enemy mentality. Some of them, and perhaps other white people, too, brought their families along. There was one white boy at Gila who came to school wearing a hunting knife on his belt. We Japanese children assumed he wore it to protect himself against us. His family either left Gila or the boy was sent away because he stopped coming to school after the first year. We were glad to be rid of him. He and his knife were a constant reminder of what some white people thought of us.

When my father, my mother, and I were the only ones left from our family at Gila, we were allowed to transfer to Poston, where my sister Hiroko and her family were. The desert surrounding Poston was not nearly as beautiful as Gila. Unlike Gila with its red and white barracks, Poston had the same tar-papered barracks as Tulare. The people had planted castor and other bushes and flowers, but none of that could overcome the oppressive ugliness of the black, smutty tar paper.

The Colorado River was seven miles away, but by the time I got to Poston most of the children had already been there several times and did not want to make the long hike again. They said the river was dangerous, with strong undercurrents, and one boy had drowned swimming in it. But the main reason why the river was not as attractive as it might have been was that there was a swimming pool at Poston. It was actually a small reservoir the people had made by digging an L-shaped hole in the ground and diverting water to it from an irrigation canal. It had high and low diving boards, wooden railings, and a rough-hewn pavilion with benches for people who wanted to just sit and watch. During my two summers in Poston, every day was spent at the pool where we dove for pennies, played tag, and even wrestled in deep water.

Food was served "family style" at Poston. Each family was assigned a table and the food was brought to the tables by girls serving as waitresses, so there was no standing in line. My mother got a job as a dishwasher, for which she was paid $16 a month. I don't think the amount made much of a difference to her. She simply liked the idea of getting paid for her work. When she got her first paycheck, she said, "I don't want to cash it. I want to keep it forever. I've been working all my life and this is the first time anybody has paid me." Working in the mess hall had other benefits. From time to time she brought home leftover milk, bread, and apple butter. The milk soured quickly in the heat and it made me a little nauseous but I drank it anyway. In Poston I gained back much of the weight I lost at Gila.

Goro, after he finished his basic training, came to visit us at Poston. He looked good in his Army uniform and a lot stronger. We went on walks by the irrigation canal and he would tell me about Camp Shelby. "You know, in Mississippi," he said, "if you talk to a Negro guy, a *hakujin* will come and tap you on the shoulder and say, 'Hey, don't talk to those guys.'" Goro used swear words, something he had never done before. About the strongest expression he used before he went into the Army was "holy mackerel," but now he peppered his talk with "goddamn" and "son-of-a-bitch." Once, while we were on a walk, Goro said, "You know, it's kids like you who are suffering the most from this experience. You have to spend your formative years in a camp in the desert. For Yosh and me it doesn't matter that much. Our characters are already formed, but you, you're missing a lot. If I were you, I'd sue the goddamn government for a million dollars after the war."

Goro was known as "the joker" in the family because he was always saying amusing things in his quiet way. I thought he might be making another one of his jokes, but he was very serious. After he left, I thought about what he said, especially the words, "formative years," which sounded deep and full of complicated meaning. Long after the war I asked Goro if he remembered telling me those things and he laughed and said he had no recollection of it.

In Poston, I was twelve years old, in the third year of the internment, and Goro made me think more about what the government had done to us. I memorized the Gettysburg Address, in part for the fun of it because I remembered Goro going around the house in Guadalupe, with his chest out, saying very solemnly, "Fourscore and seven years ago . . ." But I memorized it mainly because I liked the words. I did not understand some parts of it, but I could understand the founding of "a new nation, conceived in liberty and dedicated to the proposition that all men are created equal." When I told Mrs. Evans, our sixth-grade teacher, that I knew the Gettysburg Address by heart, she had me recite it in front of the class.

Several weeks later, when President Roosevelt died, Mrs. Evans asked me to recite the Gettysburg Address at a special memorial service we were having at the school. I agreed to do it, but as the time for the service approached I became increasingly troubled by the idea. I could not see any connection between what Lincoln said during the Civil War and President Roosevelt's death. I went to Mrs. Evans to tell her I didn't want to recite the Gettysburg Address because it did not make any sense at a service for President Roosevelt. Mrs. Evans argued that it did, but could not persuade me to change my mind.

At the service the children from both the elementary and high school gathered outside with each class standing together in rows as in a military formation. As I listened to the speeches I was glad I was not taking part in the ceremonies. It made me uncomfortable to hear Japanese students delivering eulogies. President Roosevelt might have been a great man and a great president, but he was the one who had put us in the camp. I experienced no sorrow at his death; I felt no emotion whatsoever.

When the war ended, Poston began gradually to empty. In the block next to ours a family of Hopi Indians moved into one of the barracks. They had chickens and a pair of goats in a makeshift pen made of chicken wire. They were very friendly people and allowed us children to pat the goats. One of my friends took the teat of the she-goat and squirted milk at me. I thought the owners would be upset, but they only laughed. The grandfather of the family liked to talk to us and he told us how the white man had taken their land away. One day, he said, there would be a great Indian uprising and they would take all the land back. Later, other Indian families began to move into the camp and sometimes late at night you could hear an Indian brave shouting what might have been a war chant at the top of his lungs. It seems eerie when I think back on our final days in Poston, on a community of imprisoned Japanese beginning to scatter, the barracks taking on a look of deterioration as the desert reasserted its claim, and the Hopi Indians, the true owners of the land, gathering slowly, prophesying war. Toward the end of our stay I thought I could hear coyotes howling at night.

The government began a resettlement program and helped my brother-in-law Nobuo get a job in Los Angeles as a truck driver for a paint company. After several weeks, he was able to rent an apartment in a housing project in nearby Long Beach where the rest of us joined him. And so, in late summer of 1945, three years after it began, our internment ended.

from *QUIET ODYSSEY:*
A PIONEER KOREAN WOMAN IN AMERICA

Mary Paik Lee (1900–   )

edited with an introduction by
Sucheng Chan

I*n the following excerpt from* Quiet Odyssey, *Mary Paik Lee describes the struggles of her Korean American family during the early 1910s in Northern California. During this period, Korean Americans were too few in number to develop their own communities, unlike Chinese and Japanese Americans who were able to help each other in many ways. Social and economic isolation combined with severe discrimination against Asian Americans, forced her family to live an itinerant, financially impoverished existence. Consequently, the author was forced to assume adult responsibilities at a young age.* Quiet Odyssey *won the 1991 Outstanding Book Award in History and Social Science from the Association for Asian American Studies.*

Ms. Paik Lee's memoir spans most of the twentieth century, from her birth in Pyongyang, Korea, in 1900 through the 1980s. At the age of five, she immigrated with her family to Hawaii, and then a year and a half later to Riverside, California. She began working at the age of eleven as a maid, to help her family, and continued to work until she was eighty-five. Despite laboring long and arduous hours as a youth, she managed to be educated in American public schools. After her marriage to H. M. Lee, she and her husband farmed, sold produce, and managed apartments together. She is now retired and lives in San Francisco.

Sucheng Chan is professor of history and Asian American studies at the University of California, Santa Barbara.

CLAREMONT AND COLUSA

We lived in Riverside for four or five years, but Father became concerned about Mother's health—the work of cooking for thirty men was too much for her. She was a small woman, only four feet eleven inches tall, and she was expecting another baby. So we paid off the Chinese merchants who had helped us get started, paid all our debts to friends, and moved to Claremont, not too far away. It was a quiet college town with many school buildings. We moved into a duplex building, where an old friend, Martha Kim, was living with her parents. It was across the street from the railroad station and a huge citrus-packing house. Those were the days before frozen fruit juices, so after the choice fruit was packed, the culls were piled up in boxes in back of the buildings to be taken to the dump once a week. Because of this, we were fortunate that we could enjoy all the discarded fruit.

Our move to Claremont turned out to be our first experience with the American way of living. The new house seemed huge after our little shack. It had several rooms with beds, chairs, and other furniture. The kitchen had a gas stove, electric lights, and a sink with faucets for cold and hot water. But all that was as nothing compared with what we found in the bathroom. There was a big white tub with faucets at one end—I couldn't believe it was the place for taking our baths. And the biggest surprise of all was the toilet. Father flushed it to show us how it operated. He must have seen these wonders before somewhere, because he wasn't surprised at anything. For the first time, I felt glad that we had come to America.

Father found a job as a janitor in the nearby apartment buildings. He told Meung and me to ask the tenants if we could do their laundry, and also to ask our schoolteachers the same thing. On foot, Meung had to pick up the dirty laundry in a big basket and return it later. I helped with the laundry before and after school and with the ironing at night. In Claremont we had our first experience with an electric iron. Before this we had heated the old "sad irons," as they were called in those days, on the wood stove. It was such a relief to use the electric iron. No more going back and forth to the wood stove for a hot iron. No more kerosene lamps, hunting for firewood, and outhouses.

Life was getting better. Every Saturday Father bought a beef roast, and every Sunday we had pot roast with mashed potatoes and bread. This was our introduction to American food, and it tasted wonderful. A small group of Koreans lived in Claremont. They came together to worship on Sundays in an old building. There was no minister, so Father preached there several times. Arthur was born in Claremont on December 2, 1910. The memory of our short stay there is a pleasant one.

Unfortunately Father's wages were so low in Claremont that it was difficult to make a living. So, a year later, we moved to Colusa in northern California, hoping to find work there. It turned out we had made a disastrous move. Father could not find any kind of work. There was a depression in 1911, and the situation was so bad the Salvation Army offered a bowl of soup and a piece of bread to each hungry person in town. But when I asked if we could go and get some, Father said no. He didn't want us to be humiliated by asking for help.

The feeling towards Orientals in southern California had not been friendly, but we had been tolerated. In the northern part of the state, we found the situation to be much worse. Although we found a house on the outskirts of town, the townspeople's attitude towards us was chilling. Father told Meung and me to ask our schoolteachers for their laundry. Once again, Meung had to fetch and deliver, carrying a basket on foot. Since we lived on the outskirts of town, it was a hard job for him, but he never complained. But because of the negative feeling towards Orientals in Colusa, we never got enough clothes to launder, and we could not earn enough money to meet our needs.

After paying the rent, light, water, and other bills, we had very little left over for food. Mother would tell me to buy a five-pound sack of flour, a small can of baking powder, salt, and two cans of Carnation milk for the baby. The two cans of milk had to last for one week: it was diluted with so much water, it didn't look like anything nourishing. Mother made tiny biscuits each morning and served one biscuit and a tin cup of water to each of us three times a day. During the time we lived in Colusa, we had no rice, meat, or anything besides biscuits to eat. Nonetheless, when we sat down to eat, Father would pray, thanking God for all our blessings. This used to irritate me. At the age of eleven years, I couldn't think of anything to be thankful for. Once he was sitting out on the porch smoking after dinner, and I asked him what we had to be so thankful for. He said, "Don't you remember why we came here?" I had forgotten that the fate of our family in Korea was much worse than ours. Nevertheless, my stomach ached for lack of food, and I had severe cramps. One evening the pain was so bad I got up to fill myself with water, which helped somewhat. As I neared the kitchen, I saw Father and Mother sitting across from each other at the table holding hands, with tears flowing down their faces. I realized then how much agony they were suffering, and that my own feelings were as nothing compared with theirs. I had been so absorbed in myself that the thought of my parents' suffering had never entered my mind. Seeing them that way made me realize how ignorant I was. It awakened me to the realities of life.

I thought maybe I could get work cleaning someone's home to help out. Since my schoolteacher was the only one I could talk to, I asked her if she knew where I could get housework. She said that the principal lived in a big house, that his wife might need someone to help her. So I went to the principal and asked if his wife needed someone to do the cleaning in his home. He said that he would find out and let me know.

The next day I went to his office and found out that his wife was willing to try me. She said I should work before and after school, and all day Saturdays and Sundays. The wages were to be one dollar a week. In my ignorance, that sounded good to me. I asked where he lived and walked past it on my way home. It was a big, beautiful house, quite far from ours, with a large lawn in front and colorful flowers all around. When I told Father about it, he shook his head and didn't say a word. As if he didn't know it, I said that one dollar would buy twenty loaves of bread, and that it would help feed the younger children who were hungry. Bread cost five cents a loaf then. He said it was too much work for me, but I could try it. Father left the room and went outside to smoke his pipe. Many years later, he told me he had felt humiliated to hear his eleven-year-old daughter tell him that her one-dollar-a-week wages were needed to feed the family. I was too young and ignorant to know how my words had hurt him.

I was totally ignorant of what my employers expected of me,

but I was stubborn enough to make the attempt. My secret reason for wanting this job was that I was hoping to get something more than a tiny biscuit and water to eat, but my punishment came in an unexpected way. Before I left home in the morning, Father gave me advice about how I was to behave in my first American home. He showed me how to set a table with napkins, and so forth. He said I should eat in the kitchen, never with the family. I left home at 6 A.M., reached the principal's house before 7 A.M., and was surprised to see his wife. She looked like the pictures of the fat lady in the circus—a huge woman. I also met her son, who was about twenty years old. I helped the woman prepare breakfast and I set the table. Before they sat down to eat, she gave me a cup of black coffee with no sugar, milk, or cream, and she took the trouble to slice a piece of bread so thin that, when I held it up to the light of the window, I could see the outline of the tree outside. That was about the same amount of food I would have had at home. I had to laugh at myself.

After the family finished eating, I cleared the table, washed the dishes, and cleaned up in the kitchen. Then I had to walk to school while the principal drove in his car. His son had a car also. Very few people in town owned cars, so two cars in one home was certainly unusual. When I told Father about it, he said that it *was* surprising, considering the low salaries of teachers. About fifteen years later, as I was passing a newsstand, I saw the principal's name in the headline of a paper. I stopped to read it. The article stated that Mr. So-and-So had been arrested for embezzling school funds. This had apparently been going on for years. No wonder he had a big, beautiful home and two cars in the family.

After school I went back to the principal's house, helped his wife prepare dinner, and set the table. Then I cleaned the other rooms while dinner was being prepared. She gave me a piece of bread and a few spoons of this and that for my meal. When I cleared the table, she put all the leftovers in dishes, covered them tightly, and put them in the ice box. I guess she was afraid I would eat their food. After washing the dishes and cleaning up the kitchen, I was told I could leave.

On Saturdays, I had to wash all the sheets, pillowcases, towels, and clothes in a big washtub, scrubbing them on a washboard in the backyard, rinsing them, hanging them on a line to dry, and taking them into the house after they were dry. There were no washing machines in those days. Everything had to be done by hand. On Sunday mornings, I sprinkled all the clothes that needed ironing and ironed all day. By nightfall, I was so tired I could hardly walk home. I had to admit to myself that the work was too much for me. Finally, summer vacation came. Father said that he was going to Dinuba, near Fresno, to work in the fruit orchards there to try to make some money. Thus, I should stay home and help Mother while he was away. I was really glad to have an excuse to quit my job. After that, I learned to listen to my elders and not to be such a stubborn fool over things I knew nothing about.

One day we heard music outside the house. Looking out the window, we saw a small truck painted in bright colors with a big picture of an ice cream cone filled with white ice cream. All my younger brothers had their faces pressed against the window, wondering what the truck was. We had never tasted ice cream. Seeing so many children, the man thought that surely someone would come out to buy from him. After waiting several minutes, he gave up and left. The children looked around at Father with questions in their eyes, not daring to say a word. That must have been an agonizing moment for my parents. I looked at their sad, desperate faces and felt sorry for them. Father asked all of us to come into the kitchen and sit down at the table. He took out all the money he had and said that we were not earning enough money to buy everything we wanted, and that we had to pay for several things before we could even buy food to eat. Picking up a few coins, he said, "We have to save this much every week in order to pay the rent for this house, otherwise the owner will not let us live here. Then we have to pay so much for the electric lights, gas for the stove, water, and laundering supplies. That is why we cannot buy enough food to eat three times a day. There is nothing left for such things as ice cream cones." It was a lesson in economics that even a five-year-old child could understand. There were five children in the family then, and ice cream cones cost five cents apiece. Twenty-five cents was a lot of money when one did not have it. From then on, the children never looked out the window when the music sounded, and the ice cream man

never stopped at our house. The children never asked for anything after that.

When Father left for Dinuba, Mother, Meung, and I tried to
keep going as usual, but we could not do any better. We still
had just one biscuit with a cup of water three times a day. Father
came back from Dinuba in September, looking so sick and tired
it was pitiful. We were shocked at his appearance and wished
he had not left home. After paying for his room, board, and the
train fare home, there was little left over, but he said he had just
enough for us to move out of Colusa.

ROBERTS ISLAND

WHILE FATHER WAS WORKING IN DINUBA, HE MET A FRIEND, A
Mr. Kim, who was looking for someone to help him on a farm
that raised potatoes. They made plans to grow Burbank potatoes
on Roberts Island, a big island in the Sacramento-San Joaquin
Delta. So in 1912 we took the train to Stockton, where we
boarded a small motor boat and traveled for several hours to
Roberts Island. We didn't have much to take with us, only our
bedding and a few kitchen utensils and clothes. It was a relief
to leave Colusa, even though we didn't know where we were
going. But, as Mother always said, God was surely leading us
to the right place. Moving to Roberts Island saved our lives and
prevented our starving to death.

The motorboat ride was exciting. We saw many trees but
very few houses along the banks of the river. After several
hours, the boat stopped, and the crew put up a plank of wood
so we could land. As I walked up the plank, I looked at a branch
on a nearby tree and saw a green snake staring at me. That was
our welcome to the farm, an indication of things to come.

We had never seen a vegetable farm before. It looked like a
heavenly paradise to us. Fish jumped up and down in the river,
and the banks were full of various vegetables growing wild
from seeds scattered by former farmers. We had plenty to eat
and to be really thankful for. The farmhouse was an ancient,
wooden two-story building, barely standing. There was also a
big old barn with some hay in it, a few chickens, rats, and
numerous snakes. All of a sudden we were in a new world. We

felt alive and eager to see everything. The younger children ran towards the barn, but they stopped suddenly. They just stood there, looking in. I wondered why and went to see for myself. Their noisy approach had startled the creatures living there: rats and snakes of all sizes and kinds were running around trying to avoid one another in their haste to leave the barn. It was our first look at such wildlife. The sight fascinated as well as frightened us. We backed off to join our parents, who were more interested in the old house. They were trying to figure out how to arrange things to make it comfortable for everyone. Father told us children that Mr. Kim would arrive in a day or two with twenty single men to work on the farm and all the groceries we needed for cooking. The kitchen and dining areas took about two-thirds of the ground floor of the house; the rest of the space became our bedroom. We were back to using kerosene lamps, a water pump outside, and outhouses, but the house was about twice the size of our old shack in Riverside.

We were so hungry that we pulled up the vegetables growing on the banks, washed them at the pump, then cooked and ate everything. It felt good to have something solid to chew on. Father found some white butcher string and some old fish hooks. He said he would show us how to catch fish. He cut a long, slim branch from the willow tree, tied the string to the branch's tip, and tied the hook to the other end of the string. Then he dug up enough worms to fill a coffee can and put one of the worms on the hook. An old rowboat belonging to the farm was tied with a long rope to a tree. He told us to sit in the boat and to let the worm fall into the river. In a few seconds there was a pull on the line. We saw a big grey-black catfish coming up at the end of the string. It was our first sight of a live fish—a very exciting moment. Father told Meung to take the fish off the hook and to put another worm on it. A large grey cat living on the farm jumped into the rowboat and sat on the back seat as we were fishing. When Meung pulled up his fish, the cat stood up, trying to grab it. Meung took the fish off the hook and put it in an old bucket that was in the boat. The cat tried to eat it. It must have been very hungry, because although there were plenty of rats around, they were so big and strong the cat was afraid of them and never went near the barn.

When Meung took the fish out of the bucket and gave it to the cat, she ate it right away.

The river seemed to be crowded with fish that kept jumping up as though looking for something to eat. I didn't want to put my hand in a can full of worms, so Father made some dough with flour and water. He told me to make a small ball like a marble with it and press it over the hook. The fish didn't seem to care what they ate: they liked my bait just as well as the worms. It didn't take long to catch enough for our supper. Father made an open fire, put a piece of chicken wire over it, and cooked the fish for dinner. We also had lettuce, celery, and carrots that grew along the river banks. What a wonderful experience after our ordeal in Colusa! We all felt happy again.

Though vegetables grew wild on the property, the only trees in the area were the willow trees growing along the river banks, which were too green to use for firewood. Father said he would have to buy wood by the cord. Whenever we ordered wood, a loaded barge came by and threw the logs on the river bank. Then we had to pile them up outside the kitchen door.

Father solved the problem of our beds just as he had in Riverside. He built shelves along the walls, gathered hay from the barn, put blankets over the hay, rolled up some old clothes for pillows—and those became the children's beds. Our parents slept on the floor. We used a big old tin tub on the property for our bathtub. We had to heat the water in a bucket on a fire outside the house. We never had toothbrushes or toothpaste— just a spoonful of salt and our forefinger for a brush. Perhaps because we didn't have sugar in the house, no one ever had toothaches or any other dental problems.

There was no furniture in the house. Upstairs, where the men were going to sleep, there were no beds. Father said twenty men would have just enough room to sleep on the floor with their blankets. After all the excitement of the day, the little children were tired, so we heated the water for their baths and prepared for bed.

As I stretched my legs on my shelf bed, I felt a cold, rough object against my toes. I threw back the blanket and saw a red snake coiled up. It was as surprised as I was and slithered off outside. After that, we always pounded our beds with a long stick before jumping in. Then I woke up one night feeling a sharp pain on my nose and found myself staring at two black, beady eyes. I screamed. Father came running to see what was wrong. A big rat about the size of a baby kitten had tried to eat my nose. No wonder the cat was afraid of the rats.

The morning after we arrived, Meung and I got up early and caught enough catfish for our breakfast. Then we looked into the problem of cooking for twenty men. The house evidently had been occupied by Chinese before we came. There were big cast-iron pots, pans, and a Chinese-style *wok*—all the heavy equipment they had not wanted to take with them. It was our good fortune to find almost everything we needed to get started. Mr. Kim and his friends arrived that afternoon with the supplies we needed for cooking—rice, soy sauce, and so forth. Suddenly there was a crowd. We had so much to do! Everyone helped. We filled all the huge wine barrels with water from the pump so the red clay from the river could settle before we drank it or cooked with it. Some men went fishing so there would be enough to eat for several days; others helped clean up everything around the house and barn and chased all the rats and snakes away; yet others cleaned the outhouse. There were a few chickens, so the men made a place for them to lay their eggs; but we had to watch them and get their eggs before the snakes did. After a while, the big rats and snakes stayed away. Maybe they came back at night, but we seldom saw them during the day. Some men started a garden, planting corn, cucumbers, Chinese cabbage, and watermelons.

To ensure a regular supply of fish, Father made a fish trap with a bushel basket. He put chicken wire around it, made an opening on top, then tied a rope around it and attached it to a tree. He put several fish heads and scraps in the basket, stood in the rowboat, and threw it into the river. I always got up early to pull it out, curious to see what had been caught during the night. There were several other kinds of fish besides catfish, small crabs, and lobsters. On weekends, some of the men took the rowboat somewhere to dig clams. Once, Meung caught a striped bass about a foot long. It tasted better than catfish, but that species rarely came our way.

At harvest time, when more men were needed, the extra help stayed in tents. I remember one man had a guitar; it was the first time we ever had seen such a thing. Father sometimes hired twenty or so Sikhs to help us with the harvest. They would sit around a large pot of melted butter and garlic, dipping into it with tortillas made of flour and water. The children had the job of weeding and irrigating plants in the garden. Mother and I were relieved to find that she would not have to pack lunches for the men. The field was close by, so they could come home for lunch. Plenty of good food helped all of us to recover our strength, and there was much to be thankful for.

Meung and I went to school on the other side of Roberts Island. One teacher taught all eight grades, and the whole school had only about thirty children. The teacher came to school on horseback. She looked very young, about eighteen or twenty years old. We noticed that the boys and some of the girls were barefoot, so we asked Father if we could go barefoot, too. We said our shoes were getting worn out. He told us it was all right if the others were also barefoot. The soft soil on the island, known as peat, didn't have rocks or anything in it to hurt our feet. It felt so good to walk without shoes.

One evening Father woke us up in the middle of the night and told us to hurry, put on our clothes, and come to the river bank. He wanted us to see something wonderful that happened only once a year, in June. We rushed up the bank and looked down at a mass of shining silver glittering in the moonlight. At first we were so startled we couldn't tell what we were looking at. A solid silvery mass completely covered the water. Our cat, who was with us, of course, seemed to know what it was. She went berserk at the sight. She ran down the bank, jumped on top of the silvery mass, and ran back and forth over to the little island in the middle of the river. Then we could see that a mass of very large fish were so jammed together that the water was hidden from view. Father said they were shad coming from the ocean to spawn in the river. He had brought a long pole with a chicken-wire basket that looked like a huge soup ladle tied to one end. The pressure of the fish had pushed our rowboat halfway up the bank. Father stood at the end of the boat and forced the pole into the water. He brought up several huge white fish and dropped them in the boat. He told us to go get some men to help us. He had evidently prepared everything for this occasion. The men laid the fish on a long board, rubbed off their scales and took out the roe, which was large and long. Then they filleted the fish and cut them into pieces about three inches wide. The roe and fish were carefully laid in wine barrels, where Mother salted them. This went on all night until several barrels were filled.

The salted roe is a favorite Korean delicacy, served with a special hot sauce. Before cooking, the fillets are soaked in water to reduce the salt content. Then they are drained dry and cooked over an open fire. They are very delicious, and we enjoyed them all that year on Roberts Island.

One day Ernest, who was six years old, became ill and refused to eat for several days. I knew he would not tell Mother what he wanted, so I asked him when no one else was in the room. He said he would like some canned peaches, which surprised me because we had never eaten such a thing. Mother gave me some money when I told her his desire; she sent me with Meung to a small store on the other side of the island. It took us a long time to find the store, asking people along the way how to get there. We bought a can of peaches and started for home. On the way back, we came to an irrigation ditch with just a narrow board across it. As we crossed, Meung dropped the can of peaches. We were scared stiff. The water was about six feet deep, and neither one of us could swim. We just stood there frozen with fear, staring at the can of peaches on the bottom of the ditch. Meung was fifteen years old then, but he acted like a man. He jumped into the water, grabbed the can of peaches, and struggled to the side, where I helped pull him out. We both gave a big sigh of relief and rested for a while. We did not dare say a word about what had happened, and we were relieved when Mother did not ask why we were so late or why Meung was all wet. She just said she had been worried and left it at that. Ernest was surprised and happy, and he ate the peaches. Maybe that was the medicine he needed, because he felt better the next day and got out of bed.

Another member of our family arrived about then. Ralph was born on Roberts Island on February 16, 1913.

Our potato plants that year were big and healthy looking. Instead of men digging them up with pitchforks, as they used to do, we now had a machine to make the work easier. As the horses pulled the machine, the plants were uprooted. All the potatoes were exposed, so it was easy to pick them up and put them into sacks. Almost as many snakes as potatoes came out of the ground. They were nonpoisonous, but we were afraid of them anyway. The men had to work longer hours at harvest time, so they needed a "snack" between meals. Mother made yeast doughnuts, which Meung and I took out to them with wine.

We had had a big harvest and were expecting a good profit from it, but Mr. Kim took a barge load to Stockton one morning and returned a week later with a sad story. He said the market price had dropped to ten cents for a hundred-pound sack of potatoes. He had not found even one buyer and had had to dump the load in the river. The depression that had caused us to move from Colusa was still in full force. We were so isolated from the rest of the world, we didn't know what was happening outside. No one came to Roberts Island and none of us went outside. Father had never farmed before, so he didn't know about watching the wholesale market prices. It was a heartbreaking situation. Everyone had worked so hard all year, only to find that no one wanted to buy our crop. We learned that just raising a good crop did not mean success.

Father became desperate. He wrote to friends everywhere, trying to find another place where we could make a living. We were sorry to see the men leave; we had all become good friends. A letter soon came from Mr. Byung Joon-lee, who was working for a quicksilver mining company in Idria, San Benito County, California. He said to come quickly, that a few jobs were available. Once again we had nothing to take with us, only our few clothes and blankets. The kitchen things did not belong to us, and we could not take the food. We left them so that whoever should come after us would find everything with which to start farming.

"FATHER CURES A PRESIDENTIAL FEVER"
from *FATHER AND GLORIOUS DESCENDANT*

Pardee Lowe (1904–   )

F ather and Glorious Descendant *is Pardee Lowe's*
autobiographical account of his early life in the San Francisco area
during the first decades of the twentieth century. Many of Mr.
Lowe's memories revolve around growing up Chinese American in
East Belleville and his special relationship to his father.

The significance of names—Chinese and American—played an
important part in Mr. Lowe's childhood, and is explained
throughout the book. In addition to their "foreordained" Chinese
names, Pardee and four of his siblings were given "Western aliases"
after famous Americans. While Pardee was named for a governor of
California, his twin brothers were named after President Woodrow
Wilson and his vice president, Thomas Riley Marshall.

The naming of his brothers attracted much attention from the
press and subsequently from the president's office. This strange event
belies the precarious position of Asian Americans during the 1910s
and 1920s. As Mr. Lowe noted, "[It was] a decided change from
the usual newspaper headlines clamoring for anti-Oriental state and
national legislation."

Mr. Lowe was born in San Francisco and grew up in East
Belleville in the Bay Area. He graduated from Stanford University
in 1930 and the Harvard University Graduate School of Business
Administration with an MBA in 1932. His articles and personal
essays have been published in The Atlantic, Asia, *the* Yale
Review, Survey Graphic, *and numerous anthologies. He served*
as a Lieutenant Colonel in the U.S. Air Force during the Second
World War and was decorated with a Bronze Star. Since the

1930s, he has worked for many international relations institutions, corporations, and United States government offices. From 1965–1973, he served as the State Department Officer in charge of UNESCO affairs for Asia, Africa, and the Middle East. Since the 1970s, Mr. Lowe has been special consultant and visiting professor of business management communications for the Tatung Institute in Taipei, Taiwan. When not in Taipei, he lives in Menlo Park, California.

HOW I CAME TO BE INFECTED WITH PRESIDENTITIS EVEN NOW I find somewhat difficult to explain. That it was not congenital was amply demonstrated by Father's matter-of-fact superiority over such divine foolishness. And Mother, bless her realistic Chinese soul, never affected awareness of such mundane matters until the political clubs of our neighborhood (we lived in the toughest one in East Belleville) celebrated under her very nose with torchlight parades, drunken sprees, black eyes, and cracked skulls the glorious victories of their Men of the People. Whenever this happened she would exclaim, "My, my, what queer people the Americans are!"

The first time Father discovered how long the firstborn man child of his household had been exposed to the ravages of this dread disease, he was horrified. "Unbelievable!" he stormed. But Mother, who had a strong will of her own, flew right back at him. And when she cried aloud, with Heaven as her witness, that she did not know how I caught it or how she could have prevented it, Father recognized the justice of her remarks. She couldn't. Kwong Chong, our own neighborhood dry-goods store, household duties, and two new babies kept Mother so harassed that she had no time to chase us about the streets or down the back alleys. Later, to still her flow of tears, Father even grudgingly admitted his full responsibility. By moving our family to an American neighborhood, according to Mother, he had needlessly exposed us all to the malady.

That this was the source of the trouble, probably no one knew better than Father. When the 1906 San Francisco earthquake and fire consumed all his worldly goods and forced him to flee Chinatown with his wife, two babies in arms, and a motley feudal retinue of kinsmen, relatives, and garment-sewing employees, he merely considered it more or less a blessing in disguise. From the ashes of this catastrophe, which represented for Mother the end of her Chinatownian world, Father's thoughts and plans for the future soared like a phoenix.

At long last the visions and dreams for his offspring, present and potential, would be realized. His family would rub shoulders with Americans. They would become good American citizens albeit remaining Chinese. They would inhabit a hyphenated world. By some formula, which he never was able to explain, they would select only the finest attributes of each contributory culture. They would reflect everlasting credit on him and on the name of Lowe.

(Even then, Father's faith passed all human understanding. He expected us somehow to muddle through. We did—but in a manner totally unexpected.)

From Father's point of view, we children were to be raised at home according to the old and strict Chinese ideal. But in that ever-widening circle of American neighborhood life beyond the narrow confines of our home, Father had no control. A daily commuter to his shop in San Francisco's Chinatown, an hour's ride away by steam train and ferry, he was never fully apprised of our actions until too late.

He was ignorant, for instance, of what transpired in the large wooden public school situated some three short blocks from our home. He was confident we were in good hands. If he had only known what was awaiting his son there, he might not have been so eager to have me acquire an American schooling.

When at the age of five I entered the portals of this mid-Victorian architectural firetrap, surrounded by its iron-spiked fence and tall trees, for the first time, I recognized it as an international institution in which I was free to indulge my own most un-Chinese inclinations—and, unintentionally to be sure, to undermine Father's high hopes.

I can still vividly remember the strange excitement of the first morning roll call, which was to be repeated daily for many years to come. Clumsily, the teacher pronounced our names. As we rose, she checked our nationality.

"Louisa Fleishhacker—*Austrian.*" She underlined the word *Austrian.* "Elsie Forsythe—*English.* Penelope Lincoln—*Ameri-*

can Negro. Yuri Matsuyama—*Japanese*. Nancy Mullins—*Irish*. Maria Pucinelli—*Italian*. Stella Saceanu—*Rumanian*. Anna Zorich—*Serbian*." Finishing with the girls, she turned the page. "Michael Castro—*Portuguese*. Heinz Creyer—*German*. Thorvald Ericson—*Swedish*. Philippe Etienne—*French*. Nicholas Katanov—*Russian*. Pardee Lowe—*Chinese*. Robert MacPherson—*Scotch*. And Francisco Trujillo—*Mexican*."

There we stood. In the company of fifteen other beginners no two in the entire group of the same nationality, I was embarking upon a new and glorious adventure, the educational melting pot, which was to make every one of us, beyond peradventure, an American.

It pleased Father no end to know that I liked to go to American school. He informed Mother proudly that it denoted a scholarly spirit well becoming a Chinese. If he had only glimpsed what lay back of my mind as I saw him gaily off on the morning seven-forty commuters' train he might have derived much less satisfaction.

No sooner was Father's back turned than I would dash madly to the streetcar line. On my way I would stop and pick a bunch of posies from our neighbors' back yards, praying fervently that I would be the only pupil waiting for Miss McIntyre, our teacher. Disappointment invariably awaited me, for I was not alone. Anna, Nancy, Penelope, and Robert, sharing exactly the same sentiments, always managed to get there ahead of me.

As soon as we spotted Miss McIntyre's tall figure alighting from the car, we sprang forward. With a warm smile of affection which enfolded us all, she allowed us to grab her hands, snatch her books from her arms and literally drag her from the rear step of the car to the front steps of the school, happily protesting every step of the way: "Now, children! . . . Now *children!*"

Coming mainly from immigrant homes where parents were too preoccupied with earning a living to devote much time to their children, we transferred our youthful affections to this one person who had both the time and the disposition to mother us. We showered upon our white-haired teacher the blind, wholehearted loyalty of the young. Our studies we readily absorbed, not because we particularly liked them so much as because it was "she" who taught us. Thus, with the three R's, games, stories, a weekly bath which she personally administered in the school's bathroom—two pupils at a time—and her love, she whom we staunchly enshrined in our hearts laid the rudimentary but firm foundation of our personal brand of American culture.

Then, one day it happened. Miss McIntyre, herself the daughter of an Irish immigrant who had come to California during the Gold Rush, read to us with deep emotion the life of George Washington. The virtues displayed by the Father of Our Country, particularly when confessing his act of chopping down the cherry tree, were, she led us to believe, the very ones which would, if faithfully practiced, win us equal fame. Concluding the narrative, she looked in turn at Anna, Penelope, and Robert. She was challenging us to higher things. As her eyes caught mine, she added with conviction, "And every single one of you can be President of the United States someday!"

I shall never forget that occasion. To be President in our minds was like being God, with the difference that everybody knew what the President looked like. His pictures were in every newspaper. Even in the funny sheets, I sometimes saw him. Big as life, with his grinning mouthful of teeth, eyeglasses gleaming, and his mustache bristling in the breeze of the political opposition—he looked the spitting image of Father. The only difference I could detect was that Father preferred the bamboo duster to the "Big Stick," and "*Jun Ho Ah!*" was as near as he ever came to "Bully!"

Everything I did from this moment on served only to strengthen the grandiose dream whose chief interlocking threads included myself, Father, and the Presidency. Much to the disgust of my more active playmates and the envy of my bookworm friends, I became a walking encyclopedia of American history. I could repeat the full names and dates of every President of these United States. And I knew the vivid, gory details, authentic and apocryphal, of every important military engagement in which Americans took part—and always victoriously.

I hounded the settlement librarian for books, and more books. Like one famished, I devoured all of James Fenimore Cooper's novels. Lodge and Roosevelt's *Hero Tales from American History* fascinated me. As I read Abbot's *The Story of Our Navy* and Johnston's *Famous Scouts, Including Trappers, Pioneers and Soldiers of the Frontier*, my sense of patriotism quickened. So stirred was I by Tomlinson's narrative that in my childish imagination I followed George Washington as a young scout, or marched resolutely forward to engage the Iroquois and Red Coats. Of all the books, however, Coffin's *Boys of '76* was my favorite. And many were the evenings in which I descended from the New Hampshire hills with sixteen-year-old Elijah Favor to fight at Lexington and Concord and finally to share the fruits of Revolutionary victory at Yorktown.

However, by the time I could recite with relish and gusto Scott's lines:—

> Breathes there the man, with soul so dead,
> Who never to himself hath said,
> This is my own, my native land! . . .

the President's picture had changed. In the course of the years, he had become huge, the size of a bear, but he still wore a mustache. He was less like Father now. And while I found it difficult to imagine myself becoming as stout, I felt that even flabby avoirdupois, if associated with the Presidency, had its compensations. No matter what his shape, I told myself, everybody still loved and worshiped the President of the United States.

Of this deadly and insidious fever that racked my chubby frame, Father was totally ignorant. Nor would he have ever divined my secret if it had not been for our journey to the Mother Lode country.

It was our first long overnight trip away from home together. The train ride, needless to say, was nothing short of glorious. For two whole days I had all to myself a father whom I seldom saw, but to whom I was thoroughly devoted. Besides, a city boy, I had never seen mountains so tall or sights so strange and fleeting. But the most enjoyable part of all was to bounce on the redplush train seats and stop the vendor whenever he passed by with his hamper filled with peanuts, candies and soda pop.

After a full day's ride, we arrived at our destination, a small silver-mining town in the Sierra Nevada. At the station platform, Father and I were met by a roly-poly Westerner dressed in baggy clothes, riding boots, and a huge sombrero and mouthing ominously an equally formidable black cigar. After "How-de-doing" us, the stranger offered Father a cigar. A "cheroot" I think he called it. Then followed a ritual that filled me with amazement.

While Mr. Brown sized up Father skeptically, Father planted himself firmly on both feet, rolled the unlighted cigar in his hands, stroked it gently, and drew it slowly beneath his nose. With a deep sigh of satisfaction, he inhaled deeply.

"Havana Perfecto?" inquired Father, more as a statement of fact than a question.

"Splendid!" assented Mr. Brown with a vigorous nod. Smiling broadly for the first time, he slapped Father approvingly on the back and swept me up into his arms. As we drove majestically down the dusty street in his creaky cart, our now genial host vouchsafed that Father was one of the few "damned furriners" and certainly the first "Chinaman" to pass this unusual inspection.

By the way that Father puffed at his cigar and blew magnificent smoke rings, I could see that he was pleased with Mr. Brown's compliment. But never a word did he mention about his being the proprietor of Sun Loy, the largest tobacco shop in Chinatown. Since he didn't, neither did I.

Arriving at a large two-story hotel, resembling in size, shape, and color an old Southern mansion, Mr. Brown, whom we now knew to be the proprietor, roared from his sagging wagon seat: "Hi there, folks! I've picked up my Chinamen!"

Out trooped the few American residents of the hotel, glad to witness anything that would break the monotony of a long hot summer's day, followed by six white-clad Chinese domestics who greeted us with an explosion of the Fragrant Mountain dialect. "*Ah Kung Ah!*" (Respected Great-Uncle!) "We hope all is well with you!"

It gave me a great thrill to see everybody, even the Americans, so deferential to Father. There was something about him that commanded universal respect. Chinese in Western clothes, especially of the latest cut, were a decided rarity in those days. And Father in his first suit of tailor-mades from a nobby American clothier looked simply grand. Tall, well-built, and sporting a bushy mustache, he looked every inch a distinguished personage. I could well understand why his American business associates persisted in nicknaming him "The Duke."

Mr. Brown, having already been informed of the purpose of

our visit, drew quietly aside. So did the Americans, no longer interested in a group of jabbering, gesticulating Orientals. This gave a few of my kinsmen an opportunity to converse with me in our dialect, which I understood, but, much to their chagrin, could not speak. Shocked that a Chinese boy should be ignorant of his own dialect, the eldest exclaimed, "*Chow Mah!*" (Positively disgraceful!) The way he said it made me more than a little ashamed of myself.

However, Father cut short my uncomfortable moment by introducing me to the object of our visit. "This—" indicating a short, slender chap who appeared exceedingly glum—"is your Fourth Paternal Uncle, Precious Fortune."

Fourth Uncle, despite his title, was only a distant kinsman and, from his point of view, had every reason for sulkiness. Just as he had conveniently forgotten about his grieving mother and childless wife in China for the pleasures of Chinatown's gambling tables, Father appeared—and Fourth Uncle didn't like it one bit. Father was the personification of outraged Chinese family conscience on the warpath. To him, in place of his own father, Fourth Uncle had to account for his glaring lapses in filial piety. He had to explain, for example, why he had not written them in three years; why he never sent them money; and, worst of all, why he persisted in leaving his aging mother grandchildless.

As the Clan's Senior Elder Uncle, Father took his Greater Family responsibilities very seriously. All through dinner, he informed Mr. Brown spiritedly that Fourth Uncle would have to leave. At first, Mr. Brown replied that he hated to part with an excellent cook, but when we came to dessert he finally agreed that in view of Fourth Uncle's wicked profligacy, it appeared the wisest course.

Having disposed of the fried chicken, apple pie, and Fourth Uncle so satisfactorily, Mr. Brown next turned to me. "Son," he inquired, "what are you studying to become? Would you like to stay with me and be my cook, taking your uncle's place?"

The last question passed me by completely; I answered the first one. "I want to be President," I said.

A sharp silence smote the mellow dining room. Now the secret was out. I was amazed at my own stupidity. Happily absorbed with my second helping of apple pie and fresh rich country milk, I had recklessly given vent to my Presidential aspirations. Now what would Father say?

Father, uncertain of the exact nature of the enchantment that had suddenly ensnared his son, looked at me queerly as though he doubted his ears. Mr. Brown laughed long and loud with a strange catch in his voice. "Sure, son, that's right," he added. "Study hard and you'll be President someday."

I wondered then why Mr. Brown's laughter sounded so odd, but I never associated this with pity until much, much later. By then, however, I had been thoroughly cured by Father.

Homeward bound Father said precious little. Not even to Fourth Uncle, still glum, whom we brought home with us to start life anew. Father's silence was disturbing and he attempted to cloak it, and his thoughts, with liberal benefactions. When we reached Belleville Junction I had no further use for the newspaper vendor and his basket of allurements—and Father no use for silence. In his own mind he had worked out a series of special therapeutic treatments to counteract my desperate malady, Presidentitis.

A few days after our return from the Sierra Nevada, Father said gently, "Glorious Descendant, how would you like to go to a private boarding school in China?"

I shuddered at the full significance of his suggestion. To be separated from America and from my family? And never to see them again for years and years? "No! no!" I wailed. "I don't want to go!" Rejecting the idea with all the vehemence at my command, I added, "I want to stay in America!"

Father dwelt patiently on all the advantages of such a schooling but to no avail. Nothing he said moved me. What about my future, inquired Father, didn't I care? Of course, I replied, but I didn't want to be a mandarin or a Chinese merchant prince at such a terrific sacrifice. Father's questions became more penetrating; they stripped the future of everything but realities. Could I, as a Chinese, ever hope to find a good job in American society? At this, I laughed. Miss McIntyre, I told him, had plainly said that I could even be President.

In these sessions, I revealed to Father the seriousness of my infection. I opened the gates to that part of my youthful life he had never known. I told him in no uncertain terms that I loved America, particularly East Belleville, which I considered to be the grandest place in all the world. Besides, I continued, why would I wish to go to China? All the things I had heard from our kinsfolk about the old country were bad, with no redeeming features. After all, I added as my clinching argument, if this were not so, why should our kinsmen wish to come to the United States?

Our cousins and uncles, Father tried desperately to explain, really wanted to stay at home with their wives and children, but because times seemed so difficult in China they were compelled, by economic necessity, to come and work in the Golden Mountains. "Don't think you're the only one who loves his family and hates to leave it," concluded Father somewhat angrily.

The argument became endless. The more Father pleaded, the more determined I became. America, I swore, was God's own country. It abounded in free public schools, libraries, newspapers, bathtubs, toilets, vaudeville theaters, and railroad trains. On the other hand, I reminded him, China was a place where anything might happen: One might be kidnapped, caught in a revolution, die from the heat, perish from the cold, or even pick up ringworm diseases which left huge bald patches on one's scalp.

Finally Father was convinced. Since I did not personally regard his idea with favor, trying to send me to China was hopeless. This by no means exhausted Father's remedial efforts on my behalf. Plan number one having failed, Father put number two into operation. He decided that if I wouldn't go to China I was to spend an extra hour each day on my Chinese studies for Tutor Chun.

Now I knew leisure no longer. My American playmates, and endless trips to the settlement library, were given up—but not forgotten. And I discovered to my painful sorrow that I had only substituted one necessary evil for another. Every evening from five to eight I despondently memorized, recited, and copied endless columns of queer-shaped characters which bore not the slightest resemblance to English. As I went to this school on Saturday mornings and studied my lessons on Sunday, I envied Penelope, Heinz and Francisco, my poorest foreign playmates, their luxurious freedom. They did not have to learn Chinese.

Unlike my American education, my Chinese one was not crowned with success. It was not that I was entirely unwilling to learn, but simply that my brain was not ambidextrous. Whenever I stood with my back to the teacher, my lips attempted to recite correctly in poetical prose Chinese history, geography or ethics, while my inner spirit was wrestling victoriously with the details of the Battle of Bunker Hill, Custer's Last Stand, or the tussle between the *Monitor* and *Merrimac*.

When it became apparent to Tutor Chun that, in spite of my extra hour a day, I was unable to balance cultural waters on both shoulders, he mercifully desisted flailing me with the bamboo duster. No amount of chastising, he informed me bitterly, would ever unravel the cultural chop suey I was making of my studies. But, in the long run, even the gentle soul of the Chinese teacher could not tolerate my muddle-headedness. One day after a particularly heart-rending recitation on my part, he telephoned Mother in despair. "Madame," he exclaimed in mortal anguish, "never have I had a pupil the equal of your son. I strain all my efforts but, alas, I profoundly regret that I am unable to teach him anything!"

Father was appalled at this news, but since he was not the kind of man who gave up easily, his determination waxed all the stronger. Subtler methods, bribery, were tried. Perhaps, he reasoned, I might develop a taste for Chinese as well as English literature if it were only made financially worth my while. Each Sunday a shining quarter would be mine, he said, if I would present him with a daily ten-minute verbal Chinese translation of the latest newspaper reports on European war developments.

Lured by this largess, I made my translations. They were, to be sure, crude and swiftly drawn. But then, ten minutes was all too brief a period in which to circumnavigate the globe and report on its current events. I endowed the military movements of von Kluck's, Foch's and Haig's armies with the élan of Sheridan's sweep down the Shenandoah, unencumbered with the intricate mechanized paraphernalia of modern warfare. And long before Wilson, Clemenceau and Lloyd George assembled at Versailles, I had made and remade the map of Europe a dozen times.

Father's clever scheme not only worked, but it proved mutually beneficial. During the four years of the war, we kept it up. Thanks to the revolutionary *Young China*, and the *Christian Chinese Western Daily*, he was never entirely in the dark as to which armies won which campaign and who finally won the war. Naturally, Father learned a great deal about history that wasn't so, but he did not particularly mind. I was improving my Chinese.

During this period my youthful cup of patriotism was filled to overflowing. In the first place our Americanism had finally reached the ears of the White House. The christening of my twin brothers brought two important letters of congratulation from Washington, which Father proudly framed and hung conspicuously in his private office. As might be imagined, they exerted a profound influence on all our lives.

When I felt particularly in need of encouragement, I would go to the back wall of Father's office and read aloud Vice President Marshall's letter to Father. It was a human one, glowing with warmth and inspiration. There was one sentence which stood out: "To be a good American citizen, in my judgment, is about the best thing on earth, and while I cannot endow your children with any worldly goods, I can bless them with the hope that they may grow up to be an honor to their parents and a credit to the commonwealth."

I recall this Vice-Presidential blessing so vividly because it was the crux of our family problem. It summed up our difficulties as well as our goal. For me, at least, it was difficult to be a filial Chinese son and a good American citizen at one and the same time. For many years I used to wonder why this was so, but I appreciate now it was because I was the eldest son in what was essentially a pioneering family. Father was pioneering with Americanism—and so was I. And more often than not, we blazed entirely different trails.

When America finally entered the War, even Father's sturdy common sense softened somewhat under the heat waves of patriotism that constantly beat down upon us. I was in paradise. My youthful fancies appreciated that only strife and turmoil made heroes. When I recalled that practically every great President—Washington, Jackson, Lincoln, Grant, and Roosevelt—

had once been a soldier, I bitterly lamented the fact that I was not old enough. I'd show those "Huns" (by this time I had already imbibed freely at the fount of propaganda) a thing or two, I informed Father. But Father only snorted something about waiting until I could shoulder a gun, and studying Chinese.

The next summer, my thirteenth, I decided to go to work during vacation. I needed spending money badly for my first term in high school. Father applauded this show of independence until I informed him that I intended, if possible, to become an office boy in an American business firm. Then he was seized with profound misgivings. "Would they hire you?" Father inquired.

Why shouldn't they, I replied, with overweening self-confidence. "See!" I pointed to the Sunday editions of the *San Francisco Chronicle*. "I can hold any of these jobs."

Father looked at the classified advertisements I had checked. Whether he knew what all the abbreviations meant, I wasn't certain. I didn't, but that was totally immaterial. The world was new, I was young, and for $40 a month I was willing to learn the ins. or exp. bus., work for good opps., be ready to asst. on files, and, for good measure, do gen. off. wk. for perm. adv.

Father remarked that he wasn't so certain that the millennium had arrived, but he was open to conviction. He agreed to let me proceed on one condition: If I failed to find a job I was to return to Tutor Chun and study my Chinese lessons faithfully.

Blithely one sunny July morning I went forth job hunting, well-scrubbed, wearing my Sunday suit and totally unaware of the difficulties that confronted me. In my pocket were ten clipped newspaper advertisements, each one, I thought, with a job purposely made for me.

I took out the most promising one. It was for seven enterp. boys, between the ages of 12 and 16; and they were wanted at once for a bond house which offered good opps. as well as $50 per month. The address was on California Street.

Stopping in front of an imposing marble palace of San Francisco finance, I compared the address with the clipping. It checked. How simply grand it would be to work for such a firm, I thought, as the elevator majestically pulled us up to the ninth floor. I trembled with eager anticipation as I pushed open the glass door of Richards and Mathison, for it seemed as though a new world were swimming into view.

"Wad-a-ya-wunt?" barked the sharp voice of a young lady. I looked in her direction. There she sat behind a shiny, thin brass cage, just like a bank teller—or a monkey, for above her head hung a sign. It read INFORMATION.

"Please, ma'am," I asked, "can you tell me where I can find Mr. Royal?"

"Humph!" she snorted, as she looked me up and down as if to say I didn't have a chance. "He's busy, you'll have to wait."

After what seemed hours, the girl threw open the office gate and motioned me to enter. I followed her down a long aisle of desks, every one as large as a kitchen table. At each desk sat a man or a girl shuffling large cards or scribbling on long sheets of paper. As we passed, they stopped their work and looked at me queerly. I noticed several boys of my own age putting their heads together. I knew they were talking about me. And when they snickered, I wanted to punch their noses.

Opening a door marked PRIVATE, the girl announced: "Mr. Royal, here is another boy." He raised his head.

There it was. On Mr. Royal's lean, smooth-shaven face was the same look of incredulity that I had once noticed on Mr. Brown's. But only for a moment. For he suddenly reached for a cigarette, lit it and looked at me quizzically, while I hopped on one foot and then on the other.

"Young man," he said, "I understand you would like to work for us? Well then, you'd better tell us something of yourself."

"Why, of course," I said, "of course." And impulsively I told everything: all about my graduation from grammar school, my boy-scout training, and my desire to earn my own keep during the summer.

Mr. Royal seemed visibly impressed. When a faint smile replaced his frown, I stopped fidgeting. I fully expected him to ask me to come to work in the morning. Therefore, I was appalled when he told me that he was sorry, but all the jobs were taken. It never occurred to me that our interview would end like this.

My face fell. I hadn't expected such an answer. To soften the blow, Mr. Royal added that if I filled out an application he would call me if there were any openings.

I filled out the application under the unsympathetic eyes of the information girl, and stumbled miserably out of the office, vaguely sensible of the fact that there would never be any opening.

The feeling was intensified as I made the round of the other nine firms. Everywhere I was greeted with perturbation, amusement, pity or irritation—and always with identically the same answer. "Sorry," they invariably said, "the position has just been filled." My jaunty self-confidence soon wilted. I sensed that something was radically, fundamentally wrong. It just didn't seem possible that overnight all of the positions could have been occupied, particularly not when everybody spoke of a labor shortage. Suspicion began to dawn. What had Father said? "American firms do not customarily employ Chinese." To verify his statement, I looked again in the newspaper the next morning and for the week after and, sure enough, just as I expected, the same ten ads were still in the newspaper.

For another week, I tried my luck. By now I was thoroughly shellshocked. What had begun as a glorious adventure had turned into a hideous, long-drawn nightmare.

Father during this trying period wisely said nothing. Then, one morning, he dusted off my dog-eared paperbound Chinese textbooks. When I came to breakfast I found them on my desk, mute but eloquent reminders of my promise. I looked at them disconsolately. A bargain was a bargain.

When our clock struck nine, I picked up my bundle of books. Fortunately for me, Father had already commuted to work. Only Mother saw me off. Patting me sympathetically on the shoulder, she regarded me reflectively. It was an invitation for me to unburden my heart. But not even for her would I confess my full recovery from a nearly fatal disease. That moment was reserved for my long walk to language school.

I marched out of the house insouciant. When I wasn't whistling I was muttering to myself a Jewish slang phrase I had just picked up. It was "Ishkabibble" and it meant that I didn't care. And I didn't until I reached the park where all my most vivid daydreaming periods were spent. There, I broke down and

wept. For the first time I admitted to myself the cruel truth—
I didn't have a "Chinaman's chance" of becoming President of
the United States. In this crash of the lofty hopes which Miss
McIntyre had raised, it did not occur to me to reflect that the
chances of Francisco Trujillo, Yuri Matsuyama, or Penelope
Lincoln were actually no better than mine. But after a good cry
I felt better—anyway, I could go to an American school again
in the fall.

"THE TASTE OF INDEPENDENCE"
from *FIFTH CHINESE DAUGHTER*
Jade Snow Wong (1922–)

In Fifth Chinese Daughter, *first published in 1950, Jade Snow Wong chronicles her early life in San Francisco's Chinatown during the 1920s and 1930s. The following chapter recounts her junior high experiences in both American and Chinese school, where she studied Chinese language, literature, and other subjects.* Fifth Chinese Daughter *won the Commonwealth Club's Silver Medal for Non-Fiction in 1951, and was made into an award winning PBS special for the 1976 Bicentennial.*

Ms. Wong was born in San Francisco. Her family owned a Chinatown store and later ran a denim overall factory. She graduated from City College of San Francisco and Mills College, from which she received her B.A. in 1942 and an honorary Doctor of Humane Letters in 1976. Her second book, No Chinese Stranger, *was published in 1975, and her writings have appeared in many anthologies.*

Ms. Wong is also renowned as a ceramist. Her enamels and pottery have been exhibited at many galleries and museums including the Chicago Art Institute, the San Francisco Museum of Modern Art, the Metropolitan Museum of Art, the Smithsonian Institution, the Museum of Modern Art in New York City, and internationally. Her honors include a Fine Design award from the Museum of Modern Art, Award of Merit for Outstanding Public Service from the City and County of San Francisco, and a Woman Warrior Award for Outstanding Contribution in Literature and Service from the Pacific Asian Women Bay Area Coalition. She lives in San Francisco where she enamels and runs a travel business and gift shop.

IN CHINESE SCHOOL, JADE SNOW HAD NOW PASSED BEYOND THE vocabulary stage to the study of essays, which she was required to memorize by both oral recitation and writing. The correct spelling of a word could not be hazarded from the sound, but depended on one's remembering the exact look of a character, including the location of the tiniest dot.

The only subject which permitted students to exercise their imaginations and to demonstrate their knowledge of the language was composition. Once a week they were given a subject title, such as "The Value of Learning," or "The Necessity of Good Habits," and the class hummed with anticipation as the words were written on the blackboard. They worked first on a rough draft, and afterward copied the draft with fine brushes onto the squares of a tablet page, which they submitted for correction.

On Saturday mornings, an assembly was held in the chapel of the Chinese Presbyterian Church, where members of the advanced classes took turns in practicing public speaking before the student body. Their talks were usually moral clichés, many patterned after sermons heard from their minister. Patiently, the students suffered with the speakers through such subjects as "It Is Time for China to Unite," "The Little Boy Who Cried Wolf-Wolf and Betrayed Only Himself," or "You Can Trust Some Animals More Than You Can Trust Some People."

Sometimes at these assemblies, they heard sermons or guest speakers. But always the meeting began with prayer and hymns; Jade Snow and Jade Precious Stone learned to sing in Chinese the words to such melodies as "Bringing in the Sheaves," "Day Is Dying in the West." "He Arose," and the stirring "Onward, Christian Soldiers."

Order, in the most uncompromising Chinese sense, was enforced strictly. Not a sound was tolerated from the rows of black-topped heads in the audience. A dean or disciplinarian preserved order and punished offenders for a multitude of infringements—from assembly misconduct to cheating in class.

During assembly, this unpopular man paced up and down the aisles with a long rod held menacingly in his hand. At the slightest noise he was instantly there, and the guilty one was told to stand in the aisle to be shamed publicly for misbehavior. The boys were seated on the right side of the hall, with the girls on the left, arranged by grade. Several boys were notorious for disrupting the peace at almost any assembly. They seemed to enjoy their brief sojourn in the limelight as they stood in disgrace. Rarely was a girl stood out for punishment, but when she was, all heads turned toward her as if by signal.

One Saturday morning, Jade Snow's most humiliating Chinese school experience occurred in this setting. Simply for the pleasure of outwitting the disciplinarian, Mr. Dong, some of the girls had agreed upon the idea of passing notes surreptitiously from one aisle to the other. One assembly passed off successfully; another assembly found the girls still triumphant. The third week, Mr. Dong, who was conscious of a disturbance, decided that he must find a culprit or suffer a serious loss of face. Unfortunately he decided to pull out a culprit exactly at the moment when the note slid into Jade Snow's hand.

The next move was swift—the long rod tapped Jade Snow's shoulder. Shrinking, she looked up to find Mr. Dong, his face wreathed in triumph, motioning unmistakably for her to come out and stand in the aisle.

Jade Snow had never before been mortified so completely, suddenly, and publicly. Slowly she made her way from her seat to the aisle. She stood, perspiring and blushing, keeping her eyes down to screen her agony. She wished that her straight bangs were long enough to conceal her whole face from the curious eyes that she knew were turned to stare in surprise, disapproval, and sympathy. Her tears gathered, hung, and finally dropped unchecked. The green Victorian design on the faded red aisle carpet stamped itself indelibly on her memory during the interminable wait until the end of the assembly.

As usual, her first thought was "What would Daddy and Mama say?" Mostly it was "What would Daddy say?" Daddy probably would never have been party to passing notes. He would not mind refusing to co-operate in a project to which all others had agreed, if he thought it was not exactly right. But as just another little girl in a whole row of classmates with whom one had to get along every evening of the week, Jade Snow had not felt equal to resistance. It was her own fault, as usual.

Finally, the last hymn was sung, the students received the benediction, and as the assembly was dismissed, Mr. Dong announced, "All those who have been stood out at assembly will go to the principal's office immediately to receive their punishment."

"To receive punishment"—wasn't standing out enough? This aftermath had not occurred to Jade Snow. She picked up her books from her seat and trailed out after the dwindling crowd, turning off to enter the principal's office instead of going downstairs to the street as usual.

Guilty boys were waiting inside the office, which held two old-fashioned desks and a couple of old wooden chairs. Into this colorless, cluttered-looking place, Mr. Dong hustled with brisk anticipation. He went to his desk and found a long cane switch, heavier and tied more securely than Daddy's salvages from the bindings of rice bundles. Evidently the boys were seasoned to this routine, for they quickly stepped up to Mr. Dong and held out their right palms. The switch cut the air and cracked down loudly three times on the open palms. The boys did not cry out, but stuck out their chests manfully before their lone female audience, and nonchalantly scampered off.

Mr. Dong began his treatment of Jade Snow more ceremoniously. "Wong Jade Snow, I am surprised at such misbehavior in a young lady, and you must be punished to teach you a lesson."

Jade Snow was terrified. Then indignation routed terror as it suddenly occurred to her that she need not necessarily submit. Nobody except her parents had ever whipped her. It was one thing to be stood out as a martyr for her friends, but nobody should whip her for it. According to Mama's and Daddy's instructions, she had never before argued with a teacher, but she needed no practice for the scornful words which she flung recklessly because she knew that they were righteous.

"Yes, I did pass a note, and for that perhaps I deserve to be stood out. But I am no more guilty than the girl who passed it to me, or the girl who had passed it to her, and even less at fault are we than the girl who started it. If you whip me, you should also have here all the girls from my row, with their palms outstretched. And I won't hold out my hand until I see theirs held out also!"

There was a stunned silence. Mr. Dong could not have been any more surprised than Jade Snow herself. From where had all those words tumbled, so suddenly and so forcefully?

Mr. Dong recovered somewhat and clutched his vanishing dignity. "So you dare to question me!"

The new Jade Snow spoke again, "I speak only for what is right, and I will always question wrong in the way my Daddy has taught me. I am willing to bring him here to submit this matter to his judgment. Until then, I hold out no hand."

There Mr. Dong was held. Obviously he did not wish to have a director of the school board brought in to arbitrate between the disciplinarian and his own daughter, Jade Snow. He generously waved his hand. "Very well, I shall let you off gently this time, but don't take advantage of my good nature to let this happen again!"

As Jade Snow went home that Saturday afternoon, her thoughts were not concerned with her victory, unprecedented as it was. She was struck with this new idea of speaking for what she knew was right. All the vague remarks which Mama and her older sisters had dropped from time to time, and the stories they had told about Daddy's well-known habit of speaking out forthrightly and fearlessly for what he believed was right, no matter what everyone else thought, had borne their first fruit in Jade Snow.

At the American day school, Jade Snow was now ready for junior high school. Most of her classmates went on to a local junior high school where the student body was a mixture of Italian-American and Chinese-American youngsters. Daddy, however, made some investigations first, having heard rumors that this was a "tough" school, not in the sense of academic requirements, which would have been pleasing to him, but in the behavior of the boy students.

Although the accuracy of this report could not be ascertained, Daddy judiciously was not taking any chances on undermining the delicate sensibilities and disciplined character which he and Mama had so carefully and strictly forged in Jade Snow. At eleven, this daughter could hardly find a moment of her life which was not accounted for, and accounted for properly, by Mama or Daddy. She had not yet been allowed to visit any friend, of any age or sex, unaccompanied. She had never even gone to the playground, a block away from home, without a grown-up relative or friend in attendance. When she was old enough to go alone to school, to the barber shop, or to the grocery, she either took Younger Sister, or was allowed exactly enough time to accomplish her purpose and return without any margin for loitering on the streets.

About this time, Jade Snow and Jade Precious Stone together suffered their last whipping at Daddy's hands, to teach them unforgettably the importance of keeping a promise and the necessity of accounting to their parents for their time and their activities.

Oldest Sister Jade Swallow was organizing the citizens of Chinatown to roll bandages for shipment to the Chinese front in the Sino-Japanese war. One Saturday evening she asked her two younger sisters to come over to the Y.W.C.A. to help her. Jade Snow asked Mama for permission to go.

"It is all right with me as long as you get all your household duties done before you leave. But you must also obtain your father's permission," said Mama.

Jade Snow went to Daddy.

Daddy debated, "I do not like to have you begin the habit of going out at night. However, it is a worthy cause. Be back not later than nine."

The Y.W.C.A. was about four blocks away. There the sisters had a fine time rolling bandages. It was fun to chat with Oldest Sister again, for they did not see one another often. Before they knew it, it was nine o'clock, but Jade Snow and Jade Precious Stone were loath to depart. Tomorrow would be Sunday, and only a few more bandages were needed before their quota would be filled.

"We are supposed to be home by now, Big Sister," Jade Snow anxiously reminded.

"If you stay a little longer to finish this job, I will telephone Daddy and tell him that you are still working here and will be home a half hour later."

This Oldest Sister did. She reported that he had consented.

In happy confidence that all was well, the two sisters finished their bandages and went home at 9:30.

They raced down the flight of entrance stairs, walked through the store, and just as they were entering the hallway to their room, they saw Daddy rise from his desk in his office cubicle. He came out to meet them, and they saw that he held in his hand the bundle of whipping cane.

"Look at the clock and observe the time!" was all he said.

They looked. The big old-fashioned Seth Thomas wall-piece gave the date of the month, the day of the week, and its time hands leered down at them. Nine-thirty-seven, they read.

Daddy loomed large and menacing; there was no kindness in his face. Swiftly the switch cut the air and whistled sharply just before it landed across the back of Jade Snow's bare calves.

"You are older and you must be punished first," thundered Daddy angrily. "You are responsible for leading your younger sister, and I shall teach you not to disregard the time and your word to me again."

Down whistled the switch again on little nine-year-old Jade Precious Stone's bare legs. "And you are to learn not to follow your Older Sister in her sins."

Across Jade Snow's thighs, then against Jade Precious Stone's, again and again both children were roundly whipped; but Mama had put one limitation on her own and on Daddy's whippings— the children were never to be struck near or on their heads, because such blows might affect their brain and injure their intelligence!

"Are you not ashamed that big girls like you must be taught by physical punishment! Now off to bed quickly before I become more angered," said Daddy in a roar.

The girls jumped and winced under the strokes but knew that it was best to submit silently. Jade Snow knew that Daddy's generation in China were whipped even more severely—they were suspended from their wrists while receiving punishment. The girls limped off and climbed into one bed for mutual comfort, and under the covers they rubbed each other's sore, red welts. With heavy hearts, they quietly sobbed themselves to sleep.

The daughters of the Wong family were born to requirements exacting beyond their understanding. These requirements were not always made clear, until a step out of bounds brought the parents' swift and drastic correction.

Now after eleven years of continuous vigilance, Daddy was not going to let Jade Snow go to any school that "tough" boys might be attending. He called upon Oldest Sister for assistance. Oldest Sister suggested a junior high school eight blocks from home which she thought superior to the other school. As it had no Chinese students, Jade Snow would be forced to learn more English, Oldest Sister convinced Daddy.

Complying with their decision, Jade Snow found herself the only Chinese student in a small neighborhood school. Here she did not make new friends. She missed her grammar school companions, but she hesitated to take the initiative in making friends with the first "foreign" classmates of her own age. She was not invited to any of their homes or parties. Being shy anyway, she quietly adjusted to this new state of affairs; it did not occur to her to be bothered by it.

Since the new school was a little farther than comfortable walking distance over the steepest part of Nob Hill, Jade Snow received fifty cents from Mama twice a month to buy a car ticket. On nice days, however, Jade Snow usually walked home from school to save two-and-a-half cents.

It was on one of these solitary walks home soon after she had transferred to the new school that Jade Snow was introduced for the first time to racial discrimination.

She had been delayed after school. Everyone had gone except herself and a little boy to whom she had never paid much attention—a very pale, round-faced boy with puffy cheeks, an uncombed thatch of sandy hair, freckles, and eyes which strangely matched the color of his hair.

"I've been waiting for a chance like this," Richard said excitedly to Jade Snow. With malicious intent in his eyes, he burst forth, "Chinky, Chinky, Chinaman."

Jade Snow was astonished. She considered the situation and decided to say nothing.

This placidity provoked Richard. He picked up an eraser and threw it at her. It missed and left a white chalk mark upon the floor. A little puff of white dust sifted up through the beam of the afternoon sun streaming through the window.

Jade Snow decided that it was time to leave. As she went out of the doorway, a second eraser landed squarely on her back. She looked neither to the right nor left, but proceeded sedately down the stairs and out the front door. In a few minutes, her tormentor had caught up with her. Dancing around her in glee, he chortled, "Look at the eraser mark on the yellow Chinaman. Chinky, Chinky, no tickee, no washee, no shirtee!"

Jade Snow thought that he was tiresome and ignorant. Everybody knew that the Chinese people had a superior culture. Her ancestors had created a great art heritage and had made inventions important to world civilization—the compass, gunpowder, paper, and a host of other essentials. She knew, too, that Richard's grades couldn't compare with her own, and his home training was obviously amiss.

After following her for a few blocks, Richard reluctantly turned off to go home, puzzled and annoyed by not having provoked a fight. Jade Snow walked on, thinking about the incident. She had often heard Chinese people discuss the foreigners and their strange ways, but she would never have thought of running after one of them and screaming with pointed finger, for instance, "Hair on your chest!" After all, people were just born with certain characteristics, and it behooved no one to point a finger at anyone else, for everybody was or had something which he could not help.

She concluded that perhaps the foreigners were simply unwise in the ways of human nature, and unaware of the importance of giving the other person "face," no matter what one's personal opinion might be. They probably could not help their own insensibility. Mama said they hadn't even learned how to peel a clove of garlic the way the Chinese did.

When she arrived home, she took off her coat and brushed off the chalk mark. Remembering the earlier incident of the neighborhood boy who spit on her and its outcome, she said nothing about that afternoon to anyone.

During the next two years, Jade Snow found in eager reading her greatest source of joy and escape. As she now understood a fair amount of English, she stopped at the public library every few days after school to return four books and choose four new ones, the number allowed on one library card. Every day she read one book from cover to cover while with one ear she listened to her teachers. Temporarily she forgot who she was, or the constant requirements of Chinese life, while she delighted in the adventures of the Oz books, the *Little Colonel, Yankee Girl,* and Western cowboys, for in these books there was absolutely nothing resembling her own life.

About this time, to help her in her studies, Daddy bought Jade Snow her own desk. It was exactly like his, of yellow oak, with a kneehole, a set of three drawers on the right side, pigeonholes facing on the back, and a cover of flexible slats which could be rolled down to lock the desk. Daddy believed firmly in providing each of his children with a personal desk, light, and pair of scissors. He hated to have anyone disturb his belongings, and to teach his children the importance of leaving other people's personal property alone, he saw to it that each had his own essential tools for orderly living and studying.

Thus well equipped, Jade Snow had no excuse for not doing her homework to perfection. Because of this and because her last name began with "W," which seated her at the back of the classroom, she was able to manage those two fancy-full happy, daydreaming years in her storybooks while she obviously sailed through junior high, received a blue-and-white block sweater emblem for outstanding citizenship, and woke up to find that her teachers had skipped her half a grade. At twelve she was qualified to enter high school.

"RAILROAD STANDARD TIME"
Frank Chin (1940–   )

T he title of Frank Chin's short story refers to the building of the transcontinental railroad by Chinese American men during the 1860s. From 1865–1869, thousands of Chinese American men were hired by the Central Pacific Railroad Company to build the Western half of the transcontinental line from Sacramento eastward. Representing 90 percent of the company's employees, these men worked as both physical and technical laborers, laying tracks, clearing trees and rocks, handling explosives, and boring tunnels in the Sierra Nevada. The reclamation of this neglected history as a part of Chinese American heritage is a theme in many of Mr. Chin's stories, essays, and plays.

Mr. Chin was born in Berkeley, California, and grew up primarily in the Chinatowns of Oakland and San Francisco. He graduated from the University of California at Santa Barbara and won a fellowship to the Writers' Workshop at Iowa State University. He is the recipient of the 1992 Lannan Literary Fellowship for fiction, the Joseph Henry Jackson Award, the James T. Phelan Award for short fiction, and a National Endowment for the Arts creative writing grant.

Eight of his stories are collected in his book, The Chinaman Pacific and Frisco R.R. Co., which won a Before Columbus Foundation American Book Award in 1989. He is the author of two novels, Donald Duk, published in 1991 and Gunga Din. His plays, The Chickencoop Chinaman, The Year of the Dragon, and Gee, Pop! . . . A Real Cartoon have also won him acclaim, including the East-West Players Playwriting Award in 1971 and a

Rockefeller Playwright's grant in 1974. He co-edited the Asian American anthologies, Aiiieeeee! *(1974) and* The Big Aiiieeeee! *(1991) with Jeffery Paul Chan, Lawson Fusao Inada, and Shawn Wong. His stories and essays have been published in* The New York Times, Bridge, *and* Y'Bird Magazine. *He lives in the Los Angeles area.*

"THIS WAS YOUR GRANDFATHER'S," MA SAID. I WAS TWELVE, maybe fourteen years old when Grandma died. Ma put it on the table. The big railroad watch, Elgin. Nineteen-jewel movement. American made. Lever set. Stem wound. Glass face-cover. Railroad standard all the way. It ticked on the table between stacks of dirty dishes and cold food. She brought me in here to the kitchen, always to the kitchen to loose her thrills and secrets, as if the sound of running water and breathing the warm soggy ghosts of stale food, floating grease, old spices, ever comforted her, as if the kitchen was a paradise for conspiracy, sanctuary for us *juk sing* Chinamen from the royalty of pure-talking China-born Chinese, old, mourning, and belching in the other rooms of my dead grandmother's last house. Here, private, to say in Chinese, "This was your grandfather's," as if now that her mother had died and she'd been up all night long, not weeping, tough and lank, making coffee and tea and little foods for the brokenhearted family in her mother's kitchen, Chinese would be easier for me to understand. As if my mother would say all the important things of the soul and blood to her son, me, only in Chinese from now on. Very few people spoke the language at me the way she did. She chanted a spell up over me that conjured the meaning of what she was saying in the shape of old memories come to call. Words I'd never heard before set me at play in familiar scenes new to me, and ancient.

She lay the watch on the table, eased it slowly off her fingertips down to the tabletop without a sound. She didn't touch me, but put it down and held her hands in front of her like a bridesmaid holding an invisible bouquet and stared at the watch. As if it were talking to her, she looked hard at it, made faces at it, and did not move or answer the voices of the old, calling her from other rooms, until I picked it up.

A two-driver, high stepping locomotive ahead of a coal tender and baggage car, on double track between two semaphores showing a stop signal was engraved on the back.

"Your grandfather collected railroad watches," Ma said. "This one is the best." I held it in one hand and then the other, hefted it, felt out the meaning of "the best," words that rang of meat and vegetables, oils, things we touched, smelled, squeezed, washed, and ate, and I turned the big cased thing over several times. "Grandma gives it to you now," she said. It was big in my hand. Gold. A little greasy. Warm.

I asked her what her father's name had been, and the manic heat of her all-night burnout seemed to go cold and congeal. "Oh," she finally said, "it's one of those Chinese names I . . ." in English, faintly from another world, woozy and her throat and nostrils full of bubbly sniffles, the solemnity of the moment gone, the watch in my hand turned to cheap with the mumbling of a few awful English words. She giggled herself down to nothing but breath and moving lips. She shuffled backward, one step at a time, fox trotting dreamily backward, one hand dragging on the edge of the table, wobbling the table, rattling the dishes, spilling cold soup. Back down one side of the table, she dropped her butt a little with each step then muscled it back up. There were no chairs in the kitchen tonight. She knew, but still she looked. So this dance and groggy mumbling about the watch being no good, in strange English, like an Indian medicine man in a movie.

I wouldn't give it back or trade it for another out of the collection. This one was mine. No other. It had belonged to my grandfather. I wore it braking on the Southern Pacific, though it was two jewels short of new railroad standard and an outlaw watch that could get me fired. I kept it on me, arrived at my day-off courthouse wedding to its time, wore it as a railroad relic/family heirloom/grin-bringing affectation when I was writing background news in Seattle, reporting from the shadows of race riots, grabbing snaps for the 11:00 P.M., timing today's happenings with a nineteenth-century escapement. (Ride with me, Grandmother.) I was wearing it on my twenty-seventh birthday, the Saturday I came home to see my son asleep in the back of a strange station wagon, and Sarah inside, waving, shouting through an open window, "Goodbye, Daddy," over and over.

I stood it. Still and expressionless as some good Chink, I watched Barbara drive off, leave me, like some blonde white goddess going home from the jungle with her leather patches and briar pipe sweetheart writer and my kids. I'll learn to be a sore loser. I'll learn to hit people in the face. I'll learn to cry when I'm hurt and go for the throat instead of being polite and worrying about being obnoxious to people walking out of my house with my things, taking my kids away. I'll be more than quiet, embarrassed. I won't be likable anymore.

I hate my novel about a Chinatown mother like mine dying, now that Ma's dead. But I'll keep it. I hated after reading *Father and Glorious Descendant, Fifth Chinese Daughter, The House That Tai Ming Built.* Books scribbled up by a sad legion of snobby autobiographical Chinatown saps all on their own. Christians who never heard of each other, hardworking people who sweat out the exact same Chinatown book, the same cunning "Confucius says" joke, just like me. I kept it then and I'll still keep it. Part cookbook, memories of Mother in the kitchen slicing meat paper-thin with a cleaver. Mumbo jumbo about spices and steaming. The secret of Chinatown rice. The hands come down toward the food. The food crawls with culture. The thousand-year-old living Chinese meat makes dinner a safari into the unknown, a blood ritual. Food pornography. Black magic. Between the lines, I read a madman's detailed description of the preparation of shrunken heads. I never wrote to mean anything more than word fun with the food Grandma cooked at home. Chinese food. I read a list of what I remembered eating at my grandmother's table and knew I'd always be known by what I ate, that we come from a hungry tradition. Slop eaters following the wars on all fours. Weed cuisine and mud gravy in the shadow of corpses. We plundered the dust for fungus. Buried things. Seeds plucked out of the wind to feed a race of lace-boned skinnys, in high-school English, become transcendental Oriental art to make the dyke-ish spinster teacher cry. We always come to fake art and write the Chinatown book like bugs come to fly in the light. I hate my book now that ma's dead, but I'll keep it. I know she's not the woman I wrote up like my mother, and dead, in a book that was like everybody else's Chinatown book. Part word map of Chinatown San Francisco, shop to shop down Grant Avenue. Food again. The wind sucks the shops out and you breathe warm roast ducks dripping fat, hooks into the neck, through the head, out an eye. Stacks of iced fish, blue and fluorescent pink in the neon. The air is thin soup, sharp up the nostrils.

All mention escape from Chinatown into the movies. But we all forgot to mention how stepping off the streets into a faceful of Charlie Chaplin or a Western on a ripped and stained screen that became caught in the grip of winos breathing in unison in their sleep and billowed in and out, that shuddered when cars went by . . . we all of us Chinamans watched our own MOVIE ABOUT ME! I learned how to box watching movies shot by James Wong Howe. Cartoons were our nursery rhymes. Summers inside those neon-and-stucco downtown hole-in-the-wall Market Street Frisco movie houses blowing three solid hours of full-color seven-minute cartoons was school, was rows and rows of Chinamans learning English in a hurry from Daffy Duck.

When we ate in the dark and recited the dialogue of cartoon mice and cats out loud in various tones of voice with our mouths full, we looked like people singing hymns in church. We learned to talk like everybody in America. Learned to need to be afraid to stay alive, keeping moving. We learned to run, to be cheerful losers, to take a sudden pie in the face, talk American with a lot of giggles. To us a cartoon is a desperate situation. Of the movies, cartoons were the high art of our claustrophobia. They understood us living too close to each other. How, when you're living too close to too many people, you can't wait for one thing more without losing your mind. Cartoons were a fine way out of waiting in Chinatown around the rooms. Those of our Chinamans who every now and then break a reverie with, "Thank you, Mighty Mouse," mean it. Other folks thank Porky Pig, Snuffy Smith, Woody Woodpecker.

The day my mother told me I was to stay home from Chinese school one day a week starting today, to read to my father and teach him English while he was captured in total paralysis from a vertebra in the neck on down, I stayed away from cartoons. I went to a matinee in a white neighborhood looking for the

MOVIE ABOUT ME and was the only Chinaman in the house. I liked the way Peter Lorre ran along non-stop routine hysterical. I came back home with Peter Lorre. I turned out the lights in Pa's room. I put a candle on the dresser and wheeled Pa around in his chair to see me in front of the dresser mirror, reading Edgar Allan Poe out loud to him in the voice of Peter Lorre by candlelight.

The old men in the Chinatown books are all fixtures for Chinese ceremonies. All the same. Loyal filial children kowtow to the old and whiff food laid out for the dead. The dead eat the same as the living but without the sauces. White food. Steamed chicken. Rice we all remember as children scrambling down to the ground, to all fours and bonking our heads on the floor, kowtowing to a dead chicken.

My mother and aunts said nothing about the men of the family except they were weak. I like to think my grandfather was a good man. Even the kiss-ass steward service, I like to think he was tough, had a few laughs and ran off with his pockets full of engraved watches. Because I never knew him, not his name, nor anything about him, except a photograph of him as a young man with something of my mother's face in his face, and a watch chain across his vest. I kept his watch in good repair and told everyone it would pass to my son someday, until the day the boy was gone. Then I kept it like something of his he'd loved and had left behind, saving it for him maybe, to give to him when he was a man. But I haven't felt that in a long time.

The watch ticked against my heart and pounded my chest as I went too fast over bumps in the night and the radio on, on an all-night run downcoast, down country, down old Highway 99, Interstate 5. I ran my grandfather's time down past road signs that caught a gleam in my headlights and came at me out of the night with the names of forgotten high school girlfriends, BELLEVUE KIRKLAND, ROBERTA GERBER, AURORA CANBY, and sang with the radio to Jonah and Sarah in Berkeley, my Chinatown in Oakland and Frisco, to raise the dead. Ride with me, Grandfather, this is your grandson the ragmouth, called Tampax, the burned scarred boy, called Barbecue, going to San Francisco to bury my mother, your daughter, and spend Chinese New Year's at home. When we were sitting down and into our dinner after Grandma's funeral, and ate in front of the table set with white food for the dead, Ma said she wanted no white food and money burning after her funeral. Her sisters were there. Her sisters took charge of her funeral and the dinner afterwards. The dinner would most likely be in a Chinese restaurant in Frisco. Nobody had these dinners at home anymore. I wouldn't mind people having dinner at my place after my funeral, but no white food.

The whiz goes out of the tires as their roll bites into the steel grating of the Carquinez Bridge. The noise of the engine groans and echoes like a bomber in flight through the steel roadway. Light from the water far below shines through the grate, and I'm driving high, above a glow. The voice of the tires hums a shrill rubber screechy mosquito hum that vibrates through the chassis and frame of the car into my meatless butt, into my tender asshole, my pelvic bones, the roots of my teeth. Over the Carquinez Bridge to CROCKETT MARTINEZ closer to home, roll the tires of Ma's Chevy, my car now, carrying me up over the water southwest toward rolls of fog. The fat man's coming home on a sneaky breeze. Dusk comes a drooly mess of sunlight, a slobber of cheap pawnshop gold, a slow building heat across the water, all through the milky air through the glass of the window into the closed atmosphere of a driven car, into one side of my bomber's face. A bomber, flying my mother's car into the unknown charted by the stars and the radio, feels the coming of some old night song climbing hand over hand, bass notes plunking as steady and shady as reminiscence to get on my nerves one stupid beat after the other crossing the high rhythm six-step of the engine. I drive through the shadows of the bridge's steel structure all over the road. Fine day. I've been on the road for sixteen hours straight down the music of Seattle, Spokane, Salt Lake, Sacramento, Los Angeles, and Wolfman Jack lurking in odd hours of darkness, at peculiar altitudes of darkness, favoring the depths of certain Oregon valleys and heat and moonlight of my miles. And I'm still alive. Country'n' western music for the night road. It's pure white music. Like "The Star-Spangled Banner," it was the first official American music out of school into my jingling earbones sung by sighing white big tits in front of the climbing promise of FACE and Every Good Boy Does Fine chalked on the blackboard.

She stood up singing, one hand cupped in the other as if to catch drool slipping off her lower lip. Our eyes scouted through her blouse to elastic straps, lacy stuff, circular stitching, buckles, and in the distance, finally some skin. The color of her skin spread through the stuff of her blouse like melted butter through bread nicely to our tongues and was warm there. She sat flopping them on the keyboard as she breathed, singing "Home on the Range" over her shoulder, and pounded the tune out with her palms. The lonesome prairie was nothing but her voice, some hearsay country she stood up to sing *a capella* out of her. Simple music you can count. You can hear the words clear. The music's run through Clorox and Simonized, beating so insistently right and regular that you feel to sing it will deodorize you, make you clean. The hardhat hit parade. I listen to it a lot on the road. It's that get-outta-town beat and tune that makes me go.

Mrs. Morales was her name. Aurora Morales. The music teacher us boys liked to con into singing for us. Come-on opera, we wanted from her, not them Shirley Temple tunes the girls wanted to learn, but big notes, high long ones up from the navel that drilled through plaster and steel and skin and meat for bone marrow and electric wires on one long titpopping breath.

This is how I come home, riding a mass of spasms and death throes, warm and screechy inside, itchy, full of ghostpiss, as I drive right past what's left of Oakland's dark wooden Chinatown and dark streets full of dead lettuce and trampled carrot tops, parallel all the time in line with the tracks of the Western Pacific and Southern Pacific railroads.

"KUBOTA"

Garrett Hongo (1951–   )

Garrett Hongo's personal essay focuses on his special
relationship with his grandfather, known by his last name, Kubota.
As a third-generation Japanese American, the author inherits his
grandfather's internment stories and the impetus to tell them. As he
explains, this is a most unusual situation for a Sansei growing up in
the Gardena, California, of the 1950s. "Kubota" was included in
the Best American Essays of 1991.

    Mr. Hongo was born in the village of Volcano, Hawaii, and
grew up on the North Shore of Oahu and, later, in Los Angeles.
He was educated at Pomona College, The University of Michigan,
and the University of California at Irvine, where he earned his
MFA. His first collection of poems, Yellow Light, was published
in 1982. His second book, The River of Heaven, won the 1987
Lamont Poetry Prize of the Academy of American Poets for a
distinguished second book of poems and was a finalist for the 1989
Pulitzer Prize in poetry. Most recently, he is editor of The Open
Boat: Poems from Asian America.

    Mr. Hongo's honors include a Rockefeller Fellowship, a
Discovery/The Nation Award, two NEA fellowships, and a
Guggenheim fellowship. His work has been published in The New
Yorker, Antaeus, The American Poetry Review, Bamboo
Ridge, Field, The Nation, and Ploughshares. He has taught at
Houston, Irvine, and elsewhere, and is now professor of English
and director of creative writing at the University of Oregon. For
part of each year, he returns to Volcano, where he is at work on a
memoir about Hawaii.

ON DECEMBER 8, 1941, THE DAY AFTER THE JAPANESE ATTACK ON Pearl Harbor in Hawaii, my grandfather barricaded himself with his family—my grandmother, my teenage mother, her two sisters and two brothers—inside of his home in La'ie, a sugar plantation village on Oahu's North Shore. This was my maternal grandfather, a man most villagers called by his last name, Kubota. It could mean either "Wayside Field" or else "Broken Dreams," depending on which ideograms he used. Kubota ran La'ie's general store, and the previous night, after a long day of bad news on the radio, some locals had come by, pounded on the front door, and made threats. One was said to have brandished a machete. They were angry and shocked, as the whole nation was in the aftermath of the surprise attack. Kubota was one of the few Japanese Americans in the village and president of the local Japanese language school. He had become a target for their rage and suspicion. A wise man, he locked all his doors and windows and did not open his store the next day, but stayed closed and waited for news from some official.

He was a *kibei*, a Japanese American born in Hawaii (a U.S. territory then, so he was thus a citizen) but who was subsequently sent back by his father for formal education in Hiroshima, Japan, their home province. *Kibei* is written with two ideograms in Japanese: one is the word for "return" and the other is the word for "rice." Poetically, it means one who returns from America, known as the Land of Rice in Japanese (by contrast, Chinese immigrants called their new home Mountain of Gold).

Kubota was graduated from a Japanese high school and then came back to Hawaii as a teenager. He spoke English—and a Hawaiian creole version of it at that—with a Japanese accent. But he was well liked and good at numbers, scrupulous and hard working like so many immigrants and children of immigrants. Castle & Cook, a grower's company that ran the sugarcane business along the North Shore, hired him on first as a stock boy and then appointed him to run one of its company stores. He did well, had the trust of management and labor—not an easy accomplishment in any day—married, had children, and had begun to exert himself in community affairs and excel in his own recreations. He put together a Japanese community organization that backed a Japanese language school for children and sponsored teachers from Japan. Kubota boarded many of them, in succession, in his own home. This made dinners a silent affair for his talkative, Hawaiian-bred children, as their stern *sensei*, or teacher, was nearly always at table and their own abilities in the Japanese language were as delinquent as their attendance. While Kubota and the *sensei* rattled on about things Japanese, speaking Japanese, his children hurried through their suppers and tried to run off early to listen to the radio shows.

After dinner, while the *sensei* graded exams seated in a wicker chair in the spare room and his wife and children gathered around the radio in the front parlor, Kubota sat on the screened porch outside, reading the local Japanese newspapers. He finished reading about the same time as he finished the tea he drank for his digestion—a habit he'd learned in Japan—and then he'd get out his fishing gear and spread it out on the plank floors. The wraps on his rods needed to be redone, gears in his reels needed oil, and, once through with those tasks, he'd painstakingly wind on hundreds of yards of new line. Fishing was his hobby and his passion. He spent weekends camping along the North Shore beaches with his children, setting up umbrella tents, packing a rice pot and hibachi along for meals. And he caught fish. *Ulu'a* mostly, the huge surf-feeding fish known on the mainland as the jack crevalle, but he'd go after almost anything in its season. In Kawela, a plantation-owned bay nearby, he fished for mullet Hawaiian-style with a throw net, stalking the bottom-hugging, gray-backed schools as they gathered at the stream mouths and in the freshwater springs. In an outrigger out beyond the reef, he'd try for *aku*—the skipjack tuna prized for steaks and, sliced raw and mixed with fresh seaweed and cut onions, for *sashimi* salad. In Kahaluu and Ka'awa and on an offshore rock locals called Goat Island, he loved to go torching, stringing lanterns on bamboo poles stuck in the sand to attract *kumu'u*, the red goatfish, as they schooled at night just inside the reef. But in Lai'e on Laniloa Point near Kahuku, the northernmost tip of Oahu, he cast twelve-and fourteen-foot surf rods for the huge, varicolored, and fast-running *ulu'a* as they ran for schools of squid and baitfish just beyond the biggest breakers and past the low sand flats wadable from the shore to nearly a half mile out. At sunset, against the western light, he looked as if he walked on water as he came back, fish and rods slung over

his shoulders, stepping along the rock and coral path just inches
under the surface of a running tide.

When it was torching season, in December or January, he'd
drive out the afternoon before and stay with old friends, the
Tanakas or Yoshikawas, shopkeepers like him who ran stores
near the fishing grounds. They'd have been preparing for weeks,
selecting and cutting their bamboo poles, cleaning the hurricane
lanterns, tearing up burlap sacks for the cloths they'd soak with
kerosene and tie onto sticks they'd poke into the soft sand of
the shallows. Once lit, touched off with a Zippo lighter, these
would be the torches they'd use as beacons to attract the schooling fish. In another time, they might have made up a dozen
paper lanterns of the kind mostly used for decorating the summer folk dances outdoors on the grounds of the Buddhist church
during O-Bon, the Festival for the Dead. But now, wealthy
and modern and efficient killers of fish, Tanaka and Kubota
used rag torches and Colemans and cast rods with tips made of
Tonkin bamboo and butts of American-spun fiberglass. After
just one good night, they might bring back a prize bounty of a
dozen burlap bags filled with scores of bloody, rigid fish delicious to eat and even better to give away as gifts to friends,
family, and special customers.

It was a Monday night, the day after Pearl Harbor, and there
was a rattling knock at the front door. Two FBI agents presented
themselves, showed identification, and took my grandfather in
for questioning in Honolulu. He didn't return home for days.
No one knew what had happened or what was wrong. But
there was a roundup going on of all those in the Japanese-
American community suspected of sympathizing with the enemy and worse. My grandfather was suspected of espionage,
of communicating with offshore Japanese submarines launched
from the attack fleet days before war began. Torpedo planes
and escort fighters, decorated with the insignia of the Rising
Sun, had taken an approach route from northwest of Oahu
directly across Kahuku Point and on toward Pearl. They had
strafed an auxiliary air station near the fishing grounds my
grandfather loved and destroyed a small gun battery there, killing three men. Kubota was known to have sponsored and har-
bored Japanese nationals in his own home. He had a radio. He
had wholesale access to firearms. Circumstances and an under-

tone of racial resentment had combined with wartime hysteria in the aftermath of the tragic naval battle to cast suspicion on the loyalties of my grandfather and all other Japanese Americans. The FBI reached out and pulled hundreds of them in for questioning in dragnets cast throughout the West Coast and Hawaii.

My grandfather was lucky; he'd somehow been let go after only a few days. Others were not as fortunate. Hundreds, from small communities in Washington, California, Oregon, and Hawaii, were rounded up and, after what appeared to be routine questioning, shipped off under Justice Department orders to holding centers in Leuppe on the Navaho reservation in Arizona, in Fort Missoula in Montana, and on Sand Island in Honolulu Harbor. There were other special camps on Maui in Ha'iku and on Hawaii—the Big Island—in my own home village of Volcano.

Many of these men—it was exclusively the Japanese-American men suspected of ties to Japan who were initially rounded up—did not see their families again for more than four years. Under a suspension of due process that was only after the fact ruled as warranted by military necessity, they were, if only temporarily, "disappeared" in Justice Department prison camps scattered in particularly desolate areas of the United States designated as militarily "safe." These were grim forerunners of the assembly centers and concentration camps for the 120,000 Japanese-American evacuees that were to come later.

I am Kubota's eldest grandchild, and I remember him as a lonely, habitually silent old man who lived with us in our home near Los Angeles for most of my childhood and adolescence. It was the fifties, and my parents had emigrated from Hawaii to the mainland in the hope of a better life away from the old sugar plantation. After some success, they had sent back for my grandparents and taken them in. And it was my grandparents who did the work of the household while my mother and father worked their salaried city jobs. My grandmother cooked and sewed, washed our clothes, and knitted in the front room under the light of a huge lamp with a bright three-way bulb. Kubota raised a flower garden, read up on soils and grasses in gardening books, and planted a zoysia lawn in front and a dichondra one in back. He planted a small patch near the rear block wall with green onions, eggplant, white Japanese radishes, and cucumber. While he hoed and spaded the loamless, clayey earth of Los Angeles, he sang particularly plangent songs in Japanese about plum blossoms and bamboo groves.

Once, in the mid-sixties, after a dinner during which, as always, he had been silent while he worked away at a meal of fish and rice spiced with dabs of Chinese mustard and catsup thinned with soy sauce, Kubota took his own dishes to the kitchen sink and washed them up. He took a clean jelly jar out of the cupboard—the glass was thick and its shape squatty like an old-fashioned. He reached around to the hutch below where he kept his bourbon. He made himself a drink and retired to the living room where I was expected to join him for "talk story," the Hawaiian idiom for chewing the fat.

I was a teenager and, though I was bored listening to stories I'd heard often enough before at holiday dinners, I was dutiful. I took my spot on the couch next to Kubota and heard him out. Usually, he'd tell me about his schooling in Japan where he learned judo along with mathematics and literature. He'd learned the *soroban* there—the abacus, which was the original pocket calculator of the Far East—and that, along with his strong, judo-trained back, got him his first job in Hawaii. This was the moral. "Study *ha-ahd*," he'd say with pidgin emphasis. "Learn read good. Learn speak da kine *good* English." The message is the familiar one taught to any children of immigrants: succeed through education. And imitation. But this time, Kubota reached down into his past and told me a different story. I was thirteen by then, and I suppose he thought me ready for it. He told me about Pearl Harbor, how the planes flew in wing after wing of formations over his old house in La'ie in Hawaii, and how, the next day, after Roosevelt had made his famous "Day of Infamy" speech about the treachery of the Japanese, the FBI agents had come to his door and taken him in, hauled him off to Honolulu for questioning, and held him without charge for several days. I thought he was lying. I thought he was making up a kind of horror story to shock me and give his moral that much more starch. But it was true. I asked around. I brought it up during history class in junior high school, and my teacher, after silencing me and stepping me off to the back of the room, told me that it was indeed so. I asked my mother and she said it was true. I asked my schoolmates, who laughed and ridiculed me for being so ignorant. We lived in a Japanese-American community, and the parents of most of my classmates were the *nisei* who had been interned as teenagers all through the war. But there was a strange silence around all of this. There was a hush, as if one were invoking the ill powers of the dead when one brought it up. No one cared to speak about the evacuation and relocation for very long. It wasn't in our history books, though we were studying World War II at the time. It wasn't in the family albums of the people I knew and whom I'd visit staying over weekends with friends. And it wasn't anything that the family talked about or allowed me to keep bringing up either. I was given the facts, told sternly and pointedly that "it was war" and that "nothing could be done." "*Shikatta ga nai*" is the phrase in Japanese, a kind of resolute and determinist pronouncement on how to deal with inexplicable tragedy. I was to know it but not to dwell on it. Japanese Americans were busy trying to forget it ever happened and were having a hard enough time building their new lives after "camp." It was as if we had no history for four years and the relocation was something unspeakable.

But Kubota would not let it go. In session after session, for months it seemed, he pounded away at his story. He wanted to tell me the names of the FBI agents. He went over their questions and his responses again and again. He'd tell me how one would try to act friendly toward him, offering him cigarettes while the other, who hounded him with accusations and threats, left the interrogation room. Good cop, bad cop, I thought to myself, already superficially streetwise from stories black classmates told of the Watts riots and from my having watched too many episodes of *Dragnet* and *The Mod Squad*. But Kubota was not interested in my experiences. I was not made yet, and he was determined that his stories be part of my making. He spoke quietly at first, mildly, but once into his narrative and after his drink was down, his voice would rise and quaver with resentment and he'd make his accusations. He gave his testimony to me and I held it at first cautiously in my conscience like it was an heirloom too delicate to expose to strangers and anyone outside of the world Kubota made with his words. "I give you story now," he once said, "and you learn speak good, eh?" It was my job, as the disciple of his preaching I had then become, Ananda to his Buddha, to reassure him with a promise. "You learn speak good like the Dillingham," he'd say another time, referring to the wealthy scion of the grower family who had once run, unsuccessfully, for one of Hawaii's first senatorial seats. Or he'd then invoke a magical name, the name of one of his heroes, a man he thought particularly exemplary and righteous. "Learn speak dah good Ing-rish like *Mistah Inouye*," Kubota shouted. "He *lick* dah Dillingham even in debate. I saw on *terre-bision* myself." He was remembering the debates before the first senatorial election just before Hawaii was admitted to the Union as its fiftieth state. "You *tell* story," Kubota would end. And I had my injunction.

The town we settled in after the move from Hawaii is called Gardena, the independently incorporated city south of Los Angeles and north of San Pedro harbor. At its northern limit, it borders on Watts and Compton, black towns. To the southwest are Torrance and Redondo Beach, white towns. To the rest of L.A., Gardena is primarily famous for having legalized five-card draw poker after the war. On Vermont Boulevard, its eastern border, there is a dingy little Vegas-like strip of card clubs with huge parking lots and flickering neon signs that spell out "The Rainbow" and "The Horseshoe" in timed sequences of varicolored lights. The town is only secondarily famous as the largest community of Japanese Americans in the United States outside of Honolulu, Hawaii. When I was in high school there, it seemed to me that every *sansei* kid I knew wanted to be a doctor, an engineer, or a pharmacist. Our fathers were gardeners or electricians or nurserymen or ran small businesses catering to other Japanese Americans. Our mothers worked in civil service for the city or as cashiers for Thrifty Drug. What the kids wanted was a good job, good pay, a fine home, and no troubles. No one wanted to mess with the law—from either side—and no one wanted to mess with language or art. They all talked about getting into the right clubs so that they could go to the right schools. There was a certain kind of sameness, an intensely enforced system of conformity. Style was all. Boys wore moccasin-sewn shoes from Flagg Brothers, black A-1 slacks, and Kensington shirts with high collars. Girls wore their hair up in stiff bouffants solidified in hairspray and knew all the latest dances from the slauson to the funky chicken. We did well in chemistry and in math, no one who was Japanese but me spoke in English class or in history unless called upon, and no one talked about World War II. The day after Robert Kennedy was assassinated, after winning the California Democratic primary, we worked on calculus and elected class co-ordinators for the prom, featuring the 5th Dimension. We avoided grief. We avoided government. We avoided strong feelings and dangers of any kind. Once punished, we tried to maintain a concerted emotional and social discipline and would not willingly seek to fall out of the narrow margin of protective favor again.

But when I was thirteen, in junior high, I'd not understood why it was so difficult for my classmates, those who were themselves Japanese American, to talk about the relocation. They had cringed, too, when I tried to bring it up during our discussions of World War II. I was Hawaiian-born. They were mainland-born. Their parents had been in camp, had been the ones to suffer the complicated experience of having to distance themselves from their own history and all things Japanese in order to make their way back and into the American social and economic mainstream. It was out of this sense of shame and a fear of stigma I was only beginning to understand that the *nisei* had silenced themselves. And, for their children, among whom I grew up, they wanted no heritage, no culture, no contact with a defiled history. I recall the silence very well. The Japanese-American children around me were burdened in a way I was not. Their injunction was silence. Mine was to speak.

Away at college, in another protected world in its own way as magical to me as the Hawaii of my childhood, I dreamed about my grandfather. Tired from studying languages, practicing German conjugations or scripting an army's worth of Chinese ideograms on a single sheet of paper, Kubota would come to me as I drifted off into sleep. Or I would walk across the newly mown ball field in back of my dormitory, cutting through a street-side phalanx of ancient eucalyptus trees on my way to visit friends off campus, and I would think of him, his anger, and his sadness.

I don't know myself what makes someone feel that kind of need to have a story they've lived through be deposited somewhere, but I can guess. I think about *The Illiad, The Odys-*

sey, The Peloponnesian Wars of Thucydides, and a myriad of the works of literature I've studied. A character, almost a *topoi* he occurs so often, is frequently the witness who gives personal testimony about an event the rest of his community cannot even imagine. The sibyl is such a character. And Procne, the maid whose tongue is cut out so that she will not tell that she has been raped by her own brother-in-law, the king of Thebes. There are the dime novels, the epic blockbusters Hollywood makes into miniseries, and then there are the plain, relentless stories of witnesses who have suffered through horrors major and minor that have marked and changed their lives. I myself haven't talked to Holocaust victims. But I've read their survival stories and their stories of witness and been revolted and moved by them. My father-in-law, Al Thiessen, tells me his war stories again and again and I listen. A Mennonite who set aside the strictures of his own church in order to serve, he was a Marine codeman in the Pacific during World War II, in the Signal Corps on Guadalcanal, Morotai, and Bougainville. He was part of the island-hopping maneuver MacArthur had devised to win the war in the Pacific. He saw friends die from bombs which exploded not ten yards away. When he was with the 298th Signal Corps attached to the Thirteenth Air Force, he saw plane after plane come in and crash, just short of the runway, killing their crews, setting the jungle ablaze with oil and gas fires. Emergency wagons would scramble, bouncing over newly bulldozed land men used just the afternoon before for a football game. Every time we go fishing together, whether it's in a McKenzie boat drifting for salmon in Tillamook Bay or taking a lunch break from wading the riffles of a stream in the Cascades, he tells me about what happened to him and the young men in his unit. One was a Jewish boy from Brooklyn. One was a foul-mouthed kid from Kansas. They died. And he *has* to tell me. And I *have* to listen. It's a ritual payment the young owe their elders who have survived. The evacuation and relocation is something like that.

Kubota, my grandfather, had been ill with Alzheimer's disease for some time before he died. At the house he'd built on Kamehameha Highway in Hau'ula, a seacoast village just down the road from La'ie where he had his store, he'd wander out from the garage or greenhouse where he'd set up a workbench, and trudge down to the beach or up toward the line of pines he'd planted while employed by the Work Projects Administration during the thirties. Kubota thought he was going fishing. Or he thought he was back at work for Roosevelt, planting pines as a windbreak or soilbreak on the windward flank of the Ko'olau Mountains, emerald monoliths rising out of sea and cane fields from Waialua to Kaneohe. When I visited, my grandmother would send me down to the beach to fetch him. Or I'd run down Kam Highway a quarter mile or so and find him hiding in the cane field by the roadside, counting stalks, measuring circumferences in the claw of his thumb and forefinger. The look on his face was confused or concentrated, I didn't know which. But I guessed he was going fishing again. I'd grab him and walk him back to his house on the highway. My grandmother would shut him in a room.

Within a few years, Kubota had a stroke and survived it, then he had another one and was completely debilitated. The family decided to put him in a nursing home in Kahuku, just set back from the highway, within a mile or so of Kahuku Point and the Tanaka Store where he had his first job as a stock boy. He lived there three years, and I visited him once with my aunt. He was like a potato that had been worn down by cooking. Everything on him—his eyes, his teeth, his legs and torso—seemed like it had been sloughed away. What he had been was mostly gone now and I was looking at the nub of a man. In a wheelchair, he grasped my hands and tugged on them—violently. His hands were still thick and, I believed, strong enough to lift me out of my own seat into his lap. He murmured something in Japanese—he'd long ago ceased to speak any English. My aunt and I cried a little, and we left him.

I remember walking out on the black asphalt of the parking lot of the nursing home. It was heat-cracked and eroded already, and grass had veined itself into the interstices. There were coconut trees around, a cane field I could see across the street, and the ocean I knew was pitching a surf just beyond it. The green Ko'olaus came up behind us. Somewhere nearby, alongside the beach, there was an abandoned airfield in the middle of the canes. As a child, I'd come upon it playing one day, and my friends and I kept returning to it, day after day, playing war or sprinting games or coming to fly kites. I recognize it even now when I see it on TV—it's used as a site for action scenes in the detective shows Hollywood always sets in the islands: a helicopter chasing the hero racing away in a Ferrari, or gun dealers making a clandestine rendezvous on the abandoned runway. It was the old airfield strafed by Japanese planes the day the major flight attacked Pearl Harbor. It was the airfield the FBI thought my grandfather had targeted in his night fishing and signaling with the long surf poles he'd stuck in the sandy bays near Kahuku Point.

Kubota died a short while after I visited him, but not, I thought, without giving me a final message. I was on the mainland, in California studying for Ph.D. exams, when my grandmother called me with the news. It was a relief. He'd suffered from his debilitation a long time and I was grateful he'd gone. I went home for the funeral and gave the eulogy. My grandmother and I took his ashes home in a small, heavy metal box wrapped in a black *furoshiki*, a large silk scarf. She showed me the name the priest had given to him on his death, scripted with a calligraphy brush on a long, narrow talent of plain wood. Buddhist commoners, at death, are given priestly names, received symbolically into the clergy. The idea is that, in their next life, one of scholarship and leisure, they might meditate and attain the enlightenment the religion is aimed at. "*Shaku Shūchi*," the ideograms read. It was Kubota's Buddhist name, incorporating characters from his family and given names. It meant "Shining Wisdom of the Law." He died on Pearl Harbor Day, December 7, 1983.

After years, after I'd finally come back to live in Hawaii again, only once did I dream of Kubota, my grandfather. It was the same night I'd heard HR 442, the redress bill for Japanese Americans, had been signed into law. In my dream that night Kubota was "torching," and he sang a Japanese song, a querulous and wavery folk ballad, as he hung paper lanterns on bamboo poles stuck into the sand in the shallow water of the lagoon behind the reef near Kahuku Point. Then he was at a work table, smoking a hand-rolled cigarette, letting it dangle from his lips Bogart-style as he drew, daintily and skillfully, with a narrow trim brush, ideogram after ideogram on a score of paper lanterns he had hung in a dark shed to dry. He had painted a talismanic mantra onto each lantern, the ideogram for the word "red" in

Japanese, a bit of art blended with some superstition, a piece of sympathetic magic appealing to the magenta coloring on the rough skins of the schooling, night-feeding fish he wanted to attract to his baited hooks. He strung them from pole to pole in the dream then, hiking up his khaki worker's pants so his white ankles showed and wading through the shimmering black waters of the sand flats and then the reef. "The moon is leaving, leaving," he sang in Japanese. "Take me deeper in the savage sea." He turned and crouched like an ice racer then, leaning forward so that his unshaven face almost touched the light film of water. I could see the light stubble of beard like a fine, gray ash covering the lower half of his face. I could see his gold-rimmed spectacles. He held a small wooden boat in his cupped hands and placed it lightly on the sea and pushed it away. One of his lanterns was on it and, written in small neat rows like a sutra scroll, it had been decorated with the silvery names of all our dead.

from *THE JOY LUCK CLUB*
Amy Tan (1952–)

Amy Tan's debut novel tells the stories of four Chinese American women and their daughters living in contemporary San Francisco. The four older women are members of the Joy Luck Club, a group they formed in 1949 to play mah-jongg and tell stories both of their pasts in China and their present lives in the United States. Their vignettes alternate with those of their American-born daughters. The following excerpt is narrated by Lindo Jong's daughter, Waverly.

Amy Tan was born in Oakland, California, and grew up in Fresno, Oakland, and Berkeley, as well as the suburbs of the Bay Area. From 1969 to 1976, she attended five colleges, receiving both a B.A. and an M.A. from San Jose State University.

The Joy Luck Club *was on* The New York Times *bestseller list for over nine months in 1989, and was a finalist for both the National Book Award and the National Book Critics Circle Award. It received the Bay Area Book Reviewers Award for Fiction and the Commonwealth Club Gold Award, and was translated into seventeen languages, including Chinese. She wrote the screenplay for the movie version of* The Joy Luck Club, *directed by Wayne Wang. Her acclaimed second novel,* The Kitchen God's Wife, *was published in 1991, and her children's book,* The Moon Lady, *in 1992. Her stories have been published in magazines such as* The Atlantic, Grand Street, *and* Lear's. *Her essays have appeared in* Life, The Threepenny Review, The State of the Language, *and* The Best American Essays of 1991. *She lives in San Francisco.*

I HAD TAKEN MY MOTHER OUT TO LUNCH AT MY FAVORITE CHI-nese restaurant in hopes of putting her in a good mood, but it was a disaster.

When we met at the Four Directions Restaurant, she eyed me with immediate disapproval. "*Ai-ya!* What's the matter with your hair?" she said in Chinese.

"What do you mean, 'What's the matter,' " I said. "I had it cut." Mr. Rory had styled my hair differently this time, an asymmetrical blunt-line fringe that was shorter on the left side. It was fashionable, yet not radically so.

"Looks chopped off," she said. "You must ask for your money back."

I sighed. "Let's just have a nice lunch together, okay?"

She wore her tight-lipped, pinched-nose look as she scanned the menu, muttering, "Not too many good things, this menu." Then she tapped the waiter's arm, wiped the length of her chopsticks with her finger, and sniffed: "This greasy thing, do you expect me to eat with it?" She made a show of washing out her rice bowl with hot tea, and then warned other restaurant patrons seated near us to do the same. She told the waiter to make sure the soup was very hot, and of course, it was by her tongue's expert estimate "not even *lukewarm.*"

"You shouldn't get so upset," I said to my mother after she disputed a charge of two extra dollars because she had specified chrysanthemum tea, instead of the regular green tea. "Besides, unnecessary stress isn't good for your heart."

"Nothing is wrong with my heart," she huffed as she kept a disparaging eye on the waiter.

And she was right. Despite all the tension she places on her-self—and others—the doctors have proclaimed that my mother, at age sixty-nine, has the blood pressure of a sixteen-year-old and the strength of a horse. And that's what she is. A Horse, born in 1918, destined to be obstinate and frank to the point of tactlessness. She and I make a bad combination, because I'm a Rabbit, born in 1951, supposedly sensitive, with tendencies toward being thin-skinned and skittery at the first sign of criti-cism.

After our miserable lunch, I gave up the idea that there would ever be a good time to tell her the news: that Rich Schields and I were getting married.

★ ★ ★

"Why are you so nervous?" my friend Marlene Ferber had asked over the phone the other night. "It's not as if Rich is the scum of the earth. He's a tax attorney like you, for Chrissake. How can she criticize that?"

"You don't know my mother," I said. "She never thinks anybody is good enough for anything."

"So elope with the guy," said Marlene.

"That's what I did with Marvin." Marvin was my first husband, my high school sweetheart.

"So there you go," said Marlene.

"So when my mother found out, she threw her shoe at us," I said. "And that was just for openers."

My mother had never met Rich. In fact, every time I brought up his name—when I said, for instance, that Rich and I had gone to the symphony, that Rich had taken my four-year-old daughter, Shoshana, to the zoo—my mother found a way to change the subject.

"Did I tell you," I said as we waited for the lunch bill at Four Directions, "what a great time Shoshana had with Rich at the Exploratorium? He—"

"Oh," interrupted my mother, "I didn't tell you. Your father, doctors say maybe need exploratory surgery. But no, now they say everything normal, just too much constipated." I gave up. And then we did the usual routine.

I paid for the bill, with a ten and three ones. My mother pulled back the dollar bills and counted out exact change, thirteen cents, and put that on the tray instead, explaining firmly: "No tip!" She tossed her head back with a triumphant smile. And while my mother used the restroom, I slipped the waiter a five-dollar bill. He nodded to me with deep understanding. While she was gone, I devised another plan.

"*Choszle!*"—Stinks to death in there!—muttered my mother when she returned. She nudged me with a little travel package of Kleenex. She did not trust other people's toilet paper. "Do you need to use?"

I shook my head. "But before I drop you off, let's stop at my place real quick. There's something I want to show you."

★ ★ ★

My mother had not been to my apartment in months. When I was first married, she used to drop by unannounced, until one day I suggested she should call ahead of time. Ever since then, she has refused to come unless I issue an official invitation.

And so I watched her, seeing her reaction to the changes in my apartment—from the pristine habitat I maintained after the divorce, when all of a sudden I had too much time to keep my life in order—to this present chaos, a home full of life and love. The hallway floor was littered with Shoshana's toys, all bright plastic things with scattered parts. There was a set of Rich's barbells in the living room, two dirty snifters on the coffee table, the disemboweled remains of a phone that Shoshana and Rich took apart the other day to see where the voices came from.

"It's back here," I said. We kept walking, all the way to the back bedroom. The bed was unmade, dresser drawers were hanging out with socks and ties spilling over. My mother stepped over running shoes, more of Shoshana's toys, Rich's black loafers, my scarves, a stack of white shirts just back from the cleaner's.

Her look was one of painful denial, reminding me of a time long ago when she took my brothers and me down to a clinic to get our polio booster shots. As the needle went into my brother's arm and he screamed, my mother looked at me with agony written all over her face and assured me, "Next one doesn't hurt."

But now, how could my mother *not* notice that we were living together, that this was serious and would not go away even if she didn't talk about it? She had to say something.

I went to the closet and then came back with a mink jacket that Rich had given me for Christmas. It was the most extravagant gift I had ever received.

I put the jacket on. "It's sort of a silly present," I said nervously. "It's hardly ever cold enough in San Francisco to wear mink. But it seems to be a fad, what people are buying their wives and girlfriends these days."

My mother was quiet. She was looking toward my open closet, bulging with racks of shoes, ties, my dresses, and Rich's suits. She ran her fingers over the mink.

"This is not so good," she said at last. "It is just leftover strips. And the fur is too short, no long hairs."

"How can you criticize a gift!" I protested. I was deeply wounded. "He gave me this from his heart."

"That is why I worry," she said.

And looking at the coat in the mirror, I couldn't fend off the strength of her will anymore, her ability to make me see black where there was once white, white where there was once black. The coat looked shabby, an imitation of romance.

"Aren't you going to say anything else?" I asked softly.

"What should I say?"

"About the apartment? About *this*?" I gestured to all the signs of Rich lying about.

She looked around the room, toward the hall, and finally she said, "You have career. You are busy. You want to live like mess, what I can say?"

My mother knows how to hit a nerve. And the pain I feel is worse than any other kind of misery. Because what she does always comes as a shock, exactly like an electric jolt that grounds itself permanently in my memory. I still remember the first time I felt it.

I was ten years old. Even though I was young, I knew my ability to play chess was a gift. It was effortless, so easy. I could see things on the chessboard that other people could not. I could create barriers to protect myself that were invisible to my opponents. And this gift gave me supreme confidence. I knew what my opponents would do, move for move. I knew at exactly what point their faces would fall when my seemingly simple and childlike strategy would reveal itself as a devastating and irrevocable course. I loved to win.

And my mother loved to show me off, like one of my many trophies she polished. She used to discuss my games as if she had devised the strategies.

"I told my daughter, Use your horses to run over the enemy," she informed one shopkeeper. "She won very quickly this way." And of course, she had said this before the game—that and a hundred other useless things that had nothing to do with my winning.

To our family friends who visited she would confide, "You don't have to be so smart to win chess. It is just tricks. You blow from the North, South, East, and West. The other person becomes confused. They don't know which way to run."

I hated the way she tried to take all the credit. And one day I told her so, shouting at her on Stockton Street, in the middle of a crowd of people. I told her she didn't know anything, so she shouldn't show off. She should shut up. Words to that effect.

That evening and the next day she wouldn't speak to me. She would say stiff words to my father and brothers, as if I had become invisible and she was talking about a rotten fish she had thrown away but which had left behind its bad smell.

I knew this strategy, the sneaky way to get someone to pounce back in anger and fall into a trap. So I ignored her. I refused to speak and waited for her to come to me.

After many days had gone by in silence, I sat in my room, staring at the sixty-four squares of my chessboard, trying to think of another way. And that's when I decided to quit playing chess.

Of course I didn't mean to quit forever. At most, just for a few days. And I made a show of it. Instead of practicing in my room every night, as I always did, I marched into the living room and sat down in front of the television set with my brothers, who stared at me, an unwelcome intruder. I used my brothers to further my plan; I cracked my knuckles to annoy them.

"Ma!" they shouted. "Make her stop. Make her go away."

But my mother did not say anything.

Still I was not worried. But I could see I would have to make a stronger move. I decided to sacrifice a tournament that was coming up in one week. I would refuse to play in it. And my mother would certainly have to speak to me about this. Because the sponsors and the benevolent associations would start calling her, asking, shouting, pleading to make me play again.

And then the tournament came and went. And she did not come to me, crying, "Why are you not playing chess?" But I was crying inside, because I learned that a boy whom I had easily defeated on two other occasions had won.

I realized my mother knew more tricks than I had thought. But now I was tired of her game. I wanted to start practicing for the next tournament. So I decided to pretend to let her win. I would be the one to speak first.

"I am ready to play chess again," I announced to her. I had imagined she would smile and then ask me what special thing I wanted to eat.

But instead, she gathered her face into a frown and stared into my eyes, as if she could force some kind of truth out of me.

"Why do you tell me this?" she finally said in sharp tones. "You think it is so easy. One day quit, next day play. Everything for you is this way. So smart, so easy, so fast."

"I said I'll play," I whined.

"No!" she shouted, and I almost jumped out of my scalp. "It is not so easy anymore."

I was quivering, stunned by what she said, in not knowing what she meant. And then I went back to my room. I stared at my chessboard, its sixty-four squares, to figure out how to undo this terrible mess. And after staring like this for many hours, I actually believed that I had made the white squares black and the black squares white, and everything would be all right.

And sure enough, I won her back. That night I developed a high fever, and she sat next to my bed, scolding me for going to school without my sweater. In the morning she was there as well, feeding me rice porridge flavored with chicken broth she had strained herself. She said she was feeding me this because I had the chicken pox and one chicken knew how to fight another. And in the afternoon, she sat in a chair in my room, knitting me a pink sweater while telling me about a sweater that Auntie Suyuan had knit for her daughter June, and how it was most unattractive and of the worst yarn. I was so happy that she had become her usual self.

But after I got well, I discovered that, really, my mother had changed. She no longer hovered over me as I practiced different chess games. She did not polish my trophies every day. She did not cut out the small newspaper items that mentioned my name. It was as if she had erected an invisible wall and I was secretly groping each day to see how high and wide it was.

At my next tournament, while I had done well overall, in the end the points were not enough. I lost. And what was worse, my mother said nothing. She seemed to walk around with this satisfied look, as if it had happened because she had devised this strategy.

I was horrified. I spent many hours every day going over in my mind what I had lost. I knew it was not just the last tournament. I examined every move, every piece, every square. And I could no longer see the secret weapons of each piece, the magic within the intersection of each square. I could see only my mistakes, my weaknesses. It was as though I had lost my magic armor. And everybody could see this, where it was easy to attack me.

Over the next few weeks and later months and years, I continued to play, but never with that same feeling of supreme confidence. I fought hard, with fear and desperation. When I won, I was grateful, relieved. And when I lost, I was filled with growing dread, and then terror that I was no longer a prodigy, that I had lost the gift and had turned into someone quite ordinary.

When I lost twice to the boy whom I had defeated so easily a few years before, I stopped playing chess altogether. And nobody protested. I was fourteen.

from TURNING JAPANESE: MEMOIRS OF A SANSEI
David Mura (1952–   )

urning Japanese *is David Mura's memoir of his year in contemporary Japan and his early life in America. His introspective accounts of living in Japan with his wife, Susan, are based on his travels there in 1984 on a U.S./Japan Creative Artist Exchange Fellowship. In the following excerpt, Mr. Mura recalls growing up as a third-generation Japanese American in a primarily Jewish American Chicago suburb.* Turning Japanese *won a 1991 Josephine Miles Book Award from the Oakland PEN, and has been translated into Japanese and Dutch.*

Mr. Mura was born in Great Lakes, Illinois. He was educated at Grinnell College, the University of Minnesota, and Vermont College, where he received his M.F.A. in creative writing. His collection of poetry, After We Lost Our Way, *won the National Poetry Series competition in 1989. He has also written* A Male Grief: Notes on Pornography & Addiction *(1987). He wrote and performed* Relocations: Images from a Sansei *in 1990, and his play,* Invasion, *premiered at Minneapolis's Pillsbury House Theater in 1993.*

His awards include two NEA Literature Fellowships, several Minnesota State Arts Board grants, a Discovery/The Nation Award, two Loft-McKnight awards, and two Bush Foundation Fellowships. His poems have been published in The Nation, The American Poetry Review, The New England Review, Crazyhorse, The New Republic, *and several anthologies. His essays and criticism have appeared in* Mother Jones, The New York Times, The Utne Reader, The Graywolf Annual, The

Boston Review, *and many other publications. Mr. Mura has
taught at the University of Minnesota, the University of Oregon,
St. Olaf College, and the Loft. He lives in St. Paul, Minnesota,
where he co-founded the Asian American Renaissance, an arts
organization.*

MY FATHER NEVER SLEPT WITH A WHITE WOMAN; NEVER, I THINK,
slept with anyone but my mother. Still, I know he must have
thought of crossing that line, must have been aware it was there
to cross.

One fall afternoon, I am home from eighth grade, with a
slight fever. My mother is out shopping. For some reason, I
start rummaging in my parents' closet, pushing back the pumps
and flats, all lined in a row on the rack, unzipping the garment
bags. (What am I looking for? Years later, my therapist will tell
me that news travels quickly and silently in families; no one has
to speak of it.) From beneath a stack of folded sweaters, I pull
a *Playboy* magazine. I start moving through the pages, the ads
for albums and liquor, cartoons, the interview with Albert
Schweitzer, with photos of the great man in pith helmet and
bow tie, his famous walrus mustache. And then the foldout
undoes itself, flowing before me with its glossy shine.

I have seen a *Playboy* someone brought into the locker room
at school. But now I am alone, in my parents' bedroom. I worry
about when my mother is coming back, I forget she is gone. I
am entranced by the woman's breasts, the aureoles seem large
as my fists. She is blond, eighteen, a U.C.L.A. coed. She leans
against a screen, half her body exposed to the camera.

And so, like many other American boys, I discover my sexu-
ality in the presence of a picture. And, like many other American
boys, I do not think of the color of the woman's skin. Of course,
if she were black or brown or yellow . . . but she is white, her
beauty self-evident. I sense somehow that she must be more
beautiful than Asian women, more prestigious. But the forbidden quality of sex overpowers any thought of race. I do not
wonder why my father looks at these pictures, these women
who are not my mother. The sensations of pleasure, of momen-

tary possession and shame, flood over me quickly, easily, sliding through my body.

A few minutes later, I pick up the magazine, slip it back in the garment bag beneath the sweaters.

My mother, I remember, never touched me. In that way we were very Japanese. Or very puritan. In fact, I don't remember playing with her. When Saturdays came, I ran instead to the room of my aunt Miwako, who lived with us. She was the maiden aunt, the one who had time. She took me to movies, the zoo, bought me ice cream, candy.

The strongest childhood memory I have of conversing with my mother has her standing at the stove, cutting carrots or celery, letting slices slip into the pot of stew. I am sitting at the table, saying the multiplication table. I get frustrated every time I miss one; there is pleasure only in getting every one right. It is not a game, it is a performance. And it must be perfect. I look up and see her there, the steam rising in her face, her hair pulled behind her head, her slightly hooked nose freckled, not yet beginning to show the spots of age. The bones of her cheeks are angular, almost Spanish rather than Japanese. I know now she was beautiful, but I did not think so then. The distance between us, about ten feet, seems right, comfortable.

I don't know what she said to my father when she found I had gotten into his *Playboys*. I only know that later my father summoned me to the kitchen table and gave me a lecture that would serve as a model for the ones to come all through my adolescence, whenever she discovered pornography in my room. I see my father in his T-shirt and tortoiseshell glasses; his hair is shiny, brushed off his forehead. He is a little older than I am now. Some part of me must know he is uncomfortable, but I am only aware that some knot I can't untie is growing in my stomach, its strands tightening, engorging, twisting together.

He does not say much. He tells me, simply, "You will burn yourself out." I should stay away from girls; he can have the magazine because he is an adult, I must wait till I'm seventeen, eighteen—years away. And then he hands me a pamphlet from the AMA, where he works. "If you have any questions after you read this . . ."

I have no questions.

Later, I do manage to observe technically my father's ban on dates. After all, I am going to a Jewish high school; most of the girls are not allowed to date "goyim." They can hardly pass me off to their parents as David Steinberg. And I am awkward, socially backward, more adept in the classroom or on the basketball court than at a dance. Once, in senior year, Laurie Brandt, she of the long legs, does agree to go out with me, but at the end of the second date, at her doorstep, she bursts into tears. "I can't go out with you," she says, "my dad found out you weren't Jewish." I am dumbfounded. It feels like my fate. I do not go to homecoming or prom.

At nineteen—a late age for that period of "free love"—I lose my virginity to an upper-class woman at college. It is brief, joyless, done mainly because neither of us sees a reason not to. I feel relieved, the deed is done. But it does not wash away the feelings of inadequacy, the barriers I feel are there because of my looks. Is it my race or my own features? I cannot separate them; the matter is too hazy, too fraught with complications.

After this slow start, I break my father's ban with a vengeance. Steadily, surely, even after I meet Susie at the age of twenty, I come to woman after woman. My desires seem limitless. I take my father at his word. I begin to burn myself out.

"What Means Switch"
Gish Jen (1955–)

In "What Means Switch," Gish Jen humorously depicts the trials and wiles of protagonist Mona Chang, a Chinese American newcomer to a junior high school in Scarsdale, New York. Among other themes, this story explores the sometimes tense relations between Japanese and Chinese Americans deriving from the Second World War and centuries-long antagonism between Japan and China.

Born in New York City, Ms. Jen graduated from Harvard University and the Iowa Writers' Workshop, where she earned an M.F.A. Her first novel, Typical American, *was published in 1991 and was nominated for the National Book Critics Circle Award. She has received writing grants from the NEA, the Guggenheim Foundation, the Radcliffe Bunting Institute, the James Michener/Copernicus Society, and the Massachusetts Artists' Foundation. Ms. Jen's short fiction has appeared in numerous anthologies including* The Best American Short Stories of 1988. *Her work has also been published in magazines including* The New Yorker, The Atlantic, The Yale Review, Fiction International, *and* The Southern Review. *She lives in Cambridge, Massachusetts.*

THERE WE ARE, NICE CHINESE FAMILY—FATHER, MOTHER, TWO born-here girls. Where should we live next? My parents slide the question back and forth like a cup of ginseng neither one wants to drink. Until finally it comes to them, what they really want is a milkshake (chocolate) and to go with it a house in Scarsdale. What else? The broker tries to hint: the neighborhood, she says. Moneyed. Many delis. Meaning rich and Jewish. But someone has sent my parents a list of the top ten schools nation-wide (based on the opinion of selected educators and others) and so *many-deli* or not we nestle into a Dutch colonial on the Bronx River Parkway. The road's windy where we are, very charming; drivers miss their turns, plow up our flower beds, then want to use our telephone. "Of course," my mom tells them, like it's no big deal, we can replant. We're the type to adjust. You know—the lady drivers weep, my mom gets out the Kleenex for them. We're a bit down the hill from the private plane set, in other words. Only in our dreams do our jacket zippers jam, what with all the lift tickets we have stapled to them, Killington on top of Sugarbush on top of Stowe, and we don't even know where the Virgin Islands are—although certain of us do know that virgins are like priests and nuns, which there were a lot more of in Yonkers, where we just moved from, than there are here.

This is my first understanding of class. In our old neighborhood everybody knew everything about virgins and non-virgins, not to say the technicalities of staying in between. Or almost everybody, I should say; in Yonkers I was the laugh-along type. Here I'm an expert.

"You mean the man . . . ?" Pig-tailed Barbara Gugelstein spits a mouthful of Coke back into her can. "That is *so* gross!"

Pretty soon I'm getting popular for a new girl. The only problem is Danielle Meyers, who wears blue mascara and has gone steady with two boys. "How do *you* know," she starts to ask, proceeding to edify us all with how she French-kissed one boyfriend and just regular kissed another. ("Because, you know, he had braces.") We hear about his rubber bands, how once one popped right into her mouth. I begin to realize I need to find somebody to kiss too. But how?

Luckily, I just about then happen to tell Barbara Gugelstein I know karate. I don't know why I tell her this. My sister Callie's the liar in the family; ask anybody. I'm the one who doesn't see why we should have to hold our heads up. But for some reason

I tell Barbara Gugelstein I can make my hands like steel by thinking hard. "I'm not supposed to tell anyone," I say.

The way she backs away, blinking, I could be the burning bush.

"I can't do bricks," I say—a bit of expectation management. "But I can do your arm if you want." I set my hand in chop position.

"Uhh, it's okay," she says. "I know you can, I saw it on TV last night."

That's when I recall that I too saw it on TV last night—in fact, at her house. I rush on to tell her I know how to get pregnant with tea.

"With *tea?*"

"That's how they do it in China."

She agrees that China is an ancient and great civilization that ought to be known for more than spaghetti and gunpowder. I tell her I know Chinese. "*Be-yeh fa-foon,*" I say. "*Shee-veh. Ji nu.*" Meaning, "Stop acting crazy. Rice gruel. Soy sauce." She's impressed. At lunch the next day, Danielle Meyers and Amy Weinstein and Barbara's crush, Andy Kaplan, are all impressed too. Scarsdale is a liberal town, not like Yonkers, where the Whitman Road Gang used to throw crabapple mash at my sister Callie and me and tell us it would make our eyes stick shut. Here we're like permanent exchange students. In another ten years, there'll be so many Orientals we'll turn into Asians; a Japanese grocery will buy out that one deli too many. But for now, the mid-sixties, what with civil rights on TV, we're not so much accepted as embraced. Especially by the Jewish part of town—which, it turns out, is not all of town at all. That's just an idea people have, Callie says, and lots of them could take us or leave us same as the Christians, who are nice too; I shouldn't generalize. So let me not generalize except to say that pretty soon I've been to so many bar and bas mitzvahs, I can almost say myself whether the kid chants like an angel or like a train conductor, maybe they could use him on the commuter line. At seder I know to forget the bricks, get a good pile of that mortar. Also I know what is schmaltz. I know that I am a goy. This is not why people like me, though. People like me because I do not need to use deodorant, as I demonstrate in the locker room before and after gym. Also, I can explain to them, for example, what is tofu (*der-voo*, we say at home). Their mothers invite me to taste-test their Chinese cooking.

"Very authentic." I try to be reassuring. After all, they're nice people, I like them. "De-lish." I have seconds. On the question of what we eat, though, I have to admit, "Well, no, it's different than that." I have thirds. "What my mom makes is home style, it's not in the cookbooks."

Not in the cookbooks! Everyone's jealous. Meanwhile, the big deal at home is when we have turkey pot pie. My sister Callie's the one introduced them—Mrs. Wilder's, they come in this green-and-brown box—and when we have them, we both get suddenly interested in helping out in the kitchen. You know, we stand in front of the oven and help them bake. Twenty-five minutes. She and I have a deal, though, to keep it secret from school, as everybody else thinks they're gross. We think they're a big improvement over authentic Chinese home cooking. Oxtail soup—now that's gross. Stir-fried beef with tomatoes. One day I say, "You know Ma, I have never seen a stir-fried tomato in any Chinese restaurant we have ever been in, ever."

"In China," she says, real lofty, "we consider tomatoes are a delicacy."

"Ma," I say. "Tomatoes are *Italian*."

"No respect for elders." She wags her finger at me, but I can tell it's just to try and shame me into believing her. "I'm tell you, tomatoes *invented* in China."

"*Ma.*"

"Is true. Like noodles. Invented in China."

"That's not what they said in *school*."

"In *China*," my mother counters, "we also eat tomatoes uncooked, like apple. And in summertime we slice them, and put some sugar on top."

"Are you sure?"

My mom says of course she's sure, and in the end I give in, even though she once told me that China was such a long time ago, a lot of things she can hardly remember. She said sometimes she has trouble remembering her characters, that sometimes she'll be writing a letter, just writing along, and all of a sudden she won't be sure if she should put four dots or three.

"So what do you do then?"

"Oh, I just make a little sloppy."

"You mean you *fudge*?"

She laughed then, but another time, when she was showing me how to write my name, and I said, just kidding, "Are you sure that's the right number of dots now?" she was hurt.

"I mean, of course you know," I said. "I mean, *oy*."

Meanwhile, what *I* know is that in the eighth grade, what people want to hear does not include how Chinese people eat sliced tomatoes with sugar on top. For a gross fact, it just isn't gross enough. On the other hand, the fact that somewhere in China somebody eats or has eaten or once ate living monkey brains—now that's conversation.

"They have these special tables," I say, "kind of like a giant collar. With a hole in the middle, for the monkey's neck. They put the monkey in the collar, and then they cut off the top of its head."

"Whadda they use for cutting?"

I think. "Scalpels."

"*Scalpels*?" says Andy Kaplan.

"Kaplan, don't be dense," Barbara Gugelstein says. "The Chinese *invented* scalpels."

Once a friend said to me, You know, everybody is valued for something. She explained how some people resented being valued for their looks; others resented being valued for their money. Wasn't it still better to be beautiful and rich than ugly and poor, though? You should be just glad, she said, that you have something people value. It's like having a special talent, like being good at ice-skating, or opera-singing. She said, You could probably make a career out of it.

Here's the irony: I am.

Anyway. I am ad-libbing my way through eighth grade, as I've described. Until one bloomy spring day, I come in late to homeroom, and to my chagrin discover there's a new kid in class.

Chinese.

So what should I do, pretend to have to go to the girls' room, like Barbara Gugelstein the day Andy Kaplan took his ID back? I sit down; I am so cool I remind myself of Paul Newman. First thing I realize, though, is that no one looking at me is thinking of Paul Newman. The notes fly:

"*I* think he's cute."

"Who?" I write back. (I am still at an age, understand, when I believe a person can be saved by aplomb.)

"I don't think he talks English too good. Writes it either."

"Who?"

"They might have to put him behind a grade, so don't worry."

"He has a crush on you already, you could tell as soon as you walked in, he turned kind of orangeish."

I hope I'm not turning orangeish as I deal with my mail; I could use a secretary. The second round starts:

"What do you mean who? Don't be weird. Didn't you *see* him??? Straight back over your right shoulder!!!!"

I have to look; what else can I do? I think of certain tips I learned in Girl Scouts about poise. I cross my ankles. I hold a pen in my hand. I sit up as though I have a crown on my head. I swivel my head slowly, repeating to myself, *I* could be Miss America.

"Miss Mona Chang."

Horror raises its hoary head.

"Notes, please."

Mrs. Mandeville's policy is to read all notes aloud.

I try to consider what Miss America would do, and see myself, back straight, knees together, crying. Some inspiration. Cool Hand Luke, on the other hand, would, quick, eat the evidence. And why not? I should yawn as I stand up, and boom, the notes are gone. All that's left is to explain that it's an old Chinese reflex.

I shuffle up to the front of the room.

"One minute please," Mrs. Mandeville says.

I wait, noticing how large and plastic her mouth is.

She unfolds a piece of paper.

And I, Miss Mona Chang, who got almost straight A's her whole life except in math and conduct, am about to start crying in front of everyone.

★ ★ ★

I am delivered out of hot Egypt by the bell. General pandemonium. Mrs. Mandeville still has her hand clamped on my shoulder, though. And the next thing I know, I'm holding the new boy's schedule. He's standing next to me like a big blank piece of paper. "This is Sherman," Mrs. Mandeville says.

"Hello," I say.

"*Non how a*," I say.

I'm glad Barbara Gugelstein isn't there to see my Chinese in action.

"*Ji nu*," I say. "*Shee veh.*"

Later I find out that his mother asked if there were any other Orientals in our grade. She had him put in my class on purpose. For now, though, he looks at me as though I'm much stranger than anything else he's seen so far. Is this because he understands I'm saying "soy sauce rice gruel" to him or because he doesn't?

"Sher-man," he says finally.

I look at his schedule card. Sherman Matsumoto. What kind of name is that for a nice Chinese boy?

(Later on, people ask me how I can tell Chinese from Japanese. I shrug. You just kind of know, I say. *Oy!*)

Sherman's got the sort of looks I think of as pretty-boy. Monsignor-black hair (not monk brown like mine), bouncy. Crayola eyebrows, one with a round bald spot in the middle of it, like a golf hole. I don't know how anybody can think of him as orangeish; his skin looks white to me, with pink triangles hanging down the front of his cheeks like flags. Kind of delicate-looking, but the only truly uncool thing about him is that his spiral notebook has a picture of a kitty cat on it. A big white fluffy one, with a blue ribbon above each perky little ear. I get much opportunity to view this, as all the poor kid understands about life in junior high school is that he should follow me everywhere. It's embarrassing. On the other hand, he's obviously even more miserable than I am, so I try not to say anything. Give him a chance to adjust. We communicate by sign language, and by drawing pictures, which he's better at than I am; he puts in every last detail, even if it takes forever. I try to be patient.

A week of this. Finally I enlighten him. "You should get a new notebook."

His cheeks turn a shade of pink you mostly only see in hyacinths.

"Notebook." I point to his. I show him mine, which is psychedelic, with big purple and yellow stick-on flowers. I try to explain he should have one like this, only without the flowers. He nods enigmatically, and the next day brings me a notebook just like his, except that this cat sports pink bows instead of blue.

"Pret-ty," he says. "You."

He speaks English! I'm dumbfounded. Has he spoken it all this time? I consider: Pretty. You. What does that mean? Plus actually, he's said *plit-ty*, much as my parents would; I'm assuming he means pretty, but maybe he means pity. Pity. You.

"Jeez," I say finally.

"You are wel-come," he says.

I decorate the back of the notebook with stick-on flowers, and hold it so that these show when I walk through the halls. In class I mostly keep my book open. After all, the kid's so new; I think I really ought to have a heart. And for a livelong day nobody notices.

Then Barbara Gugelstein sidles up. "Matching notebooks, huh?"

I'm speechless.

"First comes love, then comes marriage, and then come chappies in a baby carriage."

"Barbara!"

"Get it?" she says. "Chinese Japs."

"Bar-*bra*," I say to get even.

"Just make sure he doesn't give you any *tea*" she says.

Are Sherman and I in love? Three days later, I hazard that we are. My thinking proceeds this way: I think he's cute, and I think he thinks I'm cute. On the other hand, we don't kiss and we don't exactly have fantastic conversations. Our talks *are* getting better, though. We started out, "This is a book."

"Book." "This is a chair." "Chair." Advancing to, "What is this?" "This is a book." Now, for fun, he tests me.

"What is this?" he says.

"This is a book," I say, as if I'm the one who has to learn how to talk.

He claps. "Good!"

Meanwhile, people ask me all about him. I could be his press agent.

"No, he doesn't eat raw fish."

"No, his father wasn't a kamikaze pilot."

"No, he can't do karate."

"Are you sure?" somebody asks.

Indeed he doesn't know karate, but judo he does. I am hurt I'm not the one to find this out; the guys know from gym class. They line up to be flipped, he flips them all onto the floor, and after that he doesn't eat lunch at the girls' table with me anymore. I'm more or less glad. Meaning, when he was there, I never knew what to say. Now that he's gone, though, I seem to be stuck at the "This is a chair" level of conversation. Ancient Chinese eating habits have lost their cachet; all I get are more and more questions about me and Sherman. "I dunno," I'm saying all the time. *Are* we going out? We do stuff, it's true. For example, I take him to the department stores, explain to him who shops in Alexander's, who shops in Saks. I tell him my family's the type that shops in Alexander's. He says he's sorry. In Saks he gets lost; either that, or else I'm the lost one. (It's true I find him calmly waiting at the front door, hands behind his back, like a guard.) I take him to the candy store. I take him to the bagel store. Sherman is crazy about bagels. I explain to him that Lender's is gross, he should get his bagels from the bagel store. He says thank you.

"Are you going steady?" people want to know.

How can we go steady when he doesn't have an ID bracelet? On the other hand, he brings me more presents than I think any girl's ever gotten before. Oranges. Flowers. A little bag of bagels. But what do they mean? Do they mean thank you, I enjoyed our trip; do they mean I like you; do they mean I decided I liked the Lender's better even if they are gross, you can have these? Sometimes I think he's acting on his mother's instructions. Also I know at least a couple of the presents were supposed to go to our teachers. He told me that once and turned red. I figured it still might mean something that he didn't throw them out.

More and more now, we joke. Like, instead of "I'm thinking," he always says, "I'm sinking," which we both think is so funny, that all either one of us has to do is pretend to be drowning and the other one cracks up. And he tells me things—for example, that there are electric lights everywhere in Tokyo now.

"You mean you didn't have them before?"

"Everywhere now!" He's amazed too. "Since Olympics!"

"Olympics?"

"1960," he says proudly, and as proof, hums for me the Olympic theme song. "You know?"

"Sure," I say, and hum with him happily. We could be a picture on a UNICEF poster. The only problem is that I don't really understand what the Olympics have to do with the modernization of Japan, any more than I get this other story he tells me, about that hole in his left eyebrow, which is from some time his father accidentally hit him with a lit cigarette. When Sherman was a baby. His father was drunk, having been out carousing; his mother was very mad but didn't say anything, just cleaned the whole house. Then his father was so ashamed he bowed to ask her forgiveness.

"Your mother cleaned the house?"

Sherman nods solemnly.

"And your father *bowed*?" I find this more astounding than anything I ever thought to make up. "That is so weird," I tell him.

"Weird," he agrees. "This I no forget, forever. *Father* bow to *mother*!"

We shake our heads.

As for the things he asks me, they're not topics I ever discussed before. Do I like it here? Of course I like it here, I was born here, I say. Am I Jewish? Jewish! I laugh. *Oy!* Am I American? "Sure I'm American," I say. "Everybody who's born here is American, and also some people who convert from what they were before. You could become American." But he says no, he could never. "Sure you could," I say. "You only have to learn some rules and speeches."

"But I Japanese," he says.

"You could become American anyway," I say. "Like I *could* become Jewish, if I wanted to. I'd just have to switch, that's all."

"But you Catholic," he says.

I think maybe he doesn't get what means switch.

I introduce him to Mrs. Wilder's turkey pot pies. "Gross?" he asks. I say they are, but we like them anyway. "Don't tell anybody." He promises. We bake them, eat them. While we're eating, he's drawing me pictures.

"This American," he says, and he draws something that looks like John Wayne. "This Jewish," he says, and draws something that looks like the Wicked Witch of the West, only male.

"I don't think so," I say.

He's undeterred. "This Japanese," he says, and draws a fair rendition of himself. "This Chinese," he says, and draws what looks to be another fair rendition of himself.

"How can you tell them apart?"

"This way," he says, and he puts the picture of the Chinese so that it is looking at the pictures of the American and the Jew. The Japanese faces the wall. Then he draws another picture, of a Japanese flag, so that the Japanese has that to contemplate. "Chinese lost in department store," he says. "Japanese know how go." For fun, he then takes the Japanese flag and fastens it to the refrigerator door with magnets. "In school, in ceremony, we this way," he explains, and bows to the picture.

When my mother comes in, her face is so red that with the white wall behind her she looks a bit like the Japanese flag herself. Yet I get the feeling I better not say so. First she doesn't move. Then she snatches the flag off the refrigerator, so fast the magnets go flying. Two of them land on the stove. She crumples up the paper. She hisses at Sherman, "*This is the U.S. of A., do you hear me!*"

Sherman hears her.

"You call your mother right now, tell her come pick you up."

He understands perfectly. *I*, on the other hand, am sty-
mied. How can two people who don't really speak English
understand each other better than I can understand them? "But
Ma," I say.

"Don't *Ma* me," she says.

Later on she explains that World War II was in China, too.
"Hitler," I say. "Nazis. Volkswagens." I know the Japanese
were on the wrong side, because they bombed Pearl Harbor.
My mother explains about before that. The Napkin Massacre.
"*Nan*-king," she corrects me.

"Are you sure?" I say. "In school, they said the war was
about putting the Jews in ovens."

"Also about ovens."

"About both?"

"Both."

"That's not what they said in school."

"Just forget about school."

Forget about school? "I thought we moved here for the
schools."

"We moved here," she says, "for your education."

Sometimes I have no idea what she's talking about.

"I like Sherman," I say after a while.

"He's nice boy," she agrees.

Meaning what? I would ask, except that my dad's just come
home, which means it's time to start talking about whether we
should build a brick wall across the front of the lawn. Recently
a car made it almost into our living room, which was so scary,
the driver fainted and an ambulance had to come. "We should
have discussion," my dad said after that. And so for about a
week, every night we do.

"Are you just friends, or more than just friends?" Barbara Gugelstein is giving me the cross-ex.

"Maybe," I say.

"Come on," she says, "I told you *everything* about me and
Andy."

I actually *am* trying to tell Barbara everything about Sherman,
but everything turns out to be nothing. Meaning, I can't locate
the conversation in what I have to say. Sherman and I go places,

we talk, one time my mother threw him out of the house because of World War II.

"I think we're just friends," I say.

"You think or you're sure?"

Now that I do less of the talking at lunch, I notice more what other people talk about—cheerleading, who likes who, this place in White Plains to get earrings. On none of these topics am I an expert. Of course, I'm still friends with Barbara Gugelstein, but I notice Danielle Meyers has spun away to other groups.

Barbara's analysis goes this way: To be popular, you have to have big boobs, a note from your mother that lets you use her Lord & Taylor credit card, and a boyfriend. On the other hand, what's so wrong with being unpopular? "We'll get them in the end," she says. It's what her dad tells her. "Like they'll turn out too dumb to do their own investing, and then they'll get killed in fees and then they'll have to move to towns where the schools stink. And my dad should know," she winds up. "He's a broker."

"I guess," I say.

But the next thing I know, I have a true crush on Sherman Matsumoto. *Mis*ter Judo, the guys call him now, with real respect; and the more they call him that, the more I don't care that he carries a notebook with a cat on it.

I sigh. "Sherman."

"I thought you were just friends," says Barbara Gugelstein.

"We were," I say mysteriously. This, I've noticed, is how Danielle Meyers talks; everything's secret, she only lets out so much, it's like she didn't grow up with everybody telling her she had to share.

And here's the funny thing: The more I intimate that Sherman and I are more than just friends, the more it seems we actually are. It's the old imagination giving reality a nudge. When I start to blush; he starts to blush; we reach a point where we can hardly talk at all.

"Well, there's first base with tongue, and first base without," I tell Barbara Gugelstein.

In fact, Sherman and I have brushed shoulders, which was equivalent to first base I was sure, maybe even second. I felt as though I'd turned into one huge shoulder; that's all I was, one huge shoulder. We not only didn't talk, we didn't breathe. But how can I tell Barbara Gugelstein that? So instead I say, "Well there's second base and second base."

Danielle Meyers is my friend again. She says, "I know exactly what you mean," just to make Barbara Gugelstein feel bad.

"Like *what* do I mean?" I say.

Danielle Meyers can't answer.

"You know what I think?" I tell Barbara the next day. "I think Danielle's giving us a line."

Barbara pulls thoughtfully on one of her pigtails.

If Sherman Matsumoto is never going to give me an ID to wear, he should at least get up the nerve to hold my hand. I don't think he sees this. I think of the story he told me about his parents, and in a synaptic firestorm realize we don't see the same things at all.

So one day, when we happen to brush shoulders again, I don't move away. He doesn't move away either. There we are. Like a pair of bleachers, pushed together but not quite matched up. After a while, I have to breathe, I can't help it. I breathe in such a way that our elbows start to touch too. We are in a crowd, waiting for a bus. I crane my neck to look at the sign that says where the bus is going; now our wrists are touching. Then it happens: He links his pinky around mine.

Is that holding hands? Later, in bed, I wonder all night. One finger, and not even the biggest one.

Sherman is leaving in a month. Already! I think, well, I suppose he will leave and we'll never even kiss. I guess that's all right. Just when I've resigned myself to it, though, we hold hands all five fingers. Once when we are at the bagel shop, then again in my parents' kitchen. Then, when we are at the playground, he kisses the back of my hand.

He does it again not too long after that, in White Plains.

I invest in a bottle of mouthwash.

Instead of moving on, though, he kisses the back of my hand again. And again. I try raising my hand, hoping he'll make the jump from my hand to my cheek. It's like trying to wheedle an inchworm out the window. You know, *This way, this way.*

All over the world, people have their own cultures. That's what we learned in social studies.

If we never kiss, I'm not going to take it personally.

It is the end of the school year. We've had parties. We've turned in our textbooks. Hooray! Outside the asphalt already steams if you spit on it. Sherman isn't leaving for another couple of days, though, and he comes to visit every morning, staying until the afternoon, when Callie comes home from her big-deal job as a bank teller. We drink Kool-Aid in the backyard and hold hands until they are sweaty and make smacking noises coming apart. He tells me how busy his parents are, getting ready for the move. His mother, particularly, is very tired. Mostly we are mournful.

The very last day we hold hands and do not let go. Our palms fill up with water like a blister. We do not care. We talk more than usual. How much airmail is to Japan, that kind of thing. Then suddenly he asks, will I marry him?

I'm only thirteen.

But when old? Sixteen?

If you come back to get me.

I come. Or you can come to Japan, be Japanese.

How can I be Japanese?

Like you become American. Switch.

He kisses me on the cheek, again and again and again.

His mother calls to say she's coming to get him. I cry. I tell him how I've saved every present he's ever given me—the ruler, the pencils, the bags from the bagels, all the flower petals. I even have the orange peels from the oranges.

All?

I put them in a jar.

I'd show him, except that we're not allowed to go upstairs to my room. Anyway, something about the orange peels seems to choke him up too. *Mister* Judo, but I've gotten him in a soft spot. We are going together to the bathroom to get some toilet paper to wipe our eyes when poor tired Mrs. Matsumoto, driving a shiny new station wagon, skids up onto our lawn.

"Very sorry!"

We race outside.

"Very sorry!"

Mrs. Matsumoto is so short that about all we can see of her is a green cotton sun hat, with a big brim. It's tied on. The brim is trembling.

I hope my mom's not going to start yelling about World War II.

"Is all right, no trouble," she says, materializing on the steps behind me and Sherman. She's propped the screen door wide open; when I turn I see she's waving. "No trouble, no trouble!"

"No trouble, no trouble!" I echo, twirling a few times with relief.

Mrs. Matsumoto keeps apologizing; my mom keeps insisting she shouldn't feel bad, it was only some grass and a small tree. Crossing the lawn, she insists Mrs. Matsumoto get out of the car, even though it means trampling some lilies-of-the-valley. She insists that Mrs. Matsumoto come in for a cup of tea. Then she will not talk about anything unless Mrs. Matsumoto sits down, and unless she lets my mom prepare her a small snack. The coming in and the tea and the sitting down are settled pretty quickly, but they negotiate ferociously over the small snack, which Mrs. Matsumoto will not eat unless she can call Mr. Matsumoto. She makes the mistake of linking Mr. Matsumoto with a reparation of some sort, which my mom will not hear of.

"Please!"

"No no no no."

Back and forth it goes: "No no no no." "No no no no." "No no no no." What kind of conversation is that? I look at Sherman, who shrugs. Finally Mr. Matsumoto calls on his own, wondering where his wife is. He comes over in a taxi. He's a heavy-browed businessman, friendly but brisk—not at all a type you could imagine bowing to a lady with a taste for tie-on sun hats. My mom invites him in as if it's an idea she just this moment thought of. And would he maybe have some tea and a small snack?

Sherman and I sneak back outside for another farewell, by the side of the house, behind the forsythia bushes. We hold hands. He kisses me on the cheek again, and then—just when I think he's finally going to kiss me on the lips—he kisses me on the neck.

Is this first base?

He does it more. Up and down, up and down. First it tickles, and then it doesn't. He has his eyes closed. I close my eyes too. He's hugging me. Up and down. Then down.

He's at my collarbone.

Still at my collarbone. Now his hand's on my ribs. So much for first base. More ribs. The idea of second base would probably make me nervous if he weren't on his way back to Japan and if I really thought we were going to get there. As it is, though, I'm not in much danger of wrecking my life on the shoals of passion; his unmoving hand feels more like a growth than a boyfriend. He has his whole face pressed to my neck skin so I can't tell his mouth from his nose. I think he may be licking me.

From indoors, a burst of adult laughter. My eyelids flutter. I start to try and wiggle such that his hand will maybe budge upward.

Do I mean for my top blouse button to come accidentally undone?

He clenches his jaw, and when he opens his eyes, they're fixed on that button like it's a gnat that's been bothering him for far too long. He mutters in Japanese. If later in life he were to describe this as a pivotal moment in his youth, I would not be surprised. Holding the material as far from my body as possible, he buttons the button. Somehow we've landed up too close to the bushes.

What to tell Barbara Gugelstein? She says, "Tell me what were his last words. He must have said something last."

"I don't want to talk about it."

"Maybe he said, Good-bye?" she suggests. "Sayonara?" She means well.

"I don't want to talk about it."

"Aw, come on, I told you everything about—"

I say, "Because it's private, excuse me."

She stops, squints at me as though at a far-off face she's trying to make out. Then she nods and very lightly places her hand on my forearm.

The forsythia seemed to be stabbing us in the eyes. Sherman said, more or less, *You will need to study how to switch.*

And I said, *I think you should switch. The way you do everything is weird.*

And he said, *You just want to tell everything to your friends. You just want to have boyfriend to become popular.*

Then he flipped me. Two swift moves, and I went sprawling through the air, a flailing confusion of soft human parts such as had no idea where the ground was.

It is the fall, and I am in high school, and still he hasn't written, so finally I write him.

I still have all your gifts, I write. *I don't talk so much as I used to. Although I am not exactly a mouse either. I don't care about being popular anymore. I swear. Are you happy to be back in Japan? I know I ruined everything. I was just trying to be entertaining. I miss you with all my heart, and hope I didn't ruin everything.*

He writes back, *You will never be Japanese.*

I throw all the orange peels out that day. Some of them, it turns out, were moldy anyway. I tell my mother I want to move to Chinatown.

"Chinatown!" she says.

I don't know why I suggested it.

"What's the matter?" she says. "Still boy-crazy? That Sherman?"

"No."

"Too much homework?"

I don't answer.

"Forget about school."

Later she tells me if I don't like school, I don't have to go every day. Some days I can stay home.

"Stay home?" In Yonkers, Callie and I used to stay home all the time, but that was because the schools there were *waste of time.*

"No good for a girl be too smart anyway."

★ ★ ★

For a long time I think about Sherman. But after a while I
don't think about him so much as I just keep seeing myself
flipped onto the ground, lying there shocked as the Matsu-
motos get ready to leave. My head has hit a rock; my brain
aches as though it's been shoved to some new place in my
skull. Otherwise I am okay. I see the forsythia, all those
whippy branches, and can't believe how many leaves there
are on a bush—every one green and perky and durably itself.
And past them, real sky. I try to remember about why the
sky's blue, even though this one's gone the kind of indescrib-
able gray you associate with the insides of old shoes. I smell
grass. Probably I have grass stains all over my back. I hear
my mother calling through the back door, "Mon-a! Everyone
leaving now," and "Not coming to say good-bye?" I hear
Mr. and Mrs. Matsumoto bowing as they leave—or at least
I hear the embarrassment in my mother's voice as they bow.
I hear their car start. I hear Mrs. Matsumoto directing Mr.
Matsumoto how to back off the lawn so as not to rip any
more of it up. I feel the back of my head for blood—just a
little. I hear their chug-chug grow fainter and fainter, until it
has faded into the whuzz-whuzz of all the other cars. I hear
my mom singing, "*Mon-a! Mon-a!*" until my dad comes
home. Doors open and shut. I see myself standing up, brushing myself off so I'll have less explaining to do if she comes
out to look for me. Grass stains—just like I thought. I see
myself walking around the house, going over to have a look
at our churned-up yard. It looks pretty sad, two big brown
tracks, right through the irises and the lilies of the valley, and
that was a new dogwood we'd just planted. Lying there like
that. I hear myself thinking about my father, having to go
dig it up all over again. Adjusting. I think how we probably
ought to put up that brick wall. And sure enough, when I go
inside, no one's thinking about me, or that little bit of blood
at the back of my head, or the grass stains. That's what they're
talking about—that wall. Again. My mom doesn't think it'll
do any good, but my dad thinks we should give it a try.
Should we or shouldn't we? How high? How thick? What
will the neighbors say? I plop myself down on a hard chair.

And all I can think is, we are the complete only family that has to worry about this. If I could, I'd switch everything to be different. But since I can't, I might as well sit here at the table for a while, discussing what I know how to discuss. I nod and listen to the rest.

from THE FLOATING WORLD
Cynthia Kadohata (1956–   )

Cynthia Kadohata's first novel portrays the experiences of a Japanese American family working and living throughout the Pacific Northwest and Midwest of the 1950s and 1960s. The family moves frequently, sometimes traveling with other families; and the young narrator, Olivia Osaka, calls their environment "the floating world," referring to the "gas station attendants, restaurants, and jobs we depended on, the motel towns floating in the middle of fields and mountains." She explains that this nomadic life was due in part to the difficulty Japanese Americans had finding jobs "even into the fifties and sixties." The following chapter takes place in California. The reader needs to know that the previous night the narrator encountered a threatening stranger, whom her grandmother scared off.

Ms. Kadohata was born in Chicago. Her stories have been published in The New Yorker, Grand Street, and The Pennsylvania Review. She is the author of two other novels, In the Heart of the Valley of Love published in 1992 and the forthcoming Dragon Road. A recipient of the 1991 Whiting Writers' Award and an NEA grant, she lives in Los Angeles.

SOMETIMES OBĀSAN SLEPT FOR HOURS AND HOURS, UNTIL WE thought she was sick, while other times she required no sleep at all. Though she and I had returned late the night before, she woke my brothers and me at six, as usual, for our morning hike. We always had to go with her, unless we weren't feeling well. But I didn't mind. Some days, the people we met on those mornings would be the only people I talked to besides my family and whatever family we were traveling with. Those walks were some of my favorite times growing up.

It was still dark gray out. She wanted to take a long walk. My father's job wouldn't be finished until evening, and we had nothing to do all day. We put Peter into a stroller and headed off through a sloping field and some orchards. Peter was used to bumping along. He could sleep through anything. A fine mist broke up our view, as if each drop of mist were a dot of paint. The mist sprayed coolly on our cheeks as we walked through the field, and the long misted grass brushed our ankles. I could feel the blood flowing to my face as I tried to keep up with Obāsan, who always walked briskly.

We saw some kids outside a farm. They'd probably be going to school later. "What's today?" said Walker.

"Wednesday,"

"Wednesday." He didn't say anything else. Walker hardly ever talked, except to repeat something just said. Sometimes we called him Echo.

Obāsan had a cigar and stopped to blow smoke rings into the air. The sky, white-gray, showed through the rings.

"Will you smoke when you get older?" Ben asked me.

"I'll never smoke. I want to be the opposite of Obāsan. Anything she does, I never will."

"She eats," said Ben. "And you have to eat." He crossed his eyes at me.

I chased him through the grass, but he stopped abruptly and knelt, and I fell over him. I rolled, just for fun, through the damp field. When I got dizzily to my feet, my grandmother and brothers were watching me. With them stood an old man. That is, his face didn't appear old, but he had wispy white hair that stood on end, seeming to move and fly of its own accord, like something alive. He'd appeared out of nowhere—all around us were fields. I sort of salivated inside whenever I met someone new. I was nosy, and I thought new people might tell me interesting things.

Obāsan didn't speak. There was something imperial about the way she held herself, the way she ignored the man. She appeared to be looking through him, at the sky and the fields. I could see she wasn't going to speak, so I told the man I hoped we weren't trespassing.

He chewed on something and glanced over the beautiful misted fields. The fields were full of varied greens. They were his fields, I felt sure. "Maybe you're trespassing," he said. I felt a brief fear, probably just left over from the night before.

"Sorry."

He chewed some more. The wind blew at his hair. I thought the wispy strands might fly away. "But maybe you're not," he said.

Obāsan continued to gaze through him. "We'll go now," I said. We turned and began to leave. I noticed Obāsan's cigar was gone. I noticed something burning a hole in her pocket. Obāsan, so brave last night, was scared of this man. She was scared of what he might think of her cigar.

"Hey," the man called, and we turned around. "I'll sell you some apples cheap."

Everyone looked at me expectantly. "What kind of apples?"

"What kind do you want?"

"Well, are they good?"

"The best."

The hole in my grandmother's pocket had stopped smoking.

We went with the man to buy some apples. Men had come out to work some of the fields. The men touched their hats when they said "Good morning" to me and my grandmother, and I felt very grown up.

"Where are you all from?" said the man.

"Here and there." My grandmother had told me once never to tell people where I came from or what my name was.

He nodded at her. "She speak English?"

I considered this question. Maybe she didn't want me to tell. "I'm not sure," I said, stupidly.

Behind a barn sat several bushels, a couple of them filled with large golden delicious apples, sunbursts of pale rose and green on the rich yellow skins. We pooled our money—Obāsan had most—and bought two dozen apples. My grandmother owned a magic purse that never emptied, though she didn't work and had never made much money. She always had a couple of dollars.

"You know how to pick good apples?" said the man.

"Color?" said Ben.

"Nope."

"Smell?"

"Nope." He paused before saying with mock impatience, "Do you want me to tell you or not?" He paused again, throwing an apple into the air. Finally he said triumphantly: "Sound." He squeezed and rubbed the apple between his large hands until it squeaked. "Good one," he said. "It sings. Never buy an apple unless it sings." He added hurriedly, "Of course the ones you just bought are all good." He rubbed and rubbed, making three distinct notes, enough for "Mary Had a Little Lamb" and another song I didn't recognize, and he moved his head in time with the music, his hair following the movement of his head. We also tried to play the apples, but ours sounded like tiny sick cows.

We headed back without the man. I felt very happy, almost elated, for no real reason, just for the way the morning had started. The workers in the fields stopped again to touch their hats.

"Hey!"

We turned around, saw the man standing in the distant mist.

"Someday you teach your kids that apple trick!" he called. He tapped at the space above his head as if he wore a hat, and then walked off with his dancing hair, and with his singing apple still in hand.

He'd given us no bags, so we had trouble carrying the apples. Obāsan walked way ahead with Peter. We kept dropping the apples, but soon we were having so much fun chasing after the falling fruit that we began to drop it deliberately. As I chased a stray apple, I saw Obāsan stop walking, and I thought she wanted to scold us. But she was staring out over the fields, the way you might stare at someone who is leaving you. She had worked on a celery farm a few seasons, and I wondered whether she was remembering that. Today when I think back on how she looked, I believe she knew then she would die soon. I bit into an apple, and she turned to glare at me. My brothers had run way ahead with the stroller. "Give me that apple." She walked toward me. "Don't eat that."

"How come?"

"It's dirty."

Every time she took a step toward me I took a step back. Sometimes I ran from her, but I never ran hard. I didn't want her to catch and hit me, but I didn't want to lose her, either. It was our responsibility to keep an eye on each other. I continued eating my apple but rolled up the rest of the fruit in my skirt and hurried home, making sure never to lose sight of Obāsan. By the time we got to the house, her face was all evil and anger. I felt scared now, so I ran inside, chained the door, and sat on the bed to finish the apple. I jumped when the door jerked partway open, stopped by the chain. One of Obāsan's eyes peered in. If I squinted, she looked like a Cyclops. I chomped into a new apple, still staring at her. She reached her hand in, jiggling the chain while my heart pounded, but she couldn't open the door. She cajoled, she bribed, she threw kisses. She jangled her purse, suddenly full of coins. "Livvie, my sweet, I have to use the bathroom," she said. But I knew she was lying. I could have closed the door or hidden from sight, and my body jerked with the impulse to get up. Instead I bit into my third apple and felt mesmerized by my grandmother's face.

"I can't open it," I said. "You'll hit me."

She stood there, her arthritic knee clicking. Finally she left, and I didn't hear any clicking or tinkling or muttering. I sneaked to the door and slowly opened it. She was sitting on a little bench on the porch. She had a peaceable look on her face. I went to put the remaining apples next to her and sat on a stair. The mist had risen, covering the sky with gray lace. Something pounded across my ear, knocking me over. "Why did you give that man my money?" Obāsan said.

When my father finished work that evening, we started driving immediately. We were going to visit with relatives in Los Angeles, then head to Arkansas. The Shibatas, a family we'd met that week, were traveling with us to L.A. We stopped for the night at a small motel. That was a long time ago—the motel cost two dollars a night. It had a lighted pink vacancy sign, and another sign reading Cal-Inn. The view was lovely: almond groves made jagged black lines on the horizon, and I thought I smelled almonds in the air. After supper, everyone sat on the curb outside the motel. There were only two cars besides ours and the Shibatas' in the parking lot. My brothers and I and the Shibata children played strings, cards, and jan ken po—the Japanese version of paper-scissors-rock. Then we sat briefly bored, scraping and rapping our bare feet restlessly on the parking-lot concrete.

Susie Shibata and I got up to sing for everyone. We did a little dance. I sang more on key, yet her voice held more sweetness, so I sat back and listened. I was singing softly along when Obāsan pushed me from my place at the curb—she'd been sitting behind me, I suppose. Ordinarily I wouldn't have felt indignant, because it had always been a rule that we either must offer our elders our seats or expect to be forcibly removed. But Obāsan had pushed me especially hard this time. And she'd been mean to me while we were cooped up in the car all day. Several times she'd boxed the side of my head and told me to quiet down.

"You made me scrape my knee," I said. I held up my knee, my foot dangling in the air. "See the blood? You're in my seat, and please move now."

"What did you say?" she said. She rubbed her fingers together. I could just hear the dry skin scraping.

She reached out and grabbed my wrist, but I tried to pull it away and run. She held fast, though. I wouldn't have thought she was so strong, but I couldn't get away. We called her Pincher Obāsan behind her back. One of her methods of punishment was to smile as if she loved you with her full heart, all the while squeezing you inside the wrist. You were supposed to smile back as best you could. We had a funny picture of Ben getting pinched. With that smile, he looked like a lunatic. Now I opened my lips, pressed my teeth hard together, and tried to keep my eyes opened wide. Obāsan smiled easily back at me as she pinched. The lighting made her gums look brown, and I knew her top teeth were dentures. I was determined to outsmile her. Once, when she'd got mad at Ben and pinched him for something like fifteen minutes, he outsmiled her, and finally she broke down, patted his head, and gave him a nickel. I would make her give me a nickel, too. But she didn't stop, and after a while I felt my pulse between her fingers. I thought a vein would burst, or my skin might fall off in her hands.

"You've got the record!" encouraged Ben. Meaning it had been more than fifteen minutes.

Obāsan seemed to pinch more tightly. "All right!" I said. She let go, and I went off to sit by myself. My mother came over and ran her hand across my head. When I felt I could talk without crying, I said, "Mom, I was just sitting there. She pushed me. You saw."

"She's old," said my mother. "But I'll tell her not to be so hard on you. Okay?"

"She's evil," I said. "When she smiles I see she's a devil." I sucked on my wrist.

My mother laughed. "Oh, you never even knew her during her pinching prime. I could tell you stories."

"Obāsan pinching stories!" I said. "That's the last thing I want to hear."

My father rose to go in, as did Mr. Shibata. "Seven o'clock?" said my dad. Mr. Shibata nodded. Seven was when we would start out the next day. Before he went in, my father knelt beside me and my mother. "How'd you like to sit in front with us tomorrow?"

"Okay."

"You can have the window if you want or the middle if you want," said my mother.

"Thank you," I said. But I wasn't appeased.

My father went in. My mother followed with Peter, and I followed her. I didn't want to sit outside with Obāsan.

My mother sat on the bed and leafed through a book about presidents' wives. She admired presidents' wives and liked to know what they ate and wore, liked to know the odd fact that made them human. For instance, she liked knowing that Andrew Jackson's wife married him mistakenly, thinking she'd obtained a divorce from her first husband, or knowing that Mrs. Polk, who was very religious, prohibited liquor and dancing in the White House—"No wonder the Polks had no children," she would say. She'd probably inherited her interest in first ladies from Obāsan, who used to revere the Japanese emperor and his wife. "The emperor was a moron," Obāsan once said, "but he was still the emperor."

My grandmother came inside; I went out.

It was always a relief when she went in for the evening, but it felt especially wonderful that night. My brothers and I played tag back of the motel, and later we peeked into the rooms of strangers, but saw nothing. When we'd finished playing, only Mrs. Shibata and Susie still sat on the curb.

Though Obāsan always went inside early, she usually came to the door when a car approached the motel office. "Get in. What will people think, with Japanese hanging around like hoodlums at night?" We would all go in, watch until the car had left, then wander out, continuing this wandering in and out until time for bed. But tonight a car drove up and I waited expectantly for Obāsan's voice. When it didn't come I figured she'd gone to sleep, and I turned around, idly, to glance through the open door. I was really quite shocked to see my grandmother, looking cadaverous in the neon, standing in the doorway silently watching the car. She came out and sat with us briefly, an event unprecedented at that hour. She talked of her life. "My memories are a string of pearls and rocks," she said. I thought that was a line she'd memorized to say to us, but then she stretched her bony hands through the air, so for a moment I seemed to see the glitter of the string extended over the concrete lot. But the next moment she turned to me in one of her furies. "*I* don't know," she cried. But I didn't know what she was talking about. It was like the night Isamu got upset because his daughter had failed him. With all the older people I knew, even my parents, I occasionally saw that fierce expression as they exclaimed over something that had happened years ago, losses in a time and place as far removed from my twelve-year-old mind as the dates in a schoolbook.

Later I lay on the floor under the sheets. My wrist still hurt. I couldn't sleep. I watched as my grandmother walked to the bathroom. Obāsan was in there for a long time, and after a while I started to hear noises like coughing. I got up and knocked on the bathroom door, but Obāsan didn't answer.

The door was unlocked, though. Obāsan lay in her housedress on a towel she must have placed on the floor. Though I know now it was just my imagination, at the time I thought she seemed to have been expecting me. She was already not of this world, and she spoke with a fury unnatural even for her. "You! Get your mother," she said. It was a hiss, a rasp, and a cracked whisper all at once. I felt cold, as if there were ghosts in the room. But it was my own body, making me cold in the warm night. I reached back to close the door and turned to watch her again.

"Get your mother," Obāsan said. Still with fury but, now, something else, too. The hint of a "please" in her voice.

I saw in the mirror that I was crying and shaking. I had hated my grandmother for so long.

"Get your mother." This time Obāsan sounded desperate, pleading.

She said it two more times, once with draining hope and the last time peacefully. "Get your mother," she said, with calm, peaceful resignation. She closed her eyes and I left. I got under the sheets again. Dim light shone through the sheet over my head, a glow like very early morning. Sometimes, when I couldn't quite place what I was feeling, I would search through my body, from my toes up to my calves, between my legs, and on up to my head. Now my stomach hurt. I thought I heard noise from the bathroom. Obāsan was ready to die, I thought. And then I felt very sleepy.

When I next woke, Walker had just found Obāsan dead on the bathroom floor. He clung to me as we stood at the door. My mother stood over her mother, horrified. My father was grim.

"She made me kill her!" I said.

"She made me kill her!" Walker echoed.

My parents just thought I was crazy with grief.

We sent Obāsan's body to Wilcox, California, which was where her third husband was buried, and drove there for the funeral. As I watched the casket buried, I felt surrounded by a cool, choking swirl of air that made me cough up phlegm and made my eyes smart and water, and I knew that Obāsan was there. But the coldness went away, and it never returned. I looked toward the sky, to see whether my grandmother's ghost might be heading heavenward. "No, she must have gone down there," I said, pointing with my thumb toward the ground. I automatically braced myself for the ear boxing I always got when I said something I knew I shouldn't say; but there would be no more of that. I placed a bouquet of red plastic flowers on the gravestone.

Peter pointed at the flowers. "Obāsan?" he said—as if the

whole of her life had been distilled into the flash of color in the gray cemetery.

We headed for Los Angeles to visit relatives. On the drive down we had some of Obāsan's riches—enameled boxes, painted fans, and old journals filled with graceful Japanese writing. We had her purse, empty now, and a picture of her as a striking woman in her twenties. As we drove, I played the last time I'd talked to her over and over in my mind, changing the end so that in my fantasies I went to get my parents for help. But when I emerged from my fantasy and thought about how evil I had been, I got a feeling I get sometimes even today, that there are things I am scared to know. My mother had cut off her mother's long braid and given one strand each to Ben, Walker, and me. The strands were black at one end and white at the other. I tied a string around mine and folded it into one of the enameled boxes. All the windows in the car were open. It was early evening, and we were halfway between Wilcox and Los Angeles. I stuck my head out the window. I was free. But I didn't feel free.

"Whatever Happened to Harry?"

Susan Ito (1959–   )

Like other fiction by new writers, "Whatever Happened to Harry?" involves issues that have only recently surfaced as discussable subjects. This short story depicts the dark side of sexual coming of age. The narrator, Diane, is an adult looking back on growing up in the early 1970s.

Susan Ito was born in New Rochelle, New York, and grew up in Park Ridge, New Jersey. Her short fiction has been published in numerous anthologies and journals, including Hurricane Alice and American Way. Her short story, "Hiroko," won first prize in the Somersault Press short story contest and was nominated for the 1991 Pushcart Prize. She is an M.F.A. candidate in the Creative Writing Program at Mills College. Ms. Ito lives in Oakland, where she hosts a monthly café reading for fiction writers and teaches at the Asian American Women Writers' Workshop.

MY MOTHER CALLED TODAY AND TOLD ME ABOUT THE TROUBLE in your family. "Those poor Yoshidas," she sighed. "So sad." She talked in a hushed voice about how your father finally died of stomach cancer, how for the last year of his life he ate nothing more than vanilla pudding and okai, boiled rice soup. Then she told me about your mother's diabetes, how it made her go blind, how it turned her feet into swollen purple eggplants.

She was right; it *was* really sad, and I told her not to tell me any more. But then she told me about you, how you go to your mother's house every day, bringing groceries and clean laundry. She told me you give her a hot bath, that you lean over the steaming water and scrub her yourself.

"Poor Harry," she sighed. "All alone, no wife, just taking care of the mother. Sad life, *neh?*"

I brightened at this mention of your name. "He's all alone?" I asked. "Never got married?"

"No. *Kawai soh, neh?* I feel sorry for him. Think about it, all day working at that advertising company, then all night and weekend nursing her. Terrible."

I thought about it. The image of you, driving across the Golden Gate Bridge in the evening, carrying paper bags full of cereal and TV dinners, made me smile. It softened the hard core of rage that I usually feel when I hear your name. Perfect penance, I thought. The idea of you serving a life sentence taking care of your parents, good people I had always liked, is more satisfying than the violence I usually wish on you.

Usually, I think about grabbing your collar with both hands and slamming you up against a wall like they do in the movies. Your feet would dangle down helplessly, your flimsy glasses tossed to the side of your face. My fist would grow to the size of a honeydew melon and I would punch your belly until your eyes popped. This is what I would have done to you, back when I was twelve, if I had known what you were going to do to me.

But I didn't know. You were twenty-two years old when I met you, Harry Yoshida, almost too old for the Japanese American Community Youth. I was eager to leave the children's program to join that hip group of teenagers. I had just had the braces taken off my teeth, and I had traded my black horn-rimmed glasses for contact lenses. That summer, I felt myself filling with possibility. I had a low-cut peasant blouse to go over my new breasts. I had hot pants, nothing more than denim panties. I hung on the edges of the Youth, tantalized by the jokes, the laughing, the talk that was a maze of unopened secrets.

I was especially taken with you, with the wooden box of paints you carried everywhere, the wild bright colors that bounced off the walls of the Community Center rec room. They let you paint murals there, over the Ping-Pong table: fluorescent paintings of Japanese samurai warriors in tie-dyed robes. I stood next to you for entire afternoons while you painted, inhaling the smell of linseed oil and turpentine. I washed your brushes. We didn't talk much, but I knew you were aware of me.

One Saturday, you asked my parents if you could take me to the Museum of Modern Art.

My mother was impressed. "How nice, Harry's taken such an interest in Diane," she said. "Like a big brother."

I knew it was really a date, and I fretted excitedly in my room, trying on every combination of clothing that my wardrobe held. I had never been kissed by a boy, and I wondered if you would hold my hand. You did.

First you bought me a cup of coffee, and we sat in a small café outside the museum. I tossed my hair back and drank the stuff black, sipping it slowly through my teeth. It tasted terrible but I knew that to ask for milk or sugar would make me look like a little girl. You talked about the exhibit we were going to see, names of painters I had never heard of. I just nodded. I was staring at you, your hair brushing the edges of your shoulders, the black bandana around your neck, and I wished my girl-friends from Taylor Middle School could see how cool you were.

"You should know good art," you said, and I nodded solemnly. Then we stood up and went into the gallery and you took my hand, slowly swinging my arm as we walked in front of the large framed paintings. That would have been enough for me. I would have written about you in my diary, Harry, I would have scribbled your name in the margins of my three-ring binder for months to come.

But I never wrote your name down; I never wrote a word about what happened, not until now. You drove me back to my street, out in the Avenues, and parked the car fifty yards from the house. We lived in one of those pale boxy houses the color of Necco Wafers, right at the edge of Golden Gate Park. Some song was on the radio, *Mah beautiful woh-man*, and you grinned, looking over at me. "Just like you, Diane." You touched my cheek and said those words, told me I was beautiful.

I nearly fainted. Here it was, the romantic life, right at my doorstep. I tilted my head back slightly, the way I knew women did, and felt your heat moving toward me. *A kiss*, I thought. *I'm going to have my first kiss.* But your mouth, so gentle with flattery, was nearly violent on contact, huge and wet and full of teeth. Your tongue was a crazy snake, slithering over the roof of my mouth. I made myself respond with enthusiasm, even though I wanted to gag, to push you away. I was desperate for you not to figure out what a child I really was, a baby without a clue. You were smooth, professional, the way you unhooked my bra with one hand and slipped off my shirt. I lifted my arms obediently, like an infant, and then sat there, bright white under the light of the streetlamp.

You pushed your face into the side of my neck, moaning and saying, "God, Diane, you're fantastic." I believed you, giddy and terrified. You clawed at my pants, the zipper opening with a tearing sound. Your fingers, with jagged unclipped nails, kneaded the flesh through my cotton panties.

You gasped into my neck, "Does it feel good? Yes? Do you like this?" Your eyes were closed, and it seemed you could barely breathe.

It didn't feel good, Harry, not in the remotest sense. It was red pain. But it appeared that this grinding thing you were doing, this mashing down on my sex, was supposed to feel good. I whispered, "Yes."

As you crawled over me, licking and biting like an animal, I lay with my head pressed against the car door. I didn't say anything until, like a lucid nightmare, I heard a familiar voice pierce through the thick wet fog of the windshield.

"Wait," I whispered. "Stop."

It was my father, walking our shepherd mutt, Yakamashi, right past the car. They were taking their usual route through the park, where I knew they would take one lap around the polo fields. My father was singing radio jingles. "K-EZY," he crooned. "Easy, soft and lo-ow . . ."

Immediately you disowned me. You flung yourself to the opposite door, muttering, "Shit, oh shit, he's going to kill me." I trembled on the vinyl seat, pale and absolutely naked. My twisted pants clung around one ankle. I saw the outline of my father through the fog, walking briskly, pulling the chain around Yakamashi's neck.

I prayed to God to let me die at that moment, but I didn't die. My father didn't peer in the windows. He didn't rescue me or kill you, as I was partially hoping he would. He kept walking, pulling the sniffing dog away from the car door, and then his voice dimmed and disappeared through the sweating glass.

You waited just a second or two after my father dissolved into the darkness. I thought that would be the end of it, but you came back to me, renewed and unashamed. This time you unzipped your own pants and took out this thing, poking out underneath your shirt. I had never seen an adult one, not alive like that, so large and tough and shiny. You told me to touch it, and I patted its hardness like the head of a cat, with the flat surfaces of my fingers held tightly together. I had no idea what I was doing, that was obvious. You became impatient and said, accusingly, "You don't have much experience, do you?" Ashamed, discovered, I shook my head.

You rolled your eyes. You tucked yourself back into your pants and quietly told me to put on my clothes. While you combed your hair, looking up into the rearview mirror, you said, "There's this really good book. I think you could get a lot out of it, Diane."

I liked to read, and I was relieved to have a conversation to distract me from the humiliation of trying to work the clasp of my bra. "Really? What's it called?" I was expecting a title about modern art, something I could learn about the paintings we'd seen.

You told me to look for *The Sensuous Woman*. "It's out in paperback," you said. "You can probably even find it at that bookstore near the museum, in Opera Plaza."

I nodded obediently, making a note of it in my head, and lifted my white T-shirt from the dashboard. For a moment I thought of waving it out the window, like a surrender flag.

You picked up my hand, kissed it on the palm. "Listen, Diane," you said, "maybe you're a little young for me. Let's try this again, maybe, when you're, let's say sixteen?"

I wept into my bathwater that night, Harry. I didn't want to wait until I was sixteen. I had crossed a line that night with you, an invisible border to the other side of childhood, and there was no going back. I thought of the way you had kissed me, like a drowning person, and it made me shiver. I felt as if I had failed some critical exam in your car, and I vowed to buy *The Sensuous Woman*, and that I would study all the things you had found so lacking in me.

After my parents went to bed, talking about how much they liked you, I lay on the carpet, tracing my finger around the cut-out heart shapes on the Matisse postcard you had bought me. My boyfriend, I thought. I have a boyfriend named Harry Yoshida. But that was the last time you called me, or took me anywhere.

A month after our date, you showed up at Community Youth with a new girlfriend, someone close to your age: Pamela Shimizu, the college girl who had tutored me in math one summer. I was devastated. I wondered if Pamela did those things with you in the back seat of your car, those things that I couldn't. I almost asked her, but then a month after that, you were alone again and she had a new boyfriend, a white Jewish guy named Neil. I guess you know they got married, a long time ago, and they have two little boys.

After a while, your insistence on being part of the Youth seemed pathetic. You were so much older than any of us junior high and high school kids. There was that day during the Cherry Blossom festival. You and I were going up in the elevator of the community center. We hadn't spoken in years. I remember the way you looked at me, and then you said, "Didn't you just have a birthday, Diane?"

"Yes." I looked up at the crawling numbers as the elevator lurched its way to the sanctuary.

"How old are you now?"

I held my breath. "Sixteen."

"You've sure grown up, Di." You reached out, pulled my arm so fast it hurt, and then that sensation of your mouth on my face made me feel like throwing up. The door opened then, and the light from the auditorium flooded in as I jumped away. Your mother was there, browsing the crafts table.

She waved a Japanese paper kite at me as I stepped out, and called my name. "Diane-chan! Did you get a new haircut? You look so pretty today."

That was the last time I saw you, Harry. You know that I finished high school and went on to the University in Hawaii. I don't come home that often. There are lots of men here with dark, spiky hair like yours, and sometimes I think it's you on the street, or standing in line in front of me at the market. I get a tight, burning feeling high in my stomach until they turn to face me, and I realize it's someone else.

My mother sees you every now and then when she goes to the Community Center. She tells me that you paint all the banners for the festivals, flying like brilliant, airborne fish over Post Street. No matter how old you are, you're still her favorite Japanese boy, and she calls to tell me what you're doing, little things about your family.

I'm sorry about your parents, Harry, I really am. But I can't help feeling satisfied when I think of you, sitting on the edge of the tub next to your mom, and she's running her hands quietly over the surface of the water. The way you gently, gently lift off her kimono, and sponge the soft pale skin underneath, and then scoop the rinse water over her back with a plastic teacup. How you go to her, every evening, to help her bathe, while the neighborhood girls walk by under the window, and you hear their high sweet whistles, calling their dogs home.

GROWING UP

"THE PARROT'S BEAK"

Kartar Dhillon (1915–   )

In "The Parrot's Beak," Kartar Dhillon portrays the experiences
of her pioneering Indian American family in Northern California
during the 1910s and 1920s. Although her growing up was
hastened by the demands of both poverty and tradition, she has
described her life with ebullience.

Born in Simi Valley, California, Ms. Dhillon grew up in
Oregon and California, where her father worked in lumber mills
and her family farmed. Her father emigrated from India during the
1890s, and her mother became one of the first Indian women to live
in the United States when she immigrated in 1910. As an activist
for social justice, Ms. Dhillon has supported a broad range of causes
including freedom for India from British colonization, antiapartheid
efforts in South Africa, and Korean reunification. She lives in
Berkeley, California.

MY MOTHER WAS SURE SHE WOULD DIE AFTER SURGERY. A DOCTOR
told her she would have to go to the county hospital in Fresno
to have a tumor removed. Her first sight of the doctor in the
hospital confirmed her fears.

"That man does not like Indians," she told us. "He is the one
who let Labh Singh die."

She had never before been a patient in a hospital. Her eight
children had been born at home with the help of midwives. The
day before entering the hospital she lay in her bed and brooded

275

about the fate of her children. She was forty-one years old, widowed for five years. Her youngest child, born after the death of our father, was five years old, and her first-born, delivered a few weeks after her arrival in the United States in 1910, was twenty-one. Her husband had promised his brother in India that his first-born son would be his son because he had no children of his own. So they taught their first-born to call them "uncle" and "aunt," which he did, and the other children, all seven of us, hearing these terms, called our father and mother uncle and aunt also. "Chacha" and "Chachi" were our names for them, uncle and aunt on the father's side.

My parents had five sons and three daughters, and it was the daughters who worried our mother the most. Whatever we did that was different from the proper behavior of young girls in her village in India signified danger. And because most things here were different, I was in constant trouble.

At a very early age, I became convinced that my mother hated me. It seemed to me that whatever I did, or didn't do, was wrong. She cursed and beat me so much that I automatically ducked if she lifted her hand. When entering a room, I kept to the edges to stay out of her arm's reach.

"Get up, you black-faced witch," was a usual eye-opener for me in the morning. And throughout the day, it was, "You parrot's beak," to remind me of my long, ugly nose.

Sometimes when I was no more than six or seven years old, I would wonder why she hated me so much. Watching her nurse the newest baby, I would wonder what she felt about having carried me in her body.

She frequently talked to us about God. "He made parents to be as God over their children," she explained once. "If children do not obey their parents, they will surely go to hell after they die." Hell was a place, she said, where the disobedient would have to pass through walls set so close together it would be almost impossible to squeeze through them, and she would indicate a tiny space with her thumb and forefinger. I wasn't able to envision my soul, so I suffered endlessly imagining my body trying to squeeze through that tiny space.

Sometimes when she was particularly exasperated with me, she would say, "God must have given you to me to punish me for something I did in my previous life."

I went about feeling guilty most of the time, but I was never sure what I had done wrong. In time, I decided my crime was being a girl.

One day before she entered the hospital, she summoned me to her bedside, like a sovereign might summon a serf. I entered her room braced for a scolding. I knew she wouldn't hit me, because as I had grown older—I was sixteen then—she had given up on physical punishment, saying, "You are too old for whippings now. I can only appeal to your reason." The truth was, I had grown a head taller than my mother; I was too big.

I had learned long before not to speak when she scolded me for something. If I ever dared to protest an unjust accusation, she shouted, "Do not speak back to your elders."

At first I did not speak back because of her order; later I found not speaking to be a useful form of resistance. I would stand mute before her at times, even when being questioned, which added to her rage and frustration.

I went into her bedroom that day, tall and gangly, head hanging, waiting for an outpouring of abuse. But it did not come. Instead she said, "You probably know that I don't expect to come out of the hospital alive. You will be alone now, with neither father nor mother to guide you."

She had never spoken to me in a confiding manner before. I felt a rush of sorrow for her, this frail woman lying before me out of whose body I had come, and I felt guiltier than ever. Two days earlier she had paid a doctor in Merced with chickens, eggs, and vegetables, to learn that her tumor, grown to the size of a melon, had to be surgically removed.

"Your father wanted to arrange marriages for you and your sisters before he died," she continued, "but I absolutely refused. I told him, 'We came to this country to give our children an education. What good will it do them if they have to marry men they do not know and perhaps might not like?' You were only eleven years old when he died, you know."

"Oh yes, Chachi," I wanted to cry out to her, "I know. How well I know. But I thought it was only he who cared about me; it was only he who was kind to me. He would stop you from beating me, and when you pointed out my faults, he would say, she will learn better when she gets older, and you would reply, I doubt it. And yet it was you who saved me from a commitment I would have hated." I wanted to pour out words of gratitude, I wanted to comfort her, but I was too confused to say anything, and I remained silent.

"You will marry whom you please," she went on, "but it is my duty to teach you how to conduct yourself in marriage.

"You must remember that a woman is subservient to a man. When she is a child, she obeys her father; if he should die, then she must obey her oldest brother.

"When a woman marries, her husband is her master.

"If she becomes a widow, then she must defer to her sons."

The year was 1932. My mother did die in the hospital, a few days after the surgery. Her youngest child, my brother, was not old enough for grade school yet, so we took him to high school with us for the remainder of my senior term.

I had dreams of becoming an artist; I planned to work actively for India's freedom from British rule. I looked upon marriage as a prison. But even though I abhorred the idea of marriage, that same year, right out of high school, I got married.

My oldest brother already had planned to send me to India to marry the "right person." But the man I married, a political activist, born and raised in India, warned me, "You will have no rights in India. Your brother can force you to marry anyone he chooses. Marry me, then he will have no power over you."

I idolized this man. I had been impressed from the start by his fiery speeches at meetings of the Gadar Party, an organization formed to fight British rule in India. He already had a degree in political science from the University of California in Berkeley.

"But I want to go to the university," I said.

"You can do both," he insisted. "I will help you."

We got married secretly so that I could go on caring for my younger brothers and sister. But I did not keep my secret for long, because soon I had morning sickness and was frequently running out of the house to throw up behind the trees and bushes. "No children," I had said to my husband. "Political activism and babies don't go together." Though he had agreed with me, I found myself pregnant nonetheless.

My oldest brother was so furious when he found out that he kicked me out of the house. "Go live off your husband," he said, though he had bragged to people earlier about how much I did for the family. "Give her two empty bowls," he would say, "and she can produce a delicious dinner for the whole family."

I wanted to take the two youngest children with me, but my next oldest brother said, "You will have problems enough being married." A month later, all four of the younger children were brought to live with me and my husband—one of them had accidentally burned down the house.

Caring for the family was nothing new to me. When we were no more than seven and eight years old, my mother used to assign a baby apiece to me and my sister to watch for the day. At twelve, I was doing the entire family's wash on a washboard by hand, and taking turns with my sister to cook meals. By high school, the job of milking thirty cows every morning and night was tacked onto my other duties.

When I was in my eighth month of pregnancy, I had had no medical care. The clinics in the area where my husband leased land on a sharecrop basis had refused me because I had not been in that county a full year. So in an effort to obtain care, all the children and I had moved back to the farm that my brothers sharecropped. We slept on large raisin boxes under the open sky, and I cooked meals on a grill placed over a hole in the ground for the wood fire.

A family friend was shocked to learn I was not getting medical treatment and took me to the director of the same county hospital where my mother had died. But she also refused me admission, saying, "If these people can afford to farm, they can afford medical care." My friend pointed out that we did not have any money, that we could not even buy enough milk for all the children. "They buy one quart of milk a day, and take turns drinking one cup every other day." She told her that my teeth were breaking off in pieces for lack of calcium, but the director remained adamant.

"She can't have her baby on the street," my friend said.

The hospital official fixed her eyes on my friend and asked, "Then why do these people have babies?"

As we walked out the door, a nurse who had been in the room whispered to us, "The hospital can't turn you away in an emergency. Come in when you are in labor."

And that's what I did. My joy was great at learning my baby was a girl. Because I was slipping in and out of the anesthesia,

I asked three times to be assured I had heard right. I had indeed. I was so happy it was a girl because I wanted to prove to the world that she could be the equal of any boy ever born. Above that, I wanted a girl to give her the love and understanding that had been withheld from me.

In the hospital the nurses wouldn't believe that I was married because I wore no wedding ring and I gave my own last name instead of my husband's. I told them my mother had not worn a wedding ring, that it was a cultural thing. Also, I saw no reason for changing my name to someone else's.

One day the superintendent of nurses came into my ward, sat down on the edge of my bed, and took my hand in hers. "You can tell me, dear," she said gently. "You're really not married, are you?"

"But I am," I said.

"Then why don't you use your husband's name?"

"Why doesn't he use mine?"

She let go of my hand. "Is your husband English?"

"No, we're both Indian."

"But his name is Sharman. He must have borrowed it from the English."

"The English probably borrowed it from us," I replied. "After all, the Indian civilization has been here much longer."

I eventually lost the battle to keep my identity when I went to work in a war plant and was asked once too often why, if I was really married, I didn't use my husband's name and wear a wedding ring. I went to the dime store and bought a "gold" ring which I wore until the day I decided not to be married anymore.

My husband couldn't understand.

"What have I done wrong?" he begged to know.

I didn't have the courage to confront him, to tell him how he cheated me out of an education. You see, the day I was to sign up for classes at the university, he accused me of wanting to be around other men.

I didn't confront him about how he put an end to my political work either. The day I was to cover a strike for the workers' paper, he asked me, "And who will take care of the children if you are arrested?"

When he asked me what had he done wrong, I only told him,

"Last week when I asked you to buy me some white sewing thread, you said you had bought some another time, and what had I done with it."

He looked at me as if I was crazy. "We've been married eleven years, and when I ask you what is wrong, you tell me I wouldn't buy you five cents' worth of thread."

"That's it exactly," I said. "It cost only five cents, but I didn't have even *that* much money of my own. I had to ask you for it."

I had been in the habit of keeping silent about my real feelings for too many years and was unable to articulate all my grievances. I decided at that moment that I was not going to be a servant any longer—and an unpaid one at that.

Freedom from marriage at the age of twenty-seven with no job skills and three children to support is not quite the stuff of dreams, but I had finally taken my destiny into my own hands. I could wait on tables, and my typing ability could get me work in offices. Most important, I could live in a city to avail myself of evening classes and guarantee a good education for my children.

My cardinal rules for raising children were: no physical punishment, no discrimination between boys and girls, and no unfairness. When I was a child, my mother sometimes punished me for someone else's misdeed because she thought I looked guilty. I decided to believe my children.

In the house where I lived with my son and two daughters in San Francisco, there was no girls' work and no boys' work. The three of them helped me according to their ability. My son became the best cook because he started learning how the earliest.

Education topped the list of priorities for us. We took classes in everything that was available. I studied shorthand and bookkeeping to increase my earning power, and art and literature to fulfill my real aspirations. The children took classes in dance, art, and biology. They attended lectures by prominent world figures, went to the symphony with donated tickets, and took music lessons on the second-hand piano and violin I had purchased. With the leanest of budgets, we could be seated in only the top rows of the theaters and opera house, but we enjoyed the performances of many talented artists nevertheless.

In high school I had always been on the outside looking in.

When my classmates stayed after school to rehearse plays, take part in sports, or play musical instruments, I went home to do housework and milk cows. I was determined to help my children expand their horizons by taking advantage of all the things the city offered. On weekends we rented bicycles and rode through Golden Gate Park; we picnicked on the ocean beaches; we visited the zoo; we saw the exhibits at the museums. At home, when our studies were done, we played chess. When I was a child, if I was not studying, I had to be working, or if I was not working, I had to be studying. So now I played with my children—chess, tennis, swimming. I believed that life was meant to be enjoyed, not suffered.

We may have lived in the slums at times, but our apartments were sunny with life. Our rooms were filled with books and music, social activity, and intellectual endeavor. No matter how shabby a place we moved into, I could make it beautiful with paint and paintings. I sometimes think back to the many homes I lived in as a child. I cannot recall a single house that had running water or a rug on the floor. But I can recall vignettes of my mother and father seated at the rough kitchen table. On one occasion my mother was drawing a scroll of birds and flowers entwined with leafy vines around the borders of a letter to her family written in Punjabi script. On another occasion my father sat at the table in the light of a kerosene lamp writing poetry on a schoolchild's lined tablet.

Was that where my interest in art and literature was born? Was it their artistic creativity which sustained them in the harsh reality of their barren existence? Sometimes, when I look beyond my own hurts, I try to envision my mother's life before I arrived. I marvel at her survival as the family trekked around California and Oregon, living as they could wherever my father found work. He had the company of other men, friends and workers on the job. My mother had no one, no other Indian women to keep her company, no sisters or relatives to give her a hand with the housework. She had to do it all—all, that is, until her daughters grew old enough to help.

Both my father and mother were pioneers in those days of the early West. My father arrived at the port of San Francisco in 1899 as a matter of choice, an economic choice. He left his village in India of his own volition. Yet when my mother came to California, it was not her choice, but her husband's. My father had returned to India, and brought back to the United States the wife selected for him by his father. At the age of seventeen, she had been picked up virtually like a piece of baggage and taken off to a foreign land by a man whom she never saw before her marriage.

It was her good fortune that he was a kind and generous man who taught her to write in Punjabi so that she could communicate with the family she left behind, the family she would never see again. Neither of my parents went to school, but my father had learned to read and write both Punjabi and English in the course of his years of service in the British army. His was the vision that motivated me to educate my children.

With what wisdom I have gained, I now realize that some of the bitterness my mother projected onto me came from her status as a woman in a world controlled by men. I think my mother would agree, if she could: I consider my greatest accomplishment summed up in a compliment paid to one of my children: "She is not afraid to think."

"SEVENTEEN SYLLABLES"

Hisaye Yamamoto (1921–)

L*ike much of Hisaye Yamamoto's fiction, "Seventeen Syllables" takes place in a small, rural, pre–Second World War community in Southern California. This short story was first published in* The Partisan Review *in 1949 and is the title story of her first fiction collection. Emiko Omori's film,* Hot Summer Winds, *which aired on PBS's* American Playhouse, *is loosely based on "Seventeen Syllables" and Ms. Yamamoto's short story "Yoneko's Earthquake."*

Ms. Yamamoto was born in Redondo Beach, California. She attended Compton Junior College, where she studied French, Spanish, German, and Latin. She and her family were interned in the Poston, Arizona, concentration camp from 1942 to 1945. During the internment, she wrote for the relocation camp newspaper, The Poston Chronicle. *After the war she worked for the* Los Angeles Tribune, *an African American weekly.*

She is the author of Five Stories of Japanese American Life, *published in Tokyo. Her fiction and nonfiction have been published in many journals since the 1930s, including* Kenyon Review, Harper's Bazaar, Furioso, Gidra, Asian America, Amerasia Journal, *and* Arizona Quarterly. *Her poetry and prose have also been published in numerous Japanese American, Japanese Canadian, and Japanese publications including* Rafu Shimpo, Pacific Citizen, Kashu Mainichi, New Canadian, Rikka, Ashai Shimbun, Pan, *and* Hokubei Mainichi. *Her work has been reprinted in numerous anthologies, including* The Best American Short Stories of 1952. *She received the John Hay Whitney Foundation Opportunity Fellowship in 1950, the American Book Award for Lifetime*

Achievement from the Before Columbus Foundation in 1986, and an Association of Asian American Studies literature award in 1989. She lives in Los Angeles.

THE FIRST ROSIE KNEW THAT HER MOTHER HAD TAKEN TO WRITING poems was one evening when she finished one and read it aloud for her daughter's approval. It was about cats, and Rosie pretended to understand it thoroughly and appreciate it no end, partly because she hesitated to disillusion her mother about the quantity and quality of Japanese she had learned in all the years now that she had been going to Japanese school every Saturday (and Wednesday, too, in the summer). Even so, her mother must have been skeptical about the depth of Rosie's understanding, because she explained afterwards about the kind of poem she was trying to write.

See, Rosie, she said, it was a *haiku*, a poem in which she must pack all her meaning into seventeen syllables only, which were divided into three lines of five, seven, and five syllables. In the one she had just read, she had tried to capture the charm of a kitten, as well as comment on the superstition that owning a cat of three colors meant good luck.

"Yes, yes, I understand. How utterly lovely," Rosie said, and her mother, either satisfied or seeing through the deception and resigned, went back to composing.

The truth was that Rosie was lazy; English lay ready on the tongue but Japanese had to be searched for and examined, and even then put forth tentatively (probably to meet with laughter). It was so much easier to say yes, yes, even when one meant no, no. Besides, this was what was in her mind to say: I was looking through one of your magazines from Japan last night, Mother, and toward the back I found some *haiku* in English that delighted me. There was one that made me giggle off and on until I fell asleep—

> *It is morning, and lo!*
> *I lie awake, comme il faut,*
> *sighing for some dough.*

Now, how to reach her mother, how to communicate the melancholy song? Rosie knew formal Japanese by fits and starts, her mother had even less English, no French. It was much more possible to say yes, yes.

It developed that her mother was writing the *haiku* for a daily newspaper, the *Mainichi Shimbun*, that was published in San Francisco. Los Angeles, to be sure, was closer to the farming community in which the Hayashi family lived and several Japanese vernaculars were printed there, but Rosie's parents said they preferred the tone of the northern paper. Once a week, the *Mainichi* would have a section devoted to *haiku*, and her mother became an extravagant contributor, taking for herself the blossoming pen name, Ume Hanazono.

So Rosie and her father lived for awhile with two women, her mother and Ume Hanazono. Her mother (Tome Hayashi by name) kept house, cooked, washed, and, along with her husband and the Carrascos, the Mexican family hired for the harvest, did her ample share of picking tomatoes out in the sweltering fields and boxing them in tidy strata in the cool packing shed. Ume Hanazono, who came to life after the dinner dishes were done, was an earnest, muttering stranger who often neglected speaking when spoken to and stayed busy at the parlor table as late as midnight scribbling with pencil on scratch paper or carefully copying characters on good paper with her fat, pale-green Parker.

The new interest had some repercussions on the household routine. Before, Rosie had been accustomed to her parents and herself taking their hot baths early and going to bed almost immediately afterwards, unless her parents challenged each other to a game of flower cards or unless company dropped in. Now if her father wanted to play cards, he had to resort to solitaire (at which he always cheated fearlessly), and if a group of friends came over, it was bound to contain someone who was also writing *haiku*, and the small assemblage would be split in two, her father entertaining the non-literary members and her mother comparing ecstatic notes with the visiting poet. If they went out, it was more of the same thing. But Ume

Hanazono's life span, even for a poet's, was very brief—perhaps three months at most.

One night they went over to see the Hayano family in the neighboring town to the west, an adventure both painful and attractive to Rosie. It was attractive because there were four Hayano girls, all lovely and each one named after a season of the year (Haru, Natsu, Aki, Fuyu), painful because something had been wrong with Mrs. Hayano ever since the birth of her first child. Rosie would sometimes watch Mrs. Hayano, reputed to have been the belle of her native village, making her way about a room, stooped, slowly shuffling, violently trembling (*always* trembling), and she would be reminded that this woman, in this same condition, had carried and given issue to three babies. She would look wonderingly at Mr. Hayano, handsome, tall, and strong, and she would look at her four pretty friends. But it was not a matter she could come to any decision about.

On this visit, however, Mrs. Hayano sat all evening in the rocker, as motionless and unobtrusive as it was possible for her to be, and Rosie found the greater part of the evening practically anaesthetic. Too, Rosie spent most of it in the girls' room, because Haru, the garrulous one, said almost as soon as the bows and other greetings were over, "Oh, you must see my new coat!"

It was a pale plaid of grey, sand, and blue, with an enormous collar, and Rosie, seeing nothing special in it, said, "Gee, how nice."

"Nice?" said Haru, indignantly. "Is that all you can say about it? It's gorgeous! And so cheap, too. Only seventeen ninety-eight, because it was a sale. The saleslady said it was twenty-five dollars regular."

"Gee," said Rosie. Natsu, who never said much and when she said anything said it shyly, fingered the coat covetously and Haru pulled it away.

"Mine," she said, putting it on. She minced in the aisle between the two large beds and smiled happily. "Let's see how your mother likes it."

She broke into the front room and the adult conversation and went to stand in front of Rosie's mother, while the rest watched from the door. Rosie's mother was properly envious. "May I inherit it when you're through with it?"

Haru, pleased, giggled and said yes, she could, but Natsu reminded gravely from the door, "You promised me, Haru."

Everyone laughed but Natsu, who shamefacedly retreated into the bedroom. Haru came in laughing, taking off the coat. "We were only kidding, Natsu," she said. "Here, you try it on now."

After Natsu buttoned herself into the coat, inspected herself solemnly in the bureau mirror, and reluctantly shed it, Rosie, Aki, and Fuyu got their turns, and Fuyu, who was eight, drowned in it while her sisters and Rosie doubled up in amusement. They all went into the front room later, because Haru's mother quaveringly called to her to fix the tea and rice cakes and open a can of sliced peaches for everybody. Rosie noticed that her mother and Mr. Hayano were talking together at the little table—they were discussing a *haiku* that Mr. Hayano was planning to send to the *Mainichi*, while her father was sitting at one end of the sofa looking through a copy of *Life*, the new picture magazine. Occasionally, her father would comment on a photograph, holding it toward Mrs. Hayano and speaking to her as he always did—loudly, as though he thought someone such as she must surely be at least a trifle deaf also.

The five girls had their refreshments at the kitchen table, and it was while Rosie was showing the sisters her trick of swallowing peach slices without chewing (she chased each slippery crescent down with a swig of tea) that her father brought his empty teacup and untouched saucer to the sink and said, "Come on, Rosie, we're going home now."

"Already?" asked Rosie.

"Work tomorrow," he said.

He sounded irritated, and Rosie, puzzled, gulped one last yellow slice and stood up to go, while the sisters began protesting, as was their wont.

"We have to get up at five-thirty," he told them, going into the front room quickly, so that they did not have their usual chance to hang onto his hands and plead for an extension of time.

Rosie, following, saw that her mother and Mr. Hayano were

sipping tea and still talking together, while Mrs. Hayano concentrated, quivering, on raising the handleless Japanese cup to her lips with both her hands and lowering it back to her lap. Her father, saying nothing, went out the door, onto the bright porch, and down the steps. Her mother looked up and asked, "Where is he going?"

"Where is he going?" Rosie said. "He said we were going home now."

"Going home?" Her mother looked with embarrassment at Mr. Hayano and his absorbed wife and then forced a smile. "He must be tired," she said.

Haru was not giving up yet. "May Rosie stay overnight?" she asked, and Natsu, Aki, and Fuyu came to reinforce their sister's plea by helping her make a circle around Rosie's mother. Rosie, for once having no desire to stay, was relieved when her mother, apologizing to the perturbed Mr. and Mrs. Hayano for her father's abruptness at the same time, managed to shake her head no at the quartet, kindly but adamant, so that they broke their circle and let her go.

Rosie's father looked ahead into the windshield as the two joined him. "I'm sorry," her mother said. "You must be tired." Her father, stepping on the starter, said nothing. "You know how I get when it's *haiku*," she continued, "I forget what time it is." He only grunted.

As they rode homeward silently, Rosie, sitting between, felt a rush of hate for both—for her mother for begging, for her father for denying her mother. I wish this old Ford would crash, right now, she thought, then immediately, no, no, I wish my father would laugh, but it was too late: already the vision had passed through her mind of the green pick-up crumpled in the dark against one of the mighty eucalyptus trees they were just riding past, of the three contorted, bleeding bodies, one of them hers.

Rosie ran between two patches of tomatoes, her heart working more rambunctiously than she had ever known it to. How lucky it was that Aunt Taka and Uncle Gimpachi had come tonight, though, how very lucky. Otherwise she might not have really kept her half-promise to meet Jesus Carrasco. Jesus was going to be a senior in September at the same school she went to, and his parents were the ones helping with the tomatoes this year. She and Jesus, who hardly remembered seeing each other at Cleveland High where there were so many other people and two whole grades between them, had become great friends this summer—he always had a joke for her when he periodically drove the loaded pick-up up from the fields to the shed where she was usually sorting while her mother and father did the packing, and they laughed a great deal together over infinitesimal repartee during the afternoon break for chilled watermelon or ice cream in the shade of the shed.

What she enjoyed most was racing him to see which could finish picking a double row first. He, who could work faster, would tease her by slowing down until she thought she would surely pass him this time, then speeding up furiously to leave her several sprawling vines behind. Once he had made her screech hideously by crossing over, while her back was turned, to place atop the tomatoes in her green-stained bucket a truly monstrous, pale green worm (it had looked more like an infant snake). And it was when they had finished a contest this morning, after she had pantingly pointed a green finger at the immature tomatoes evident in the lugs at the end of his row and he had returned the accusation (with justice), that he had startlingly brought up the matter of their possibly meeting outside the range of both their parents' dubious eyes.

"What for?" she had asked.

"I've got a secret I want to tell you," he said.

"Tell me now," she demanded.

"It won't be ready till tonight," he said.

She laughed. "Tell me tomorrow then."

"It'll be gone tomorrow," he threatened.

"Well, for seven hakes, what is it?" she had asked, more than twice, and when he had suggested that the packing shed would be an appropriate place to find out, she had cautiously answered maybe. She had not been certain she was going to keep the appointment until the arrival of mother's sister and her husband.

Their coming seemed a sort of signal of permission, of grace, and she had definitely made up her mind to lie and leave as she was bowing them welcome.

So as soon as everyone appeared settled back for the evening, she announced loudly that she was going to the privy outside, "I'm going to the *benjo!*" and slipped out the door. And now that she was actually on her way, her heart pumped in such an undisciplined way that she could hear it with her ears. It's because I'm running, she told herself, slowing to a walk. The shed was up ahead, one more patch away, in the middle of the fields. Its bulk, looming in the dimness, took on a sinisterness that was funny when Rosie reminded herself that it was only a wooden frame with a canvas roof and three canvas walls that made a slapping noise on breezy days.

Jesus was sitting on the narrow plank that was the sorting platform and she went around to the other side and jumped backwards to seat herself on the rim of a packing stand. "Well, tell me," she said without greeting, thinking her voice sounded reassuringly familiar.

"I saw you coming out the door," Jesus said. "I heard you running part of the way, too."

"Uh-huh," Rosie said. "Now tell me the secret."

"I was afraid you wouldn't come," he said.

Rosie delved around on the chicken-wire bottom of the stall for number two tomatoes, ripe, which she was sitting beside, and came up with a left-over that felt edible. She bit into it and began sucking out the pulp and seeds. "I'm here," she pointed out.

"Rosie, are you sorry you came?"

"Sorry? What for?" she said. "You said you were going to tell me something."

"I will, I will," Jesus said, but his voice contained disappointment, and Rosie fleetingly felt the older of the two, realizing a brand-new power which vanished without category under her recognition.

"I have to go back in a minute," she said. "My aunt and uncle are here from Wintersburg. I told them I was going to the privy."

Jesus laughed. "You funny thing," he said. "You slay me!"

"Just because you have a bathroom *inside*," Rosie said. "Come on, tell me."

Chuckling, Jesus came around to lean on the stand facing her. They still could not see each other very clearly, but Rosie noticed that Jesus became very sober again as he took the hollow tomato from her hand and dropped it back into the stall. When he took hold of her empty hand, she could find no words to protest; her vocabulary had become distressingly constricted and she thought desperately that all that remained intact now was yes and no and oh, and even these few sounds would not easily out. Thus, kissed by Jesus, Rosie fell for the first time entirely victim to a helplessness delectable beyond speech. But the terrible, beautiful sensation lasted no more than a second, and the reality of Jesus' lips and tongue and teeth and hands made her pull away with such strength that she nearly tumbled.

Rosie stopped running as she approached the lights from the windows of home. How long since she had left? She could not guess, but gasping yet, she went to the privy in back and locked herself in. Her own breathing deafened her in the dark, close space, and she sat and waited until she could hear at last the nightly calling of the frogs and crickets. Even then, all she could think to say was oh, my, and the pressure of Jesus' face against her face would not leave.

No one had missed her in the parlor, however, and Rosie walked in and through quickly, announcing that she was next going to take a bath. "Your father's in the bathhouse," her mother said, and Rosie, in her room, recalled that she had not seen him when she entered. There had been only Aunt Taka and Uncle Gimpachi with her mother at the table, drinking tea. She got her robe and straw sandals and crossed the parlor again to go outside. Her mother was telling them about the *haiku* competition in the *Mainichi* and the poem she had entered.

Rosie met her father coming out of the bathhouse. "Are you through, Father?" she asked. "I was going to ask you to scrub my back."

"Scrub your own back," he said shortly, going toward the main house.

"What have I done now?" she yelled after him. She suddenly felt like doing a lot of yelling. But he did not answer, and she went into the bathhouse. Turning on the dangling light, she removed her denims and T-shirt and threw them in the big carton for dirty clothes standing next to the washing machine. Her other things she took with her into the bath compartment to wash after her bath. After she had scooped a basin of hot water from the square wooden tub, she sat on the grey cement of the floor and soaped herself at exaggerated leisure, singing "Red Sails in the Sunset" at the top of her voice and using da-da-da where she suspected her words. Then, standing up, still singing, for she was possessed by the notion that any attempt now to analyze would result in spoilage and she believed that the larger her volume the less she would be able to hear herself think, she obtained more hot water and poured it on until she was free of lather. Only then did she allow herself to step into the steaming vat, one leg first, then the remainder of her body inch by inch until the water no longer stung and she could move around at will.

She took a long time soaking, afterwards remembering to go around outside to stoke the embers of the tin-lined fireplace beneath the tub and to throw on a few more sticks so that the water might keep its heat for her mother, and when she finally returned to the parlor, she found her mother still talking *haiku* with her aunt and uncle, the three of them on another round of tea. Her father was nowhere in sight.

At Japanese school the next day (Wednesday it was), Rosie was grave and giddy by turns. Preoccupied at her desk in the row for students on Book Eight, she made up for it at recess by performing wild mimicry for the benefit of her friend Chizuko. She held her nose and whined a witticism or two in what she considered was the manner of Fred Allen; she assumed intoxication and a British accent to go over the climax of the Rudy Vallee recording of the pub conversation about William Ewart Gladstone; she was the child Shirley Temple piping, "On the Good Ship Lollipop"; she was the gentleman soprano of the Four Inkspots trilling, "If I Didn't Care." And she felt reasonably satisfied when Chizuko wept and gasped, "Oh, Rosie, you ought to be in the movies!"

Her father came after her at noon, bringing her sandwiches of minced ham and two nectarines to eat while she rode, so that she could pitch right into the sorting when they got home. The lugs were piling up, he said, and the ripe tomatoes in them would probably have to be taken to the cannery tomorrow if they were not ready for the produce haulers tonight. "This heat's not doing them any good. And we've got no time for a break today."

It *was* hot, probably the hottest day of the year, and Rosie's blouse stuck damply to her back even under the protection of the canvas. But she worked as efficiently as a flawless machine and kept the stalls heaped, with one part of her mind listening in to the parental murmuring about the heat and the tomatoes and with another part planning the exact words she would say to Jesus when he drove up with the first load of the afternoon. But when at last she saw that the pick-up was coming, her hands went berserk and the tomatoes started falling in the wrong stalls, and her father said, "Hey, hey! Rosie, watch what you're doing!"

"Well, I have to go to the *benjo*," she said, hiding panic.

"Go in the weeds over there," he said, only half-joking.

"Oh, Father!" she protested.

"Oh, go on home," her mother said. "We'll make out for awhile."

In the privy Rosie peered through a knothole toward the fields, watching as much as she could of Jesus. Happily she thought she saw him look in the direction of the house from time to time before he finished unloading and went back toward the patch where his mother and father worked. As she was heading for the shed, a very presentable black car purred up the dirt driveway to the house and its driver motioned to her. Was this the Hayashi home, he wanted to know. She nodded. Was she a Hayashi? Yes, she said, thinking that he was a good-looking man. He got out of the car with a huge, flat package and she saw that he warmly wore a business suit. "I have something here for your mother then," he said, in a more elegant Japanese than she was used to.

She told him where her mother was and he came along with her, patting his face with an immaculate white handkerchief and saying something about the coolness of San Francisco. To her surprised mother and father, he bowed and introduced himself as, among other things, the *haiku* editor of the *Mainichi Shimbun*, saying that since he had been coming as far as Los Angeles anyway, he had decided to bring her the first prize she had won in the recent contest.

"First prize?" her mother echoed, believing and not believing, pleased and overwhelmed. Handed the package with a bow, she bobbed her head up and down numerous times to express her utter gratitude.

"It is nothing much," he added, "but I hope it will serve as a token of our great appreciation for your contributions and our great admiration of your considerable talent."

"I am not worthy," she said, falling easily into his style. "It is I who should make some sign of my humble thanks for being permitted to contribute."

"No, no, to the contrary," he said, bowing again.

But Rosie's mother insisted, and then saying that she knew she was being unorthodox, she asked if she might open the package because her curiosity was so great. Certainly she might. In fact, he would like her reaction to it, for personally, it was one of his favorite *Hiroshiges*.

Rosie thought it was a pleasant picture, which looked to have been sketched with delicate quickness. There were pink clouds, containing some graceful calligraphy, and a sea that was a pale blue except at the edges, containing four sampans with indications of people in them. Pines edged the water and on the far-off beach there was a cluster of thatched huts towered over by pine-dotted mountains of grey and blue. The frame was scalloped and gilt.

After Rosie's mother pronounced it without peer and somewhat prodded her father into nodding agreement, she said Mr. Kuroda must at least have a cup of tea after coming all this way, and although Mr. Kuroda did not want to impose, he soon agreed that a cup of tea would be refreshing and went along with her to the house, carrying the picture for her.

"Ha, your mother's crazy!" Rosie's father said, and Rosie laughed uneasily as she resumed judgment on the tomatoes.

She had emptied six lugs when he broke into an imaginary conversation with Jesus to tell her to go and remind her mother of the tomatoes, and she went slowly.

Mr. Kuroda was in his shirtsleeves expounding some *haiku* theory as he munched a rice cake, and her mother was rapt. Abashed in the great man's presence, Rosie stood next to her mother's chair until her mother looked up inquiringly, and then she started to whisper the message, but her mother pushed her gently away and reproached, "You are not being very polite to our guest."

"Father says the tomatoes . . ." Rosie said aloud, smiling foolishly.

"Tell him I shall only be a minute," her mother said, speaking the language of Mr. Kuroda.

When Rosie carried the reply to her father, he did not seem to hear and she said again, "Mother says she'll be back in a minute."

"All right, all right," he nodded, and they worked again in silence. But suddenly, her father uttered an incredible noise, exactly like the cork of a bottle popping, and the next Rosie knew, he was stalking angrily toward the house, almost running in fact, and she chased after him crying, "Father! Father! What are you going to do?"

He stopped long enough to order her back to the shed. "Never mind!" he shouted. "Get on with the sorting!"

And from the place in the fields where she stood, frightened and vacillating, Rosie saw her father enter the house. Soon Mr. Kuroda came out alone, putting on his coat. Mr. Kuroda got into his car and backed out down the driveway onto the highway. Next her father emerged, also alone, something in his arms (it was the picture, she realized), and, going over to the bathhouse woodpile, he threw the picture on the ground and picked up the axe. Smashing the picture, glass and all (she heard the explosion faintly), he reached over for the kerosene that was used to encourage the bath fire and poured it over the wreckage. I am dreaming, Rosie said to herself, I am dreaming, but her father, having made sure that his act of cremation was irrevocable, was even then returning to the fields.

Rosie ran past him and toward the house. What had become of her mother? She burst into the parlor and found her mother at the back window watching the dying fire. They watched together until there remained only a feeble smoke under the blazing sun. Her mother was very calm.

"Do you know why I married your father?" she said without turning.

"No," said Rosie. It was the most frightening question she had ever been called upon to answer. Don't tell me now, she wanted to say, tell me tomorrow, tell me next week, don't tell me today. But she knew she would be told now, that the telling would combine with the other violence of the hot afternoon to level her life, her world to the very ground.

It was like a story out of the magazines illustrated in sepia, which she had consumed so greedily for a period until the information had somehow reached her that those wretchedly unhappy autobiographies, offered to her as the testimonials of living men and women, were largely inventions: Her mother, at nineteen, had come to America and married her father as an alternative to suicide.

At eighteen she had been in love with the first son of one of the well-to-do families in her village. The two had met whenever and wherever they could, secretly, because it would not have done for his family to see him favor her—her father had no money; he was a drunkard and a gambler besides. She had learned she was with child; an excellent match had already been arranged for her lover. Despised by her family, she had given premature birth to a stillborn son, who would be seventeen now. Her family did not turn her out, but she could no longer project herself in any direction without refreshing in them the memory of her indiscretion. She wrote to Aunt Taka, her favorite sister in America, threatening to kill herself if Aunt Taka would not send for her. Aunt Taka hastily arranged a marriage with a young man of whom she knew, but lately arrived from Japan, a young man of simple mind, it was said, but of kindly heart. The young man was never told why his unseen betrothed was so eager to hasten the day of meeting.

The story was told perfectly, with neither groping for words nor untoward passion. It was as though her mother had memorized it by heart, reciting it to herself so many times over that its nagging vileness had long since gone.

"I had a brother then?" Rosie asked, for this was what seemed to matter now; she would think about the other later, she assured herself, pushing back the illumination which threatened all that darkness that had hitherto been merely mysterious or even glamorous. "A half-brother?"

"Yes."

"I would have liked a brother," she said.

Suddenly, her mother knelt on the floor and took her by the wrists. "Rosie," she said urgently, "promise me you will never marry!" Shocked more by the request than the revelation, Rosie stared at her mother's face. Jesus, Jesus, she called silently, not certain whether she was invoking the help of the son of the Carrascos or of God, until there returned sweetly the memory of Jesus' hand, how it had touched her and where. Still her mother waited for an answer, holding her wrists so tightly that her hands were going numb. She tried to pull free. Promise, her mother whispered fiercely, promise. Yes, yes, I promise, Rosie said. But for an instant she turned away, and her mother, hearing the familiar glib agreement, released her. Oh, you, you, you, her eyes and twisted mouth said, you fool. Rosie, covering her face, began at last to cry, and the embrace and consoling hand came much later than she expected.

from CLAY WALLS

Kim Ronyoung
(a.k.a. Gloria Hahn) (1926–1987)

Kim Ronyoung's novel tells the story of Haesu and Chun, a wife and husband who immigrate to the United States during the decade before World War II. The couple escape political persecution in Japanese-occupied Korea. Settling in Los Angeles, Haesu and Chun struggle to survive and raise a family while dealing with class issues from their pasts. Although Chun is a poor farmer's son, Haesu is a yangban or member of the traditional Korean scholar-noble class. The following excerpt is from the last part of the novel, which is narrated by Faye, the Chuns' youngest child and only daughter.

Ms. Kim was born in Los Angeles and grew up in a tiny Korean community which over several decades became Los Angeles's Koreatown. After graduating from Manual Arts High School, she attended Los Angeles City College. While a student, she helped her mother make neckties to sell to local department stores and worked at a Disney studios assembly plant. At the age of nineteen she married Richard Hahn, and became a housewife and mother. After raising her children, she studied Asian art and literature and Chinese language, receiving a B.A. from San Francisco State University in 1975. Nominated for a Pulitzer Prize, Clay Walls developed out of Ms. Kim's desire to write about her parents and their generation. The novel has been translated into Korean and was published in Seoul in 1989.

DID YOU GET THAT, FAYE?" MISS SONG RASPED. "YOU WRITE THAT it was moved by Lily Yun and seconded by Gracie Park that in

July we are to have a day hike at Elysian Park, including a tour through the Hires Root Beer plant."

"I got most of that," I said, scribbling quickly in the black notebook where we kept the minutes of the meeting. Miss Song had told us that root beer flowed from the taps at the Hires bottling plant and Lily had said that sounded like the goose that laid the golden egg. I thought all that should have gone into the minutes, but Miss Song said I should only record decisions our club made.

"Pay attention. We're going to take a vote now," Miss Song said. The club was her idea. After she was graduated from U.C.L.A. with a degree in Sociology, Eleanor Song became a social worker and called all teenage Korean girls together to form an organization. We named ourselves after the national flower of Korea, The Mugunghwa Club.

I thought Miss Song should have been a P.E. teacher. She was stocky and stood with her feet apart like a coach of a football team. Her voice was deep and raspy. Once, Gracie called her "Mr. Song" by mistake. Some of us cringed with embarrassment while others laughed.

"Miss Song, Miss Song," Nancy Lee called, waving her hand in the air. "When are we going to give the Tin Can Hop?"

"Just a minute. There's a motion on the floor. The president is supposed to call for a vote. That's you, Alice."

Under Miss Song's prompting, Alice called for a vote and the motion was passed.

"Record the results in the minutes, Faye."

"Yes, Miss Song."

She waited while I wrote everything down. "Now we'll discuss the Tin Can Hop," she said. The Hop was her idea; one had been given at her high school. Admission to the dance would be cans of food that were to be distributed to needy families on Thanksgiving.

I raised my hand. "Miss Song, what do you mean by needy?"

"Poor people," she said and looked for another question.

"Where are we going to find them?" Lily Yun asked. Her father had bought Papa's business and owned a packing house in Reedley.

"Don't worry, we'll find them," Miss Song assured her.

I hoped she did not mean us. Momma wouldn't stand for that. Papa's funeral was four years ago and she still owed people money for it. But according to her, we weren't poor; we just did not have enough money.

The motion to have the dance in early November was passed.

When we heard the sound of scuffling feet and the scraping of chairs on the other side of the partition, I hastily wrote, ". . . made a motion to adjourn the meeting" and filled in Gracie's name as her hand went up.

Several hands from both sides of the movable wall pushed the partition aside, opening up the hall of the United Korean Association. The boys had formed a club of their own, calling themselves "Cavaliers." Like us, they met on Friday nights.

The girls in charge of the refreshments fluttered around the kitchen uncapping bottles of Par-T-Pak sodas and ripping open bags of potato chips. The girls in charge of music plugged in the turntable and put on a Glenn Miller record. The boys sat around.

I had on a new dress and looked for ways to show it off without drawing attention to my feet. My saddle shoes were covered with layers of polish and looked as if they were made of chalk. The ghostly whiteness exaggerated their size, reducing my ankles to spindles. When I helped push the chairs and tables against the wall, I moved quickly, giving no one a chance to get a good look at my shoes.

"Who is he?" Gracie's voice drifted to my ears. "He looks like Dennis Morgan."

Dennis Morgan was one of my favorite actors. I turned to look. Boys from out of town often came to the N.A.K. building on Friday nights. Word had gotten around that it was a place where young Koreans met to socialize. The out-of-towners were usually from the San Joaquin Valley. Muscular and tan from working in the fields, they could be distinguished from the city boys of the Cavalier club. This one was no exception, only he was handsomer than most.

"Somebody ask him to dance. You do it, Alice," Gracie suggested. Alice was the girl the Cavaliers voted they most wanted to be marooned with on a deserted island.

"Why should I? It's not my idea," Alice protested.

Someone changed the record and turned up the volume.

When I hear that serenade in blue.
I'm somewhere in another world alone with you . . .

While the girls were still arguing, *he* walked toward me. I was sitting on the edge of a table and drew my two limestone blocks of saddle shoes into the shadows under the table.

"Hi!" His face broke into a broad grin. His white teeth glistened against his bronze skin.

"Hi," I answered back.

"Wanna dance?"

"Okay." In one move, I stepped onto the floor and put my hand on his shoulder. His eyes never fell to my feet. I thanked God it was a slow piece; I could not jitterbug. Only savages dance like that, Momma said.

"My name's Willie Koo. I'm from Reedley," he said.

"Oh, really?"

"No, Reedley. Willie's my name." His eyes twinkled as he laughed at his own play on words. He started right in talking about himself. I listened until I forgot about my shoes. He lived with his uncle and worked at the Yun's packing house until he was old enough to drive his uncle's truck. He wanted to get out of "hicktown," he said, and see the world. This was his first trip to L.A.

"Don't your parents ever come to L.A.?" I asked.

"I haven't any," he answered. "They're both dead."

I forgot to move my feet and he stepped on my shoes. "Oops, sorry," he said, breaking away to see if he had damaged anything. I quickly drew him close to resume the two step. "My father's dead too," I said. As soon as I said it, I regretted it. It was a terrible thing to have in common. But Willie was the only young person I had met who did not have a father.

"No kidding? I don't remember my mom. She died when I was born." He looked around the room. "This is really great. You guys always get together like this?"

"Every Friday night. Don't you belong to a club?"

"Ain't that many Koreans in Reedley. How old are you, anyway?"

His question took me by surprise. "Me? Fifteen, uh, going on sixteen."

"You don't happen to have a sister, do you?"

"What? Why?"

"I'm eighteen. Just graduated. Ready to see the world. And here I am. L.A. is really something."

"Uh huh." I said. No one seemed to think me old enough for anything.

Serenade, serenade in blue . . .

Willie did a fancy turn and dipped. As I fell toward him, the hard contours of his leg pressed through my dress. I had never felt a boy against me before. The blood rushed to my cheeks.

"What's your name?" he asked.

I told him.

"Fay? Like in Fay Wray?"

"With an 'e' " I said, "F-a-y-e."

"No kidding? Well, I'll be seeing you, Faye with an 'e.' "

Willie began showing up regularly on Friday nights. As an out-of-towner, he could not join the Cavaliers but they allowed him to draw from the pool of girls for dates. All of us knew how it worked: the boys decided among themselves who would ask whom to be his date. By gentlemen's agreement, no one stole another's claim. The arrangement may have been to the boys' liking, but a girl had little choice. If she refused an invitation, she was doomed to stay at home.

Willie began asking me to be his date. I had no way of knowing if it was because he wanted me or because no one else did. Anyway, I fell into being his girl.

Being Willie's girl meant that I would be included when the boys took their girls bowling, or to movies, or to Simon's Drive-in for a hamburger. I wanted to be the kind of girl boys liked to be with so, while watching movies, I studied the way Hollywood stars walked and talked. I thumbed through magazines to see how starlets fixed their hair and dressed. I learned to do my own hair, but clothes required money.

"Look at these shoes, Momma." I had delayed polishing them for the occasion. "They make me look like Frankenstein's monster. I need extra money to buy clothes. I can work, get a part-time job or help you sew."

"Never. If necessary, I'll stay up all night working to give you what you want. But you will never work for money," she said.

"Why not me? What's so special about me?" I said, hoping I would find the words that would change her mind.

"Not just you. Because of your family. Women of the *yangban* class do not work for money."

"You do."

"Because I have no choice. But here in my house where no one can see me."

"In America, it's all right to work for money, for girls to work like boys. It's nothing to be ashamed of," I insisted.

She put down her sewing to wave her finger at me. "You are not like other American girls. If you try to be like them, you will be nothing special." She picked up her sewing. "You don't need new clothes to be a lady."

"Who wants to be a lady?" As soon as I said it, I knew I was in for it. She was going to remind me about our family position in Korea, about the Japanese depriving us of our rightful due. "Oh, never mind," I said and walked to the back porch. She was right about one thing: I wasn't like other American girls. No one at school spoke to me or behaved toward me as if I were like any American girl. Most of them were nice enough. I even considered Ruth Johnson one of my best friends until she told me, "You know, Faye, I don't think of you as being Korean anymore," as if there was something wrong with being Korean. We never double dated. She went to school dances but I was never asked. If it wasn't for Miss Song, I wouldn't be anyone's girl.

I found an old paring knife and scraped off the layers of white polish from my shoes, then applied a new coat of milky paint. They still looked ragged. I could not help wondering what good it was to be a *yangban* if I couldn't dress like one.

I used the last drop of shoe-white, then went to the carriage to drop the bottle in the box for the junkman. I looked up in time to see John climb over the fence. He dropped to the ground, then disappeared behind the garage.

Soon afterwards, the doorbell rang. "Answer the door, Faye," Momma shouted.

The policeman was sweating and breathing hard. When he saw me he said, "Well, at least I've got the right place. Do you have a brother about this tall?" He held his hand at the level of his forehead. "Wearing a light blue shirt and tan pants?"

I shrugged my shoulders. "I have two brothers," I said.

"One of them run in here a few minutes ago?" he asked.

"No."

"What is it?" Momma asked me in Korean.

"It's a policeman. He's looking for a boy," I said.

Momma came to the door. "What boy?"

The policeman showed Momma John's height and described the clothes he was wearing.

"What he do?" she asked.

"Tried to steal a bicycle. Was it your son?"

"I don't know. He's not here," she said.

"Ma'am, I saw him run into this yard. I know he belongs to you."

Momma looked at me. *"Opah pwasse ni?"*

I shook my head to indicate I had not seen my brother.

The policeman took a card from his wallet and handed it to Momma. "I'm Officer Richards. Better have a word with your boy. Tell him it's best for him to cooperate with us. The store owner said he had seen your boy hanging around when some other things had disappeared."

"Maybe he looks like someone else," Momma said. "We don't steal. We pay back what we owe. I call you . . ." she looked at the card. "Officer Richards."

After he left, Momma told me, "Go find John."

I walked through the house and out the back door. By turning sideways I was able to squeeze through the space between the fence and the garage. Step by step, I edged toward the back of the garage. I stopped when I heard John's voice.

"We've got to get rid of the stuff, man," John said.

"It's you they seen. You're the one in trouble, man," a voice replied. I did not recognize the voice.

"That's why I can't keep it here. Take it. Get rid of it," John ordered.

"I know I can count on Luke to take them," the voice said.

"Man, just don't tell him where you got them," John said.

"Gotcha."

I heard shoes kick against the fence as someone climbed over it and ran away.

Someone jumped on some loose boards in the garage, then I heard the door scrape open.

"John?" I called.

His face appeared around the corner of the garage. "What are you doing there?"

"I came to tell you a policeman came looking for you. Momma knows." I sidled out to him.

"Shit! I thought I had lost him."

"What are you up to anyway?" I asked.

"What's it to you?"

"If you get into trouble we'll all be in for it. What did you try to steal for anyway?"

He sat on the ground and picked up a handful of dirt. "Know of any other way to get a bike?"

"Work for it. Save your money," I said.

John laughed as he threw the dirt in the air. "I'd be too old to ride a bike by then. Figure it out, Faye. We won't ever have anything we want."

"Don't say that, John. Harold will find a job. He'll be able to work full time," I reminded him.

"Think all he has to do is worry about buying things for us? Why do you think he went to Fresno to look for a job?"

"I thought it was because he couldn't find anything in L.A."

"Jesus, Faye, You don't know anything. He went away to get away."

"You're lying."

"Okay, I'm lying. Have it your way."

"Better go talk to Mom. The policeman left her his card."

"What did Mom tell him?"

"You know, that she'll pay for anything you took," I said.

"Shit!" He stood up. "Go on in and tell Mom I'll be home later."

"Don't get into any more trouble," I said.

"Who are you to tell me what to do? Go on in and tell Mom what I said," he ordered, then turned and walked toward Western Avenue.

I hated keeping secrets from Momma, but I wasn't anxious to give her bad news.

"John will be home later. He says you shouldn't worry."

"We'll see," she said.

I went to the kitchen to wash the rice. The water splashed over the sink onto my shoes, sending a spray of white on the floor.

I held the door open for Willie. He was carrying a lug of cucumbers. "The first of the season, Mrs. Chun. You'll be the first lady in L.A. to make *oi kimchee*," he said. On top of the cucumbers lay a bunch of yellow daisies. "Those are for you," he said to me.

While he took the lug to the back porch, I found a vase and put the flowers in water. I didn't notice Willie creeping up on me. He turned me around and planted his mouth on my lips. "Stop that!" I said, pushing him away. He giggled silently and grabbed me around the waist.

"Yah! Faye-yah!" Momma called.

Willie let go of me like a shot. I laughed at him quietly and walked out of the kitchen. "What do you want, Momma?"

"I'm worried about John. Would you and Willie see if you can find him?"

"Sure, Mrs. Chun," Willie said. He had followed me out carrying the daisies. When he set them down, the yellow blossoms seemed to light up the whole table.

"They're very pretty," Momma said.

"I'm taking Faye bowling. We're meeting some kids at the alley. Maybe John will be there," he said.

"Tell him I want to see him right away," Momma said.

I grabbed a sweater and was about to go out the door when Momma said, "Be home by ten o'clock."

"Ten? Our tournament won't be over by then," I complained.

"Ten-thirty then."

"Alice Choy doesn't have to be in until eleven," I said. Momma always used Alice as an example for me to follow.

"Ten-thirty is late enough," she said with finality.

As we walked toward Willie's truck, I complained, "My Mom's so strict."

"I don't blame her. If you were mine, I'd watch over you like a hawk," he said, squeezing my hand.

"But she overdoes it. Feels she has to make up for Papa, I guess."

"At least you have a Mom to make up for your not having a father."

I pressed against his arm. "I shouldn't be complaining, should I?"

"It's okay, baby. Cry on my shoulders anytime. I can take it," he said boastfully.

As we drove by *Curries'* Ice Cream Parlor, I looked in to see if John was there. Whenever we had extra change in our hands, we would walk the mile to *Curries'* to have an ice cream cone. He wasn't there.

"They make the best ice cream," I told Willie.

"That's a long way to go for ice cream," he said.

"The library's right across the street. I go there a couple of times a month," I said. "I first went to look up a poem by Walt Whitman and it got to be a habit." I thought about Jane. I hadn't seen her for several years. When she joined the Japanese Culture Club and I joined the Mugunghwa, we drifted apart. But I've never forgotten her or her sisters' skit. " 'A child said, What is grass?, fetching it to me with full hands . . .'," I recited to Willie.

"You're in trouble, kid. Didn't you read the sign, 'Keep off the grass'?" Willie replied, mimicking my cadence.

I laughed. "It's really a swell poem. I don't understand all of it. It ends with, 'And to die is different from what anyone supposed, and luckier.' "

"Luckier?"

"That's what it says. I understand dying being different from what anyone supposed. Learned it the hard way. I was a mess at my father's funeral, made a fool of myself. Momma had to tell everyone, 'It's her first funeral. She doesn't know how to behave.' I wanted to die."

"I wouldn't know how to act either. I've never been to a funeral."

"Not even your father's?"

Willie hesitated, as if he were arguing with himself. "He hasn't had one," he said, finally. "I say he's dead because he never considered me alive. No one's ever owned up to being my father, but I've got a feeling I know who it is and he ain't dead."

"What are you talking about?"

He hesitated again. "Aw, forget it."

Whatever it was had made him sad. "You'd get a kick out of the book on etiquette I've read about funerals," I said cheerfully.

"There's a book on it?"

"I looked it up. It tells you what to wear, what to do, and how to think. It said that 'death has lost much of its terror.' It said that 'death is accepted with simple fortitude by sensible people.' "

Willie gave a laugh. " 'Sensible people,' " he said, as if no such thing existed.

"How do you like this one . . . 'etiquette requires complete control by the bereaved woman'?"

"You mean, crying at a funeral is a no-no? Who wrote that book anyway?"

"Can you imagine a Korean woman in 'complete control'?" I asked sardonically.

"That's like asking a Korean to hate *kimchee*," he said, chuckling. "What does 'bereaved' mean?"

"That means losing someone who died," I answered with confidence. I had looked up the word.

"You sound like you memorized the book," Willie said.

I wondered if he was teasing me. I had read the pages over and over again, trying to comprehend the reasons behind the rules. Nothing Momma had taught me helped me to understand.

"I'd feel so strange trying to think and act like that. That's why I read it so many times. It said, 'Leave the family in mourning alone with their grief.' Everyone came to the house. They helped Momma cook then sat around to eat and keep her company."

"Sounds like the best part of the funeral," Willie teased.

"I've read the book but I still think I wouldn't know how to behave at a funeral," I said with a sigh.

"Why worry about it? No Korean will be reading the book," Willie reassured me. "How'd we get on this subject, anyway?"

"Whitman's poem." I settled back into my seat. " 'All goes onward and outward, nothing collapses.' "

As Willie opened the door, the rumble of bowling balls rolling down hardwood floors and the sharp crack as they hit the ten-pins made me want to have a try at it. No other place in the world sounded like a bowling alley.

Alice waved when she saw us. "We've already reserved the lanes," she shouted.

I cupped my hands around my mouth. "Have you seen John?"

She nodded and pointed toward the pool room.

"Will you get him, Willie? He won't listen to me. Tell him he should go home right now," I said.

I sidled down the row behind Alice to talk to her. She was wearing a plaid skirt and a cardigan sweater that picked up the red in the plaid. Silver barrettes held her permanent-waved hair neatly in place. She had on rented bowling shoes, a brand new pair without a single crack in the blue number '5' painted on the back of the heels. She looked terrific.

"Whoever loses has to treat the winner. Noodles at Hang-chow Restaurant," she said.

"Who's coming?" I asked.

"C. K. is picking up Lily. Jimmy brought me. He's in there with John," she said, nodding her head toward the pool room.

"I see they finally got some decent shoes," I said, pointing my chin at her feet.

"The last pair of 5's."

"I wear 7's but I'd better get mine before they're gone." I left her to go to the registration desk.

Willie had a serious look on his face as he walked toward me. "Is something wrong?" I asked.

"I was going to ask you the same thing. John said he's going home as soon as he finishes the game. He wanted to know when I was going back to Reedley."

"Why?"

"That's what I was wondering."

"But he is going home?"

"Oh yeah. He said to tell you he's going home."

I was relieved. Momma wouldn't be worried about him much longer.

"JAMES LEE!" a voice boomed over the loudspeaker. Jimmy came out of the pool room to claim the lanes assigned to us. John followed him out. He looked at me then turned and went out the door.

"Did you get your shoes?" Willie asked.

I held up a battered pair of ecru shoes. "Seven is a popular size. The man said they're all beat up like this."

The sight of them made Willie laugh. "You ought to buy yourself a pair," he said.

I sighed. "My Mom would say, 'You don't need your own bowling shoes to be a good bowler.' "

Willie put his arms around my waist. "I'll get you a pair for Christmas."

By the time C. K. and Lily arrived, we had bowled a game. Willie didn't mind their being late. He did not like Lily. "She's a stuck-up little snot," he once told me. He had worse things to say about her father. "That S. O. B. is so full of himself. When he comes to the packing house, he expects everyone to kiss his you-know-what because he's given them a job. He expects gratitude for slave labor," he had said. I remember being perplexed. "Mr. Yun? He bought my father's business. He's responsible for collecting the money to build the N.A.K. building. He's a bigshot in the community. What's he done to you?" Willie had muttered to himself then told me, "I hate his guts."

Lily opened her navy blue canvas bag and took out a pair of bowling shoes. "I can't stand the thought of wearing shoes someone else has worn," she said with a shudder.

"Good idea. Think how they must feel," Willie said.

Lily ignored him. "The fit has to be exactly right or your feet begin to hurt." She bent down to untie her saddle shoes. "Aren't these a nuisance to polish? How do you keep yours so white, Faye?" I had tucked my shoes under the seat.

Before I could open my mouth, Willie said, "She read a book on it."

"Well I'm sure you didn't," she said to him.

I put a restraining hand on Willie but couldn't shut him up. "No, but Faye told me about it. It takes a special kind of spit." He hacked to bring his sputum up. "Got plenty for you," he gurgled.

"Jesus, Willie. You haven't got any class," C. K. said in disgust.

I punched Willie in the ribs. "That's repulsive," I said.

"Willie's a country hick," Lily said. "He doesn't know any better."

Alice rolled back her eyes. "Cut it out, both of you." She took a Kleenex from her purse and handed it to Willie. "Get rid of it," she said.

I looked at Lily, expecting her to say something. But she wore her expression of disapproval without saying another word. Prim in a pale blue sweater that set off her brown checked skirt, she seemed sure of herself. I had noticed earlier that the brown of her saddle shoes matched the brown of her skirt. I'd be sure of myself too, I thought, if my shoes matched my dress.

We had bowled two hours when Willie announced, "Last game if we want to eat. Faye has to be in by ten-thirty."

I could have hit him over the head with a bowling ball. "Don't let me break up the game," I said.

Jimmy began adding up the score. "Well, I know for sure that Alice and I want to eat. We left you guys in the dust. You're low man, Willie. You and C. K. will have to treat."

"That's nothing new. I'm the original low man," Willie said.

Everyone laughed but me. I saw nothing amusing in what he had said.

The streets that led to the Hangchow Restaurant went through the heart of old Los Angeles. Our voices wobbled as the wheels of the truck bounced over streetcar tracks and fell into gutted asphalt.

I grabbed the ledge of the window as we bounced over a pothole. "You shouldn't say bad things about yourself," I said.

"Why not? I beat the other guys to the punch," Willie said.

"Or give them ideas."

He took a moment to think about what I had said, then chuckled, "Do you take everything so seriously?"

Do I? I wondered. Everyone else had laughed. "Not every-thing," I said.

He put his hand on my thigh and gave it a squeeze. "Stick with me, baby. We'll have plenty of laughs."

I pushed his hand away. "That's not funny," I said.

The others were waiting when we arrived. The six of us entered the restaurant and crowded into a booth. It was difficult to see anything. The dim light barely reflected off the brown shellacked walls. We brushed off the seats of the bentwood chairs before sitting down. "Don't they ever clean this joint?" Willie grumbled.

"Whose idea was it to come here?" Lily asked.

Willie and Jimmy looked at each other in mock amazement. "We always come here," Jimmy said.

"Doesn't everybody?" Willie added.

Everyone but Lily laughed.

From the booth next to ours, the hollow sound of Chinese words sprinkled with pidgin English climbed over the top of the partition. The other cubicles were silent. The restaurant was practically empty. There would be no excuse for slow service. While we waited for attention, an old Chinese man sat behind the cash register reading his newspaper.

Willie pushed aside the dingy curtain and shouted, "Hey! Garcon!"

The man looked up. Willie held up his arm and pointed to his watch.

Scowling, the man snapped, "Next time, come early."

Willie leaned toward the center of the table and in a lowered voice said, "Next time, we won't come at all."

Everyone laughed but Lily and me.

"You have to know how to handle these guys," Willie said, after our meal was served. "Put a little pressure on and you get service. Old Yankee know-how." He gave me a wink.

C. K. pushed back on his chair to look out. "He's still reading his newspaper."

"One thing you have to say for him," I said. "He has a lot of character." I smiled and waited for the laugh.

"What?" Willie asked. He didn't get it.

"Never mind," I said. "What time is it?"

He looked at his watch. "Holy Smokes! We have to beat it." He pulled out his wallet and laid down a ten dollar bill. "This ought to do it."

"That's too much!" C. K. protested.

"Forget it," Willie said. He once told me there was nothing worse than being a cheapskate.

We ran to his truck and scrambled in. Willie turned the key to the ignition and slammed his foot on the starter. The engine whined but refused to turn over. "Damn it!" Willie said. He pulled on the choke and kept at the starter until the engine finally took fire. He grappled with the steering wheel to maneuver out of the tight parking space. "Trading in this pile of junk for a new semi. I'll be able to make a lot more money."

"That's great," I said.

At every Boulevard Stop, the engine threatened to die. We were halfway home when it finally gave up. "Shit!" Willie hissed. "We'll have to push it to the curb."

I got out to help him. When the truck was snug against the curb and in gear, we walked to the corner and stood in the dark to wait for the J car.

"We're late, Faye. What am I going to tell your Mom?" Willie asked.

"She's probably asleep. Besides, she's my Mom. You won't have to tell her anything."

He smiled so broadly that I saw his teeth glimmer in the dark. "Thanks, baby." He put his arm around me. "I wish you didn't have to go home at all." He pulled me close and snuggled his face in my hair. He ran his lips over my ears. It tickled and I pulled away. "Don't!" I said, laughing.

"Don't!" he mimicked. He took my hand and pulled me to him. I was no match for the strength of a country boy. My hands became hot from struggling with him. I felt moist all over. He pulled my hips against him to feel the hardness between his legs. He released me only to pull me against him again, repeatedly in a rhythmic movement he seemed unable to control.

Clang! Clang! I broke free and ran out to the street to wave down the approaching streetcar. I didn't wait for it to come to a complete halt before clambering aboard. I slid into the front seat where I would be in full view of the conductor. The street-car started up again as Willie dropped the coins in the box. He fell next to me and smiled. I looked out the window.

"You liked it," he insisted. "Go on, admit it."

"Stop it!" I said to him in Korean. I stared out the window, confused by the contradiction of excitement and revulsion, un-able to sort them out by the time we reached our stop. I tugged the cord to ring the bell. Willie stood up and stepped aside to let me pass, his lips curled in a smug smile. His smile was getting on my nerves.

We ran the three blocks to my house. The light in the dining room was on. "I've gotta hurry back. I'm going to see if Jimmy can give me a hand with the truck. See you next week," Willie whispered hoarsely. He started to run down the steps when the front door flew open.

"Willie! Come in here!" Momma called to him. "Why are you late?" she demanded to know.

"No, Momma . . . don't. Let him go. Don't ask him. Ask me," I pleaded.

Willie hushed me up and led me into the house. "It's my fault." He spoke to her in Korean so that she would understand, haltingly as he searched for the words. He told her about the slow service at the restaurant, about the dead engine, about the infrequent running of streetcars at night. "*Mi yan ham ni da,*" he said, ending his explanation by saying he was sorry.

"It's very important to keep promises. I said ten-thirty and you said all right. I don't know if something happened to you. Parents worry about their children," she said.

Willie nodded to show he understood. I waited for someone to say something to me.

"Next time, if we're going to be late, I'll call you," he prom-ised.

"That's good. But try not to be late. Faye has to keep a good reputation."

After Willie left, Momma began closing up the house.

"Why didn't you talk to me?" I asked.

"He has to know what I expect. He doesn't have any parents to tell him. Now go to bed," she said as she switched off the light.

She left me standing in the dark as if I wasn't there at all, cutting me off from the light, leaving me to grope my way to my room. Willie had helped himself to my body and Momma put my reputation in his hands. I wished I was rid of them both; I could take care of my own reputation.

from *The Woman Warrior: Memoirs of a Girlhood Among Ghosts*

Maxine Hong Kingston (1940–   )

T*he following excerpt from* The Woman Warrior *is the last part of the "White Tigers" section. In the first half of "White Tigers" the narrator recalls the Chinese legend of Fa Mu Lan, a woman warrior. Embellishing the tale told to her by her mother, the narrator portrays Fa Mu Lan as a girl called to her life as a swordswoman by a bird, and educated in the ways of war and magic by an elderly man and woman. After training for fifteen years, Fa Mu Lan returns to her village to take her father's place in battle against oppressive rulers and enemies. In preparation for the fight, her parents carve words of revenge and grievance on her back. In the following passage, the narrator draws inspiration from the woman warrior legend in her American life.*

Maxine Hong Kingston was born in Stockton, California. She graduated from the University of California at Berkeley in 1962 with an A.B., and has taught high school and college English in California and Hawaii. The Woman Warrior *won the National Book Critics Circle Award in 1976. Her other books are* China Men *(1980), which won the National Book Award, and a novel,* Tripmaster Monkey: His Fake Book *(1989). Her work is widely taught in American literature classes and has been translated into eight languages. She lives in Oakland, California, and is a senior lecturer in English at the University of California at Berkeley.*

MY AMERICAN LIFE HAS BEEN SUCH A DISAPPOINTMENT.

"I got straight A's, Mama."

"Let me tell you a true story about a girl who saved her village."

I could not figure out what was my village. And it was important that I do something big and fine, or else my parents would sell me when we made our way back to China. In China there were solutions for what to do with little girls who ate up food and threw tantrums. You can't eat straight A's.

When one of my parents or the emigrant villagers said, " 'Feeding girls is feeding cowbirds,' " I would thrash on the floor and scream so hard I couldn't talk. I couldn't stop.

"What's the matter with her?"

"I don't know. Bad, I guess. You know how girls are. 'There's no profit in raising girls. Better to raise geese than girls.' "

"I would hit her if she were mine. But then there's no use wasting all that discipline on a girl. 'When you raise girls, you're raising children for strangers.' "

"Stop that crying!" my mother would yell. "I'm going to hit you if you don't stop. Bad girl! Stop!" I'm going to remember never to hit or to scold my children for crying, I thought, because then they will only cry more.

"I'm not a bad girl," I would scream. "I'm not a bad girl. I'm not a bad girl." I might as well have said, "I'm not a girl."

"When you were little, all you had to say was 'I'm not a bad girl,' and you could make yourself cry," my mother says, talking-story about my childhood.

I minded that the emigrant villagers shook their heads at my sister and me. "One girl—and another girl," they said, and made our parents ashamed to take us out together. The good part about my brothers being born was that people stopped saying, "All girls," but I learned new grievances. "Did you roll an egg on *my* face like that when *I* was born?" "Did you have a full-month party for *me*?" "Did you turn on all the lights?" "Did you send *my* picture to Grandmother?" "Why not? Because I'm a girl? Is that why not?" "Why didn't you teach me English?" "You like having me beaten up at school, don't you?"

"She is very mean, isn't she?" the emigrant villagers would say.

"Come, children. Hurry. Hurry. Who wants to go out with Great-Uncle?" On Saturday mornings my great-uncle, the ex–river pirate, did the shopping. "Get your coats, whoever's coming."

"I'm coming. I'm coming. Wait for me."

When he heard girls' voices, he turned on us and roared, "No girls!" and left my sisters and me hanging our coats back up, not looking at one another. The boys came back with candy and new toys. When they walked through Chinatown, the people must have said, "A boy—and another boy—and another boy!" At my great-uncle's funeral I secretly tested out feeling glad that he was dead—the six-foot bearish masculinity of him.

I went away to college—Berkeley in the sixties—and I studied, and I marched to change the world, but I did not turn into a boy. I would have liked to bring myself back as a boy for my parents to welcome with chickens and pigs. That was for my brother, who returned alive from Vietnam.

If I went to Vietnam, I would not come back; females desert families. It was said, "There is an outward tendency in females," which meant that I was getting straight A's for the good of my future husband's family, not my own. I did not plan ever to have a husband. I would show my mother and father and the nosey emigrant villagers that girls have no outward tendency. I stopped getting straight A's.

And all the time I was having to turn myself American-feminine, or no dates.

There is a Chinese word for the female *I*—which is "slave." Break the women with their own tongues!

I refused to cook. When I had to wash dishes, I would crack one or two. "Bad girl," my mother yelled, and sometimes that made me gloat rather than cry. Isn't a bad girl almost a boy?

"What do you want to be when you grow up, little girl?"

"A lumberjack in Oregon."

Even now, unless I'm happy, I burn the food when I cook. I do not feed people. I let the dirty dishes rot. I eat at other people's tables but won't invite them to mine, where the dishes are rotting.

If I could not-eat, perhaps I could make myself a warrior like the swordswoman who drives me. I will—I must—rise and plow the fields as soon as the baby comes out.

Once I get outside the house, what bird might call me; on what horse could I ride away? Marriage and childbirth strengthen the swordswoman, who is not a maid like Joan of Arc. Do the women's work; then do more work, which will become ours too. No husband of mine will say, "I could have been a drummer, but I had to think about the wife and kids. You know how it is." Nobody supports me at the expense of his own adventure. Then I get bitter: no one supports me; I am not loved enough to be supported. That I am not a burden has to compensate for the sad envy when I look at women loved enough to be supported. Even now China wraps double binds around my feet.

When urban renewal tore down my parents' laundry and paved over our slum for a parking lot, I only made up gun and knife fantasies and did nothing useful.

From the fairy tales, I've learned exactly who the enemy are. I easily recognize them—business-suited in their modern American executive guise, each boss two feet taller than I am and impossible to meet eye to eye.

I once worked at an art supply house that sold paints to artists. "Order more of that nigger yellow, willya?" the boss told me. "Bright, isn't it? Nigger yellow."

"I don't like that word," I had to say in my bad, small-person's voice that makes no impact. The boss never deigned to answer.

I also worked at a land developers' association. The building industry was planning a banquet for contractors, real estate dealers, and real estate editors. "Did you know the restaurant you chose for the banquet is being picketed by CORE and the NAACP?" I squeaked.

"Of course I know." The boss laughed. "That's why I chose it."

"I refuse to type these invitations," I whispered, voice unreliable.

He leaned back in his leather chair, his bossy stomach opulent. He picked up his calendar and slowly circled a date. "You will be paid up to here," he said. "We'll mail you the check."

If I took the sword, which my hate must surely have forged out of the air, and gutted him, I would put color and wrinkles into his shirt.

It's not just the stupid racists that I have to do something about, but the tyrants who for whatever reason can deny my family food and work. My job is my own only land.

To avenge my family, I'd have to storm across China to take back our farm from the Communists; I'd have to rage across the United States to take back the laundry in New York and the one in California. Nobody in history has conquered and united both North America and Asia. A descendant of eighty pole fighters, I ought to be able to set out confidently, march straight down our street, get going right now. There's work to do, ground to cover. Surely, the eighty pole fighters, though unseen, would follow me and lead me and protect me, as is the wont of ancestors.

Or it may well be that they're resting happily in China, their spirits dispersed among the real Chinese, and not nudging me at all with their poles. I mustn't feel bad that I haven't done as well as the swordswoman did; after all, no bird called me, no wise old people tutored me. I have no magic beads, no water gourd sight, no rabbit that will jump in the fire when I'm hungry. I dislike armies.

I've looked for the bird. I've seen clouds make pointed angel wings that stream past the sunset, but they shred into clouds. Once at a beach after a long hike I saw a seagull, tiny as an insect. But when I jumped up to tell what miracle I saw, before I could get the words out I understood that the bird was insect-size because it was far away. My brain had momentarily lost its depth perception. I was that eager to find an unusual bird.

The news from China has been confusing. It also had something to do with birds. I was nine years old when the letters made my parents, who are rocks, cry. My father screamed in his sleep. My mother wept and crumpled up the letters. She set fire to them page by page in the ashtray, but new letters came almost every day. The only letters they opened without fear were the ones with red borders, the holiday letters that mustn't carry bad news. The other letters said that my uncles were made to kneel on broken glass during their trials and had confessed to being landowners. They were all executed, and the aunt whose thumbs were twisted off drowned herself. Other aunts, mothers-in-law, and cousins disappeared; some suddenly began writing to us again from communes or from Hong Kong. They kept asking for money. The ones in communes got four ounces of fat and one cup of oil a week, they said, and had to work from 4 A.M. to 9 P.M. They had to learn to do dances waving red kerchiefs; they had to sing nonsense syllables. The Communists gave axes to the old ladies and said, "Go and kill yourself. You're useless." If we overseas Chinese would just send money to the Communist bank, our relatives said, they might get a percentage of it for themselves. The aunts in Hong Kong said to send money quickly; their children were begging on the sidewalks, and mean people put dirt in their bowls.

When I dream that I am wire without flesh, there is a letter on blue airmail paper that floats above the night ocean between here and China. It must arrive safely or else my grandmother and I will lose each other.

My parents felt bad whether or not they sent money. Sometimes they got angry at their brothers and sisters for asking. And they would not simply ask but have to talk-story too. The revolutionaries had taken Fourth Aunt and Uncle's store, house, and lands. They attacked the house and killed the grandfather and oldest daughter. The grandmother escaped with the loose cash and did not return to help. Fourth Aunt picked up her sons, one under each arm, and hid in the pig house, where they slept that night in cotton clothes. The next day she found her husband, who had also miraculously escaped. The two of them collected twigs and yams to sell while their children begged. Each morning they tied the faggots on each other's back. Nobody bought from them. They ate the yams and some of the children's rice. Finally Fourth Aunt saw what was wrong. "We have to shout 'Fuel for sale' and 'Yams for sale,' " she said. "We can't just walk unobtrusively up and down the street." "You're right," said my uncle, but he was shy and walked in back of her. "Shout," my aunt ordered, but he could not. "They think we're carrying these sticks home for our own fire," she said. "Shout." They walked about miserably, silently, until sundown, neither of them able to advertise themselves. Fourth Aunt, an orphan since the age of ten, mean as my mother, threw her bundle down at his feet and scolded Fourth Uncle, "Starving to death, his wife and children starving to death, and he's too damned shy to raise his voice." She left him standing by himself and afraid to return empty-handed to her. He sat under a tree to think, when he spotted a pair of nesting doves. Dumping his bag of yams, he climbed up and caught the birds. That was where the Communists trapped him, in the tree. They criticized him for selfishly taking food for his own family and killed him, leaving his body in the tree as an example. They took the birds to a commune kitchen to be shared.

It is confusing that my family was not the poor to be championed. They were executed like the barons in the stories, when they were not barons. It is confusing that birds tricked us.

What fighting and killing I have seen have not been glorious but slum grubby. I fought the most during junior high school and always cried. Fights are confusing as to who has won. The corpses I've seen had been rolled and dumped, sad little dirty bodies covered with a police khaki blanket. My mother locked her children in the house so we couldn't look at dead slum people. But at news of a body, I would find a way to get out; I had to learn about dying if I wanted to become a swordswoman. Once there was an Asian man stabbed next door, words on cloth pinned to his corpse. When the police came around asking questions, my father said, "No read Japanese. Japanese words. Me Chinese."

I've also looked for old people who could be my gurus. A medium with red hair told me that a girl who died in a far country follows me wherever I go. This spirit can help me if I acknowledge her, she said. Between the head line and heart line in my right palm, she said, I have the mystic cross. I could become a medium myself. I don't want to be a medium. I don't want to be a crank taking "offerings" in a wicker plate from the frightened audience, who, one after another, asked the spirits how to raise rent money, how to cure their coughs and skin diseases, how to find a job. And martial arts are for unsure little boys kicking away under fluorescent lights.

I live now where there are Chinese and Japanese, but no emigrants from my own village looking at me as if I had failed them. Living among one's own emigrant villagers can give a good Chinese far from China glory and a place. "That old busboy is really a swordsman," we whisper when he goes by. "He's a swordsman who's killed fifty. He has a tong ax in his closet." But I am useless, one more girl who couldn't be sold. When I visit the family now, I wrap my American successes around me like a private shawl; I *am* worthy of eating the food. From afar I can believe my family loves me fundamentally. They only say, "When fishing for treasures in the flood, be careful not to pull in girls," because that is what one says about daughters. But I watched such words come out of my own mother's and father's mouths; I looked at their ink drawing of poor people snagging their neighbors' flotage with long flood hooks and pushing the girl babies on down the river. And I had to get out of hating range. I read in an anthropology book that Chinese say, "Girls are necessary too"; I have never heard the Chinese I know make this concession. Perhaps it was a saying in another village. I refuse to shy my way anymore through our Chinatown, which tasks me with the old sayings and the stories.

The swordswoman and I are not so dissimilar. May my people understand the resemblance soon so that I can return to them. What we have in common are the words at our backs. The idioms for *revenge* are "report a crime" and "report to five families." The reporting is the vengeance—not the beheading, not the gutting, but the words. And I have so many words— "chink" words and "gook" words too—that they do not fit on my skin.

from *HOMEBASE*

Shawn Wong (1949–   )

Homebase *is the story of Rainsford Chan, a fourth-generation Chinese American, growing up in the 1950s and 1960s. Rainsford's stories alternate with those of his forebears, especially his great-grandfather who helped build the transcontinental railroad through the Sierra Nevadas. The following passage describes Rainsford's life in Guam and Berkeley, California.*

Shawn Wong was born in Oakland, California, and raised in Berkeley. He graduated from the University of California at Berkeley and San Francisco State University, where he studied creative writing with Kay Boyle. Homebase *was first published in 1979 by writer Ishmael Reed's company, I. Reed Books, and won the Pacific Northwest Booksellers Award and the Washington State Governor's Writers Day Award. A recipient of an NEA creative writing fellowship, Mr. Wong is co-editor of several anthologies, including* Aiiieeeee!, The Big Aiiieeeee!, *and the Before Columbus Foundation poetry and fiction anthologies. He has taught at Mills College, University of California at Santa Cruz, and San Francisco State University. He lives in Seattle, where he is director and associate professor of Asian American Studies at the University of Washington.*

IN THE LATE NIGHTS OF SPRING, 1957, MY MOTHER DROVE HOME from Oak Knoll Naval Hospital, thrashing the night traffic, pushing the little car through its gears, and somehow returned home away from the sleepless daze and the edge of crash. She came home joking about amazing dog stories, traveling across the desert, oceans, freezing mountains all in the night without food. Her driving at night seemed to her like swimming the currents of a flooded street, her eyes unfocused on the black night, and still seeing the white hospital bed, father's pale skin and the light in the hospital's solarium that signaled his dying.

And one night she came home early, not joking, not ready to gather me up in her arms to play. She asked what color I wanted my room painted. And in her blank expression I knew that father had died. I started crying. She became angry, not looking at me, and started calling out colors.

My mother taught me how to iron clothes that night. She had a basket full of clothes that had been around for years. The basket never grew or decreased in size. She ironed only what we needed. So when I was seven she told me to iron the back of the collar on my shirt so that the collar won't show wrinkles on the top part that shows. Next, to iron the shoulder area. Then the sleeves. The flap that the buttons are sewn to. Then the left front, the back, and the right front. Hang it up and button the top two buttons. A family tradition had been passed on to me. I don't remember how long I was ironing that night but I ironed all my own shirts. When I had finished ironing my shirts I noticed she had fallen asleep on the couch. I could see her from the kitchen. That was when I started ironing my father's shirts. Most of them were at the bottom of the basket. My father used to send his shirts out to be cleaned and ironed. He would let me put on his huge shirt before he put it on so that I could hear the sound of my hand working its way down the sleeve with that tearing sound because the starch had glued the sleeves shut. He had shirt pockets that held both my hands. I didn't have any starch that night so I ironed his shirts like mine. I folded them all neatly on the kitchen table. Ten white shirts, five light blue shirts, two khaki work shirts, two plaid ones. I reached down into the basket and found myself a set of flannel pajamas. I ironed them and put them on. I took the blanket off my bed and squeezed into a small space next to my mother on the couch and fell asleep with her. The blanket trapped the smells of clean and warm cotton with her perfume and her warm breath.

I had said before that I am violent, that I had become a father to myself. But it was my mother who controlled my growing until she too died eight years after my father's death. Not a startling revelation except when I saw her burial and I discovered that she had shaped the style of my manhood in accordance with her own competitive and ambitious self. I grew up watching my mother's face for direction, the movements of her body. The features of her face shaped me. She was thirty-two years old when my father died and I was seven, and when I think of her now I remember her as a young woman and how her growing kept pace with mine. She would not let me be present at my father's funeral, she did not want to be the object of everyone's pity, the mother of a fatherless child, and she did not want my childhood shaped around the ceremony and ritual of a funeral. And now, after I had witnessed her dying in another hospital eight years later and became the prominent figure at her funeral, I did not cry. I did not want everyone's pity for an orphaned fifteen-year-old boy, but kept my eyes on the casket, kept my hands in my pockets and walked quickly through the ceremony of her death.

After she died I was no longer anyone's son. By my mother's arrangement I was to go off and live with my uncle and aunt until I was eighteen, then I could decide for myself what I wanted to do with my life. They lived along the California coast by a large lagoon. My uncle kept my mother's old Volkswagen there until I turned sixteen and learned how to drive. I suffered from dreams in that car. I remembered a lot of life driving around in my mother's car.

After my father's death, my mother took me to Carmel on weekends and only there, while I played on the beach and she walked along the ocean's edge, did she show her despair. I knew she brought me to the white sandy beaches of Carmel because it reminded her of our last happy days as a family on Guam. She merely wished that I should continue my uninterrupted childhood from one beach to another. But I had already lost my role as a child at the age of seven when I noticed her desperate efforts and private despair. A child doesn't accept tragedy in the same light as an adult because in the fantasy world of the hero in books and movies the hero has no weaknesses other than his own mortality, and sometimes even that is questionable. So out of my vacated childhood I wanted to show my mother that I had accepted Father's death and needed her real life around me. I inherited a melodramatic strength, a hero's arrogance, I was able to take care of myself, and her death further entrenched that strength. I grew up out of the ruins of a childhood, yet the fantasies and myths a child believes in fathered me through those years. When I entered high school, I entered with a stoic, not passive, acceptance of the stereotyped insane adolescent years. Whether I had known or not, I had grown beyond those years and the social life of a teenager was a blank. There were no dates, no dances, just swimming miles and miles and playing water polo. I was a poor student because that role did not fit into the concept of myself, but the direct test of my physical abilities did.

A few years after my father died, my mother opened a flower shop. She taught me the flower business until I was able to assist her and prepare the flowers for weddings, assemble corsages, and make flower arrangements for all occasions. When customers wanted something "exotic," like one of those "Japanese modernistic" flower arrangements, my mother would smile and take their order and charge them appropriately for a custom-made, one-of-a-kind arrangement dug out of our supposed misty Oriental heritage. She always let me make those floral arrangements, and I worked like a demented Dr. Frankenstein in his laboratory, twisting ti leaves into circles, shredding leaves into fountains of green splinters amid pieces of wood and stone, and arranging three lone but strategically placed flowers known by all to symbolize sun, man, and earth. The customers were always pleased by the work of art, never knowing that a four-teen-year-old kid wearing a letterman's jacket, jeans, and black tennis shoes was behind the creation.

Three mornings a week she had sent me with the driver to the flower market, and to me it had been the fulfillment of the childish gesture of bringing flowers home to mother. Except I brought home several hundred of the finest hothouse-grown flowers. And it was on those mornings that I felt vibrant and alive, stepping into the warehouse where the growers set up tables, piled high with flowers. The air was so thick with flowers that it soaked into my clothes and stayed with me for hours afterward. After she died, it was that thick sweet smell of the flower market that froze me on the edge of shock, made me sick to my stomach. That same smell followed my mother when she came out with the flowers from the storage refrigerator into the dusty smells of the warm storefront. Holidays for everyone else became hectic labor all night long for us. Mother's Day was always the worst. We boxed roses and made corsages all night long until we finished the day's orders. And at the end of all this we would go home without a single flower for my own mother, and she would always say, when I pointed out the lack of flowers in our own home, "We spend more time at the shop and that's where the flowers are. Besides, I've told you that 'the cobbler's son has no shoes.' "

In the evening following her funeral I stood in the darkened store, silent except for the refrigerator fans cooling the flowers. I did not cry at her funeral, and now standing in the tomb of her energies I wanted to cry for my loss, but with almost no sleep in the three days following her death I simply felt a moment of relief away from the relatives and friends. I walked up to the display refrigerator and opened the door to turn off the fluorescent lights. The cold sweet air pushed out at me and I started to get sick, I shut off the fans of the refrigerator but the air still filtered out as I backed away from the opened door.

My mother had brought me beyond those years. I lost myself, my role as a student, and could not grasp anything that was not relevant to my sense of tragedy, except competition. The need to compete filled my life, especially when my mother was dying and slipping from my grip. I brought to her bedside my water polo awards, the swimming medals. But she saw that I was now like my father, the track star, the basketball and ice hockey player, and whether I had realized it then or not did not matter to her, she had succeeded in forming me into her notion of manly style, and in her eyes I had become simply her husband's son. She must have seen the hints of his sensibility in my personality and their own conspicuously romantic past, because in the middle of a perfect recovery, she died in the night.

After my mother died, I never wanted to be alone. I was in competition with everyone except myself. I was driving at night. I was driving with my father. When I was three, he had decided it was time he and his family saw America. He drove a brown, clattering, stubborn Hillman Minx across the country

and back, across the plains of America, into big cities like Chicago and New York. I slept most of the way and only remember
a day in New York, a day in Washington, D.C., at the Lincoln
Memorial, a store in Oklahoma where he bought me a slingshot,
and I remember standing at the rim of the Grand Canyon. And
when we came home, he never spoke of that journey again
while I was growing up except to say that "we had done it."

Until my father died he had brought me up on all the childhood heroes. He indulged me in my fantasies and fascinations
with planes, cars, cowboys, comic book heroes, and trains. He
took me down to Berkeley's Aquatic Park two or three times a
week to watch the trains pull in to the factories bordering the
lake. We sat in the car parked under a tree watching the trains
for hours at a time. My father sat in the back seat of the car and
napped, smoked, and read the newspaper while I stood up on
the front seat watching for trains. My father always read every
page of the paper, beginning with the first page and ending on
the last page of the financial section. If stories were continued
on other pages, he wouldn't turn to them until he had read all
the stories in between. He read the paper as people do riding on
a crowded bus, folding it lengthwise and reading half of the
paper at a time instead of holding it at arm's length.

The boxcars were too far away for me to read the names on
the sides, so while they were pulling in or pulling out I called
out the names of the states and big cities I knew. I always called
the caboose "Berkeley," for our hometown. And after a while
if I saw that a train was leaving, I'd wake my father up and
make him rush to a crossing gate so that I could see, up close,
the sides of the cars, listen to them building up speed, hear the
rhythm of the iron wheels keeping time with the ringing bell at
the crossing gate in front of us.

On Guam, the bombers at the Air Force base took the place
of the trains. My father and I would stand at the end of the
runway as I plugged my ears, clenched my teeth, wrinkled my
face into what must have looked like an expression of great
pain, as the bombers thundered off the runway about a hundred
feet over us, shaking the ground and blowing two-hundred-
mile-an-hour dust at us.

I remember those bombers like friends. My father took pictures of them for the family album. The B-47s made a lot of

332

noise with their jet engines, and I always liked to see them land and their chutes pop out of their tails. But there was no real detail to the B-47s; they were sleek, fast, and efficient-looking. There were no names on the B-47s like "Rosie" or "Betty Sue," just numbers. The old B-29s were turned into weather planes and their tails were painted orange. Before the B-47s came to Guam, the base was filled with a kid's closest friend—the B-36. It looked like a giant toothpick, with a bubble cockpit up front, a straight back tail, and swept wings. It killed the enemy by making them laugh. It looked like a silver boat with six outboard engines on the rear of the wings. It was like a kid's drawing of fancy planes, except this one flew.

And when my father took pictures of those planes for me, and when we waited hours for those trains to pass by Aquatic Park, he encouraged my enthusiasm and imagination. At night, when the trains were no longer visible, he drove me down to Emeryville to see the enormous "Sherwin Williams Paints Cover the Earth" neon sign, watching the red lights pour down over the earth out of the giant, green-lighted paint can. He walked with me. He towed me up and down the sidewalks in a red wagon. He kept pace with my youth. He was Bobby to me. And when he died, my mother knew she had to tell me about his youth and the lives of my grandfathers as he had told her. She had to tell me who kept pace with his youth, what was the grief that shaped his sensibility, and who struggled to make a place for him, for me. She had to make me more than just her husband's son, more than understanding his sensibility, but rather make me realize it on my own and sometime in my life say simply that "I am the son of my father."

When the nurse dropped my mother's thick green jade bracelet into my hands, the circle of green stone moved in my hands, turned red. I could not let go of it. It was the sound of her heart. She has no shape for me now, only my echo, and she kept my youth like cool green jade. She had a lover two years after my father died who moved like a ghost around my mother, loving her like artificial heat, dry, stifling, a silent heat that kept me secret in my play. No heroes, only that dark love, that dry heated love, the smell of exhaust and warmed car heat, stifling my breath for some air outside the windows. I stayed cool by putting my ear to the window and listening to the highway air, my cheek pressed against the glass. It felt like ice in the windy forest of friends, my heroes climbing, fighting, shooting, running alongside the car, waving frantically, calling me into the forest to join their gang, ride their train, and I forgot the ceaseless hum of the car's heater. I was running on iron wheels, my face in the wind, breathing frozen air and white engine steam, the fear of my mother's love toward him moved me and made me run in my dreams, pointless, frantic, running nowhere, just to run and feel my own secret and the pain of breath. It is only when I wake that I am frightened, feeling that somehow I have progressed, leaving myself behind at the same time. I am violent. I give myself names to prove the fantasy, but the dream eludes me.

She thought that now the nights of crying could be solved by this new love. Yet her grief was still overpowering her; she held on to her grief for her dead husband and lover, crying at nights, taking her well-kept grief out of its hiding place to cry herself to sleep. I would hear her moaning and crying. Only in the first days after my father's death did I cry silently into my pillow, my lover, my hero gone, his name whispered on my lips as I cried; then one day I stopped crying for him, resolved to make my life like his; it gave me strength. And it was my resolve not to cry anymore that always drove me to my mother to comfort her in her grief. Her grief became my duty. I watched her tears fall to the pillow, asking her not to cry, impatient, knowing that all her strength was leaving her, and somehow I thought if I put my mouth to the tear-stained pillow and sucked the tears from the white case, her energy would pass to me in the warm salt of those tears. And when she died I was mad that she had failed me. She had no longer wanted to stand by my side. After my mother died I was alone, but I did not cry. My sleep tore me apart, and gave her flesh back to me in pieces, her voice with no substance, and finally nothing but a hollow sound would wake me, her jade bracelet knocking against the house as she moved around, cleaning, cooking, writing. It had become for me, in those dreams, the rhythmic beating of her heart. There was no need for me to put my head against her chest to hear the beating of her heart. The cold stone, jade in my eyes, filled my youth and kept time with the unsteady beating of my own heart.

"CARNIVAL QUEEN"
Mavis Hara (1949–   )

I*n "Carnival Queen," issues of race and definitions of beauty surface and intertwine when the narrator, Sam, enters her high school Carnival Queen contest. Most of the students and teachers in Sam's high school are Asian American. However, the standards of beauty remain Eurocentric, inspiring some of the contestants to do things like Scotch tape their eyelids to appear more European American.*

Mavis Hara was born in Honolulu. She graduated from the University of Hawaii and received her master's degree in Education from the University of California at Santa Barbara. Her fiction has been published in Bamboo Ridge *as well as in anthologies. She now lives in Japan, where she teaches English.*

MY FRIEND TERRY AND I BOTH HAVE BOY'S NICKNAMES. BUT that's the only thing about us that is the same. Terry is beautiful. She is about 5'4" tall, which is tall enough to be a stewardess. I am only 5 feet tall, which is too short, so I should know.

My mother keeps asking me why Terry is my friend. This makes me nervous, because I really don't know. Ever since we had the first senior class officers' meeting at my house and my mother found the empty tampax container in our wastebasket she has been really asking a lot of questions about Terry. Terry and I are the only girls who were elected to office. She's treasurer and I'm secretary. The president, the vice-president, and the sergeant-at-arms are all boys. I guess that's why Terry and I hang out together. Like when we have to go to class activities and meetings she picks me up. I never even knew her before we were elected. I don't know who she used to hang around with, but it sure wasn't with me and my friends. We're too, Japanese girl, you know, plain. I mean, Terry has skin like a porcelain doll. She has cheekbones like Garbo, a body like Ann Margret, she has legs like, well, like not any Japanese girl I've ever seen. Like I said, she's beautiful. She always dresses perfectly, too. She always wears an outfit, a dress with matching straw bag and colored leather shoes. Her hair is always set, combed, and sprayed, she even wears nylon stockings under her jeans, even on really hot days. Terry is the only girl I know who has her own Liberty House charge card. Not that she ever goes shopping by herself. Whenever she goes near a store, her mother goes with her.

Funny, Terry has this beautiful face, perfect body, and nobody hates her. We hate Valerie Rosecrest. Valerie is the only girl in our P.E. class who can come out of the girls' showers, wrap a towel around herself under her arms and have it stay up by itself. No hands. She always takes the longest time in the showers and walks back to her locker past the rest of us, who are already dry and fumbling with the one hook on the back of our bras. Valerie's bra has five hooks on the back of it and needs all of them to stay closed. I think she hangs that thing across the top of her locker door on purpose just so we can walk past it and be blinded by it shining in the afternoon sun. One time, my friend Tina got fed up and snatched Val's bra. She wore it on top of her head and ran around the locker room. I swear, she looked like an albino Mickey Mouse. Nobody did anything but laugh. Funny, it was Terry who took the bra away and put it back on Val's locker again.

I don't know why we're friends, but I wasn't surprised when we ended up together as contestants in the Carnival Queen contest. The Carnival Queen contest is a tradition at McKinley. They have pictures of every Carnival Queen ever chosen hanging in the auditorium corridor right next to the pictures of the senators, governors, politicians, and millionaires who graduated from the school. This year there are already five portraits of queens up there. All the girls are wearing long ball gowns and the same rhinestone crown which is placed on their heads by Mr. Harano, the principal. They have elbow length white gloves and they're carrying baby's breath and roses. The thing is, all the girls are hapa. Every one.

Every year, it is the same tradition. A big bunch of girls gets nominated to run, but everybody knows from intermediate school on which girl in the class is actually going to win. She has to be hapa.

"They had to nominate me," I try to tell Terry. "I'm a class officer, but you, you actually have a chance to be the only Japanese girl to win." Terry had just won the American Legion essay contest the week before. You would think that being fashionable and coordinated all the time would take all her energy and wear her out, but her mother wants her to be smart too. She looks at me with this sad face I don't understand.

"I doubt it," she says.

Our first orientation meeting for contestants is today in the library after school. I walk to the meeting actually glad to be there after class. The last after school meeting I went to was the one I was forced to attend. That one had no contestants. Just potential school dropouts. The first meeting, I didn't know anybody there. Nobody I know in the student government crowd is like me and has actually flunked chemistry. All the guys who were coming in the door were the ones who hang around the bathrooms that I'm too scared to use. Nobody ever threatened me though, and after a while, dropout class wasn't half bad, but I have to admit, I like this meeting better. I sit down and watch the other contestants come through the door. I know the first name of almost every girl who walks in. Terry, of course, who is wearing her blue suede jumper and silk blouse, navy stockings and navy patent leather shoes. My friend Trudye, who has a great figure for an Oriental girl but who wears braces and coke bottle glasses. My friend Linda, who has a beautiful face but a basic musubi-shaped body. The Yanagawa twins, who have beautiful hapa faces, but pretty tragic, they inherited their father's genes and have government-issue Japanese-girl legs. Songleaders, cheerleaders, ROTC sponsors, student government committee heads, I know them all. Krissie Clifford, who is small and blond, comes running in late. Krissie looks like a young version of Beaver's mother on the TV show.

She's always running like she just fell out of the screen, and if she moves fast enough, she can catch up with the TV world and jump back in. Then she walks in. Leilani Jones. As soon as she walks in the door, everybody in the room turns to look at her. Everybody in the room knows that Leilani is the only girl who can possibly win.

Lani is hapa, Japanese-haole. She inherited the best features from everybody. She is tall and slim, with light brown hair and butter frosting skin. I don't even know what she is wearing. Leilani is so beautiful it doesn't matter what she is wearing. She is smooth, and gracefully quiet. Her smile is soft and shiny. It's like looking at a pearl. Lani is not only beautiful, when you look at her all you hear is silence, like the air around her is stunned. We all know it. This is the only girl who can possibly win.

As soon as Leilani walks in, Mrs. Takahara, the teacher advisor says, "Well, now, take your seats everyone. We can begin."

We each take a wooden chair on either side of two rows of long library tables. There is a make-up kit and mirror at each of the places. Some of Mrs. Takahara's friends who are teachers are also sitting in.

"This is Mrs. Chung, beauty consultant of Kamedo cosmetics," Mrs. Takahara says. "She will show us the proper routines of skin cleansing and make-up. The Carnival Queen contest is a very special event. All the girls who are contestants must be worthy representatives of McKinley High School. This means the proper make-up and attitude. Mrs. Chung . . ."

I have to admire the beauty consultant. Even though her make-up is obvious as scaffolding in front of a building, it is so well done, kinda like the men who dance the girls' parts in Kabuki shows, you look at it and actually believe that what you are seeing is her face.

"First, we start with proper cleansing," she says. We stare into our own separate mirrors.

"First, we pin our hair so that it no longer hangs in our faces." All of the girls dig in handbags and come up with bobby pins. Hairstyles disappear as we pin our hair straight back. The teachers look funny, kind of young without their teased hair. Mrs. Chung walks around to each station. She squeezes a glop of pink liquid on a cotton ball for each of us.

"Clean all the skin well," she says. "Get all the dirt and impurities out." We scrub hard with that cotton ball, we all know that our skin is loaded with lots of stuff that is impure. My friend Trudye gets kinda carried away. She was scrubbing so hard around her eyes that she scrubbed off her Scotch tape. She hurries over to Mrs. Takahara's chair, mumbles something and excuses herself. I figure she'll be gone pretty long; the only bathroom that is safe for us to use is all the way over in the other building.

"Now we moisturize," Mrs. Chung is going on. "We use this step to correct defects in the tones of our skins." I look over at Terry. I can't see any defects in any of the tones of her skin.

"This mauve moisturizer corrects sallow undertones," Mrs. Chung says.

"What's shallow?" I whisper to Terry.

"SALLOW," she whispers back disgusted. "Yellow."

"Oh," I say and gratefully receive the large glop of purple stuff Mrs. Chung is squeezing on my new cotton ball. Mrs. Chung squeezes a little on Terry's cotton ball too. When she passes Lani, she smiles and squeezes white stuff out from a different tube.

I happily sponge the purple stuff on. Terry is sponging too but I notice she is beginning to look like she has the flu. "Next, foundation," says Mrs. Chung. She is walking around, narrowing her eyes at each of us and handing us each a tube that she is sure is the correct color to bring out the best in our skin. Mrs. Chung hands me a plastic tube of dark beige. She gives Terry a tube of lighter beige and gives Lani a different tube altogether.

"Just a little translucent creme," she smiles to Lani who smiles back rainbow bubbles and strands of pearls.

Trudye comes rushing back and Linda catches her up on all the steps she's missed. I gotta admit, without her glasses and with all that running, she has really pretty cheekbones and nice colored skin. I notice she has new Scotch tape on too, and is really concentrating on what Mrs. Chung is saying next.

"Now that we have the proper foundation, we concentrate on the eyes," She pulls out a rubber and chrome pincer machine. She stands in front of Linda with it. I become concerned.

"The eyelashes sometimes grow in the wrong direction,"

Mrs. Chung informs us. "They must be trained to bend correctly. We use the Eyelash Curler to do this." She hands the machine to Linda. I watch as Linda puts the metal pincer up to her eye and catches her straight, heavy black lashes between the rubber pincer blades.

"Must be sore if they do it wrong and squeeze the eyelid meat," I breathe to Terry. Terry says nothing. She looks upset, like she is trying not to bring up her lunch.

"Eyeshadow must be applied to give the illusion of depth," says Mrs. Chung. "Light on top of the lid, close to the lashes, luminescent color on the whole lid, a dot of white in the center of the iris, and brown below the browbone to accentuate the crease." Mrs. Chung is going pretty fast now. I wonder what the girls who have Oriental eyelids without a crease are going to do. I check out the room quickly, over the top of my make-up mirror. Sure enough, all the Oriental girls here have a nice crease in their lids. Those who don't are wearing Scotch tape. Mrs. Chung is passing out "pearlescent" eyeshadow.

"It's made of fish scales," Terry says. I have eyelids that are all right, but eyeshadow, especially sparking eyeshadow, makes me look like a gecko, you know, with protruding eye sockets that go in separate directions. Terry has beautiful deep-socketed eyes and browbones that don't need any help to look well defined. I put on the stuff in spite of my better judgment and spend the rest of the time trying not to move my eyeballs too much, just in case anybody notices. Lani is putting on all this make-up too. But in her case, it just increases the pearly glow that her skin is already producing.

"This ends the make-up session," Mrs. Chung is saying. "Now our eyes and skins have the proper preparation for our roles as contestants for Carnival Queen."

"Ma, I running in the Carnival Queen contest," I was saying last night. My mother got that exasperated look on her face.

"You think you get chance!"

"No, but the teachers put in the names of all the student council guys." My mother is beginning to look like she is suffering again.

"When you were small, everybody used to tell me you should run for Cherry Blossom contest. But that was before you got so dark like your father. I always tell you no go out in the sun or wear lotion like me when you go out but you never listen."

"Yeah, Ma, but we get modeling lessons, make-up, how to walk."

"Good, might make you stand up straight. I would get you a back brace, but when you were small, we paid so much money for your legs, to get special shoes connected to a bar. You only cried and never would wear them. That's why you still have crooked legs."

That was last night. Now I'm here and Mrs. Takahara is telling us about the walking and modeling lessons.

"Imagine a string coming out of the top of your skull and connected to the ceiling. Shorten the string and walk with your chin out and back erect. Float! Put one foot in front of the other, point your toes outward and glide forward on the balls of your feet. When you stop, place one foot slightly behind the other at a forty-five degree angle. Put your weight on the back foot . . ." I should have worn the stupid shoes when I was small. I'm bow-legged. Just like my father. Leilani is not bow-legged. She looks great putting one long straight tibia in front of the other. I look kinda like a crab. We walk in circles around and around the room. Terry is definitely not happy. She's walking pretty far away from me. Once, when I pass her, I could swear she is crying.

"Wow, long practice, yeah?" I say as we walk across the lawn heading toward the bus. Terry, Trudye, Linda, and I are still together. A black Buick pulls up to the curb. Terry's Mom has come to pick her up. Terry's Mom always picks her up. She must have just come back from the beauty shop. Her head is wrapped in a pink net wind bonnet. Kind of like the cake we always get at weddings that my mother keeps on top of the television and never lets anybody eat.

"I'll call you," Terry says.

"I'm so glad that you and Theresa do things together," Terry's mother says. "Theresa needs girlfriends like you, Sam." I'm looking at the pink net around her face. I wonder if Terry's father ever gets the urge to smash her hair down to feel the shape of her head. Terry looks really uncomfortable as they drive away.

I feel uncomfortable too. Trudye and Linda's make-up looks really weird in the afternoon sunlight. My eyeballs feel larger than tank turrets and they must be glittering brilliantly too. The Liliha Puunui bus comes and we all get on. The long center aisle of the bus gives me an idea. I put one foot in front of the other and practice walking down. Good thing it is late and the guys we go to school with are not getting on.

"You think Leilani is going to win?" Trudye asks.

"What?" I say as I almost lose my teeth against the metal pole I'm holding on to. The driver has just started up, and standing with your feet at a forty-five degree angle doesn't work on public transportation.

"Lani is probably going to win, yeah?" Trudye says again. She can hide her eye make-up behind her glasses and looks pretty much OK. "I'm going to stay in for the experience. Plus, I'm going to the orthodontist and take my braces out, and I asked my mother if I could have contact lenses and she said OK." Trudye goes on, but I don't listen. I get a seat by the window and spend the whole trip looking out so nobody sees my fish-scale eyes.

I am not surprised when I get home and the phone begins to ring.

"Sam, it's Terry. You stay in the contest. But I decided I'm not going to run."

"That's nuts, Terry," I am half screaming at her, "you are the only one of us besides Lani that has a chance to win. You could be the first Japanese Carnival Queen that McKinley ever has." I am going to argue this one.

"Do you know the real name of this contest?" Terry asks.

"I don't know, Carnival Queen. I've never thought about it I guess."

"It's the Carnival Queen Scholarship Contest."

"Oh, so?" I'm still interested in arguing that only someone with legs like Terry even has a chance.

"Why are you running? How did you get nominated?" Terry asks.

"I'm Senior Class secretary, they had to nominate me, but you . . ."

"And WHY are you secretary," she cuts me off before I get another running start about chances.

"I don't know, I guess because I used to write poems for English class and they always got in the paper of the yearbook. And probably because Miss Chuck made me write a column for the newspaper for one year to bring up my social studies grade."

"See . . . and why am I running?"

"OK, you're class officer, and sponsor, and you won the American Legion essay contest . . ."

"And Krissy?"

"She's editor of the yearbook, and a sponsor and the Yanagawa twins are songleaders and Trudye is prom committee chairman and Linda . . ." I am getting into it.

"And Lani," says Terry quietly.

"Well, she's a sponsor I think . . ." I've lost some momentum. I really don't know.

"I'm a sponsor, and I know she's not," Terry says.

"Student government? No . . . I don't think so . . . not cheering, her sister is the one in the honor society, not . . . hey, no, couldn't be . . ."

"That's right," Terry says, "the only reason she's running is because she's supposed to win." It couldn't be true. "That means the rest of us are all running for nothing. The best we can do is second place." My ears are getting sore with the sense of what she says. "We're running because of what we did. But we're going to lose because of what we look like. Look, it's still good experience and you can still run if you like."

"Nah . . ." I say, still dazed by it. "But what about Mrs. Takahara, what about your mother?" Terry is quiet.

"I think I can handle Mrs. Takahara," Terry finally says.

"I'll say I'm not running, too. If it's two of us, it won't be so bad." I am actually kind of relieved that this is the last day I'll have to put gecko eye make-up all over my face.

"Thanks, Sam . . ." Terry says.

"Yeah . . . my mother will actually be relieved. Ever since I forgot the ending at my piano recital in fifth grade, she gets really nervous if I'm in front of any audience."

"You want me to pick you up for the carnival Saturday night?" Terry asks.

"I'll ask my Mom," I say. "See you then . . ."

"Yeah . . ."

I think, "We're going to lose because of what we look like." I need a shower, my eyes are itching anyway. I'm glad my mother isn't home yet. I think best in the shower and sometimes I'm in there an hour or more.

Soon, with the world a small square of warm steam and tile walls, it all starts going through my head. The teachers looked so young in the make-up demonstration with their hair pinned back—they looked kind of like us. But we are going to lose because of what we look like. I soap the layers of make-up off my face. I guess they're tired of looking like us; musubi bodies, daikon legs, furoshiki-shaped, home-made dresses, bento tins to be packed in the early mornings, mud and sweat everywhere. The water is splashing down on my face and hair. But Krissy doesn't look like us, and she is going to lose too. Krissy looks like the Red Cross society lady from intermediate school. She looks like Beaver's mother on the television show. Too haole. She's going to lose because of the way she looks. Lani doesn't look anything like anything from the past. She looks like something that could only have been born underwater where all motions are slow and all sounds are soft. I turn off the water and towel off. Showers always make me feel clean and secure. I guess I can't blame even the teachers, everyone wants to feel safe and secure.

My mother is sitting at the table peeling an orange. She does this almost every night and I already know what she's going to say.

"Eat this orange, good for you, lots of vitamin C."

"I don't want to eat orange now, Ma." I know it is useless, but I say it anyway. My mother is the kind of Japanese lady who will hunch down real small when she passes in front of you when you're watching TV. Makes you think she's quiet and easy going, but not on the subject of vitamin C.

"I peeled it already. Want it." Some people actually think that my mother is shy.

"I not running in the contest. Terry and I going quit."

"Why?" my mother asks, like she really doesn't need to know.

"Terry said that we running for nothing. Everybody already knows Lani going win." My mother looks like she just tasted some orange peel.

"That's not the real reason." She hands me the orange and starts washing the dishes.

There's lots of things I don't understand. Like why Terry hangs out with me. Why my mother is always so curious about her and now why she doesn't think this is the real reason that Terry is quitting the contest.

"What did the mother say about Terry quitting the contest?" my mother asks without turning around.

"I donno, nothing I guess."

"Hmmmmmmm . . . that's not the real reason. That girl is different. The way the mother treats her is different." Gee, having a baby and being a mother must be really hard and it must really change a person because all I know is that my mother is really different from me.

Terry picks me up Saturday night in her brother's white Mustang. It's been a really busy week. I haven't even seen her since we quit the contest. We had to build the Senior Class Starch Throwing booth.

"Hi, Sam. We're working until ten o'clock on the first shift, OK?" Terry is wearing a triangle denim scarf in her hair, a workshirt and jeans. Her face is flushed from driving with the Mustang's top down and she looks really glamorous.

"Yeah, I thought we weren't going to finish the booth this afternoon. Lucky thing my Dad and Lenny's Dad helped us with the hammering and Valerie's committee got the cardboard painted in time. We kinda ran out of workers because most of the girls . . ." I don't have to finish. Most of the student council girls are getting dressed up for the contest.

"Mrs. Sato and the cafeteria ladies finished cooking the starch and Neal and his friends and some of the football guys are going to carry the big pots of starch over to the booth for us." Terry is in charge of the manpower because she knows everybody.

"Terry's mother is on the phone!" my mother is calling to us from the house. Terry runs in to answer the phone. Funny, her mother always calls my house when Terry is supposed to pick me up. My mother looks out at me from the door. The look on her face says, "Checking up." Terry runs past her and jumps back in the car.

"You're lucky, your mother is really nice," she says.

We go down Kuakini Street and turn onto Liliha. We pass

School Street and head down the freeway on-ramp. Terry turns on K-POI and I settle down in my seat. Terry drives faster than my father. We weave in and out of cars as she guns the Mustang down H-1. I know this is not very safe, but I like the feeling in my stomach. It's like going down hills. My hair is flying wild and I feel so clean and good. Like the first day of algebra class before the symbols get mixed up. Like the first day of chemistry before we have to learn molar solutions. I feel like it's going to be the first day forever and I can make the clean feeling last and last. The ride is too short. We turn off by the Board of Water Supply station and we head down by the Art Academy and turn down Pensacola past Mr. Feiterra's green gardens and into the parking lot of the school.

"I wish you were still in the contest tonight," I tell Terry as we walk out toward the Carnival grounds. "I mean you are so perfect for the Carnival Queen. You were the only Japanese girl that was perfect enough to win."

"I thought you were my friend," Terry starts mumbling. "You sound like my mother. You only like me because of what you think I should be." She starts walking faster and is leaving me behind.

"Wait! What? How come you getting so mad?" I'm running to keep up with her.

"Perfect, perfect. What if I'm NOT perfect. What if I'm not what people think I am? What if I can't be what people think I am?" She's not making any sense to me and she's crying. "Why can't you just like me? I thought you were different. I thought you just liked me. I thought you were my friend because you just liked ME." I'm following her and I feel like it's exam time in chemistry. I'm flunking again and I don't understand.

We get to the Senior booth and Terry disappears behind the cardboard. Valerie Rosecrest is there and hands me a lot of paper cupcake cups and a cafeteria juice ladle.

"Quick, we need at least a hundred of these filled, we're going to be open in ten minutes."

"Try wait, I gotta find Terry." I look behind the cardboard back of the booth. Terry is not there. I run all around the booth. Terry is nowhere in sight. The senior booth is under a tent in the midway with all the games. There are lots of lightbulbs strung like kernels of corn on wires inside the tent. There's lots of game booths and rows and rows of stuffed animal prizes on clotheslines above each booth. I can't find Terry and I want to look around more, but all of a sudden the merry-go-round music starts and all the lights come on. The senior booth with its handpainted signs, "Starch Throw—three script" looks alive all of a sudden in the warm Carnival light.

"Come on, Sam!" Valerie is calling me. "We're opening. I need you to help!" I go back to the booth. Pretty soon Terry comes back and I look at her kind of worried, but under the soft popcorn light, you cannot even tell she was crying.

"Terry, Mr. Miller said that you're supposed to watch the script can and take it to the cafeteria when it's full." Val's talking to her, blocking my view. Some teachers are arriving for first shift. They need to put on shower caps and stick their heads through holes in the cardboard so students can buy paper cupcake cups full of starch to throw to try to hit the teachers in the face. Terry goes in the back to help the teachers get ready. Lots of guys from my dropout class are lining up in the front of the booth.

"Eh, Sam, come on, take my money. Ogawa's back there. He gave me the F in math. Gimme the starch!" Business is getting better and better all night. Me, Val, and Terry are running around the booth, taking script, filling cupcake cups, and getting out of the way fast when the guys throw the starch. Pretty soon, the grass in the middle of the booth turns into a mess that looks like thrown-up starch, and we are trying not to slip as we run around trying to keep up with business.

"Ladies and gentlemen, McKinley High School is proud to present the 1966 Carnival Queen and her court." It comes over the loudspeaker. It must be the end of the contest, ten o'clock. All the guys stop buying starch and turn to look toward the tent. Pretty soon, everyone in the tent has cleared the center aisle. They clap as five girls in evening dresses walk our way.

"Oh, great," I think. "I have starch in my hair and I don't want to see them." The girls are all dressed in long gowns and are wearing white gloves. The first girl is Linda. She looks so pretty in a maroon velvet A-line gown. Cannot see her musubi-shaped body and her face is just glowing. The rhinestones in her tiara are sparkling under each of the hundreds of carnival lights. The ribbon on her chest says "Third Princess." It's neat!

Just like my cousin Carolyn's wedding. My toes are tingling under their coating of starch. The next is Trudye. She's not wearing braces and she looks so pretty in her lavender gown. Some of the guys are going "Wow" under their breath as she walks by. The first Princesses pass next. The Yanagawa twins. They're wearing matching pink gowns and have pink baby roses in their hair, which is in ringlets. Their tiaras look like lace snowflakes on their heads as they pass by. And last. Even though I know who this is going to be I really want to see her. Sure enough, everybody in the crowd gets quiet as she passes by. Lani looks like her white dress is made of sugar crystals. As she passes, her crown sparkles tiny rainbows under the hundreds of lightbulbs from the tent and flashbulbs popping like little suns.

The court walks through the crowd and stops at the senior booth. Mr. Harano, the principal, steps out.

"Your majesty," he's talking to Lani, who is really glowing. "I will become a target in the senior booth in your honor. Will you and your Princesses please take aim and do your best as royal representatives of our school?"

I look around at Terry. The principal is acting so stupid. I can't believe he really runs the whole school. Terry must be getting so sick. But I look at her and she's standing in front of Lani and smiling. This is weird. She's the one who said the contest was fixed. She's the one who said everyone knew who was supposed to win. She's smiling at Lani like my grandmother used to smile at me when I was five. Like I was a sweet mochi dumpling floating in red bean soup. I cannot stand it. I quit the contest so she wouldn't have to quit alone. And she yells at me and hasn't talked to me all night. All I wanted was for her to be standing there instead of Lani.

The Carnival Queen and four Princesses line up in front of the booth. Val, Terry, and I scramble around giving each of them three cupcake cups of starch. They get ready to throw. The guys from the newspaper and the yearbook get ready to take their picture. I lean as far back into the wall as I can. I know Trudye didn't have time to get contacts yet and she's not wearing any glasses. I wonder where Val is and if she can flatten out enough against the wall to get out of the way. Suddenly, a hand reaches out and grabs my ankle. I look down, and Terry, who is sitting under the counter of the booth with Val, grabs my hand and pulls me down on the grass with them. The ground here is nice and clean. The Carnival Queen and Princesses and the rows of stuffed animals are behind and above us. The air is filled with pink cupcake cups and starch as they throw. Mr. Harano closes his eyes, the flashbulbs go off, but no one comes close to hitting his face. Up above us everyone is laughing and clapping. Down below, Terry, Val, and I are nice and clean.

"Lani looks so pretty, Sam." Terry is looking at me and smiling.

"Yeah, even though the contest was juice she looks really good. Like a storybook," I say, hoping it's not sounding too fake.

"Thanks for quitting with me." Terry's smile is like the water that comes out from between the rocks at Kunawai stream. I feel so clean in that smile.

"It would have been lonely if I had to quit by myself," Terry says, looking down at our starch-covered shoes. She looks up at me and smiles again. And even if I'm covered with starch, I suddenly know that to her, I am beautiful. Her smile tells me that we're friends because I went to dropout class. It is a smile that can wash away all the F's that Mr. Low my chemistry teacher will ever give. I have been waiting all my life for my mother to give me that smile. I know it is a smile that Terry's mother has never smiled at her. I don't know where she learned it.

It's quiet now, the Carnival Queen and her Princesses have walked away. Terry stands up first as she and Val and I start to crawl out from our safe place under the counter of the booth. She gives me her hand to pull me up and I can see her out in the bright Carnival light. Maybe every girl looks like a queen at one time in her life.

"PAINT"

Darrell H. Y. Lum (1950–   )

As in many African American and Latina/o writings, questions of language are an important element of many Asian American stories. This is especially true of the literature of Hawaii.

Darrell Lum's short story is written entirely in Hawaii Creole English. This dialect evolved from the English spoken by immigrant laborers from China, Japan, the Philippines, Korea, Portugal, and other countries, who worked on Hawaii's sugar plantations from the mid-1800s through the 1940s.

Mr. Lum is a Chinese American writer born and raised in Hawaii. In 1978, he co-founded Bamboo Ridge Press, a nonprofit literary press that publishes works by and about Hawaii's people. He has published two collections of short stories, Sun, *short stories and drama in 1980 and* Pass On, No Pass Back!, *which won the National Book Award from the Association for Asian American Studies in 1992. His fiction has appeared in numerous publications and anthologies including* Seattle Review, Chaminade Literary Review, Hawaii Herald, Landmarks, *and* Hawaii Review. *He has had three plays produced in Hawaii. A recipient of an NEA fellowship, Mr. Lum lives in Honolulu.*

SOMETIMES I FEEL MEAN. I LIKE GO BUST SOMETING. SOME GUYS like bust car antennas but I only like go spray paint. I donno, I feel mean and I feel good at da same time, you know. It bad, but still yet I like spray paint. I donno why. Make me feel mean when I stay painting but feel like I stay doing someting. Someting big you know, so dat I stay big, too. I no paint swear words la dat. I paint my name and make um fancy wit curlicues undahneat. Sometimes I paint my babe's name but I no like do dat too much, bumbye everybody know, you know. Sometimes I paint one surf pickcha. One real tubular wave wit one guy jes making it . . . cranking through, you know.

When you paint on one new wall, j'like you stay da first one in da world fo spray paint. Even if you know get someting undahneat dat you went paint before, when da wall stay new, I mean, when dey jes paint up da wall fo cover da old spray paint, j'like, stay da first time you painting. You can feel da spray paint, cool on your hand. You can smell da spray, sting your nose but sweet, j'like. I no sniff, you stupid if you sniff, bumbye you come all stoned and you no can spray good. But j'like it make you feel big. Make you feel good dat your name stay ovah dere big. Like you stay *somebody*.

Coco. Ass my name. "Coco '84" is what I write. I no write um plain, I make um nice, you know. Fat lettahs. Outline um. Wit sparkles. Da kine dat you can make wit white or silvah paint, like one cross or one star. From far, j'like your name stay shiny. I stay undah da freeway aftah school fo watch my wall. I watch um from across da street by da school parking lot. Everybody who pass look at my wall every day. I try put someting new everytime so get someting new fo everybody to see. Only little bit at a time, like somemore lines on da wave or one different color outline on my name, stuff la dat. Jes about everybody look at my wall, even if dey pass um everyday, dey look. Sometimes when get some other guys by me aftah school I no can paint new stuff but da people dat pass still yet try look fo figgah out what stay new.

Aftah school I gotta wait fo my muddah pau work pick me up. Sometimes I stay by da guys when dey no mo baseball practice la dat but most times I stay by myself. Everyday gotta plan how you going paint. When you paint, you gotta plan um good. You gotta be fast. You gotta know what you going do. And you cannot get nabbed. How many times I almost got nabbed, man.

One time somebody went put "Rockerz Rule" on my wall.

Was anykine way. Wasn't nice. Had some guys hanging around da wall and I went ask dem, "You went make dat?"

"So what if we did?" one of da guys went tell me. I told dem, "Eh, I know da guy Coco, and he going bust your head if he find out you went spray on his wall. He big, you know, Coco."

Dey went look around first fo see if I had backers. Since nevah have nobody, dey went ack like dey was tough. But finally dey went go away. Deh nevah spray nutting else except fo dis one punk kid went spray and walk. Had one crooked black line all da way across my wall. I would've beefed um but I nevah like. I would've given um lickins. I could've taken um.

Nobody know I spray paint. Nobody even know I stay Coco. If they knew, they would say, "Naht, dass not you. I heard Coco stay one big guy. You too runt fo be Coco." Funny yeah, but dass me. Ass me, Coco. One time I going paint one big mural and everybody going know ass me. Would be good if you no need paint fast and hide when somebody come. Could make um nice and people would even buy da paint for me. I would make da whole wall wit spray. I would paint faces, my face ovah and ovah and I would make um look mean and tough. And I would look *bad* and I would be feeling good. I would make sparkles and you could see dem shining in my eyes. I would use silvah and some black paint. People would tink, "Who did dat nice one." Dey wouldn't paint um ovah. Dey would buy me paint. Dey would gimme money for paint da walls all ovah da place. Wouldn't need to do work in school. Da teacha would gimme one spray can, not brush and paypah, la dat. Junk, when you paint in school. Gotta do certain tings, certain way. No can be big. No mo feeling. Ass why spray paint mo bettah. Make you feel mean. And bad. And good.

One time had one lady came by da wall. She wasn't one teacha or nutting cause she had long hair and had jeans and tee-shirt la dat. I had to hide my spray can when I seen her coming. I nevah like her bust me. But you know what, she had her own spray can and went look right at me den she went spray on my wall:

REVOLUTION FOR THE 80'S
MAY DAY.

Den she went little mo down and went spray out my "Coco '84" and went put, "WORLD WITHOUT IMPERIALISM, NO IMPERIALIST WARS," right ovah my surf pickcha.

When she was pau she went look at me and say, "You know what dat means?"

"No," I told her.

"Dat means we gotta tell people to fight da government. Gotta get da people together and tell da governments not to have wars. Gotta give da poor people money and food and power la dat."

"Oh," I said, "But lady, why you went spray um ovah da wall? You nevah have to spray um ovah Coco's stuff. You could've put um on da top or on da side or write smaller. Look how you went jam up my pickcha, I mean Coco's pickcha."

"Sorry," she went tell kinda sassy.

"Why you gotta paint da kine stuff?"

"Cause I like. So what, kid." She was coming little bit piss off.

So aftah she went go away, I went try fix my wall up. But she went use red. Hard to cover, red. She nevah have to put um right ovah my writing. I wanted dem fo come paint da whole wall awready, erase um so dat could start ovah. I jes went get my can spray and I went stand in front da lady's words. I was feeling mean. Not good kine, jes mean. I went write, "LADY—HATE YOU," not nice wit fat lettahs or sparkles but jes anykine way. I nevah care. Was ugly, jes like her's one.

When my muddah came pick me up, I seen her reading da wall. "Who went do dat?" she went ask me. I told her one lady with long hair and tee-shirt. I went ask her who dat kine lady was and she went say, "Dat Commanists dat. Not Americans. Hippies." She told me, "Dey good fo nuttings." I was looking out da window when we went drive away. Couldn't even see "Coco" anymore.

I couldn't tink about anyting except what I was going paint ovah da hippie lady's words. First I thought I could paint some-more surf pictures but I went check my colors and I figgahed would be too hard fo cover da words. Da lady, she went write

354

big. I thought I could do "Coco '84" mo big but still couldn't cover da lady's words. Would use up all my paint.

Aftah school da next day, I went to my wall. Could see da lady's words from far away. I jes went look at her spray paint words. Ass all was, jes words. Ugly words dat nobody like read. Not like mines, not nice wit sparkles la dat or curlicues or one pickcha of one surfah in da tube. Jes words . . . anykine words. Everybody going say, "Whoo da ugly. Who did dat?" What if dey tink was me? Betchu da painter guys going come paint da wall fast. J'like the time somebody else went write "Sakai Sucks" and everybody knew dey was talking about Mr. Sakai, da principal. Dey came right away fo paint da wall dat time.

Nevah feel good anymore fo look at my wall. Wasn't mine anymore. Wasn't Coco's. Wasn't even da hippie lady's 'cause she no care. Was nobody's.

And den da next day had posters pasted up on da wall. Was somemore stuff about May Day and had one pickcha of one guy holding up his fist. Dey nevah only put one, but dey went line um up. Had maybe six or seven or eight all line up. Cover everyting: my surf pickcha, my name, even my "hate you" words. And dey went paste um on good. Dey went use someting dat stick real good to da cement and den dey even put paste on da top so dat da ting was stuck extra good. No can peel um off. Hardly can scrape um even. Only little bit. I seen da hippie lady aftah school looking at da posters.

"You went do dat?"

"What you tink?" she went tell me.

"I donno. You went do um, eh?"

"So."

"You shouldn't have done dat. Coco going come piss off, you know. Dis his wall. Maybe he might even call da cops or someting."

"Who's dat, Coco? Dat you? Betchu da guy no stay. If he so big, how come he no come talk to me himself? From now on dis is everybody's wall. Not only Coco can paint on dis wall. Anybody can paint. Me. You. Anybody."

She jes went keep on talking, "Eh, you no need be scared of Coco. He ain't so tough. What he going do to you?"

"Yeah but, not supposed to be writing on da walls . . ."

"Who said? Da government? Coco? Coco went paint first. He went li-bah-rate dis wall first time. But now he no can hog um. Dis wall is fo everybody I tell you. Uddahwise he stay making up anykine rules. J'like one nudda government."

"Hah?"

"Howcome you gotta watch dis wall for Coco? You jes being Coco's stooge you know. You shouldn't have to be scared of Coco. Dat's jes like da people who scared of da government. I mean you no need be oh-press by somebody else . . ."

Couldn't tell what she was saying cause one truck was going on da freeway and from far could hear one police siren. Da lady went stop talking and we went look up at da freeway listen to da siren coming closer. Went pass.

I jes told her, "No paint on top Coco's wall, eh. Or else you going be in trouble. Coco, he big, you know. He *somebody* you know." She nevah say nutting. She jes went walk away but I was still yet telling her anykine stuff, "You no can jes cover up my wall la dat. Was *my* surfah. Was *my* wave. Was *my* name! I hate you hippie lady!"

I went get my can spray and I jes started for paint one face right ovah her words. I donno who's face. Jes one face. Was black and red. Had plenny lines in da face. Was one mean and sad face. I jes went keep on adding lines to da face and came mo black and mo black until was almost like one popolo but wasn't. Jes was one face wit plenny lines on um. Da paint went run out when I was fixing up da cheek. Went drip. I couldn't finish um. I went cross da street and watch my face.

Had some guys in one truck, regular fix-da-road guys, went come and look at da posters. Dey took out anykine scrapers and some real strong kine thinner fo take da posters off.

"Awright," I went tell dem.

"Damn kids do anykine yeah," one guy went tell me.

"Naht, wasn't kids. Was da hippie lady." I went tell um.

"You know who was?"

"Yeah, da hippie lady who come around here sometimes."

"You not da one, eh?" da man went ask me.

"Nah, but da guy Coco spray."

"Coco spray dis kine words?" da man was pointing to da word "hate" between da posters. Could only see "lady" and "hate" left.

"Nah he make nice kine stuff. He no paint ugly stuff."

Dey went clean off all da posters and started to paint da wall.

"What fo you paint da wall awready. Da hippie lady only going paint um again? What fo?"

"At least going look nice fo little while," da boss guy told me.

"Eh, try look dis face," one of da guys went point to my pickcha wit his roller. "Not bad yeah? Look almost like somebody crying wit dis red drip ovah here. You know who went do this one? Pretty good artist. Too bad gotta cover um up."

I jes went turn around. I started for cry. I donno how come. . . .

"CHANG"

Sigrid Nunez (1951–)

*A*lthough *"Chang" is a work of fiction, it reflects the history of Chinese in the United States and elsewhere in the Western hemisphere. Since the mid-nineteenth century, immigrants from China settled in many places throughout the Caribbean, Central and South America, sometimes establishing communities and sometimes passing through en route to the United States. Sigrid Nunez's short story depicts growing up as the daughter of a Panamanian Shanghainese American father and a German American mother in the New York City area during the 1950s and 1960s.*

Born and raised in New York City, Ms. Nunez holds a B.A. from Barnard College and an M.F.A. from Columbia University. Her short fiction has been published in The Threepenny Review, Fiction, Iowa Review, Salmagundi, *and other journals. Her awards include two Pushcart Prizes and a G.E. Foundation Award for Younger Writers. She lives in New York City.*

THE FIRST TIME I EVER HEARD MY FATHER SPEAK CHINESE WAS AT Coney Island. I don't remember how old I was then, but I must have been very young. It was in the early days, when we still went on family outings. We were walking along the boardwalk when we ran into the four Chinese men. My mother told the story often, as if she thought we'd forgotten. "You kids didn't know them and neither did I. They were friends of your father's, from Chinatown. You'd never heard Chinese before. You didn't know what was up. You stood there with your mouths hanging open—I had to laugh. 'Why are they singing? Why is Daddy singing?' "

I remember a little more about that day. One of the men gave each of my sisters and me a dollar bill. I cashed mine into dimes and set out to win a goldfish. A dime bought you three chances to toss a ping-pong ball into one of many small fishbowls, each holding a quivering tangerine-colored fish. Overexcited, I threw recklessly, again and again. When all the dimes were gone I ran back to the grownups in tears. The man who had given me the dollar tried to give me another, but my parents wouldn't allow it. He pressed the bag of peanuts he had been eating into my hands and said I could have them all.

I never saw any of those men again or heard anything about them. They were the only friends of my father's that I would ever meet. I would hear him speak Chinese again, but very seldom. In Chinese restaurants, occasionally on the telephone, once or twice in his sleep, and in the hospital when he was dying.

So it was true, then. He really was Chinese. Up until that day I had not quite believed it.

My mother always said that he had sailed to America on a boat. He took a slow boat from China, was what she used to say, laughing. I wasn't sure whether she was serious, and if she was, why coming from China was such a funny thing.

A slow boat from China. In time I learned that he was born not in China but in Panama. No wonder I only half believed he was Chinese. He was only half Chinese.

The facts I know about his life are incredibly, unbearably few. Although we shared the same house for eighteen years, we had little else in common. We had no culture in common. It is only a slight exaggeration to say that we had no language in common. By the time I was born my father had lived almost thirty years in America, but to hear him speak you would not have believed this. About his failure to master English there always seemed to me something willful. Except for her accent—as thick as but so different from his—my mother had no such trouble.

"He never would talk about himself much, you know. That was his way. He never really had much to say, in general. Silence was golden. It was a cultural thing, I think." (My mother.)

By the time I was old enough to understand this, my father had pretty much stopped talking.

Taciturnity: they say that is an Oriental trait. But I don't believe my father was always the silent, withdrawn man I knew. Think of that day at Coney Island, when he was talking a Chinese blue streak.

Almost everything I know about him came from my mother, and there was much she herself never knew, much she had forgotten or was unsure of, and much that she would never tell.

I am six, seven, eight years old, a schoolgirl with deplorable posture and constantly cracked lips, chafing in the dollish old-world clothes handmade by my mother; a bossy, fretful, sly, cowardly child given to fits of temper and weeping. In school, or in the playground, or perhaps watching television I hear something about the Chinese—something odd, improbable. I will ask my father. He will know whether it is true, say, that the Chinese eat with sticks.

He shrugs. He pretends not to understand. Or he scowls and says, "Chinese just like everybody else."

("He thought you were making fun of him. He always thought everyone was making fun of him. He had a chip on his shoulder. The way he acted, you'd've thought he was colored!")

Actually, he said "evvybody."

Is it true the Chinese write backwards?

Chinese just like evvybody else.

Is it true they eat dog?

Chinese just like evvybody else.

Are they really all Communists?

Chinese just like evvybody else.

What is Chinese water torture? What is footbinding? What is a mandarin?

Chinese just like evvybody else.

He was not like everybody else.

361

★ ★ ★

The unbearably few facts are these. He was born in Colón, Panama, in 1911. His father came from Shanghai. From what I have been able to gather, Grandfather Chang was a merchant engaged in the trade of tobacco and tea. This business, which he ran with one of his brothers, kept him travelling often between Shanghai and Colón. He had two wives, one in each city, and, as if out of a passion for symmetry, two sons by each wife. Soon after my father, Carlos, was born, his father took him to Shanghai, to be raised by the Chinese wife. Ten years later my father was sent back to Colón. I never understood the reason for this. The way the story was told to me, I got the impression that my father was being sent away from some danger. This was, of course, a time of upheaval in China, the decade following the birth of the Republic, the era of the warlords. If the date is correct, my father would have left Shanghai the year the Chinese Communist Party was founded there. It remains uncertain, though, whether political events had anything at all to do with his leaving China.

One year after my father returned to Colón his mother was dead. I remember hearing as a child that she had died of a stroke. Years later this would seem to me odd, when I figured out that she would have been only twenty-six. Odder still, to think of that reunion between the long-parted mother and son; there's a good chance they did not speak the same language. The other half-Panamanian son, Alfonso, was either sent back with my father or had never left Colón. After their mother's death the two boys came into the care of their father's brother and business partner, Uncle Mee, who apparently lived in Colón and had a large family of his own.

Grandfather Chang, his Chinese wife, and their two sons remained in Shanghai. All were said to have been killed by the Japanese. That must have been during the Sino-Japanese War. My father would have been between his late twenties and early thirties by then, but whether he ever saw any of his Shanghai relations again before they died, I don't know.

At twelve or thirteen my father sailed to America with Uncle Mee. I believe it was just the two of them who came, leaving the rest of the family in Colón. Sometime in the next year or so my father was enrolled in a public school in Brooklyn. I remember coming across a notebook that had belonged to him in those days and being jolted by the name written on the cover: Charles Cipriano Chang. That was neither my father's first nor his last name, as far as I knew, and I'd never heard of the middle name. (Hard to believe that my father spent his boyhood in Shanghai being called Carlos, a name he could not even pronounce with the proper Spanish accent. So he must have had a Chinese name as well. And although our family never knew this name, perhaps among Chinese people he used it.)

Twenty years passed. All I know about this part of my father's life is that it was lived illegally in New York, mostly in Chinatown, where he worked in various restaurants. Then came the Second World War and he was drafted. It was while he was in the Army that he finally became an American citizen. He was no longer calling himself Charles but Carlos again, and now, upon becoming a citizen, he dropped his father's family name and took his mother's. Why a man who thought of himself as Chinese, who had always lived among Chinese, who spoke little Spanish and who had barely known his mother would have made such a decision in the middle of his life is one of many mysteries surrounding my father. My mother had an explanation: "You see, Alfonso was a Panamanian citizen, and *he* had taken his mother's name" (which would, of course, be in keeping with Spanish cultural tradition). "He was the only member of his family your father had left—the others were all dead. Your father wanted to have the same last name as his brother. Also, he thought he'd get along better in this country with a Spanish name." This makes no sense to me. He'd been a Chinatown Chang for twenty years—and now all of a sudden he wanted to pass for Hispanic?

In another version of this story, the idea of getting rid of the Chinese name was attributed to the citizenship official handling my father's papers. This is plausible, given that immigration restrictions for Chinese were still in effect at that time. But I have not ruled out the possibility that the change of names was the result of a misunderstanding between my father and this official. My father was an easily fuddled man, especially when dealing with authority, and he always had trouble understanding and making himself understood in English. And I can imagine him not only befuddled enough to make such a mistake but also too timid afterwards to try to fix it.

Whatever really happened I'm sure I'll never know. I do know that having a Spanish name brought much confusion into my father's life and have always wondered in what way my own life might have been different had he kept the name Chang.

From this point on the story becomes somewhat clearer.

With the Hundredth Infantry Division my father goes to war, fights in France and Germany and, after V-E Day, is stationed in the small southern German town where he will meet my mother. He is thirty-four and she not quite eighteen. She is soon pregnant.

Here is rich food for speculation: How did they communicate? She had had a little English in school. He learned a bit of German. They must have misunderstood far more than they understood of each other. Perhaps this helps to explain why my eldest sister was already two and my other sister on the way before my parents got married. (My sisters and I did not learn about this until we were in our twenties.)

By the time I was three they would already have had two long separations.

"I should have married Rudolf!" (My mother.)

1948. My father returns to the States with his wife and first daughter. Now everything is drastically changed. A different America this: the America of the citizen, the legal worker, the family man. No more drinking and gambling till all hours in Chinatown. No more drifting from job to job, living hand to mouth, sleeping on the floor of a friend's room or on a shelf in the restaurant kitchen. There are new, undreamed-of expenses: household money, layettes, taxes, insurance, a special bank account for the children's education. He does the best he can. He rents an apartment in the Fort Greene housing project, a short walk from the Cantonese restaurant on Fulton Street where he works as a waiter. Some nights after closing, after all the tables have been cleared and the dishes done, he stays for the gambling. He weaves home to a wide-awake wife who sniffs the whiskey on his breath and doesn't care whether he has lost or won. So little money—to gamble with any of it is a sin. Her English is getting better ("no thanks to him!"), but for what she has to say she needs little vocabulary. She is miserable. She hates America. She dreams incessantly about going home. There is something peculiar about the three-year-old: she rarely smiles; she claws at the pages of magazines, like a cat. The one-year-old is prone to colic. To her horror my mother learns that she is pregnant again. She attempts an abortion, which fails. I am born. About that attempt, was my father consulted? Most likely not. Had he been I think I know what he would have said. He would have said: No, this time it will be a boy. Like most men he would have wanted a son. (All girls—a house full of females—a Chinese man's nightmare!) Perhaps with a son he would have been more open. Perhaps a son he would have taught Chinese.

He gets another job, as a dishwasher in the kitchen of a large public health service hospital. He will work there until he retires, eventually being promoted to kitchen supervisor.

He moves his family to another housing project, outside the city, newly built, cleaner, safer.

He works all the time. On weekends, when he is off from the hospital, he waits on table in one or another Chinese restaurant. He works most holidays and takes no vacations. On his rare day off he outrages my mother by going to the racetrack. But he is not self-indulgent. A little gambling, a quart of Budweiser with his supper—eaten alone, an hour or so after the rest of us (he always worked late)—now and then a glass of Scotch, cigarettes—these were his only pleasures. While the children are still small there are occasional outings. To Coney Island, Chinatown, the zoo. On Sundays sometimes he takes us to the children's matinee, and once a year to Radio City, for the Christmas or Easter show. But he and my mother never go out alone together, just the two of them—never.

Her English keeps getting better, making his seem worse and worse.

He is hardly home, yet my memory is of constant fighting. Not much vocabulary needed to wound.

"Stupid woman. Crazy lady. Talk, talk, talk, talk—never say nothing!"

"I should have married Rudolf!"

Once, she spat in his face. Another time, she picked up a bread knife and he had to struggle to get it away from her.

They slept in separate beds.

Every few months she announced to the children that it was over: we were going "home." (And she did go back with us to Germany once, when I was two. We stayed six months. About this episode she was always vague. In years to come, whenever we asked her why we did not stay in Germany, she would say, "You children wanted your father." But I think that is untrue. More likely she realized that there was no life for her back there. She had never got on well with her family. By this time I believe Rudolf had married another.)

Even working the two jobs, my father did not make much money. He would never make enough to buy a house. Yet it seemed the burden of being poor weighed heavier on my mother. Being poor meant you could never relax, meant eternal attention to appearances. Just because you had no money didn't mean you were squalid. Come into the house: see how clean and tidy everything is. Look at the children: spotless. And people did comment to my mother—on the shininess of her floors and how she kept her children—and she was gratified by this. Still, being poor was exhausting.

One day a woman waist-deep in children knocked at the door. When my mother answered, the woman apologized. "I thought—from the name on the mailbox I thought you were Spanish, too. My kids needed to use the toilet." My mother could not hide her displeasure. She was proud of being German, and in those postwar years she was also bitterly defensive. When people called us names—spicks and chinks—she said, "You see how it is in this country. For all they say how bad we Germans are, no one ever calls you names for being German."

She had no patience with my father's quirks. The involuntary twitching of a muscle meant that someone had given him the evil eye. Drinking a glass of boiled water while it was still hot cured the flu. He saved back issues of *Reader's Digest* and silver dollars from certain years, believing that one day they'd be worth lots of money. What sort of backward creature had she married? His English drove her mad. Whenever he didn't catch something that was said to him (and this happened all the time), instead of saying "what?" he said "who?" "Who? Who?" she screeched back at him. "What are you, an owl?"

Constant bickering and fighting.

We children dreamed of growing up, going to college, getting married, getting away.

And what about Alfonso and Uncle Mee? What happened to them?

"I never met either of them, but we heard from Mee all the time those first years—it was awful. By then he was back in Panama. He was a terrible gambler, and so were his sons. They had debts up to here—and who should they turn to but your father. Uncle What-About-Mee, I called him. 'Think of all I've done for you. You owe me.' " (And though she had never heard it she mimicked his voice.) "Well, your father had managed to save a couple of thousand dollars and he sent it all to Mee. I could have died. I never forgave him. I was pregnant then, and I had one maternity dress—*one*. Mee no sooner got that money than he wrote back for more. I told your father if he sent him another dime I was leaving."

Somehow the quarrel extended to include Alfonso, who seems to have sided with Mee. My father broke with them both. Several years after we left Brooklyn, an ad appeared in the Chinatown newspaper. Alfonso and Mee were trying to track my father down. He never answered the ad, my father said. He never spoke to either man again. (Perhaps he lied. Perhaps he was always in touch with them, secretly. I believe much of his life was a secret from us.)

I have never seen a photograph of my father that was taken before he was in the Army. I have no idea what he looked like as a child or as a young man. I have never seen any photographs of his parents or his brothers, or of Uncle Mee or of any other relations, or of the houses he lived in in Colón and Shanghai. If my father had any possessions that had belonged to his parents, any family keepsakes or mementos of his youth, I never saw them. About his youth he had nothing to tell. A single anecdote he shared with me. In Shanghai he had a dog. When my father sailed to Panama, the dog was brought along to the dock to see him off. My father boarded the boat and the dog began howling. He never forgot that: the boat pulling away from the dock and the dog howling. "Dog no fool. He know I never be back."

In our house there were no Chinese things. No objects made of bamboo or jade. No lacquer boxes. No painted scrolls or fans. No calligraphy. No embroidered silks. No Buddhas. No chopsticks among the silverware, no rice bowls or tea sets. No Chinese tea, no ginseng or soy sauce in the cupboards. My father was the only Chinese thing, sitting like a Buddha himself among the Hummels and cuckoo clocks and pictures of alpine landscapes. My mother thought of the house as hers, spoke of *her* curtains, *her* floors (often in warning: "Don't scuff up my floors!"). The daughters were hers, too. To each of them she gave a Teutonic name, impossible for him to pronounce. ("*What* does your father call you?" That question—an agony to me— rang through my childhood.) It was part of her abiding nostalgia that she wanted to raise the children as Germans. She sewed dirndls for them and even for their dolls. She braided their hair, then wound the braids tightly around their ears, like hair earmuffs, in the German style. They would open their presents on Christmas Eve rather than Christmas morning. They would not celebrate Thanksgiving. Of course they would not celebrate any Chinese holidays. No dragon and firecrackers on Chinese New Year's. For Christmas there was red cabbage and sauerbraten. Imagine my father saying sauerbraten.

Now and then he brought home food from Chinatown: fiery red sausage with specks of fat like teeth embedded in it, dried fish, buns filled with bean paste which he cracked us up by calling Chinese pee-nus butter. My mother would not touch any of it. ("God knows what it really is.") We kids clamored for a taste and when we didn't like it my father got angry. ("You know how he was with that chip on his shoulder. He took it personally. He was insulted.") Whenever we ate at one of the restaurants where he worked, he was always careful to order for us the same Americanized dishes served to most of the white customers.

★ ★ ★

An early memory: I am four, five, six years old, in a silly mood, mugging in my mother's bureau mirror. My father is in the room with me but I forget he is there. I place my forefingers at the corners of my eyes and pull the lids taut. Then I catch him watching me. His is a look of pure hate.

"He thought you were making fun."

A later memory: "Panama is an isthmus." Grade-school geography. My father looks up from his paper, alert, suspicious. "Merry Isthmus!" "Isthmus be the place!" My sisters and I shriek with laughter. My father shakes his head. "Not nice, making fun of place where people born."

"*Ach*, he had no sense of humor—he never did. You couldn't joke with him. He never got the point of a joke."

It is true that I hardly ever heard him laugh. (Unlike my mother, who, despite her chronic unhappiness, seemed always to be laughing—at him, at us, at the neighbors. A great tease she was, sly, malicious, often witty.)

Chinese inscrutability. Chinese sufferance. Chinese reserve. Yes, I recognize my father in the clichés. But what about his Panamanian side? What are Latins said to be? Hot-blooded, mercurial, soulful, macho, convivial, romantic. No, he was none of these.

"He always wanted to go back, he always missed China."

But he was only ten years old when he left.

"Yes, but that's what counts—where you spent those first years, and your first language. That's who you are."

I had a children's book about Sun Yat Sen, The Man Who Changed China. There were drawings of Sun as a boy. I tried to picture my father like that, a Chinese boy who wore pajamas outdoors and a coolie hat and a pigtail down his back. (Though of course in those days after Sun's Revolution he isn't likely to have worn a pigtail.) I pictured my father against those landscapes of peaks and pagodas, with a dog like Old Yeller at his heels. What was it like, this boyhood in Shanghai? How did the Chinese wife treat the second wife's son? (My father and Alfonso would not have had the same status as the official wife's sons, I don't think.) How did the Chinese brothers treat him? When he went to school—did he go to school?—was he accepted by the other children as one of them? Is there a Chinese word for half-breed, and was he called that name as we would be? Surely many times in his life he must have wished he were all Chinese. My mother wished that her children were all German. I wanted to be an all-American girl with a name like Sue Brown.

He always wanted to go back.

In our house there were not many books. My mother's romances and historical novels, books about Germany (mostly about the Nazi era), a volume of Shakespeare, tales from Andersen and Grimm, the *Nibelungenlied*, Edith Hamilton's *Mythology*, poems of Goethe and Schiller, *Struwwelpeter*, the drawings of Wilhelm Busch. It was my mother who gave me that book about Sun Yat Sen and, when I was a little older, one of her own favorites, *The Good Earth*, a children's story for adults. Pearl Buck was a missionary who lived in China for many years. (Missionaries supposedly converted the Changs to Christianity. From what? Buddhism? Taoism? My father's mother was almost certainly Roman Catholic. He himself belonged to no church.) Pearl Buck wrote eighty-five books, founded a shelter for Asian-American children, and won the Nobel Prize.

The Good Earth. China a land of famine and plagues—endless childbirth among them. The births of daughters seen as evil omens. "It is only a slave this time—not worth mentioning." Little girls sold as a matter of course. Growing up to be concubines with names like Lotus and Cuckoo and Pear Blossom. Women with feet like little deer hooves. Abject wives, shuffling six paces behind their husbands. All this filled me with anxiety. In our house the man was the meek and browbeat one.

I never saw my father read, except for the newspaper. He did not read the *Reader's Digest*s that he saved. He would not have been able to read *The Good Earth*. I am sure he could not write with fluency in any tongue. The older I grew the more I thought of him as illiterate. Hard for me to accept the fact that he did not read books. Say I grew up to be a writer. He would not read what I wrote.

★ ★ ★

He had his own separate closet, in the front hall. Every night when he came home from work he undressed as soon as he walked in, out there in the hall. He took off his suit and put on his bathrobe. He always wore a suit to work, but at the hospital he changed into whites and at the restaurant into dark pants, white jacket and black bow tie. In the few photographs of him that exist he is often wearing a uniform—his soldier's or hospital-worker's or waiter's.

Though not at all vain, he was particular about his appearance. He bought his suits in a men's fine clothing store on Fifth Avenue, and he took meticulous care of them. He had a horror of cheap cloth and imitation leather, and an equal horror of slovenliness. His closet was the picture of order. On the top shelf, where he kept his hats, was a large assortment—a lifetime's supply, it seemed to me—of chewing gum, cough drops, and mints. On that shelf he kept also his cigarettes and cigars. The closet smelled much as he did—of tobacco and spearmint and the rosewater-glycerin cream he used on his dry skin. A not unpleasant smell.

He was small. At fourteen I was already as tall as he, and eventually I would outweigh him. A trim sprig of a man—dainty but not puny, fastidious but not effeminate. I used to marvel at the cleanliness of his nails, and at his good teeth, which never needed any fillings. By the time I was born he had lost most of his top hair, which made his domed forehead look even larger, his moon-face rounder. It may have been the copper-red cast of his skin that led some people to take him for an American Indian—people who'd never seen one, probably.

He could be cruel. I once saw him blow pepper in the cat's face. He loathed that cat, a surly, untrainable tom found in the street. But he was very fond of another creature we took in, an orphaned nestling sparrow. Against expectations, the bird survived and learned how to fly. But, afraid that it would not be able to fend for itself outdoors, we decided to keep it. My father sometimes sat by its cage, watching the bird and cooing at it in Chinese. My mother was amused. "You see: he has more to say to that bird than to us!" The emperor and his nightingale, she called them. "The Chinese have always loved their birds." (What none of us knew: at that very moment in China keeping pet birds had been prohibited as a bourgeois affectation, and sparrows were being exterminated as pests.)

It was true that my father had less and less to say to us. He was drifting further and further out of our lives. These were my teenage years. I did not see clearly what was happening then, and for long afterwards, whenever I tried to look back, a panic would come over me, so that I couldn't see at all.

At sixteen, I had stopped thinking about becoming a writer. I wanted to dance. Every day after school I went into the city for class. I would be home by 8:30, about the same time as my father, and so for this period he and I would eat dinner together. And much later, looking back, I realized that that was when I had—and lost—my chance. Alone with my father every night like that, I could have got to know him. I could have asked him all those questions that I now have to live without answers to. Of course he would have resisted talking about himself. But with patience I might have drawn him out.

Or maybe not. As I recall, the person sitting across the kitchen table from me was like a figure in a glass case. That was not the face of someone thinking, feeling, or even daydreaming. It was the clay face, still waiting to receive the breath of life.

If it ever occurred to me that my father was getting old, that he was exhausted, that his health was failing, I don't remember it.

He was still working seven days a week. Sometimes he missed having dinner with me because the dishwasher broke and he had to stay late at the hospital. For a time, on Saturdays, he worked double shifts at the restaurant and did not come home till we were all asleep.

After dinner, he stayed at the kitchen table, smoking and finishing his beer. Then he went to bed. He never joined the rest of us in the living room in front of the television. He sat alone at the table, staring at the wall. He hardly noticed if someone came into the kitchen for something. His inobservance was the family's biggest joke. My mother would give herself or one of us a new hairdo and say, "Now watch: your father won't even notice," and she was right.

My sisters and I bemoaned his stubborn avoidance of the living room. Once a year he yielded and joined us around the Christmas tree, but only very reluctantly; we had to beg him.

I knew vaguely that he continued to have some sort of social life outside the house, a life centered in Chinatown.

He still played the horses.

By this time family outings had ceased. We never did anything together as a family. But every Sunday my father came home with ice cream for everyone.

He and my mother fought less and less—seldom now in the old vicious way—but this did not mean there was peace. Never any word or gesture of affection between them, not even, "for the sake of the children," pretense of affection.

(Television: the prime-time family shows. During the inevitable scenes when family love and loyalty were affirmed, the discomfort in the living room was palpable. I think we were all ashamed of how far below the ideal our family fell.)

Working and saving to send his children to college, he took no interest in their school life. He did, however, reward good report cards with cash. He did not attend school events to which parents were invited; he always had to work.

He never saw me dance.

He intrigued my friends, who angered me by regarding him as if he were a figure in a glass case. Doesn't he ever come out of the kitchen? Doesn't he ever talk? I was angry at him, too, for what he seemed to me to be doing: *willing* himself into stereotype: inscrutable, self-effacing, funny little chinaman.

And why couldn't he learn to speak English?

He developed the tight wheezing cough that would never leave him. The doctor blamed cigarettes, so my father tried sticking to cigars. The cough was particularly bad at night. It kept my mother up, and so she started sleeping on the living-room couch.

I was the only one who went to college, and I got a scholarship. My father gave the money he had saved to my mother, who bought a brand-new Mercedes, the family's first car.

★ ★ ★

He was not like everybody else. In fact, he was not like anyone
I had ever met. But I thought of my father when I first encountered the "little man" of Russian literature. I thought of him a
lot when I read the stories of Chekhov and Gogol. Reading
"Grief," I remembered my father and the sparrow, and a new
possibility presented itself: my father not as one who would not
speak but as one to whom no one would listen.

And he was like a character in a story also in the sense that
he needed to be invented.

The silver dollars saved in a cigar box. The *Reader's Digests*
going back to before I was born. The uniforms. The tobacco-
mint-rosewater smell. I cannot invent a father out of these.

I waited too long. By the time I started gathering material
for his story, whatever there had been in the way of private
documents or papers (and there must have been some) had
disappeared. (It was never clear whether my father himself destroyed them or whether my mother later lost or got rid of
them, between moves, or in one of her zealous spring cleanings.)

The Sunday-night ice cream. The Budweiser bottle sweating
on the kitchen table. The five-, ten-, or twenty-dollar bill he
pulled from his wallet after squinting at your report card. "Who?
Who?"

We must have seemed as alien to him as he seemed to us. To
him we must always have been "others." Females. Demons.
No different from other demons, who could not tell one Asian
from another, who thought Chinese food meant chop suey and
Chinese customs matter for joking. I would have to live a lot
longer and he would have to die before the full horror of this
would sink in. And then it would sink in deeply, agonizingly,
like an arrow that has found its mark.

Dusk in the city. Dozens of Chinese men bicycle through the
streets, bearing cartons of fried dumplings, Ten Ingredients Lo
Mein, and sweet-and-sour pork. I am on my way to the drug-
store when one of them hails me. "Miss! Wait, Miss!" Not a
man, I see, but a boy, eighteen at most, with a lovely, oval,

fresh-skinned face. "You—you Chinese!" It is not the first time in my life this has happened. As shortly as possible I explain. The boy turns out to have arrived just weeks ago, from Hong Kong. His English is incomprehensible. He is flustered when he finds I cannot speak Chinese. He says, "Can I. Your father. Now." It takes me a moment to figure this out. Alas, he is asking to meet my father. Unable to bring myself to tell him my father is dead, I say that he does not live in the city. The boy persists. "But sometime come see. And then I now?" His imploring manner puzzles me. Is it that he wants to meet Chinese people? Doesn't he work in a Chinese restaurant? Doesn't he know about Chinatown? I feel a surge of anxiety. He is so earnest and intent. I am missing something. In another minute I have promised that when my father comes to town he will go to the restaurant where the boy works and seek him out. The boy rides off looking pleased, and I continue on to the store. I am picking out toothpaste when he appears at my side. He hands me a folded piece of paper. Two telephone numbers and a message in Chinese characters. "For father."

He was sixty when he retired from the hospital, but his working days were not done. He took a part-time job as a messenger for a bank. That Christmas when I came home from school I found him in bad shape. His smoker's cough was much worse, and he had pains in his legs and in his back, recently diagnosed as arthritis.

But it was not smoker's cough, and it was not arthritis.

A month later, he left work early one day because he was in such pain. He made it to the train station, but when he tried to board the train he could not get up the steps. Two conductors had to carry him aboard. At home he went straight to bed and in the middle of the night he woke up coughing as usual, and this time there was blood.

His decline was so swift that by the time I arrived at the hospital he barely knew me. Over the next week we were able to chart the backward journey on which he was embarked by his occasional murmurings. ("I got to get back to the base— they'll think I'm AWOL!") Though I was not there to hear it, I am told that he cursed my mother and accused her of never having cared about him. By the end of the week, when he spoke it was only in Chinese.

One morning a priest arrived. No one had sent for him. He had doubtless assumed from the name that this patient was Hispanic and Catholic, and had taken it upon himself to administer extreme unction. None of us had the will to stop him, and so we were witness to a final mystery: my father, who as far as we knew had no religion, feebly crossing himself.

The fragments of Chinese stopped. There was only panting then, broken by sharp gasps such as one makes when reminded of some important thing one has forgotten. To the end his hands were restless. He kept repeating the same gesture: cupping his hands together and drawing them to his chest, as though gathering something to him.

Now let others speak.

"After the war was a terrible time. We were all scared to death, we didn't know what was going to happen to us. Some of those soldiers were really enjoying it, they wanted nothing better than to see us grovel. The victors! Oh, they were scum, a lot of them. Worse than the Nazis ever were. But Carlos felt sorry for us. He tried to help. And not just our family but the neighbors, too. He gave us money. His wallet was always out. And he was always bringing stuff from the base, like coffee and chocolate—things you could never get. And even after he went back to the States he sent packages. Not just to us but to all the people he got to know here. Frau Meyer. The Schweitzers. They still talk about that." (My grandmother.)

"We know the cancer started in the right lung but by the time we saw him it had spread. It was in both lungs, it was in his liver and in his bones. He was a very sick man and he'd been sick for a long time. I'd say that tumor in the right lung had been growing for at least five years." (The doctor.)

"He drank a lot in those days, and your mother didn't like that. But he was funny. He loved that singer—the cowboy— what was his name? I forget. Anyway, he put on the music and he sang along. Your mother would cover her ears." (My grandmother.)

"I didn't like the way he looked. He wouldn't say anything

but I knew he was hurting. I said to myself, this isn't arthritis—no way. I wanted him to see my own doctor but he wouldn't. I was just about to order him to." (My father's boss at the bank.)

"He hated cats, and the cat knew it and she was always jumping in his lap. Every time he sat down the cat jumped in his lap and we laughed. But you could tell it really bothered him. He said cats were bad luck. When the cat jumped in your lap it was a bad omen." (My mother's younger brother, Karl.)

"He couldn't dance at all—or he wouldn't—but he clapped and sang along to the records. He liked to drink and he liked gambling. Your mother was real worried about that." (Frau Meyer.)

"Before the occupation no one in this town had ever seen an Oriental or a Negro." (My grandmother.)

"He never ate much, he didn't want you to cook for him, but he liked German beer. He brought cigarettes for everyone. We gave him schnapps. He played us the cowboy songs." (Frau Schweitzer.)

"Ain't you people dying to know what he's saying?" (The patient in the bed next to my father's.)

"When he wasn't drinking he was very shy. He just sat there next to your mother without speaking. He sat there staring and staring at her." (Frau Meyer.)

"He liked blondes. He loved that blond hair." (Karl.)

"There was absolutely nothing we could do for him. The amazing thing is that he was working right up till the day he came into the hospital. I don't know how he did that." (The doctor.)

"The singing was a way of talking to us, because he didn't know German at all." (My grandmother.)

"Yes, of course I remember. It was Hank Williams. He played those records over and over. Hillbilly music. I thought I'd go mad." (My mother.)

Here are the names of some Hank Williams songs: Honky Tonkin'. Ramblin' Man. Hey, Good Lookin'. Lovesick Blues. Why Don't You Love Me Like You Used To Do. Your Cheatin' Heart. (I Heard That) Lonesome Whistle. Why Don't You Mind Your Own Business. I'm So Lonesome I Could Cry. The Blues Come Around. Cold, Cold Heart. I'll Never Get Out of This World Alive. I Can't Help It If I'm Still in Love with You.

"First Love"

R. A. Sasaki (1952–   )

In "First Love" R. A. Sasaki weaves a tale of "intergenerational" love and coming of age in San Francisco and Berkeley in the late 1960s and early 1970s. The short story is one of nine in her collection, The Loom, published in 1991.

Ms. Sasaki is a third-generation Japanese American, born and raised in San Francisco. She attended the University of Kent in Canterbury, England, received a B.A. from the University of California at Berkeley, and an M.A. in creative writing from San Francisco State University. In 1983, she won the American Japanese National Literary Award for her short story, "The Loom." Her fiction has been published in Short Story Review, Pushcart Prize XVII, Story, and other journals and anthologies. She is a trainer in the field of intercultural communications and lives in Berkeley.

IT WAS WILLIAM CHIN WHO STARTED THE RUMOR. HE HAD BEEN crossing California Street on a Saturday afternoon in December when he was almost struck down by two people on a Suzuki motorcycle. As if it weren't enough to feel the brush of death on the sleeve of his blue parka, a split second before the demon passed, he had looked up and caught sight of two faces he never would have expected to see on the same motorcycle—one of which he wouldn't have expected to see on a motorcycle at all. No one would have imagined these two faces exchanging

379

words, or thought of them in the same thought even; yet there they were, together not only in physical space, but in their expressions of fiendish abandon as they whizzed by him. He was so shaken, first by his nearness to death, then by seeing an F.O.B. hood like Hideyuki "George" Sakamoto in the company of a nice girl like Joanne Terasaki, that it was a full five minutes before he realized, still standing in amazement on the corner of California and Fourth, that Joanne had been driving.

When William Chin's story got around, there was a general sense of outrage among the senior class of Andrew Jackson High—the boys, because an upstart newcomer like George Sakamoto had done what they were too shy to do (that is, he had gotten Joanne to like him), and the girls, because George Sakamoto was definitely cool and Joanne Terasaki, as Marsha Aquino objected with utter contempt, "doesn't even like to dance." Joanne's friends remained loyal and insisted that Jo would come to her senses by graduation. George's motorcycle cronies were less generous. "Dude's fuckin' crazy," was their cryptic consensus. Opinions differed as to which of the two lovers had completely lost their minds; however, it was unanimously held that the pairing was unsuitable.

And indeed, the two were from different worlds.

Hideyuki Sakamoto ("George" was his American name) was Japanese, a conviction that eight years, or half his life, in the States had failed to shake. He had transferred into Jackson High's senior class that year from wherever it was that F.O.B.s (immigrants fresh off the boat) transferred from; and though perhaps in his case the "fresh" no longer applied, the fact that he had come off the boat at one time or another was unmistakable. It lingered—rather, persisted—in his speech, which was ungrammatical and heavily accented, and punctuated by a mixture of exclamations commonly used on Kyushu Island and in the Fillmore District.

An F.O.B. at Jackson High could follow one of two routes: he could be quietly good at science or mathematics, or he could be a juvenile delinquent. Both options condemned him to invisibility. George hated math. His sympathies tended much more toward the latter option; however, he was not satisfied to be relegated to that category either. One thing was certain, and that was that George wanted no part of invisibility. As soon as his part-time job at Nakamura Hardware in Japantown afforded him the opportunity, he went out and acquired a second-hand Suzuki chopper (most hoods dreamed of owning a Harley, but George was Japanese and proud of it). He acquired threads which, when worn on his tall, wiry frame, had the effect— whether from admiration, derision, or sheer astonishment—of turning all heads, male and female alike. He had, in a short span of time, established a reputation as a "swinger." So when William Chin's story got around about George Sakamoto letting Joanne Terasaki drive his bike, the unanimous reaction among the girls who thought of themselves as swingers was voiced by Marsha Aquino: "God dog, what a waste."

Joanne Terasaki, or "Jo," as she preferred to be called, was, in popular opinion, a "brain." Although her parents were living in Japantown when she was born, soon afterwards her grandparents had died and the family moved out to "the Avenues." Jo was a product of the middle-class, ethnically mixed Richmond District. She had an air of breeding that came from three generations of city living, one college-educated parent, and a simple belief in the illusion so carefully nurtured by her parents' generation, who had been through the war, that she was absolutely Mainstream. No one, however, would have thought of her in conjunction with the word "swing," unless it was the playground variety. Indeed, there was a childlike quality about her, a kind of functional stupidity that was surprising in a girl so intelligent in other respects. She moved slowly, as if her mind were always elsewhere, a habit that boys found mysterious and alluring at first, then exasperating. Teachers found it exasperating as well, even slightly insulting, as she earned As in their classes almost as an afterthought. Her attention was like a dim but powerful beacon, slowly sweeping out to sea for—what? Occasionally it would light briefly on the world at hand, and Jo would be quick, sharp, formidable. Then it would turn out to faraway places again. Perhaps she was unable to reconcile the world around her, the world of Jackson High, with the fictional worlds where her love of reading took her. In her mind, she was Scarlett O'Hara, Lizzy Bennet, Ari Ben Canaan. Who would not be disoriented to find oneself at one moment fleeing the Yankees through a burning Atlanta, and the next moment struggling across the finish line in girls' P.E.? Tart repartee with

Mr. Darcy was far more satisfying than the tongue-tied and painful exchanges with boys that occurred in real life. Rebuffed boys thought Jo a snob, a heartless bitch. The world of Andrew Jackson High was beneath her, that was it—a passing annoyance to be endured until she went out into the wider world and entered her true element. It must be on this wider world, this future glory, that her vision was so inexorably fixed.

Or perhaps it was fixed on a point just across San Francisco Bay, on the imposing campanile of the Berkeley campus of the University of California. She had always known she would go there, ever since, as a child, she had often gone to her mother's dresser and surreptitiously opened the top drawer to take out the fuzzy little golden bear bearing the inscription in blue letters, "CAL." It was one of the few "heirlooms" that her mother had salvaged from the wartime relocation. She had taken it with her to internment camp in the Utah desert, an ineffectual but treasured symbol of a shattered life. The government could take away her rights, her father's business, her home, but they could never take away the fact that she was U.C. Berkeley, Class of '39. Jo would have that, too. People often said of Jo that she was a girl who was going places; and they didn't mean on the back (or front) of George Sakamoto's bike.

Only love or drama could bring together two people cast in such disparate roles. When auditions began for the play that was traditionally put on by the senior class before graduation, Jo, tired of being typecast as a brain, tried out for the part most alien to her image—that of the brazen hussy who flings herself at the hero in vain. For a brief moment she stood before her fellow classmates and sang her way out of the cramped cage that their imaginations had fashioned for her. The moment was indeed brief. Marsha Aquino got the part.

"You have to admit, Jo," said William Chin apologetically, "Marsha's a natural." And Jo agreed, somewhat maliciously, that Marsha was.

George, for his part, went for the lead. It was unheard of for a hood (and an F.O.B., at that) to aspire to the stage, much less the leading part. So thoroughly did George's aspect contradict conventional expectations of what a male lead should be, that the effect was quite comic. His good-natured lack of inhibition so charmed his audience that they almost overlooked the fact that his lines had been unintelligible. At the last moment, a voice of reason prevailed, and George was relegated to a nonspeaking part as one of six princes in a dream ballet, choreographed by Jo's friend Ava.

And so the two worlds converged.

"Grace," Ava was saying. "And—flair." She was putting the dream princes and princesses through their paces. "This is a ballet."

The dancers shuffled about self-consciously. After hours of work the princes and princesses, trained exclusively in soul, were managing to approximate a cross between a square dance and a track-and-field event.

"You've got to put more energy into it, or something," Jo, who was a princess, observed critically as a sheepish William Chin and Ed Bakowsky leaped halfheartedly across the floor.

"Like this, man!" George yelled suddenly, covering the stage in three athletic leaps. He landed crookedly on one knee, arms flung wide, whooping in exhilaration. There was an embarrassed silence.

"Yeah," Jo said. "Like that."

"Who is that?" she asked Ava after the rehearsal.

"I don't know," Ava said, "but what a body."

"That's George Sakamoto," said Marsha Aquino, who knew about everyone. "He's bad."

Jo, unfamiliar with the current slang, took her literally.

"Well, he seems all right to me. If it wasn't for him, our dream ballet would look more like 'The Funeral March.' Is he new?"

"He transferred from St. Francis," Marsha said. "That's where all the F.O.B.s go."

Jo had always had a vague awareness of Japanese people as being unattractively shy and rather hideously proper. Nothing could have been further from this image than George. Jo and her friends, most of whom were of Asian descent, were stunned by him, as a group of domesticated elephants born and bred in a zoo might have been upon meeting their wild African counterpart for the first time. George was a revelation to Jo, who, on the subject of ethnic identity, had always numbered among the ranks of the sublimely oblivious.

George, meanwhile, was already laying his strategy. He was not called "*Sukebe* Sakamoto" by his friends for nothing.

"This chick is the door-hanger type," he told his friend Doug. "You gotta move real slow."

"Yeah," Doug said. "Too slow for you."

"You watch, sucker."

He called her one weekend and invited her and Ava to go bowling with him and Doug. Jo was struck dumb on the telephone.

"Ha-ro, is Jo there?"

"This is Jo."

"Hey, man. This is George."

"Who?"

"George, man. Sakamoto."

"Oh." Then she added shyly, "Hi."

The idea of bowling was revolting, but Jo could bowl for love.

She told her mother that she had a date. Her mother mentally filed through her list of acquaintances for a Sakamoto.

"Is that the Sakamoto that owns the cleaner on Fillmore?"

"I don't think so," Jo said.

"Well, if Ava's going, I guess it's all right."

When George came to pick her up, Jo introduced him to her father, who was sitting in the living room watching television.

"Ha-ro," George said, cutting a neat bow to her startled father.

"Was that guy Japanese?" her father asked later when she returned.

"Yeah," Jo said, chuckling.

There was an unspoken law of evolution which dictated that in the gradual march toward Americanization, one did not deliberately regress by associating with F.O.B.s. Jo's mother, who was second generation, had endured much criticism from her peers for "throwing away a college education" and marrying Jo's father, who had graduated from high school in Japan. Even Jo's father, while certainly not an advocate of this law, assumed that most people felt this way. George, therefore, was a shock.

On their second date, Jo and George went to see Peter O'Toole in a musical. From then on, they decided to dispense with the formalities, a decision owing only in part to the fact that the musical had been wretched. The main reason was that they were in love.

They would drive out to the beach, or to the San Bruno hills, and sit for hours, talking. In the protective shell of George's mother's car they found a world where they were not limited by labels. They could be complex, vulnerable. He told her about his boyhood in Kyushu, about the sounds that a Japanese house makes in the night. He had been afraid of ghosts. His mother had always told him ghost stories. She would make her eyes go round and utter strange sounds: "*Ka-ra . . . ko-ro . . . ka-ra . . . ko-ro . . .*"—the sound made by the wooden sandals of an approaching ghost. Japanese ghosts were different from American ghosts, he said. They didn't have feet.

"If they don't have feet," Jo asked curiously, "how could they wear sandals?"

George was dumbfounded. The contradiction had never occurred to him.

They went for motorcycle rides along the roads that wound through the Presidio, at the edge of cliffs overlooking the Golden Gate. Then, chilled by the brisk winter fog, they would stop at his house in Japantown for a cup of green tea.

He lived in an old Victorian flat on the border between Japantown and the Fillmore, with his mother and grandmother and cat. His mother worked, so it was his grandmother who came from the kitchen to greet them. (But this was later. At first, George made sure that no one would be home when they went. He wanted to keep Jo a secret until he was sure of her.)

The Victorian kitchen, the green tea, all reminded Jo of her grandparents' place, which had stood just a few blocks away from George's house before it was torn down. Jo had a vague memory of her grandmother cooking fish in the kitchen. She couldn't remember her grandfather at all. The war had broken his spirit, taken his business, forced him to do day work in white people's homes, and he had died when Jo was two. After that, Jo's family moved out of Japantown, and she had not thought about the past until George's house reminded her. It was so unexpected that the swinger, the hood, the F.O.B. George Sakamoto should awaken such memories.

But they eventually had to leave the protective spaces that sheltered their love. Then the still George of the parked car and Victorian kitchen, the "real" George, Jo wanted to believe, evolved, became the flamboyant George, in constant motion, driven to maintain an illusion that would elude the cages of other people's limited imaginations.

He took her to dances Jo had never known existed. Jo had been only to school dances, where everyone stood around too embarrassed to dance. The dances that George took her to were dark, crowded. Almost everyone was Asian. Jo knew no one. Where did all these people come from? They were the invisible ones at school, the F.O.B.s. They *dressed* (unlike Jo and her crowd, who tended toward corduroy jeans). And they danced.

George was in his element here. In his skintight striped slacks flared at the calf, black crepe shirt open to the navel, billowing sleeves and satiny white silk scarf, he shimmered like a mirage in the strobe lights that cut the darkness. Then, chameleonlike, he would appear in jeans and a white T-shirt, stocking the shelves of Nakamura Hardware. At school, George shunned the striped shirts and windbreaker jackets that his peers donned like a uniform. He wore turtleneck sweaters under corduroy blazers, starched shirts in deep colors with cuff links. When he rode his bike, he was again transformed, a wild knight in black leather.

"The dudes I ride with," George confided to Jo in the car, "see me working in the store, and they say, 'Hey, what is this, man? You square a-sup'm?' Then the guys in the store, they can't believe I hang out with those suckers on bikes. 'Hey George,' they say, 'you one crazy son-of-a-bitch.' In school, man, these straight suckers can't believe it when I do good on a test. I mean, I ain't no hot shit at English, but I ain't no dumb sucker neither. 'Hey George,' they say, 'you tryin' to get into college a-sup'm?' 'Hey, why not, man?' I say. They can't take it if you just a little bit different, you know? All them dudes is like that—'cept you."

Jo was touched, and tried to be the woman of George's dreams. It was a formidable endeavor. Nancy Sinatra was the woman of George's dreams. For Christmas Jo got a pair of knee-high black boots. She wore her corduroy jeans tighter in the crotch.

"Hey, George," Doug said. "How's it goin' with Slow Jo?"

"None of your fuckin' business, man," George snapped.

"Oh-oh. Looks bad."

On New Year's Eve Jo discovered French kissing and thought it was "weird." She got used to it, though.

"You tell that guy," her father thundered, "that if he's gonna bring that motorcycle, he doesn't have to come around here anymore!"

"Jesus Christ!" Jo wailed, stomping out of the room. "I can't wait to get out of here!"

Then they graduated, and Jo moved to Berkeley in the spring.

The scene changed from the narrow corridors of Andrew Jackson High to the wide steps and manicured lawns of the university. George was attending a junior college in the city. He came over on weekends.

"Like good ice cream," he said. "I want to put you in the freezer so you don't melt."

"What are you talking about?"

They were sitting outside Jo's dormitory in George's car. Jo's roommate was a blonde from Colusa who had screamed the first time George walked into the room with Jo. ("Hey, what's with that chick?" George had later complained.)

"I want to save you," George said.

"From what?" Jo asked.

He tried another analogy. "It's like this guy got this fancy shirt, see? He wants to wear it when he goes out, man. He don't want to wear it every day, get it dirty. He wears an old T-shirt when he works under the car—get grease on it, no problem. It don't matter. You're like the good shirt, man."

"So who's the old T-shirt?" Jo asked, suddenly catching on.

"Hey, nobody, man. Nobody special. You're special. I want to save you."

"I don't see it that way," Jo said. "When you love someone, you want to be with them and you don't mind the grease."

"Hey, outasight, man."

So he brought her to his room.

George's room was next to the kitchen. It was actually the dining room converted into a young man's bedroom. It had the tall, narrow Victorian doors and windows, and a sliding door to the living room, which was blocked by bookshelves and a stereo. The glass-doored china cabinet, which should have housed Imari bowls, held tapes of soul music, motorcycle chains, Japanese comic books, and Brut. In Jo's grandparents' house there had been a black shrine honoring dead ancestors in the corner of the dining room. The same corner in George's room was decorated by a life-sized poster of a voluptuous young woman wearing skintight leather pants and an equally skintight (but bulging) leather jacket, unzipped to the waist.

George's mother and grandmother were delighted by Jo. In their eyes she was a "nice Japanese girl," something they never thought they would see, at least in conjunction with George. George had had a string of girlfriends before Jo, which had dashed their hopes. Jo was beyond their wildest expectations. It didn't seem to matter that this "nice Japanese girl" didn't understand any Japanese; George's grandmother spoke to her anyway, and gave her the benefit of the doubt when she smiled blankly and looked to George for a translation. They were so enthusiastic that George was embarrassed, and tried to sneak Jo in and out to spare her their effusions.

They would go to his room and turn up the stereo and make love to the lush, throbbing beat of soul. At first Jo was mortified, conscious of what her parents would say, knowing that "good girls" were supposed to "wait." But in the darkness of George's room, all of that seemed very far away.

So her first experiences of love were in a darkened room filled with the ghosts of missing Japanese heirlooms; in the spaces between the soul numbers with which they tried to dispel those ghostlike shadows, sounds filtered in from the neighboring kitchen: samurai music from the Japanese program on television, the ancient voice of his grandmother calling to the cat, the eternal shuffle of slippers across the kitchen floor. When his mother was home and began to worry about what they were doing in his room, he installed a lock, and when she began pounding on the door, insisting that it was getting late and that George really should take Jo home, George would call out gruffly, "Or-righ! Or-righ!"

But there was that other world, Jo's weekday world, a world of classical buildings, bookstores, coffee shops, and tear gas (for the United States had bombed Cambodia).

Jo flitted like a ghost between the two worlds so tenuously linked by a thin span of steel suspended over San Francisco

Bay. She wanted to be still, and at home, but where? On quiet weekday mornings, reading in an empty courtyard with the stillness, the early morning sun, the language of Dickens, she felt her world full of promise and dreams. Then the sun rose high, people came out, and Jo and her world disappeared in a cloak of invisibility, like a ghost.

"Her English is so good," Ava's roommate remarked to Ava. "Where did she learn it?"

"From my parents," Jo said. "In school, from friends. Pretty much the same way most San Franciscans learn it, I guess."'

Ava's roommate was from the East Coast, and had never had a conversation with an "Oriental" before.

"She just doesn't know any better," Ava apologized later.

"Well where has that chick been all her life?" Jo fumed.

Then she would long for George, and he would come on the weekend to take her away. Locked together on George's bike, hurtling back and forth between two worlds, they found a place where they could be still and at peace.

George tried to be the man of her dreams. They went on hikes now instead of soul dances. He would appear in jeans and a work shirt, and he usually had an armload of books. He was learning to type, and took great pains over his essays for Remedial English.

But they began to feel the strain. It began to bother George that Jo made twenty-five cents an hour more at her part-time job in the student dining room than he did at the hardware store. He had been working longer. He needed the money. Jo, on the other hand, never seemed to buy anything. Just books. Although her parents could afford to send her to college, her high-school record had won her a scholarship for the first year. She lived in a dream world. She had it so easy.

He asked to borrow fifty dollars, he had to fix his car, and she lent it to him immediately. But he resented it, resented his need, resented her for having the money, for parting with it so easily. Everything, so easily. And he tortured her.

"Hey, is something wrong, man?" George asked suddenly, accusing, over the phone.

"Wrong?" Jo was surprised. "What do you mean?"

"You sound funny."

"What do you mean, funny?"

"You sound real cold, man," George said. His voice was flat, dull.

"There's nothing wrong!" Jo protested, putting extra emphasis in her voice to convince him, then hating herself for doing so. "I'm fine."

"You sound real far away," George went on, listlessly.

"Hey, is something bothering *you?*"

"No," George said. "You just sound funny to me. Real cold, like you don't care." He wanted her to be sympathetic, remorseful.

And at first she was—repentant, almost hysterical. Then she became impatient. Finally, she lapsed into indifference.

"I have the day off tomorrow," George said over the phone. "Can I come?"

Jo hesitated.

"I have to go to classes," she warned.

"That's okay," he said. "I'll come with you."

There was another long pause. "Well . . . we'll see," she said.

As soon as she saw him the next day, her fears were confirmed. He had gone all out. He wore a silky purple shirt open halfway to his navel, and skintight slacks that left nothing to the imagination. There was something pathetic and vulnerable about the line of his leg so thoroughly revealed by them. As they approached the campus, George pulled out a pair of dark shades and put them on.

He was like a character walking into the wrong play. He glowed defiantly among the faded jeans and work shirts of the Berkeley campus.

Jo's first class was Renaissance Literature.

"If you want to do something else," she said, "I can meet you after class."

"That's okay, man," George said happily. "I want to see what they teaching you."

"It's gonna be real boring," she said.

"That's okay," he said. "I have my psych book."

"If you're going to study," Jo said carefully, "maybe you should go to the library."

"Hey," George said, "you tryin' to get rid of me?"

"No," Jo lied.

"Then let's go."

They entered the room. It was a seminar of about ten people, sitting in a circle. They joined the circle, but after a few minutes of discussion about *Lycidas*, George opened his psychology textbook and began to read.

Jo was mortified. The woman sitting on the other side of George was looking curiously, out of the corner of her eye, at the diagram of the human brain in George's book.

"Would you care to read the next stanza aloud?" the lecturer asked suddenly. "You—the gentleman with the dark glasses."

There was a horrible moment as all eyes turned to George, bent over his psychology textbook. He squirmed and sank down into his seat, as if trying to become invisible.

"I think he's just visiting," the woman next to George volunteered. "I'll read."

Afterwards, Jo was brutal. Why had he come to the class if he was going to be so rude? Why hadn't he sat off in the corner, if he was going to study? Or better yet, gone to the library as she had suggested? Didn't he know how inappropriate his behavior was? Didn't he care if they thought that Japanese people were boors? Didn't he know? Didn't he care?

No, he didn't know. He was oblivious. It was the source of his confidence, and that was what she had loved him for.

And so the curtain fell on their little drama, after a predictable denouement—agreeing that they would date others, then a tearful good-bye one dark night in his car, parked outside her apartment. Jo had always thought it somewhat disturbing when characters who had been left dead on the set in the last act, commanding considerable emotion by their demise, should suddenly spring to life not a minute later, smiling and bowing, and looking as unaffected by tragedy as it is possible to look. She therefore hoped she would not run into George, who would most certainly be smiling and bowing and oblivious to tragedy. She needn't have worried. Their paths had never been likely to cross.

Jo was making plans to study in New York when she heard through the grapevine that George was planning a trip to Europe. He went that summer, and when he returned, he brought her parents a gift. Jo's parents, who had had enough complaints about George when Jo was seeing him, were touched, and when Christmas came around Jo's mother, in true Japanese fashion, prepared a gift for George to return his kindness. Jo, of course, was expected to deliver it.

She had had no contact with him since they had broken up. His family was still living in Japantown, but the old Victorian was soon going to be torn down for urban renewal, and they were planning to move out to the Avenues, the Richmond District where Jo's parents lived.

As Jo's dad drove her to George's house, Jo hoped he wouldn't be home, hoped she could just leave the gift with his mother. She was thankful that she was with her father, who had a habit of gunning the engine as he sat waiting in the car for deliveries to be made, and was therefore the ideal person with whom to make a quick getaway.

George's grandmother opened the door. When she saw who it was, her face changed and she cried out with pleasure. Jo was completely unprepared for the look of happiness and hope on her face.

"Jo-chan!" George's grandmother cried; then, half-turning, she called out Jo's name twice more, as if summoning the household to her arrival.

Jo was stunned.

"This is for George," she said, thrusting the gift at George's grandmother, almost throwing it at her in her haste. "Merry Christmas."

She turned and fled down those stairs for the last time, away from the doomed Victorian and the old Japanese woman who stood in the doorway still, calling her name.

from *THE JOURNEY*
Indira Ganesan (1960–   )

T he Journey *is set on the imaginary island of Pi, an*
independent "chunk of India that is not quite India torn free to float
in the Bay of Bengal." The novel's protagonist, Renu Krishnan,
travels to Pi from Long Island after the death of her beloved "twin"
cousin, Rajesh. As Renu mourns Rajesh's death, she confronts the
belief of the women of her mother's village "that if one twin dies by
water, the other will die by fire." The following chapter takes place
in Renu's relatives' home on Pi.

Indira Ganesan was born in Srirangam, India. She was educated
at Vassar College and the University of Iowa. The Journey is her
first novel. Her work has appeared in several periodicals, including
Poughkeepsie Review, Mississippi Review, *and* Shankpainter.
She has taught at the University of Missouri and Vassar College,
and has been a fellow at the MacDowell Colony. She currently
teaches at the University of California at San Diego.

UPHOLDING THE CIRCLE THAT USED TO BE HER FAMILY WAS WHAT
Renu did. She stretched out her arms, palms cupped, and demanded they float within that span, that they be content to
remain in a freeze-frame of her needs. All those evenings spent
on Long Island after her father's death, three women in the
living room, the lethargy it inspired, seemed part of an immo-
bile tapestry. It was an especially Krishnan reaction, Renu felt, to
turn ever inward to the family, exclusive of all outside elements.

American life was different, she was convinced, feeling that difference deeply. Renu believed that American parents stood by their child's room at night, gazing with delight at the sleeping form, at the nicely matched furniture, the walls covered with pennants and posters, and the obligatory collection of athletic awards, smiling: this was their child. But knowing, too, that once the child was colleged, they could repanel the walls, cover the crayon marks, and convert the room into a needed den or exercise room. This was the American way, to raise children and let them go, an independence nurtured by the first after-school job, the first date, the carousing nights with friends (and here she always imagined teenage boys and girls eating hot dogs in a bright kitchen while parents slept trustingly upstairs). The hugs at high school graduation were traditional, taken-for-granted partings, Renu believed, partings that would never be given so willingly by island parents.

Island girls were expected to follow the rules, behave them-selves within and outside the family, save themselves for the sanctity of marriage. No boys, no questions. The early rebel-lions were reined in by their father's death, and Renu reacted by throwing herself to the task of preserving the family. She watched her mother closely for signs of crackup, taking over the cooking to assure that meals would be served regularly. Losing contact with friends, letting the phone alone, it was easy to reduce the circumference of her world. But nothing could stop the slow flush creeping up her throat in high school, in-venting excuses, I have to baby-sit, I have chores, I must study, saying no to excursions and dances. Island girls do not date, her mother had said, crisply, severely, no more nonsense. What did they do? They theorize, they rationalize, they become computer science majors if they cannot be doctors. In college, it was easy to shrug off friendships, adjust to the routine of sleeping, eating, doing coursework, working, watching television. It was the same on Pi really, a schedule of activities lazily followed, and all the necessities taken care of.

In the garden, Renu reflected on the changes precipitated by their move to America. She thought about her parents' capacity for adaptation, how her mother weathered the transition. As a young girl who had family and servants to cater to all her needs, a woman who had never been to market by herself, her mother had held her breath and willy-nilly left the island for America, land of the self-serve.

There she bravely walked down the aisles of supermarkets, taking in the seemingly endless supply of frozen foods, juice concentrates, canned cheeses, and boxes of cereal with free toys inside. She pushed the smart steel carts, marveling at their oiled smoothness, filling them with celebrated TV dinners. She tried to figure out the appliances in the kitchen, the toaster that didn't really work, the temperamental mixer, discovering she'd bought all the wrong things, trying to make a simple *dāl* with incorrect beans and dinner having to wait hours, everyone upset and bothered and hungry.

What an enormous amount she learned. Instead of handing her clothes to a waiting dhobi, she encountered monstrous machines that she must feed and empty; she had to sort and arrange clothes according to washability; select a special detergent and appropriate water temperature after consulting some charts, a bleach, a fabric softener. She could add a no-static cling paper to the load, or let it rest and hope for the best. Her mother moved through American life, tough as a pioneer, conquering dryers, parking meters, elevators, cellophane-packed goods, soda dispensers, checkout lines, gas stations, and car washes. Renu wasn't sure she could have coped, had she been in her mother's shoes.

So sat Renu thinking when her mother came outside, eyes and sari gleaming.

"Renu-ma, there you are, I've found you," said her mother.

"I was just sitting."

Renu's mother dropped into a chair nearby but couldn't resist jumping up and giving her daughter—clever perfect darling firstborn—a quick kiss.

"Oh, my darling, I'm so happy to see you. Listen, you are so young, so full of promise—you have such a good life ahead of you, such joy. I was misled by Chitra, the poor dear, but now I see. Yes, and the only happiness I have in this world is to see you happy."

Renu wondered what her mother was leading up to.

"Oh, my angel, I have decided, I have absolutely decided, it's time to get you settled." Rukmani leaned back and waited for her daughter's response.

"Marriage? Mom?"

But her mother simply beamed at her.

"I'm not even twenty yet."

"But you will be soon. You can finish your studies here, and just get *engaged* now. Then with your degree in hand, you can settle down somewhere. We'll find you a nice doctor, or a promising engineer, and why, you can even work if you want to. We are a very modern family, after all."

Getting up, the matter presumably settled, her mother kissed Renu again and left, her feet hardly touching the ground.

Rukmani thought marriage was not only proper and necessary for her daughter, but by speeding things along, it would offer a means of salvation and grace. She saw it as a party, a distracting, exciting spectacle that would take months of planning, shopping, issuing invitations, visiting, not to mention all the details to attend to in selecting a groom. With so much to do, Rukmani was certain that her daughter would be forced out of her melancholia.

Renu leaned back in her chair. What an idea. Marriage was a strange thing in her family, and disappointments were not uncommon. For one thing, most of the women tended to marry with their eyes shut. Statistics would reassure them, for as everyone knew, family-arranged marriages almost never ended in divorce. The bride's and groom's heights would nicely match, their tastes in food would be similar, their astrological signs would be in harmony—these details would be seized by the matchmakers and made much of by the parents. The bride-to-be was left to daydream, linger over a few minutes of meeting, and elaborate on her expectations. By the time of the wedding, a vision of a warrior, a shining cinema star, would dominate her thoughts as she bathed in sandalwood and rose petals. No wonder the women in her family photographs looked so grim, thought Renu—imagining Heathcliff and discovering only Kumar or Anand.

Her cousin Anu had broken the rules, marrying a German painter she'd met in Berlin. While the rest of her anthropology class wound its way to Florence, Anu ducked out from the doyenne-grip of Our Lady of Sacred Heart's sisters and remained in Germany. It had been a great scandal, but within a week, Anu had married Günter or Bruno, and had made the leap that untied her from her past.

She'd written to the Krishnans once, perhaps thinking that American relatives might be more sympathetic to her situation, but Renu's parents never discussed the letter. Renu knew of its existence only by the torn envelope with foreign stamps she'd found in a wastebasket. Copying the address, she herself had written to Anu, congratulating her and wondering if she, too, might come to Berlin. She asked Anu her opinion of the Beatles, and of Germany's attitude toward its Nazi past. She also listed twenty-three grievances against her parents and sister. She never mailed the letter.

For Anu, marrying out of caste and without approval meant exile, a complete discontinuation of the life she'd known on the island. No one attempted to contact her, and she became both a bright and extinguished light for Renu.

Her uncle Adda, however, had brought his bride back to the island, and no one could do anything about it. Aunt Bala sniffed when she told stories of the foreigner in the house, how pale and thin she was, a snob from the beginning. She died without giving Adda a child, and *that*, said Bala, was what happened when you marry out of caste. Adda himself would not speak of his wife, and Renu found herself wondering more and more about her Spanish aunt. What caused her to leave her homeland for the island, and what had she found upon arrival? Renu felt a funny closeness to this aunt; they shared the common bond of immigrants.

But there were others who had married well, who entered unions in which promises were fulfilled and wants met. It was an ancient system, based on the stars and the practical needs of each couple, and in most cases, infallible.

If Rajesh had lived, who would he have married? Someone she could get along with, that was certain. But to give up her place to some stranger girl, a housewifey type, was unthinkable. As for herself, well, it seemed implausible. Renu could not imagine marrying anyone. Maybe she was going to die soon, as everyone suspected, so perhaps marriage wasn't in her cards. Her mother seemed happy at the prospect, though, very intent on a wedding. It would be hard to disappoint her, but if she was going to die anyway, there was no reason why she shouldn't go along with the plan.

That night, Renu dreamed of a line of unmarried women partnered with apes, wandering down vast, empty lanes. When she woke up, she wondered where the image had come from, from the island or America, Art History or mythology? Did no one approve of unattached females?

When, a few days later, Rukmani approached her with a dish of her favorite sweets and a list of suitable boys, Renu could not say no. She gave her mother the okay to dispatch letters and consult horoscopes. Bala agreed with Rukmani: it was a fine idea. Only Adda shrugged and refused to comment.

AFTERWORD

As a topic of concerted critical study by writers and readers in American communities and universities, Asian American literature emerged in the late 1960s and the early and mid-1970s with the insistence that it not be confused with the literatures of Asia. Asian American literature is an American literature. It is authored by people of Asian descent who are Americans by experience or history in the Americas—though not necessarily by United States citizenship, which was denied to Asian immigrants by law until the 1940s and 1950s. With surviving works dating back to the nineteenth century, this literature is informed by sensibilities developed by the authors through their interpretations of, and responses to, their lives in America. Asian American writers have explored what it means to exist in a racial and cultural minority group that has lived as and been perceived as outsiders to American society.

Asian American literature as it emerged in the seventies worked to counteract the alienating misconceptions of those who habitually think of Asian Americans as "foreign." Rather than turning first and last to their Asian ancestral lands for self-understanding, Asian Americans began to share with one another a realization that their identities flourished in their immediate personal and communal histories—and that these histories defined their Asian American cultures as well. In attacking the mistaken perception that an Asian face must be alien to America, Asian American writers and critics asked a fundamental, unsettling, and, for some, liberating question: What does it mean to be American? What does it mean to be American if a person born and raised in America or settled there through immigration is racially, culturally, or legally considered not to be an American? Or how must the concept of American change so that it can include all the people who participate in the life and history of the United States—including Asian Americans?

In response to such questions, proponents of Asian American literature also saw that different Asian American identities— for instance, Chinese American, Japanese American, Filipino American, and Korean American—consist not in such things as customs thought typical of the group, but in the groups' and individuals' *stories*, their *narratives* of how customs came to be incorporated and developed in their American experience. This conception of Asian American literature found its source in Asian American *histories* and the learning of these histories— despite their being ignored in most systems of education in the United States. It also entailed a rejection of the kinds of "history" and "culture" Edward Said has called "Orientalism" and Frank Chin has called "the fake": misconceptions or stereotypes of the Orient that arise from imperialist, colonial interests in subjugating or economically exploiting Asian lands and peoples.

The awareness that grew in the late sixties and immediately afterward was also, in part, a celebration of the fact that Asian Americans had been creating literary works since at least the turn of the century. These include novels, short stories, poetry, and drama, proof that Asian Americans could not only record their lives in writing but could also create literary art and be taken seriously in doing so. The literature also includes chronicles and nonfiction prose narratives—for instance, autobiographies such as the one by Younghill Kang, an immigrant from Korea who gained recognition as a writer in America and who in addition to novels wrote *East Goes West* (1937) about his own journey. But even prior to Kang's achievement, autobiographies already had a peculiar prominence among Asian American writings.

One form of autobiography, practiced in the era between the Chinese Exclusion Act of 1882 and World War II, was the written, memorized, and recited response to the interrogations at the immigration station on Angel Island in San Francisco Bay, where a new arrival from China would have to satisfy the officials of the Immigration and Naturalization Service that he was truly the son of the legal resident sponsoring him, as required by the law barring the immigration of Chinese laborers. This practice of pairing older and younger men—and of creating "generations" of Chinese Americans even when American laws effectively barred the immigration of Chinese women to discourage the establishment of families—generated the term *paper son*, indicating that the relationships of the parties were literary creations. The pair would assume identities given them in "coaching books," constructing autobiographies of the would-be immigrant, his father, and their family. A member of the pair would be interrogated at Angel Island one day by officials who would ask about the pair's extended families and about details of daily life at the "home" in China. Both father and son were supposed to know these details in common: On what days of the week and month is the village marketplace open? What direction does the market face? How far is the market from the door of your house? What are your wife's and her mother's names? Later, the other member of the pair would be summoned out of detention and asked the same questions; his answers had to match the first one's. It was a test of the authenticity of the pair's story, their relationship, and their claim that the newcomer could legally immigrate through one of the exceptions allowed in the Chinese Exclusion Act. Because passing this test meant that the former identities of both "father" and "son" had to be buried and their strategy for immigration kept utterly secret, the real family histories of "paper sons and fathers" who arrived during this period are often difficult if not impossible for their descendants to tell. The writing of an "autobiography," in this period of Chinese American history, became associated with the creation of a fictional identity for strategic purposes.

Another autobiographical genre complicating Chinese American literary history took root in the personal "confessions" Chinese American women wrote under difficult circumstances. In California, these were women whom Christian missionaries rescued from prostitution during the late nineteenth century when, with a preponderance of men in places where miners and migrant laborers congregated, sexual exploitation of women was rampant. As elsewhere in missionaries' campaigns to convert "heathen" people, in California the act of teaching English literacy to rescued women was aimed at enabling the converts not only to read the Bible but also to confess their sinful, pagan pasts and to make way for a new Christian life. Whatever the Chinese American convert's past, it was thus intertwined with a culture their "rescuers" considered not simply inferior, but sinful. Writing such an "autobiography" for the missionaries had to be quite different from the "confessing" to people of the same culture; for the Chinese woman autobiographer—to save her very life, if she had been a caged prostitute in San Francisco—had to deal with how she would, by her writing, be considered a representative of her culture for an audience that believed their own culture and notions of individual virtue to be superior to hers. In such an autobiography, a confession implied an apology to a higher authority.

Chinese American autobiography today inherits this history. By 1976 when Maxine Hong Kingston's *The Woman Warrior: Memoirs of a Girlhood Among Ghosts* was published, some Asian American writers and literary critics, notably Frank Chin and his fellow editors of *Aiiieeeee! An Anthology of Asian-American Writers* (1974), were raising questions about how Asian American first-person narratives affirmed, suggested ignorance of, or were indifferent to cultures and literary histories not only of racist depictions of Asians but also of coaching books and converts' autobiographies and the like. Kingston's book could be seen and judged as an attempt at two things, perhaps both at once: It could be a critique of its narrator, a fictional first-person "I" meant to be questioned so that her confusions about Chinese American identity and the causes and consequences of her American ignorance of China might be understood; or the book could be entirely "transparent," not an interplay of hiding and revealing but a clear revelation by means of explicit, descriptive statement of what it means to grow up Chinese American and female. The selling of *Woman Warrior* as nonfiction, a marketing practice that continues today, tended to throw weight and judgment heavily on the side of the latter interpretation, so despite Kingston's disclaimers that she was not "representing" but had made very significant changes in retelling them, certain stories are generally believed to be nonfictional, transmitted as directly from Chinese tales as oral traditions allow. Contrary to many reviews that took her versions for granted, Kingston implicitly questioned how a daughter would interpret her mother's Chinese culture, given the American contexts, in which they both live, of idealism and racism, sexism, and cultural, historical ignorance. So, for instance, in "White Tigers," the narrator's belief that a woman was proscribed from being a warrior is a reflection on and critique of the prohibition in the American military, during the time the narrator is growing up, against women entering combat. The book's title, meanwhile, proclaims that unlike in America, in the mother's culture there *are* women warriors, exceedingly well-known military ones. Kingston herself has made it explicit that she considers a critique of the book's narrator and her constructs of American and Chinese cultures a key to its reading. *The Woman Warrior* in this way is a Chinese American woman's *Bildungsroman*, a narrative not aiming to present how China, Chinese, and Chinese Americans essentially are, but to plot the imaginative, psychological, ethical, and bodily development of its main character, the narrator herself. The work is, in short, an example of "growing up Asian American" in anything but a simplistic sense.

The Chinese American writings thus far alluded to do not represent typical Asian American genres of autobiography. The history of such genres in Chinese American literature is specific to that literature and the contexts of its development. However, the grouping of all Asian Americans together by race, for a variety of good and bad reasons, means that, to some degree, what happens historically to one Asian American group is bound to affect others—as indeed all of America is affected. The fact that Jade Snow Wong titled her autobiography (narrated in the third person, like Henry Adams's) *Fifth Chinese Daughter* (1950) may have influenced Monica Sone to call her Japanese American classic *Nisei Daughter* (1953), but with an interesting difference: Wong singles herself out in a ranking within her family, while Sone in her book's title names an entire generation (nisei means second-generation Japanese American). Further, the controversy over how Kingston's first published book was labeled and was to be read recalls questions over the historically specific, "confessional" nature of Wong's autobiography and its base in the ideology of assimilation. Literary debate over *Woman Warrior* also prompted re-readings of other Asian American classics in the genre, notably of Carlos Bulosan's *America Is in the Heart: A Personal History* (1946). With the questioning of boundaries between fiction and nonfiction and how these labels have affected readers' perceptions came a fresh understanding of how Bulosan meant the subtitle of his work. Whereas many readers had assumed the personal history to be Bulosan's own, others who knew him or the lives of his fellow pinoys (Filipino migrant laborers in America) saw that the narrative was of the entire group. Bulosan's "personal history" is the itinerant narrator's, and this narrator is a composite character drawn from a great many pinoys in Bulosan's experience. Unlike Bulosan, who was a poet before he left the Philippines for Seattle, the narrator undergoes an education by bodily experience in America before going on to learn to read and write. By a progressive experience and a quixotic idealism, he achieves a social and class consciousness; the quest for this informs the plot of Bulosan's fiction. Again, recognizing the author's critiquing and interpreting of the first-person narrator distances the entire narration from being simply a self-revealing, self-expressive, and—disturbingly—self-pitying and primitive statement.

What I think is most remarkable about the present anthology is its variety of selections. Some of the pieces are highly experiential, in that what their authors understand of themselves, of growing up, and of being Asian American is based mainly in experience and intuited concepts rather than in the study and reading of traditions of Asian American autobiography such as are sketched above. Other selections are based upon much learning from what are called Asian American studies in colleges and universities today. Some are not meant to be considered nonfiction, and their first-person narrators are intended to be interpreted as I suggest Kingston's and Bulosan's ought. Problems, such as in the case of Chinese American autobiographical traditions, concerning literary genre, race, gender, class, and culture still run their course in the selections: All the selections collectively and interactively call for questioning of assumptions and critical thought, and in theory the questions they inspire apply variously to instances and traditions of autobiography at large. Even if they were to be grouped by ethnicity within the general fictional category of Asian American, the selections range through a great many personal, familial, communal, and cultural histories. Reflected upon, however, they may suggest that while many variations are individual or specific to different Asian American cultural groups and histories, the authors and their subjects share or may be related to one another by positions within overarching American social, economic, cultural, and political structures in which racial concepts have served as girders and beams that structure the grouping called Asian Americans. The authors of these selections, viewing these structures from various positions, demonstrate that literary voice, culture, and race can be the creations of those who take the risk of putting themselves on the line in writing.

—Stephen H. Sumida
Ann Arbor, Michigan 1993

Suggested Further Readings

T he following list consists of prose writings about growing up
and some stories about young adulthood by Asian American authors
not included in this anthology. Some of the books are intended for
young people, as indicated. This list is in alphabetical order by
author's family name.

Appachana, Anjana. "My Only Gods." *The Forbidden Stitch: An Asian
American Women's Anthology*, ed. Shirley Geok-lin Lim, Mayumi
Tsutakawa, and Margarita Donnelly. Corvallis, OR: Calyx Books,
1989.

Bertulfo, M. G. "Windsong." *Burning Cane: Amerasia Journal*, Vol.
17, no. 2 (1991), pp. 11–15.

Castro, Luisa. "Trilliums and Rhododendrons." *Asian American Review*, Vol. 2, no. 1 (1975), pp. 170–81.

Cha, Theresa Hak Kyung. *Dictée*. New York: Tanam Press, 1982.

Chan, Jeffery Paul. "Sing Song Plain Song." *Amerasia Journal*, Vol. 3,
no. 2 (1976), pp. 23–37.

Chang, Rafael. "When I Die, I Don't Want Any Leftovers. . . ."
Lavender Godzilla: Voices of the Gay Asian Pacific Alliance, Vol. 4,
no. 1 (February/March 1991), pp. 3–4.

Chiang, Fay. "Home," from *In the City of Contradictions*. New York:
Sunbury Press, 1979.

Chin, Curtis, et al., eds. *Language of Home: Lesbian, Gay, and Bi-
Sexual Asian Pacific American Writing: The APA Journal*, Vol. 2, no. 1
(Spring 1993).

Chiu, Christina. "Roselily: Borrowed Space." *In the Heart: The APA
Journal*, Vol. 1, no. 1 (Summer 1992), pp. 10–13.

Chock, Eric. "The Mango Tree." *The Best of Bamboo Ridge: The*

Hawaii Writers' Quarterly, ed. Eric Chock and Darrell H. Y. Lum. Honolulu: Bamboo Ridge Press, 1986.

Chong, Sue Lin. "Small Endearments." *Sister Stew: Fiction and Poetry by Women*, ed. Juliet S. Kono and Cathy Song. Honolulu: Bamboo Ridge Press, 1991.

———. "Social Graces." *Paké: Writings by Chinese in Hawaii*, ed. Eric Chock and Darrell H. Y. Lum. Honolulu: Bamboo Ridge Press, 1989.

Chu, Mary. "A Laundryman's Daughter." *Bridge Magazine*, Vol. 2, no. 2 (1972), pp. 16–18.

Cobb, Nora. "Sessions." *Making Face, Making Soul: Haciendo Caras*, ed. Gloria Anzaldua. San Francisco: Aunt Lute Foundation Books, 1990.

Creef, Elena Tajima. "Notes from a Fragmented Daughter." *Making Face, Making Soul: Haciendo Caras*, ed. Gloria Anzaldua. San Francisco: Aunt Lute Foundation Books, 1990.

Davenport, Diana. "House of Skin." *Home to Stay: Asian American Women's Fiction*, ed. Sylvia Watanabe and Carol Bruchac. Greenfield Center, NY: The Greenfield Review Press, 1990.

Dunn, Ashley Sheun. "No Man's Land." *Amerasia Journal*, Vol. 5, no. 2 (1978), pp. 109–133.

Feria, Benny. *Filipino Son*. Boston: Meador Publishing, 1954.

Flowers, Ruby Reyes. "Ruby's Discovery." *The Ethnic American Woman: Problems, Protests, Lifestyle*, ed. Edith Blicksilver. Dubuque, IA: Kendall/Hunt Publishing, 1978.

Gordon, Elizabeth. "On the Other Side of the War: A Story." *Home to Stay: Asian American Women's Fiction*, ed. Sylvia Watanabe and Carol Bruchac. Greenfield Center, NY: The Greenfield Review Press, 1990.

Hamamoto, Darrell Y. "My Vietnam Syndrome." *Amerasia Journal*, Vol. 17, no. 1 (1991), pp. 129–131.

Hashimoto, Sharon. "The Mushroom Man." *Home to Stay: Asian American Women's Fiction*, ed. Sylvia Watanabe and Carol Bruchac. Greenfield Center, NY: The Greenfield Review Press, 1990.

Hirabayashi, Lane Ryo. "The Best of Both Worlds?: Reflection on the bi-cultural experience." *Echoes from Gold Mountain*, Vol. 3 (1982), pp. 77–90.

———. "On Being Hapa." *Pacific Citizen*, Vol. 101, no. 25 (December 20–27, 1985), p. A-26.

———. "Understanding the 'Happa' Experience." *Pacific Citizen*, Vol. 98, no. 15 (April 20, 1984), pp. 5, 12.

Holt, John Dominis. *Waimea Summer*. Honolulu: Topgallant Publishing, 1976.

Hong, Kyung Won. "But for You I Would Have Nothing." *Burning Cane: Amerasia Journal*, Vol. 17, no. 2 (1991), pp. 99–102.

Hongo, Garrett Kaoru; Alan Chong Lau; and Lawson Fusao Inada. *The Buddha Bandits Down Highway 99*. Mountain View, CA: Buddhahead Press, 1978.

Hosokawa, Bill. "Nostalgia" from *Thirty-Five Years in the Frying Pan*. New York: McGraw-Hill, 1978.

Houston, Velina Hasu. "On Being Mixed Japanese in Modern Times." *Pacific Citizen*, Vol. 101, no. 25. (December 20–27, 1985), Section B, pp. 1–3.

Jang, Dirk. "Return Trip." *Lavender Godzilla: Voices of the Gay Asian Pacific Alliance*, Vol. 4, no. 1 (February/March 1991), p. 5.

Joe, Jeanne. *Ying-Ying: Pieces of a Childhood*. San Francisco: East/West Publishing, 1982.

Kai, Fred S. "A Mid-Summer Incident." *Ayumi: A Japanese American Anthology*, ed. Janice Mirikitani et al. San Francisco: The Japanese American Anthology Committee, 1980.

Kam, K. "The Hopeland." *Making Waves: An Anthology of Writings by and about Asian American Women*, ed. Asian Women United of California. Boston: Beacon Press, 1989.

Kaneko, Lonny. "The Shoyu Kid." *Amerasia Journal*, Vol. 3, no. 2 (1976), pp. 1–9.

Katayama, Taro. "Haru." *Ayumi: A Japanese American Anthology*, ed. Janice Mirikatani et al. San Francisco: The Japanese American Anthology Committee, 1980.

Kikumura, Akemi. *Promises Kept: The Life of an Issei Man*. Novato, CA: Chandler & Sharp, 1991.

Koyama, Tina. "Family Dinner." *Home to Stay: Asian American Women's Fiction*, ed. Sylvia Watanabe and Carol Bruchac. Greenfield Center, NY: Greenfield Review Press, 1990.

Lang, Craig Yee Kwok. "Asian. Family. Gay. Man." *Lavender Godzilla: Voices of the Gay Asian Pacific Alliance*, Vol. 4, no. 1 (February/March 1991), pp. 15–16.

Lau, Sarah. "Long Way Home." *Home to Stay: Asian American Women's Fiction*, ed. Sylvia Watanabe and Carol Bruchac. Greenfield Center, NY: Greenfield Review Press, 1990.

Le, Phi-Oanh. "Palace Walls." *Burning Cane: Amerasia Journal*, Vol. 17, no. 2 (1991), pp. 27–35.

Lee, Ed. "Tracks." *In the Heart: The APA Journal*, Vol. 1, no. 1 (Summer 1992), pp. 63–68.

Lee, Joann Faung Jean. *Asian American Experiences in the United States: Oral Histories of First to Fourth Generation Americans from China, the*

Philippines, Japan, India, the Pacific Islands, Vietnam and Cambodia. Jefferson, NC: McFarland, 1991.

Lee, Marie G. *Finding My Voice.* Boston: Houghton Mifflin, 1992. (for young adults)

Lee, Susan K. C. "A Letter for Dar." *The Forbidden Stitch: An Asian American Women's Anthology,* ed. Shirley Geok-Lin Lim, Mayumi Tsutakawa, and Margarita Donnelly. Corvallis, OR: Calyx Books, 1989.

Lee, Suzanne Wah. "Asian and Female." *A. Magazine,* Vol. 1, no. 1 (Spring 1991), pp. 6–12.

Leyson, Rosemary Cho. "The Visit Home." *Making Face, Making Soul: Haciendo Caras,* ed. Gloria Anzaldua. San Francisco: Aunt Lute Foundation Books, 1990.

Lim, Edward. "The Long Way Home." *Lavender Godzilla: Voices of the Gay Asian Pacific Alliance,* Vol. 4, no. 1 (February/March 1991), pp. 18–19.

Lim, Genevieve. *Wings for Lai Ho.* San Francisco: East-West Publishing, 1982. (for young adults)

Lin, Adet, and Anor Lin. *Our Family.* New York: John Day, 1939.

Lin, Ed. "Ripeness." *In the Heart: The APA Journal,* Vol. 1, no. 1 (Summer 1992), pp. 32–36.

Leong, Patrick L. "Graveyard Picnics." *Burning Cane: Amerasia Journal,* Vol. 17, no. 2 (1991), pp. 57–61.

Macawili, Wesley. "Mummers." *The William and Mary Review* (Fall 1983), pp. 8–14.

Meer, Ameena. Selections from *An Evening in Paris.* In *Bomb,* (Summer 1990), pp. 84–87; and *The Portable Lower East Side,* (September 1990).

Mehta, Ved. *Sound-Shadows of the New World.* New York: W. W. Norton, 1985.

Mirikitani, Janice. *Shedding Silence.* Berkeley, CA: Celestial Arts, 1987.

Miyamoto, Kazuo. *Hawaii: End of the Rainbow.* Rutland, VT: Bridgeway Press, Charles E. Tuttle, 1964.

Mukherjee, Bharati. "Danny's Girls" from *The Middleman and Other Stories.* New York: Grove Press, 1988.

Murayama, Milton. *All I Asking for Is My Body.* Honolulu: University of Hawaii Press, 1988.

Ng, Fae Myenne. "Backdaire." *Harper's Magazine,* (April 1989), pp. 64–68.

———. *Bone.* New York, NY: Hyperion, 1993.

———. "The First Dead Man." *This World (The San Francisco Sunday Examiner & Chronicle)* (March 9, 1986), pp. 10–11.

———. "A Red Sweater." *Home to Stay: Asian American Women's*

Fiction, ed. Sylvia Watanabe and Carol Bruchac. Greenfield Center, NY: The Greenfield Review Press, 1990.

Noda, Kesaya E. "Growing Up Asian in America." *Making Waves: An Anthology of Writings by and About Asian American Women*, ed. Asian Women United of California. Boston: Beacon Press, 1989.

Nunes, Susan. "The Confession." *The Best of Bamboo Ridge: The Hawaii Writers' Quarterly,* ed. Eric Chock and Darrell H. Y. Lum. Honolulu: Bamboo Ridge Press, 1986.

———. "The Grandmother." *The Best of Bamboo Ridge: The Hawaii Writers' Quarterly*, ed. Eric Chock and Darrell H. Y. Lum. Honolulu: Bamboo Ridge Press, 1986.

Okada, John. *No-No Boy*. Seattle: The University of Washington Press, 1988.

Okubo, Mine. *Citizen 13660*. Seattle: The University of Washington Press, 1983.

On, Therese. "Strictly a 'Female' Female: Growing Up with Nancy Kwan." *A. Magazine*, Vol. 1, no. 1 (Spring 1991), pp. 50–52.

Pak, Gary. "Catching a Big Ulua." *Bamboo Ridge*, No. 47 (Summer 1990), pp. 17–27.

Pak, Ty. *Guilt Payment*. Honolulu: Bamboo Ridge Press, 1983.

Pei, Lowry Cheng-Wu. "Memories of Being an American Kid." *Bridge Magazine*, Vol. 7, no. 1 (Spring 1979), p. 50.

Pennybacker, Mindy. "Death Is a Quiet Affair." *CITY Magazine*, (1976), pp. 42–52.

Quan, Kit Yuen. "The Girl Who Wouldn't Sing." *Making Face, Making Soul: Haciendo Caras*, ed. Gloria Anzaldua. San Francisco: Aunt Lute Foundation Books, 1990.

Rno, Sung. " 'There was something in the air'." *Voices Stirring: An Anthology of Korean American Writing: The APA Journal*, Vol. 1, no. 2 (Winter 1992), p. 51.

Sone, Monica. *Nisei Daughter*. Seattle: University of Washington Press, 1979.

Suh, Grace. "The Eye of the Beholder." *A. Magazine*, Vol. 1, no. 2 (Fall 1991), pp. 56–57.

Sunaida, Mari. "Playing Samurai and the Princess." *Amerasia Journal*, Vol. 17, no. 1 (1991), pp. 171–174.

Sunoo, Brenda Paik, ed. *Korean-American Writings* (selected material from *Insight*, Korean-American bimonthly). New York: Insight, 1975.

Telemaque, Eleanor Wong. *It's Crazy to Stay Chinese in Minnesota*. Nashville: Thomas Nelson, 1978.

Terada, Wini. "Intermediate School Hapai." *The Best of Bamboo Ridge:*

The Hawaii Writers' Quarterly, ed. Eric Chock and Darrell H. Y. Lum. Honolulu: Bamboo Ridge Press, 1986.

Truong, Monique Thuy-Dung. "Kelly." *Burning Cane: Amerasia Journal*, Vol. 17, no. 2 (1991), pp. 41–48.

Tsui, Kitty. *The Words of a Woman Who Breathes Fire*. San Francisco: Spinsters, Ink, 1983.

Tsukiyama, Fuku Yokoyama. "A Cup of Flan." *Sister Stew: Fiction and Poetry by Women*, ed. Juliet S. Kono and Cathy Song. Honolulu: Bamboo Ridge Press, 1991.

Uchida, Yoshiko. *Desert Exile: The Uprooting of a Japanese American Family*. Seattle: University of Washington Press, 1982.

———. *A Jar of Dreams*. New York: Atheneum, 1981. (for young adults)

———. *Journey Home*. New York: Atheneum, 1978. (for young adults)

———. *Journey to Topaz: A Story of the Japanese American Evacuation*. New York: Scribner's, 1971. (for young adults)

Wang, James. "Asian and Male." *A. Magazine*, Vol. 1, no. 1 (Spring 1991), pp. 7–13, 43.

Wang, Wen-Wen C. "Bacon and Coffee." *Home to Stay: Asian American Women's Fiction*, ed. Sylvia Watanabe and Carol Bruchac. Greenfield Center, NY: Greenfield Review Press, 1990.

Watanabe, Sylvia. "Talking to the Dead." *Home to Stay: Asian American Women's Fiction*, ed. Sylvia Watanabe and Carol Bruchac. Greenfield Center, NY: Greenfield Review Press, 1990.

Watanna, Onoto [Winnifred Eaton Babcock]. *Me: A Book of Remembrance*. New York: Century, 1915.

Woo, Merle. "Letter to Ma." *This Bridge Called My Back: Writings by Radical Women of Color*, ed. Cherrie Moraga and Gloria Anzaldua. Latham, NY: Kitchen Table: Women of Color Press, 1983.

Yamada, Holly. "B-League Playoff." *Sister Stew: Fiction and Poetry by Women*, ed. Juliet S. Kono and Cathy Song. Honolulu: Bamboo Ridge Press, 1991.

Yamada, Mitsuye. *Desert Run: Poems and Stories*. Latham, NY: Kitchen Table: Women of Color Press, 1988.

Yamanaka, Lois-Ann. "Parts." *Sister Stew: Fiction and Poetry by Women*, ed. Juliet S. Kono and Cathy Song. Honolulu: Bamboo Ridge Press, 1991.

Yang, Jeff. "Just Family." *New York Press*, Vol. 4, no. 31 (July 31–August 6, 1991), pp. 1, 16–18.

Yep, Laurence. *Child of the Owl*. New York: Harper, 1977. (for young adults)

————. *The Lost Garden.* Englewood Cliffs, NJ: Julian Messner, Silver Burdett Press, Simon & Schuster, 1991. (for young adults)

————. *Sea Glass.* New York: Harper, 1979. (for young adults)

Young, Kathleen Ngit Jun. "Digging for Lotus Roots." *Paké: Writings by Chinese in Hawaii,* ed. Eric Chock and Darrell H. Y. Lum. Honolulu: Bamboo Ridge Press, 1989.

Young, Wynn. "Poor Butterfly!" *Burning Cane: Amerasia Journal,* Vol. 17, no. 2 (1991), pp. 113–119.

Yuen, D. Leilehua. "As How Come." *Bamboo Ridge,* No. 47 (Summer 1990), p. 69.

Yuen, Kevin. "Looking for Mana." *Hanai: An Anthology of Asian American Writings,* ed. Chris Planas et al. Berkeley, CA: Asian American Studies, Department of Ethnic Studies, University of California, 1980.

PERMISSIONS